Australian Cinema

D1616333

Australian Cinema

Edited by Scott Murray

ALLEN & UNWIN
in association with
AUSTRALIAN FILM COMMISSION

First published in 1994
Allen & Unwin Pty Ltd
9 Atchison Street, St Leonards, NSW 2065
Australia

National Library of Australia
Cataloguing-in-Publication entry:

Australian cinema.
    Bibliography.
    Includes index.
    ISBN 1 86373 311 6.
    1. Motion pictures, Australian — History and
    criticism. 2. Motion pictures — Australia — History
    and criticism. I. Murray, Scott, 1951–
791.430994

Set in 9/9½ pt Times
by Graphicraft Typesetters Ltd, Hong Kong
Printed by Southwood Press Pty Ltd, Sydney
10 9 8 7 6 5 4 3 2 1

Contents

Preface

This book is the English version of *Le Cinéma Australien* published in 1991 by the Centre Georges Pompidou in Paris, in association with the Centre's season on Australian cinema. This extensive retrospective was undertaken in collaboration with the Australian Film Commission (AFC).

All the articles, save 'Filmography: one hundred and fifty Australian films', were commissioned in Australia by Victoria Treole of the AFC and the book's Australian editor, Scott Murray. They were written in English, then sent to France where they were translated under the supervision of the French editor, Claudine Thoridnet.

The articles published here are in the original English form with the following exceptions:

* Scott Murray's 'Australian cinema in the 1970s and 1980s' has been revised, in part to take into account some new Australian films.
* A new chapter has been added, 'Australian directors overseas 1970–1992', also written by Murray.
* Claudine Thoridnet's 'Filmography' was originally compiled in French and contained review extracts from a variety of sources. The chapter has been changed by printing more extensive credits and by replacing the review selection with short synopses.
* A list of all the Australian films shown at the Centre during the season has been added.
* Some of the illustrative material is different.

Each Australian film is dated by its Australian theatrical release, which in some cases may have been preceded by an overseas release. The title of a film, where possible, is that on the film itself, reproduced here in upper and lower case. Character names, again where possible, are those given in a film's credits.

Special thanks are due to Jean-Loup Passek, Victoria Treole, Raffaele Caputo and Arthur Salton.

Contributors

Phillip Adams

Nicknamed the 'godfather' of the New Australian Cinema, Adams was commissioned to write for the Gorton government the report which led to the establishment of the Experimental Film Fund, the Australian Film and Television School, and the Australian Film Development Corporation (forerunner of the Australian Film Commission). Author of seven books, television personality and journalist in various newspapers, Adams has produced films since the mid-1960s. In 1981, he received the Raymond Longford Award for his contribution to the national cinema.

Raffaele Caputo

Assistant editor at *Cinema Papers* and of *Australian Film 1978–92: A Survey of Theatrical Features*, Caputo is an occasional lecturer in film and a contributor to a wide variety of journals and newspapers.

Debi Enker

Television and film critic, Enker has headed the *Freeze Frame* and *Video Week* magazines, worked as assistant editor for *Cinema Papers*, and was television editor for *The Herald*. She now writes television reviews for *The Sunday Age*.

Ross Gibson

Author, critic and film-maker, director and co-writer of *Dead To The World* and the documentary *Wild*, Gibson is currently working on *On This Road*.

Adrian Martin

Film critic with an interest in everything related to the media, Martin has written for various journals, including *Cinema Papers*, *Filmnews* and *Business Review Weekly*. He reviews video releases in *The Age*'s 'Green Guide' and recently edited a film issue of *Continuum*.

Megan McMurchy

Prior to being Director of Creative Development at the Australian Film Commission between 1986 and 1988, McMurchy co-produced and co-directed the documentary *For Love or Money*. More recently she has produced the features *Breathing Under Water* and *Talk*.

Graham Shirley

Scriptwriter, scientific adviser and director, Shirley conducted a major research project in television archives and restored the 1927 feature film *For The Term Of His Natural Life* for the National Film & Sound Archive. In 1983, he published, in collaboration with Brian Adams, the historical retrospective *Australian Cinema: The First Eighty Years*. He has written for *Cinema Papers*, *Lumiere* and *Filmviews*.

Edward Gough Whitlam

Lawyer, Labor MP between 1952 and 1978, and Prime Minister 1972–75. During his prime ministerial term, Whitlam took personal responsibility for cultural affairs. He enacted the first laws on the running of the Australian National Gallery, established the Australia Council, created the Australian Film and Television School and what became the Australian Film Commission. In 1978, he resigned from parliament to pursue a university career. Nominated ambassador to UNESCO, he was elected member of the executive in 1985. Between 1986 and 1991 he was president of the Australia–China Council and has sat on the board of directors for the National Gallery. In 1988, he was made an honorary member of the World Conservation Union.

The capture of Ned Kelly in Charles Tait's *The Story of the Kelly Gang* (1906), the world's first narrative film of substantial length.

Introduction

E. G. Whitlam

Australian cinema has a long history. It is almost as old as the technology of film itself, and many will find it appropriate that the French edition of this review of the past ninety years of Australian film production should bear the imprint of the Centre Georges Pompidou, one of the foremost cultural institutions in a nation largely credited with the invention of the cinema, both as an art form and as a medium of entertainment.

As in other countries, cinema in Australia has survived many challenges. The periods through which it languished—chiefly in the years after the two world wars—have served only to dramatise its more productive phases. As a source of entertainment, it has outlasted the advent of commercial radio in the 1920s, of television in the 1950s and of the video industry in the 1980s. Its renaissance in the late 1970s led to the most creative and admired phase in its history, and I am proud that the policies of my government played a part in that resurgence. It is certainly true that the promotion of a vigorous film industry and film culture in Australia is today an objective of all major political parties.

I have consistently maintained that in any civilised community the arts and associated amenities must occupy a central place. Their enjoyment should not be seen as something remote from everyday life. And, of all art forms, the cinema is undoubtedly the closest to ordinary people. That is why I am particularly pleased to be associated with this major critical overview of Australian cinema, the most comprehensive presentation of its kind ever mounted.

Cinema as an art form was born at the beginning of the twentieth century, only a hundred or so years after the European settlement of the Australian continent. It is a medium to which Australians have had much to contribute and, as we approach the centenary of the birth of cinema, it seems particularly appropriate to review Australia's contribution to this field of endeavour.

Cinema is unique among the arts in Australia in owing little to the influence of developments abroad. It is preeminently an indigenous growth. Apart from the invention of the cinematograph itself, it has grown without help from other countries as an expression of a distinctive local culture. In painting, no recognisable school of Australian-born artists began to emerge until the end of the nineteenth century, fifty years or more after artists like Conrad Martens and John Glover began painting in Australia. Even artists who were later seen as distinctively Australian neo-impressionists, such as Roberts, McCubbin, Conder and Streeton, were perpetuating and adapting an established European tradition. The emergence of an Australian school of landscape painting owed everything to British and French influence. The late Lloyd Rees, quintessentially Australian in his choice of material and in his identification with what might be called the Australian spirit or ethos, had his beginnings in this early European-based school; others like Sir Sidney Nolan were more honoured abroad than at home.

Australian musical life likewise depended on overseas influences for its early growth. In the nineteenth century, there was little creative musical activity; the ambitions of our cultural pioneers were limited to founding academic departments or conservatoriums to instruct students in the works of the great composers. Visits by the famous were the highlights of Australia's musical life. Our first conservatorium was established in Adelaide in 1885; our first symphony orchestra in Sydney in 1946. Alfred Hill, the most eminent Australian composer of the early twentieth century, wrote in a European tradition; Percy Grainger, resident in Melbourne for many years, took American citizenship. Australian museums and galleries were similarly 'Anglo-centric' in their curatorial policies and architectural styles. Although most of them used the word 'national' in their titles, they were founded by the colonial administrators of the last century. With the exception of the National Gallery in Canberra, established under legislation introduced by my government in 1975, they are still controlled by state governments.

Cinema had a distinctive Australian quality from the outset. And it was usually most successful when appealing to a popular audience eager for entertainment with authentic Australian settings and characters. The years before World War I were the most productive for Australian cinema, with a quantitative peak in 1911, when 51 feature films were produced, which has not been equalled since. In their review of the industry, *Australian Film 1900–1977: A Guide to Feature Film Production*[1], Andrew Pike and Ross Cooper record that in 1906 the first narrative film of any substantial length [4000 feet or more], *The Story of the Kelly Gang*[2], was made in Melbourne. Debate about whether it was the first feature film in Australia, or even in the world, tended to obscure the fact that in Australia there was an early flowering of feature film production from 1906 to 1912, predating the regular appearance of narrative films of similar length in other countries, especially Britain and the US. In Britain, for example, the longest film made in 1911 was 2500 feet; in Australia in the same year, at least twenty films were more than 3000 feet, and of those nearly half were over 4000 feet. But by 1913 production had declined. It did not fully recover until the introduction of significant federal government assistance to the film industry in the early 1970s.

It is notable that the cinema has tended to flourish in Australia whenever the other arts have flourished as well; to an extent it has served as an index of the nation's general cultural vitality. Its flowering at the beginning of the century coincided with a period of exceptional activity in literature and the visual arts; its moribund condition between the wars was paralleled by a similar sterility in Australian theatre and the performing arts. Apart from

1

Arthur Black (Peter Cummins) in Ken Hannam's *Sunday Too Far Away* (1975), which was selected in the 1975 Quinzaine des Réalisateurs (Directors' Fortnight) at Cannes.

a series of popular features produced by Ken G. Hall for Cinesound in the 1930s, there was little feature film production in Australia until the late 1960s. The 'new wave' of Australian cinema which began at that time was matched by an extraordinary upsurge in drama, literature and the arts generally. This owed much, I believe, to the establishment of those federal bodies under my government: the Film and Television School, the Film and Television Board of the Australia Council, and the Australian Film Development Corporation. To a large extent, they have accomplished for film in Australia what the Australian Broadcasting Commission, established in 1932, accomplished for music. They provided an institutional, entrepreneurial and funding structure for the industry, and training opportunities for its most promising practitioners. The recent establishment by the Hawke government of the Australian Film Finance Corporation has sought to rectify the crisis in film investment which overtook the industry in the late 1980s.

For my part, I saw the encouragement of the film industry as essential to the rekindling of Australian national pride and self-confidence. There were many who felt that the country had lost its old energy and idealism during the long years of conservative rule after 1949. In foreign policy, we had no distinctive voice; in domestic matters, opportunities were neglected to revitalise the cities and refurbish the basic infrastructure essential to development. Our writers and artists were despondent; many were working overseas. Despite a superficial prosperity, the nation was in need of a new direction, a new spirit. The films that flowed from the revitalised industry in the 1970s helped restore to Australians a sense of their identity, their place in both their region and the world. There will always be argument about which were the best ones at the time—more informed opinions will no doubt be found in these pages—but the films which found ready acceptance were invariably those that revealed aspects of Australian history and social conditions: *Picnic at Hanging Rock*, *Caddie*, *Between Wars*, *The Chant of Jimmie Blacksmith*, *Gallipoli*, *'Breaker' Morant*, *My Brilliant Career*.[3] All these films, and many more, presented Australian life, not only to the world, but to Australians themselves. Until they appeared, cinemagoers had little choice but to see American or British productions; the few films produced domestically found little enthusiasm with local exhibitors and distributors.

Difficult as it is to generalise in these matters, I believe the best Australian films have certain obvious qualities in common. If one were to define their essential characteristic, it would be, perhaps, a certain wholesomeness, a certain decency, a fundamental seriousness of purpose. Whatever their particular merits, they have usually been films worth making. If the industry has rarely aspired to heights of rarefied artistry or abstraction, nor has it overly resorted to crude sensationalism or base exploitation. If there has been no Australian Alain Resnais, nor has there been an Australian Rambo. Yet to say that Australian cinema occupies some safe middle ground would be to miss the point. Our films are robust, energetic, honest, frequently beautiful in pictorial terms and made with great craftsmanship. They are more often than not attuned to the lives and feelings of common people: the working class, the pioneers, the soldiers, the battlers. They are an index of our values and aspirations.

No country has a greater need than Australia, remote as we are from the great galleries of the world, to acquire works of art from other nations and civilisations. The Louvre, the Prado, the National Gallery in London and the Künsthistorisches Museum have never limited themselves to French, Spanish, British or Austrian purchases, or even given them any special priority. Overseas galleries have always recognised that the function of any gallery is to offer a comprehensive view of world culture. Clearly Australians will always want to see and enjoy the films of other countries; the film industry, after all, is a global one, and popular taste varies little from country to country. Insularity would be as foolish in matters of film appreciation as it would be in any other field of the arts.

For most Australians, however, it is a source of the greatest satisfaction that the resurgence of Australian film production, fostered by the establishment of a supportive national infrastructure, has seen Australian feature films screening to enthusiastic audiences on Australian cinema screens for the first time in decades. The impact of the early works of this revival was felt further afield than our own shores, most notably with the selection of Ken Hannam's *Sunday Too Far Away* in the Quinzaine des Réalisateurs (Directors' Fortnight) at the 1975 Cannes Festival. It seemed that foreign audiences were as curious about these uniquely Australian stories as were audiences at home. Cinema, significantly the most powerful and accessible of the art forms, was able to communicate the ideas, the stories, the history and culture of Australia to international audiences. And it continues to do so.

For many it may appear that our cinema emerged in the 1970s from out of the blue, like Mad Max from the wasteland. However, as this ambitious project bears witness, the story of Australian cinema is as long as the twentieth century. It charts the development of the very form of cinema itself, from the cumbersome wooden hand-cranked cameras of the beginning of the century to the technological sophistication of the 1990s. It is, however, the creative imagination behind the camera that endows these films with interest. Through them it is possible to see more than the high points of cinematic endeavour in Australia; it is possible to see the development of a nation, the culture, concerns, mythologies and the spirit of its people.

Notes

1 Andrew Pike and Ross Cooper, *Australian Film 1900–1977: A Guide to Feature Film Production*, Oxford University Press, in association with the Australian Film Institute, 1980.
2 *The Story of the Kelly Gang* (Charles Tait, 1906).
3 *Picnic at Hanging Rock* (Peter Weir, 1975), *Caddie* (Donald Crombie, 1976), *Between Wars* (Michael Thornhill, 1974), *The Chant of Jimmie Blacksmith* (Fred Schepisi, 1978), *Gallipoli* (Peter Weir, 1981), *'Breaker' Morant* (Bruce Beresford, 1980), *My Brilliant Career* (Gill Armstrong, 1979).

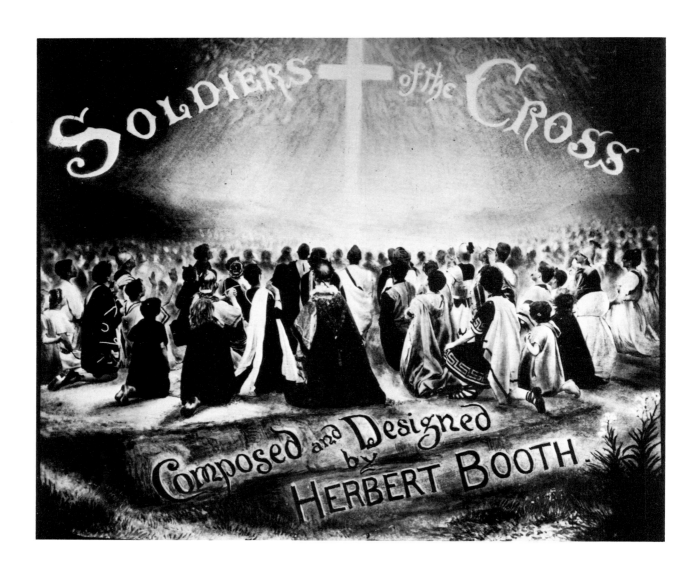

Soldiers of the Cross (1900), a compilation of short films and slides, largely directed by Joseph Perry, with input from Herbert Booth.

1
Australian cinema: 1896 to the renaissance

Graham Shirley

Until the introduction of federal government support in 1969, Australia's feature film industry found itself going through a perpetual replay of rise and fall. These cycles usually started with the discovery that Australia could and should be making features, moved into a period of public welcome for the reappearance of a national film identity, then went into a decline as that identity failed to develop or was simply taken for granted.

For many decades, the fact that the Australian feature producer survived at all was often miraculous. After a promising start, in which a number of exhibitors produced their own features, the amalgamation of exhibitors and distributors into major companies led to a decline in local output. Since it was easier and cheaper for these companies to import films, they now looked upon Australian features as something of a charity. This hardly encouraged continuity of employment among the indigenous film-makers who tried to persist. Audiences became accustomed to the predominant diet of imported films, as well as the reality that these films contained nothing of their customs, legends or day-to-day lives.

From the beginnings of cinema, most of the films screened in Australia were from overseas. Before World War I, less than half the imported films were American, but on a worldwide basis the war allowed Hollywood to achieve dominance over its European competitors. Australia's first American film exchanges were opened during the war and, by 1923, 94 per cent of all films screened locally were American. Australian exhibitors were tied increasingly to 'block booking' of the imports, with the result that it was extremely difficult to find a place for Australian films. In the late 1920s and early 1930s, this dilemma featured prominently in two well-publicised government inquiries.

There was another, much more prolific though less well publicised, film industry running parallel to feature production. This other film industry, the production of actualities—mainly documentaries and newsreels—very often supplied a career start as well as between-features sustenance for producers, directors and technicians. Indeed, when the feature industry had flickered to the point of extinction in the early 1960s, the making of actualities appeared to be in a healthier state than ever before.

Back in the mid-1890s, the earliest motion pictures to arrive in Australia were run on the Edison Kinetoscope.

On 30 November 1894, theatrical entrepreneur James McMahon opened his Kinetoscope Parlour at 148 Pitt Street, Sydney. Customers paid their shilling at the door and could peer down into the eyepieces of five successive machines, each running a 20-second Edison subject, of which 'Caicedo Dancing on the Tight rope' and a comic barber-shop scene were examples. The initial success of the Kinetoscope was phenomenal, attracting 22 000 people to McMahon's Sydney Parlour in its first five weeks.

Each Kinetoscope could only be viewed by one person, so the motion picture at this stage was not a mass medium which could be shared by hundreds, even thousands, of people simultaneously. Prophetically, it was a visiting American who was the first to project films onto a screen in Australia. This was the magician Carl Hertz, who at the Melbourne Opera House, on 22 August 1896, ran a bill of actuality and entertainment shorts including London street scenes, a segment of a boxing match, an Italian skirt dance and a scene from the play, *Trilby*. *The Age* (Melbourne) felt that projected cinema was an advance on both the Kinetoscope and the already popular magic lantern (or limelight) slides when it reported in Australia's first-ever film review that 'It is a combination in which the effects of the kinetoscope are imparted to limelight views, producing scenes of amazing realism, and giving them all the characteristics of actual moving life.'[1]

The earliest films produced in Australia were actualities. In early October 1896, the team of Lumière agent Maurice Sestier and Australian portrait photographer Walter Barnett filmed scenes around Sydney Harbour. The first of their films to be screened, *Passengers Alighting from Ferry "Brighton" at Manly*, premiered at the Salon Lumière, 237 Pitt Street, Sydney, on 27 October, making this also the first venue for the screening of an Australian film. Far more celebrated was Sestier and Barnett's filming of the Melbourne Cup on 3 November. When the Cup film premiered in Melbourne, together with the Sydney scenes and those of Melbourne's AJC Derby (filmed 31 October), *The Bulletin* magazine judged the presentation as follows: 'Artistically it is a big success in some places and a moderate one in others. Some of the pictures are painfully jumpy, and some are hazy, but, on the whole, they are a respectable collection.'[2]

Because of Sestier and Barnett's pioneering achievement, history has overlooked Australian producers who within the next several years began to film their own actualities. The first of them was the Melbourne team of E. J. Thwaites and Robert W. Harvie, who shot a Melbourne street scene as early as March 1897, but mainly covered sporting events that year and the next.

Between 1897 and 1899, the leader of film production and exhibition in Sydney was Mark Blow, a stills photographer who had a prolific output of movie shorts which he screened at his Sydney Polytechnic at 82 King Street. Characteristic of his work are *Sydney Wheel Race* (1897), *Breakers at Bondi* (1897), *Scenes of First Test Match, NSW Versus England* (1898) and *Gallop Past of Sydney Fire Brigade* (1898).

Of at least equal significance was what was probably

the first government film-making in the world, when between March and December 1899 Queensland government photographer Fred C. Wills filmed about thirty subjects to lure migrants; the films were screened soon afterward at the Greater Exhibition in London. Miraculously, most of these films, which include Brisbane and Sydney street scenes, were rediscovered in the early 1980s, and they are the most complete surviving motion-picture record of Australia late in the previous century.

First steps were also being taken in scientific film-making. In 1898, British zoologist Alfred Cord Haddon made the world's first film of an anthropological field trip when he shot the tribal customs and dances of the Torres Strait Islanders during a Cambridge University expedition.

A more ambitious local initiative was the work of Professor Walter Baldwin Spencer, who in 1901 filmed the customs and religious rites of the Aborigines of central and northern Australia. Spencer occasionally shot anthropological film until 1929, and much of his material, like that of Haddon, also survives.

Up to 1906, the leader in Australian film production, distribution and exhibition was the Melbourne-based Limelight Department of the Salvation Army. The Australian Salvation Army hierarchy was enthusiastic about the use of film for fundraising, religious propaganda and for the alleviation of the financial and moral state of the poor. The Limelight Department, under the direction of Joseph Perry, did much to serve these aims with its local and imported films, as well as lantern slides. In time, the Department set up its own film distribution network and had twenty exhibitors simultaneously touring Australia and New Zealand. This was well before the commercial film trade was anywhere near as active.

Perry's film work was a logical evolution from his earlier activities with the Department, which he had helped establish in December 1891 to produce slides on religious and social subjects. He began screening imported films in February 1897, and filmed his first local scenes in October of that year. Much of the Limelight Department's early production was for a series of 'social lectures' given on tour by Salvation Army Commandant Herbert Booth and Mrs Booth. The items included straight records as well as re-enactments of events, such as the activities of the Army's Prison Gate Brigade, and its rescue and maternity operations.

Today, the best known of the Limelight Department's output is the two-and-a-quarter-hour religious epic *Soldiers of the Cross* (1900), which was largely directed by Joseph Perry with input from Herbert Booth. Although it has often mistakenly been called a feature-length film, it was in fact a complex interweaving of thirteen 90-second dramatised films with 200 magic lantern slides, music and an accompanying lecture by Herbert Booth. The primary aim of the event was to recruit Salvation Army cadets by showing a compendium of martyrdom in the name of early Christianity.

Viewers were confronted with Christian martyrs being mauled by lions at the Colosseum, and being crucified, beheaded and putting in time as human torches for Nero.

The alternation of film and slides appears for the most part to have provided a continuous narrative, although here and there a film segment would give an emotional climax to a preceding slide series by giving life to a dramatic highlight. Much of the production was photographed against painted backdrops, and Salvation Army staff played both Romans and martyrs.

Since the premiere at the Melbourne Town Hall attracted 4000 people, the success of the event as both a showbusiness and religious phenomenon was undeniable. In reviewing the event, Salvation Army's Brigadier Philip Kyle wrote:

> It cannot fail to stir the minds and hearts of those who witness it. It is a great assault upon the conscience through eye and ear gates. While the eyes are applying the truth to the spirit, the ear is also pouring it in through the sense of sound. The devil, who often succeeds utilising the eye while the preacher is trying to reach the mind through the ear, is checkmated.[3]

The Salvation Army publicised *Soldiers of the Cross* as 'The Greatest Thing Ever Produced in the Limelight World'.[4] But far more representative of the output of the Limelight Department were its actualities. Between 1898 and late 1901, the Department shot approximately 30 000 feet of film, most of which consisted of documentary records of the Salvation Army's social work and of important events such as the proclamation of Australian nationhood and the British royal visit to open Australia's first federal parliament in 1901.

After *Soldiers of the Cross*, the Department's next ambitious production was *Under Southern Skies* (Joseph Perry, 1902). Consisting of 35 films and 200 slides, it was a detailed, two-hour documentary on the history of Australia, culminating in the recent federation proceedings.

The Salvation Army's fictional film activity increased after 1907, and a new studio was built to give greater flexibility to its productions. Early 1909 found Perry at work in this new studio, where he produced two feature-length dramas, *Heroes of the Cross* (a remake of *Soldiers of the Cross* with some new music and story elements) and *The Scottish Covenanters*. But in early 1910 the Department was abruptly closed by a puritanical new Salvation Army commandant who made no secret of his dislike for the all-too-secular role film was playing in society. Resigning from the Salvation Army, Joseph Perry worked for the remainder of his career in commercial film distribution.

Towards the end of the Limelight Department's existence, other enterprising producers were building upon the production and exhibition expertise it had established. Among them were the exhibitors Millard Johnson and William Gibson, who commissioned short and feature-length actualities before embarking on dramatised films as investors in *The Story of the Kelly Gang* (Charles Tait, 1906).

As with *Soldiers of the Cross*, *The Story of the Kelly Gang* has been subjected to a number of erroneous claims over the years, including its presumed status as 'the

Gunfight outside the Glenrowan Hotel in *The Story of the Kelly Gang* (Charles Tait, 1906).

world's first feature film', which by normal definition is a narrative film which runs for more than an hour. Today there is no certainty in knowing the exact running time of *The Story of the Kelly Gang*, beyond the fact that its length was advertised as 4000 feet and in reviews was mentioned as running between 40 minutes and more than an hour.[5] Its producer was the theatrical firm of J. and N. Tait, which in 1900 had been impressed by the audience impact of the film segments in *Soldiers of the Cross*.

From 1904, J. and N. Tait included film screenings among its theatrical activities, and the following year was sufficiently struck by the success in Australia of Edwin S. Porter's *The Great Train Robbery* (1903) to consider its involvement in production. The choice of *The Story of the Kelly Gang* was motivated by the great success of stage plays based on the real-life exploits of the horse thief and bank robber Ned Kelly, whose career had ended in 1880 with his capture and execution.

Scripting and direction of the actors in the film was by Charles Tait, while technical direction and camerawork was by Charles Byers Coates, an Englishman who also filmed such actualities as *Living Bendigo* (1907) and *Living Hawthorn* (1907) for Millard Johnson and William Gibson.[6] Great importance was placed on the authenticity of the film's events, locations and settings, and this is borne out in the eight or so minutes that survive.[7] While the emphasis on action makes it hard to evaluate performance, there is a documentary flavour to the proceedings. Reviewers of the period praised the film's realism, with the Sydney *Sunday Mail* commenting that 'The well-known features of Kate, Ned, and Dan Kelly, with Steve Hart, and Joe Byrne [members of the Kelly Gang] are all reproduced in such a remarkable manner that the onlooker could easily imagine the pictures had been photographed on the spot where and when the stirring events took place.'[8]

The Story of the Kelly Gang was an instant success, and its £1000 budget was returned by a trial run in the country.

Cozen Spencer's film studio at Rushcutter's Bay.

C. A. Jeffries and John Barr, authors of *Australia Calls* (Raymond Longford, 1913).

It went on to make a fortune for its backers and exhibitors, and this appears to have encouraged the production of even longer narrative films.

Australian film exhibition, which had seen a number of showmen come and go, began to stabilise after 1904 with the increase of imported film supplies. This period brought the appearance of a number of major exhibitors, one of whom, the British-based exhibitor T. J. West, financed Australia's first purpose-built cinema in 1906. Australian picture theatre investment was said to have made millionaires out of West and his closest rival, Cozens Spencer, and, in 1909, West built a 4000-seat cinema in Melbourne, the largest in the world yet designed for that purpose.

That same year, another prominent figure, J. D. Williams, opened Australia's first continuous cinema, the Colonial in Sydney, which ran non-stop from 11 a.m. to 11 p.m.

Australian features were popular whenever they were screened, and between 1907 and 1911 there was a ready outlet for them since the exhibitors' supply of long story films from abroad was spasmodic. This, and the existence of a multitude of independent exhibitors, helped stimulate the first 'golden' period of Australian production, which between 1910 and 1912 saw the making of almost 90 fiction films, many of them running longer than 1000m. Typical examples are the bushranging tale *Robbery Under Arms* (1907) and the colonial convict saga *For the Term of His Natural Life* (1908), both directed by Charles Byers Coates for Charles McMahon.[9]

Among other contributors were *The Story of the Kelly Gang* partners, J. and N. Tait, Millard Johnson and William Gibson, who between 1911 and early 1912 produced nine known features under the auspices of Amalgamated Pictures in Melbourne. In Sydney, there was the Australian Photo-Play Co., with at least twenty features to its credit, and Australian Life Biograph. (Appearing in most of the latter's eight features was actress Louise Carbasse, who later found fame in Hollywood as Louise Lovely.) Australian Life Biograph had a glass-roofed studio near Manly Beach, and the stories it filmed—such as *One Hundred Years Ago* and *A Tale of the Australian Bush* (both Gaston Mervale, 1911)—dealt largely with colonial Australia.

Talented directors who made their first features between 1910 and 1912 were Raymond Longford (*The Fatal Wedding*, 1911), Franklyn Barrett (*All for Gold*, 1911) and Alfred Rolfe (*Captain Midnight, the Bush King*, 1911). Rolfe and Longford were given their first directorial chances by exhibitor–producer Cozens Spencer, who in September 1912 opened a studio complex at Rushcutter's Bay, Sydney, costing in excess of £10 000. Longford made three films there, the most ambitious of which, *Australia Calls* (1913), warned of an Asiatic invasion of Australia. Sadly, along with 90 per cent of Australia's silent features (and even more of the actuality films), most of the earliest films of Longford, Barrett and Rolfe are now missing.

About half of Longford's *The Romantic Story of Margaret Catchpole* (1911) survives, showing a director with an instinctive grasp of the potentialities of the medium and an ability to make the most of locations. The story, based on fact, tells of Margaret Catchpole's transportation to New South Wales in 1801 after she had twice been sentenced to death in England for horse-stealing and escaping captivity.

The Australian colonial scenes are now missing, but those with an English setting (filmed in Australia) draw effective atmosphere from the use of coastal cliffs and inlets. Performances are variable, but there are already signs of the naturalism that was later to characterise Longford's best work. Impressive in the title role is Lottie Lyell, who was to prove an increasingly important collaborator for Longford, off and on the screen. In time, she would work as his co-director, producer, writer and editor.

All of Longford's six features for Cozens Spencer were profitable, with the first, *The Fatal Wedding*, netting £16 000 from an initial cost of £600. It was clear Longford and Spencer could have continued to expand the financial viability of local production, but in 1913 a crucial event in the Australian film industry had a marked effect on both their careers and on those of numerous others.

The period from March 1911 until January 1913 brought the formation of what became known as 'the combine', an amalgamation of two new and affiliated companies: the distributor Australasian Films and the exhibition chain Union Theatres. Both represented the former interests of a number of producer-exhibitors, including Spencer, T. J. West, J. and N. Tait, and Johnson and Gibson. From this point onward, the policy of the newly formed combine was to stress the distribution and screening of imported films. In response to producer criticism, Australasian Films occasionally embarked on short bursts of feature production, but for the most part it restricted its film-making to actualities. Cozens Spencer found himself squeezed out of the film business altogether, while Raymond Longford, who claimed his career was repeatedly and deliberately hindered by the combine, continued to direct for a number of short-lived production companies until the early sound period.

Restricted distribution and exhibition for Australian films was an undeniable problem, but almost as serious was the dilemma of finding enough stories to lure an audience accustomed to the increasing smorgasbord of overseas films. Not surprisingly, adaptations of overseas plays figured prominently in the local film-maker's repertoire, and about the only bankable genre established was bush tales. Many of these, such as *Thunderbolt* (John Gavin, 1910) and *A Tale of the Australian Bush* (1911), were bushranging adventures. But in 1912 even this guaranteed money-spinner was removed when bushranging films were banned in New South Wales. Since that state provided the largest audience, the genre virtually disappeared from local screens for another 40 years.

World War I brought temporary salvation, since the exploits of Australians at war was an obvious choice of subject. No less than sixteen Australian features dramatised aspects of the war, with some (e.g., *The Martyrdom of Nurse Cavell*, John Gavin and C. Post

Margaret Catchpole (Lottie Lyell) is courted by Lieutenant Barry (Augustus Neville) in Raymond Longford's *The Romantic Story of Margaret Catchpole* (1911).

Mason, 1916) stirring up fervour for overseas allies, others (e.g., *If the Huns Came to Melbourne*, George Coates, 1916) trying to heighten war fears for a country that was a long way from the action, and with most serving to encourage recruitment.

Two of the most avowed recruiting pieces, *Will They Never Come?* and *The Hero of the Dardanelles* (both 1915), were directed by Alfred Rolfe for Australasian Films. *The Hero of the Dardanelles*, the only one of Rolfe's 30 features to survive, shows a fluent grasp of screen grammar that is far superior to that of Longford's *Trooper Campbell*, made in 1914. The mingling of dramatic naturalism with documentary ingredients in the sequences that survive is impressive. The climax, the Australian landing at Gallipoli, is now missing but is suspected to have been re-used for the 1928 *Spirit of Gallipoli* (Keith Gatewood and William Green). If this is

the case, then it is spectacle of a high and authentic order, based as it was on official reports, drawings and photographs of the Gallipoli landing.

In contrast to the rather erratic progress of local features, the Australian newsreel had been quietly consolidating itself in the years leading up to the war. In 1909, Pathé Frères had been the first overseas film company to open a distribution office in Australia, and in November 1910 it began *Pathé's Australian Animated Gazette*, said to be one of the world's earliest regular newsreels. With the amalgamation of certain of Pathé's local interests into the Australasian Films-Union Theatres combine in 1913, *Pathé's Australian Animated Gazette* continued under the same title until it was shortened in 1914 to *The Australian Gazette*.

Within several years, *The Australian Gazette* became *Australasian Gazette*, and, in mixing news with magazine

"Tell my friends I gave my life willingly for my country. I have no fear or shrinking. I have seen death so often it is not fearful or strange to me."

Top: an illustration promoting *The Martyrdom of Nurse Cavell* (John Gavin and C. Post Mason, 1916). Bottom: Alfred Rolfe's *The Hero of the Dardanelles* (1915), the only one of Rolfe's thirty features to survive.

Top: the cast of Beaumont Smith's *Our Friends the Hayseeds* (1917). Bottom: Franklyn Barrett's lavish melodrama, *The Breaking of the Drought* (1920).

and novelty items, was much like newsreels elsewhere in the world. But from around 1915, the reel had the advantage of editorial input from the cartoonist Harry Julius, whose 'Cartoons of the Moment' offered anti-German propaganda as well as satire on such issues as Australian Prime Minister W. M. Hughes' receiving a mixed reception on his visit to London. Rarely less than inspired, the cartoons were drawn in chalk with Julius' hand moving just out of frame to create the impression of animation.

The later years of the war brought the flowering of Australian feature-film comedy, a not-so-surprising trend in the face of war weariness and growing resistance to wartime propaganda. Most characteristic were the bush farces of director Beaumont Smith. A canny showman with a background in journalism and publicity, Smith's most regular output was a series of films featuring the bucolic Hayseed family. The first, *Our Friends the Hayseeds* (1917), was so successful that Smith was to make two more that same year. In truth, the inspiration was Steele Rudd's stories, *On Our Selection*, published in 1899 and featuring the more subtly drawn Rudd family. Both the Hayseeds and the Rudds were to provide a meal ticket for Smith and other film-makers until the outbreak of World War II.

Smith's approach to film-making was often rough-and-ready, earning him the nickname 'One-Take Beau'. But his *The Adventures of Algy* (1925) and his talkie *The Hayseeds* (1933) can still entertain, particularly in the moments where comedy timing and whimsical charm are able to break through the crudeness. The former, set in Sydney and New Zealand, features Claude Dampier as Algy, a 'silly ass' Englishman who, having been swindled out of a rich land holding, strikes oil on another property. Entire tracts of the film are little more than travelogue, but the Sydney scenes, especially where a drugged Algy mistakes a Manly ferry trip for an overseas voyage, partly redeem the rest with a few belly laughs.

Far more careful about his film-making was director-writer-cameraman Franklyn Barrett, who made his first feature, *All for Gold*, in 1911 after a background in press photography and the making of actuality and dramatised shorts. Barrett's photography on his features *The Breaking of the Drought* (1920) and *A Girl of the Bush* (1921) reveal him as a brilliant cameraman, best inspired when capturing the stark beauty of the Australian outback. Both films draw their strength from Barrett's observations of the rituals of country and city life, and in each story he convincingly identifies the city with dissipation and hard times, the country with purity and regeneration.

English-born, Barrett became one of the most nationalistic of Australia's silent-era directors, and he intended to have *The Breaking of the Drought* 'illustrate to our city dwellers the brave fight of the man on the land, and make them a little more tolerant of their country cousins'. The documentary record he filmed of the 1919 drought was flawlessly incorporated into the narrative. He also recorded a vivid portrait of the Sydney slums and bohemian club land.

If Barrett's casting of stage-trained actors was apt to let him down on *The Breaking of the Drought*, his use of actors in *A Girl of the Bush* was far more assured. His rural scenes contribute to legend building, and there is an exciting climax reminiscent of the parallel cutting of D. W. Griffith's *Intolerance* (1916). But the banning of *The Breaking of the Drought* for export (because to portray drought showed the nation in an unfavourable light) was a big financial blow for Barrett. His position wasn't helped when *Know Thy Child* (1921) and *A Rough Passage* (1922) failed to return production costs. After the latter film, Barrett abandoned production and spent the rest of his career as a film exhibitor.

Australian society was experiencing a mood of post-war nationalism, a consolidation of identity for a country which had only officially been a nation since 1901. The new confidence was reflected in not only the films of Franklyn Barrett, but also those of Raymond Longford whose career peaked during this period. Longford was already an accomplished film-maker by the time he worked on *The Woman Suffers* (1918), a melodrama about a family's revenge for the jilting of an unwed mother. The first half of the film tends to be fairly uninvolving, but it gathers considerable force in the second, with scenes of multiple revelations being genuinely exciting while not overplayed. Water as an elemental and symbolic device is effectively used to steer and underline the fate of the characters, and the very mood of the outback is seen to provide strong motivation for what occurs.

Longford's *The Sentimental Bloke* (1919) is the earliest Australian feature to be regarded as a classic. Adapted from C. J. Dennis' *Songs of a Sentimental Bloke*, it effectively fleshed out much that had only been suggested in Dennis' book of verse, creating characters of great dimension and humour in the adroitly cast central roles of the Bloke (Arthur Tauchert) and his true love, Doreen (Lottie Lyell). Much of the story concerns their courtship, which is temporarily broken when they argue over the attentions of a rival for Doreen's hand. Their marriage is tested when the Bloke reverts to boozing with old mates, but the couple is assured a more stable future when they are given the chance to manage an orchard in the country.

If *The Woman Suffers* had sometimes looked too much an alliance between film and theatre, then Longford was at pains with *The Sentimental Bloke* to present characters that were unmistakably of their environment. Longford encouraged all his actors to prepare for filming in areas like the Sydney working-class suburb of Woolloomooloo by spending days in the district to mix with its people. Indicating why this worked as well as it did, Longford told *The Lone Hand*: 'The true art of acting is not to act. . .That's what I have drummed into the ears of my characters and I think it has had its effect in the naturalness of my productions. It is the little things that count, the little human touches that build up a big production, and to these I have given most thought.'[10]

With *The Sentimental Bloke*, Longford had clearly hit his stride, knowing and making use of every nuance of

Oswald Keane (Herbert Linden) and Lorna Denver (Vera James). Franklyn Barrett's *A Girl of the Bush* (1921).

Stephen Manton (Charles H. Francis) with Marion Masters (Connie Martyn) and her children (Doris Wadham and Harry Goodfellow). Raymond Longford's *The Woman Suffers* (1918).

screen grammar. In a café scene, the Bloke's pretended indifference to the antics of his rival is destroyed by his mounting fury, and the film-maker subtly emphasises this with well-timed cutting between the characters. To stress the film's remove from run-of-the-mill melodramas, actual moments of melodrama are saved for a farcical dream sequence. The Bloke's discomfort on several other occasions, such as a formal visit to Doreen's mother, is rendered with every claustrophobic moment intact. The film only falters toward the end when the move to the country gives the characters little chance to further develop.

On its release, *The Sentimental Bloke* earned greater praise and more money than any other Australian film to date, and until the end of the silent era it was quoted as a benchmark of quality by other film-makers and the trade.

Between 1919 and 1921, Longford went on to make two more successful films for the Southern Cross Feature Film Company, the Adelaide concern which had backed *The Woman Suffers* and *The Sentimental Bloke*. The second, *The Blue Mountains Mystery* (Longford and Lyell, 1921), had almost double the budget of *The Sentimental Bloke* and gave Lottie Lyell her first official credit as co-director. For exhibitor–producer E. J. Carroll, Longford and Lyell also made the first screen adaptation of Steele Rudd's *On Our Selection* (Longford, 1920) and a sequel, *Rudd's New Selection* (Longford, 1921).

After occasional involvement in early Australian features, E. J. Carroll had joined forces with his brother Dan, Olympic sportsman Snowy Baker and the Southern Cross Feature Film Company to produce films for the overseas market. In pursuit of this objective, they

ME PAL 'E TROTS 'ER UP AN' DOES THE TOFF.
'E ALLUS WUS A BLOKE FER SHOWIN' OFF.
"THIS 'ERE'S DOREEN,"'E SEZ. — "THIS 'ERE'S THE KID."
— I DIPS ME LID —

Top: Bill (Arthur Tauchert), Ginger Mick (Gilbert Emery) and Doreen (Lottie Lyell). Raymond Longford's *The Sentimental Bloke* (1919). Bottom: Raymond Longford's *On Our Selection* (1920), based on the stories by Steele Rudd.

imported American director Wilfred Lucas and his scriptwriter wife, Bess Meredyth. The team made three films starring Snowy Baker, of which only *The Man from Kangaroo* (1920) has survived. A slick and likeable action thriller, it plumbs no depths and is largely reliant on the cheery smiles and wild chases of the stunt-loving Baker.

The Man from Kangaroo was followed, also in 1920, by *The Shadow of Lightning Ridge* and *The Jackeroo of Coolabong* (both Lucas). So confident were the Carrolls in the future of Australian production that they set up a studio in the Sydney mansion 'Palmerston', where for a time they had Longford's and Baker's units working simultaneously. But problems began to loom after the success of the first two Baker films. The Carroll features began taking longer to return money, particularly from the overseas market, and E. J. Carroll decided to terminate production after Longford and Lyell had finished *The Blue Mountains Mystery*. Longford later claimed that Carroll was warned that, unless he abandoned production, Australasian Films would cripple his exhibition work by cutting off overseas film supplies.

Cast adrift from substantial backing, Longford and Lyell formed two companies for the making of another four films. The first two, *The Dinkum Bloke* (Longford, 1923) and *Fisher's Ghost* (Longford, 1924), did well at the box office, but the critical response to *The Bushwhackers* (Longford, 1925) and *Peter Vernon's Silence* (Longford, 1926) made it clear that meagre budgets had led them to apply their talents too thinly. The persistent refusal of Australasian to release their films hardly helped matters, and Longford and Lyell found themselves the victims of an industry which had been in financial crisis since mid-1922.

In September 1925, there appeared to be a reasonable chance their fortunes would revive when Longford was appointed director of productions for Australasian Films. He was to make two low-budget films for the company before he suggested that he embark on a £15 000 remake of *For the Term of his Natural Life* for the English market. But Australasian Films, having accepted this proposal, then re-assigned *For the Term of his Natural Life* to visiting American director Norman Dawn in the hope of a broader market. This was effectively the end of Longford's career. Lottie Lyell, his essential collaborator, had spent the early 1920s in declining health, and she died in December 1925. After the Australasian fiasco, Longford directed only one more film, a rather halting talkie called *The Man They Could Not Hang* (1934).

Norman Dawn's *For the Term of his Natural Life* (1927) ranks with Longford's *The Sentimental Bloke* as a landmark in Australian production. Its most notable aspects were its unprecedented budget (which climbed to £60 000) and its impressive scale of production, with Dawn— originally a documentary, feature and optical-effects cameraman—making the most of the widespread locations, particularly the penal ruins of Tasmania's Port Arthur.

This writer (who did a restoration of the film for Australia's National Film & Sound Archive in 1981) has to admit to affection for the strengths and weaknesses of *For the Term of his Natural Life*, and the latter includes an overly complicated plot and too much melodrama. But much of the film is redeemed by an authenticity, power and momentum that has much to do with inspiration from the Marcus Clarke novel from which it was adapted. *For the Term of his Natural Life* went on to earn more money at home than any other Australian film to that time.

For Australasian, Dawn next embarked on a Pacific island romance, *The Adorable Outcast* (1928), but this film failed to reap anywhere near the box-office rewards of its predecessor. The introduction of sound films destroyed high hopes for the release of both films abroad, and Australasian Films halted production to watch developments in the new technology.

By the mid-1920s, just as a batch of new feature directors was entering the field, a number of the older guard— among them Longford, Franklyn Barrett and Beaumont Smith—had virtually withdrawn. But actuality filmmakers were forging ahead much as they had before. In December 1911, the federal government had embarked on a regular schedule of publicity films and records of prominent events when it appointed an official Commonwealth Cinematographer. His work was expanded with the formation of the Commonwealth Cinema and Photographic Branch in 1921, and with various name changes the organisation continued its work until replaced by the Film Division of the Department of Information in the 1940s.

Up until World War II, the Cinema Branch's output was mostly pedestrian, but every so often a gem emerged, such as *Through Australia with the Prince of Wales* (Bert Ive, 1920) or *Among the Hardwoods* (Lyn Maplestone, 1936). The latter, a film of astonishing beauty, captured the work of timber-getters in south-west Western Australia. With inter-titles instead of commentary and with an emphasis on natural sound, the film has a timeless lyricism that has partly to do with the location, partly with the way its timber-getting techniques are filmed with anthropological fascination. In contrast to such workaday Cinema Branch titles as *Australian Apples* and *Australian Eggs*, it was an example of what the Branch might have done with more imaginative guidance.

By far the most celebrated Australian documentary film-maker of the silent and early sound periods was Frank Hurley. Like his closest counterpart, Francis Birtles (whose final film was the dramatised *Coorab in the Island of Ghosts*, 1929), Hurley made his name by filming journeys to regions still largely unexplored. If Birtles had been the first to establish a long tradition of factual films about outback adventure, then Hurley's fame grew rapidly as a result of his superb and hard-won record of the trips of noted explorers, particularly those of the Antarctic pioneers Douglas Mawson (*Home of the Blizzard*, 1913) and Ernest Shackleton (*In the Grip of the Polar Ice*, 1917).

18

Norman Dawn's £60 000 *For the Term of his Natural Life* (1927).

In 1921, Hurley enhanced his reputation with *Pearls and Savages*, a record of two exploratory and scientific expeditions around Papua New Guinea. His record of tribal lifestyles and ceremonies astonished audiences when he toured the film through Australia, the US, Canada and Britain.

In 1926, with the backing of British film and theatre magnate Oswald Stoll, Hurley made two narrative features before suspending production to await the outcome of a federal Royal Commission being conducted into Australia's motion picture industry.

The Royal Commission, which had been upgraded from a Select Committee established in March 1927, was created in response to wide community opposition to the dominance of American cinema. A broad spectrum

of British Empire loyalists, Australian producers and women's groups all had their reasons for wanting restrictions placed on the incoming torrent of American films, and since the early 1920s Australian film-makers had pressed federal and state governments to impose a quota which favoured the screening of Australian and British films. In originally moving for a Royal Commission, Senator John Grant had talked about the restrictive nature of block booking which made it almost impossible to squeeze Australian and British films in among the American ones. In Grant's opinion, government film taxes, tariffs and quotas were ideal remedies. Amid such talk, the mood among local producers was optimistic.

In April 1928, after eight months of collecting evidence in every state capital and many country centres, the

19

Top: James Carson (Gaston Mervale), Karl Rossi (Arthur McLaglen) and Cherry Carson (Marie Lorraine). Paulette McDonagh's *The Far Paradise* (1928). Bottom left: Paula Marsh (Marie Lorraine) and Lee Travers (Josef Bambach). Paulette McDonagh's *The Cheaters* (1930). Bottom right: Cherry Carson in *The Far Paradise*.

Commission's report was tabled in federal parliament. But despite the feeling expressed by Raymond Longford that the report was 'a work of truly constructive merit'[11], the only resulting legislation to assist local film-makers were a pair of cash prizes for the best Australian production and scenario, and a five per cent rejection clause in distribution and exhibition contracts to allow the release of Australian productions.

Since most producers and investors had delayed their plans until the results of the Commission were known, investment in feature production plummeted from £100 000 in 1927 to virtually nothing by the end of 1929. The release of one of the few Australian silents to be completed that year, *The Cheaters* (1930), was indefinitely suspended while its producers hastened to have it converted to a part-talkie.

Involved in *The Cheaters* was the family team of the McDonagh sisters: Paulette as writer-director, Isabel as leading actress (appearing under the stage name Marie Lorraine) and Phyllis, who served as art director, production manager and publicist. With their first feature, *Those Who Love* (P. J. Ramster and Paulette McDonagh, 1926), the McDonaghs enjoyed great commercial success, and achieved dramatic and technical standards comparable with the quality output of the American films that were their inspiration. This success was repeated with *The Far Paradise* (Paulette McDonagh, 1928), the better of their two surviving films and ranking as one of the best-directed of all Australian features prior to the coming of sound.

Aiming to compete with Hollywood at home and abroad, the McDonagh sisters chose initially to produce society dramas of a kind familiar to their audiences. Both *The Far Paradise* and *The Cheaters* saddled their heroines with feelings of conflicting loyalty between criminal fathers and would-be lovers. *The Far Paradise* starts with the return home from finishing school of Cherry (Marie Lorraine), who not only discovers her father is a dissolute drunk and swindler but also that he is the sworn enemy of the father of her lover (Paul Longuet). Paulette McDonagh ensures that the emotions felt by the lovers are both palpable and realistic. The intensity of her direction can be felt in her refinement of Marie Lorraine's instinctive performance, her handling of support players, and the unerring judgement in framing, lighting and editing. Not surprisingly, *Smith's Weekly* felt that the McDonaghs' work on this film 'has something of the art that conceals art; that makes you forget you are watching a film and so lets you judge the drama on its own merits'.[12]

The Cheaters used a similar device of lovers separated by parental differences. The story is at times over-eventful and its ending too convenient, but otherwise the film confirms Paulette McDonagh as a knowing and consistent manipulator of film form. There is a deliberately cynical, often world-weary edge to the proceedings, revealing that the McDonaghs were now prepared to eschew star-crossed romances for a darker complexity not unlike that of the silent films of Erich von Stroheim

and Fritz Lang. Marie Lorraine's heroine, sweet and unquestioning in *The Far Paradise*, has by this time developed a healthy capacity for self-doubt.

The Cheaters marked a turning point for the McDonaghs. First converted to a part-talkie, then to a 1931 full-talkie with re-shot close-ups, it appears to have had very few screenings—mostly, one gathers, because by that time it had become *passé*.

For their final film, *Two Minutes Silence* (McDonagh, 1933 or 1934), the sisters courageously turned to Leslie Haylen's anti-war play to make what became the first Australian talkie with a theme of social concern. Paulette McDonagh later said it was the best film she had ever made. But when box-office returns were unsatisfactory, the McDonaghs—a gifted team with the right material—withdrew from the field. Like *Those Who Love*, *Two Minutes Silence* is now a lost film.

Another imaginative director of the late silent period was Tal Ordell, who with *The Kid Stakes* (1927) made what was possibly the fastest, wittiest local comedy up to that time. Based on Syd Nicholls' cartoon strip 'Fatty Finn', *The Kid Stakes* mixes the energetic style of the American 'Our Gang' comedies with the unmistakably Australian character of Ordell's mostly child cast. Its setting, like that of *The Sentimental Bloke*, is the working-class milieu of Sydney's Woolloomooloo. As Longford and Lyell had, Ordell shows an immediate empathy with the district and its people, drawing satiric contrasts between working-class children and the rich in their Potts Point mansions on the hill above. The film is climaxed by a hilarious goat-drawn billycart race which is made almost audible by inter-titles that jump, spin and leap to convey the yelling of spectators.

While *The Kid Stakes* made a slight profit, from the late 1920s it became progressively harder for independents like Ordell, who had no substantial backing, to remain in production. The main reason for this was the high production cost associated with the coming of sound.

Following various experiments in Australian talkie production in the early 1920s, the first real activity came in 1927 when De Forest Phonofilms (Australia) filmed news and actuality items using imported American gear. After August 1929, Australian sound production of a more regular kind started when Fox Movietone (Australia) imported sound equipment for the shooting of Australian Movietone items. On 2 November, the first *Australian Movietone News* issue, merging local with overseas items, included a speech by Prime Minister J. H. Scullin, and on 6 November the Melbourne Cup was the subject of the first full-reel Australian special. January 1931 brought the debut of an entirely Australian edition, and from this point on the Australian reel appeared alongside a weekly international reel edited 'with due appreciation of Australian values'[13] by Movietone boss Harry Guinness.

Because of competition from Movietone, the final Sydney issue of the silent *The Australasian Gazette* had appeared in March 1929. For about fifteen months from June 1930, Union Theatres' Melbourne branch produced

Tal Ordell's *The Kid Stakes* (1927).

a sound-on-disc *The Australian Talkies Newsreel* (later *The Australian Sound Gazette*). Another contender was the Melbourne-based *The Herald Newsreel*. Produced by *The Herald* (Melbourne) in collaboration with Herschells Films, *The Herald Newsreel* was established following a suggestion by *The Herald* proprietor Keith Murdoch, who had been impressed by the way in which newspapers had been affiliated with talkie newsreels abroad. Premiered in September 1931, the newsreel ran for exactly twelve months, after which it was absorbed by a more ambitious competitor, *Cinesound Review*, headed by Ken G. Hall.

Hall, who had a background in film publicity for Union Theatres and the Australian branch of First National Pictures (Australasia), had been sent to the US by the latter in 1925 to observe production. In 1928, First National gave him his first taste of film-making when he directed Australian replacement sequences for the imported German film, *Unsere Emden* (Louis Ralph, 1926), released locally as *The Exploits of the Emden*. The re-

sult, which meant virtually half a re-make of the German film, had a lucrative run in Sydney. Hall subsequently worked as personal assistant to Union Theatres-Australasian Films' managing director Stuart F. Doyle, who appears to have taken into account the success of *The Exploits of the Emden* when, in 1931, he gave Hall the chance to direct Australasian's first talkie feature, *On Our Selection* (1932). Using sound equipment developed by local inventor Arthur Smith, the film cost a mere £6000.

As co-writer and producer of the play from which *On Our Selection* was adapted, Bert Bailey (who played the central role of Dad) had had twenty years in which to refine his routines and build up an excellent stock company of supporting players. Nearly all the bits of business and the cast remained intact for Hall's film, and as co-writer and director Hall worked closely with Bailey to convert them to cinema. Most of the actors had previously made the roles their own, and this, within the context of *On Our Selection*, gives the performances an authentic edge rare in Australian films of the 1930s. It also makes for inspired comedy timing, although certain other ingredients, such as those of melodramatic confrontation, have dated badly. Welding the uncertainties together is a showcasing of the Australian bush which also gives the film much of its atmosphere. An introductory 'bush symphony' of birdcalls and an interlude of cattle fording a river caused early audiences to applaud. One reviewer wrote that 'You hear the loveliness of the bushland, and hear its shy birds calling in the soft, clear dawn, and you know that here is the real Australia.'[14]

On release, *On Our Selection's* distinctively Australian characters and setting helped give it immense local appeal, and by the late 1930s it had netted a record return of £50 000, an amount unequalled by any other Australian film until the early 1970s. This success was particularly good news for Stuart Doyle, whose Union Theatres had otherwise been battered by the Depression. Because of this, in October 1931 Union Theatres was liquidated and replaced by the newly created Greater Union Theatres. In June the following year, Doyle had enough faith in the yet-to-be released *On Our Selection* to establish Cinesound Productions to take over the film-making operations of Australasian Films. Under Cinesound's auspices, Hall was to make another sixteen profitable features up until the outbreak of World War II. All had a guaranteed release through Greater Union Theatres and distribution through another affiliate, British Empire Films.

Commenced by Hall when he was halfway through shooting *On Our Selection*, the newsreel *Cinesound Review* first appeared on 7 November 1931 featuring the ubiquitous Melbourne Cup. From here on, the Cinesound reel closely rivalled *Australian Movietone News*, and the two continued to compete earnestly each year to be the first on screen with the Cup. Each had other notable scoops, such as Movietone's filming the arrival in Brisbane of Amy Johnson at the end of her 1930 England-to-Australia flight, and *Cinesound Review's* catching the moment when Captain Francis De Groot charged his horse to prematurely open the Sydney Harbour Bridge in March 1932.

Hall had the showman's touch, and he carefully studied —as the McDonagh sisters had—exactly why certain feature film ingredients worked for an audience. Bucolic comedies were Cinesound's surest earner, and *On Our Selection* was followed by three more Dad 'n' Dave films, all of them directed by Hall: *Grandad Rudd* (1935), *Dad and Dave Come to Town* (1938) and *Dad Rudd M.P.* (1940).

Of these, *Dad and Dave Come to Town* (written by Frank Harvey and Bert Bailey from a story by Hall) can still win across the most critical of audiences. There is nothing new about its premise of contrasting rural with slick city ways, but the pacing is assured, the dialogue worldly-wise and the majority of situations inventively handled. Bert Bailey's role as Dad shows a more human face than in the earlier films, and he is given several key speeches that extend the nationalistic legend-building that had been an ingredient of *On Our Selection*.

The other stand-out Ken G. Hall features of the late 1930s were the George Wallace comedy *Let George Do It* (1938), which climaxes with an ingeniously staged speedboat chase around Sydney Harbour, and the comedy-drama *Mr. Chedworth Steps Out* (1939). In the latter, arguably Hall's best all-round film, Cecil Kellaway plays a suburban 'little man' who is the victim of family expectations. Much of the drama, like the comedy, is subtly downplayed, giving all the more impact to the several moments of slapstick and those of genuine menace. *Mr. Chedworth Steps Out,* written by Frank Harvey, is also significant for being the only 1930s feature to reflect the suburban life and aspirations of most Australians.

While other film-makers envied Cinesound's guaranteed distribution and exhibition, Hall was to claim over the years that he had been assured continuity of output for only as long as his features continued to make money. In fact, by the late 1930s a downturn in the film trade meant that the Cinesound films were taking longer to return money, something that failed to impress former chartered accountant Norman Rydge soon after he took over from Stuart Doyle as Greater Union's chairman and managing director in 1937. Following the June 1940 release of *Dad Rudd M.P.*, Rydge announced that all Cinesound feature production would be suspended for the duration of the war.

Attracting far more personal publicity than Ken G. Hall was producer-director-writer Charles Chauvel, who worked in partnership with wife Elsa from the time of their first film in 1926. Whereas Ken G. Hall made his last feature in 1946, Chauvel was able to keep going for another decade, and for a long time *was* the Australian film industry in the minds of the public. The epic and nationalistic subjects he chose undoubtedly helped this image, for Chauvel spent much of his career exploring the traditional Australian themes of pioneering and mateship.

There was a freshness in Chauvel's use of rural locations in his first two films, *The Moth of Moonbi* and *Greenhide* (both 1926), but his first talkie, *In the Wake of the Bounty* (1933), proved the least typical of his work. A partly dramatised documentary, it was planned as the first in a series of travel films, a genre to which Chauvel would not return until the end of his career with the *Walkabout* (1958) series for the BBC. The re-enacted scenes of *In the Wake of the Bounty* featured an extremely raw Errol Flynn in his first film role, helping to throw into relief the far superior documentary coverage which the Chauvels and cameraman Tasman Higgins filmed across three months on remote Pitcairn Island.

Chauvel next turned to the pioneering epic, *Heritage* (1935), followed by *Uncivilised* (1936), a 'Sanders of the River'-meets-'Tarzan' type of tale which was his most deliberate attempt to win the American market. Despite the potential for cardboard characters, they are—in contrast to those of *Bounty* and *Heritage*—alive and interesting, particularly as sexual tension builds between the film's girl reporter (Margot Rhys) and the wild white man (Dennis Hoey) she has followed into remotest north-western Australia. The use of landscape is again vivid,

AUSTRALIAN CINEMA

Top left: Dave (Fred McDonald) and Dad Rudd (Bert Bailey). Ken G. Hall's *On Our Selection* (1932). Top right: Dave (Fred McDonald) and Dad Rudd (Bert Bailey). Ken G. Hall's *Dad and Dave Come to Town* (1938). Bottom left and right: George Chedworth (Cecil Kellaway) in Ken G. Hall's *Mr. Chedworth Steps Out* (1939).

Fletcher Christian (Errol Flynn) in Charles Chauvel's *In the Wake of the Bounty* (1933).

Charles Chauvel's *Forty Thousand Horsemen* (1940).

starting with an eerie canoe trip through primeval mangrove trees.

By the time Chauvel embarked on *Forty Thousand Horsemen* (1940), his final film of the decade, there were other Australian producers—most of them new to the industry with the coming of sound—who had found the struggle to stay in business too great. They included two generously capitalised studios, F. W. Thring's Efftee Film Productions in Melbourne and Sir Hugh Denison's National Studios in Sydney. Thring, former managing director of Hoyts Theatres (the major rival chain to Greater Union), had founded his own company within weeks of resigning from Hoyts, when a controlling interest in that concern was purchased by the Fox Film Corporation. Between 1931 and 1934, Thring produced and mostly directed an output of seven features and more than 80 shorts. The most ambitious of the features was a remake of *The Sentimental Bloke* in 1932, but more successful were knockabout comedies such as *Diggers* (1931), starring vaudevillian Pat Hanna, and several with George Wallace, the best of which is *His Royal Highness* (1932).

Adapted by C. J. Dennis from an idea by George Wallace, *His Royal Highness* is an operetta film about what happens when a clumsy stagehand (Wallace) dreams about inheriting the crown of the fantasy kingdom of Betonia. Much is made of contrasts between the poker-faced Englishness of the Betonians and the haphazard Australianness of Wallace, who horrifies the palace élite by playing cards with the footmen and insisting that geriatric staff wear roller-skates. The film generates a few good laughs, but, like most of the other Efftee features, suffers from a snail's pace and stodgy direction.

Thring's output of short films was to prove far more an achievement, especially when one considers they were made in less than half the three years he was making features. Thring embarked on these shorts to provide exhibitors with supports for his features. They can be broadly divided into vaudeville and variety routines, stage recitations, VIP speeches, general documentaries and 'Australian Educational Films' shorts, the latter being nature-study films co-produced by Thring and the naturalist Noel Monkman. Two of Monkman's most accomplished documentaries are *Catching Crocodiles* and *Nature's Little Jokes*, both shot in tropical Queensland and comparing well with more recent natural history films for skilled observation of rare and often hard-to-film subjects. When the Efftee films were sold to England in 1932, Monkman's 'Australian Marvelogue' series, as they were known, was a decided drawcard.

Alarmed at a deteriorating release position for Australian producers, Thring suspended Efftee production in early 1934. His announcement came a quarter of the way through a fresh inquiry into the film industry, this time by the New South Wales government, which wanted to determine whether there was need for an Australian film quota.

Part of the problem had been a 'film war' between the local exhibition chains, Greater Union and Hoyts on the one side, and American-linked distributors on the other. The Americans for their part were alarmed by the formation of a new company, the General Theatres Corporation, in January 1933 to pool the theatre and film-buying interests of Hoyts and Greater Union. None of this looked too healthy for the Australian producer, particularly when the Americans announced they would establish their own local cinemas on a wide scale.

In June 1934, the report of the NSW film inquiry recommended a five-year distribution and exhibition quota for Australian films. When it became law in September 1935, the *NSW Cinematograph Films (Australian Quota) Act* demanded that 5 per cent of all films handled by distributors and 4 per cent of all those screened by exhibitors in its first year should be of local origin. But the quota act was too late for F. W. Thring, who died in 1936 while planning to relocate his production interests to Sydney.

The well-designed Sydney complex of National Studios was based on the Gaumont–British studios in London, and was built in the expectation that Australian production would mushroom in the wake of the Quota Act. Indeed, a sister company, National Productions, was formed a month after the act became law, but the fact that each of the National companies produced only a single feature, *The Flying Doctor* (Miles Mander, 1936) and *Rangle River* (Clarence Badger, 1936), served as an omen for the wider fortunes of the industry.

As it transpired, *The Flying Doctor*, *Rangle River* and Charles Chauvel's *Uncivilised* were the only three features to result directly from the 1935 NSW Quota Act. The NSW government was prevailed upon to adjust the quota twice before 1939, but most of the trade interests (particularly overseas distributors) found reasons for non-compliance. In December 1938, the government finally turned to the guarantee of bank overdrafts to assist the

making of four Australian features. One of these, Charles Chauvel's *Forty Thousand Horsemen*, was to be the most significant Australian film since Ken Hall's *On Our Selection* and the first Australian feature of international renown.

Although none of *Forty Thousand Horsemen* was set in Australia, its characters represented the clearest articulation of Australian national character to date. Its central theme, like that of Peter Weir's *Gallipoli* 41 years later, was how Australian mateship had been forged and tested under the battle conditions of World War I. This kind of legend-building had been around since the time of *The Hero of the Dardanelles*, but Chauvel took it a few steps further, shaping through the central performance of Chips Rafferty a classic image of the Australian soldier. The film's most obvious claim to fame was its brilliantly staged cavalry charge at Beersheba, covered and edited from numerous perspectives which provide the grand panorama as well as individual effort of the event.

Another film-maker encouraged by the NSW government guarantee was Noel Monkman. After his wildlife and underwater films of the early 1930s, he made his first feature, *Typhoon Treasure,* in 1938. With the outbreak of war, he went on to direct an accomplished propaganda piece, *The Power and the Glory* (1941), featuring Peter Finch as a German fifth columnist. Although budget deficiencies sometimes give the film a ragged edge, Monkman worked effectively within these limitations, and his direction of actors and action scenes show him to have been an intuitive director. The struggle for funds behind this film had been more than usually arduous and, demoralised by efforts to raise more, Monkman returned to Queensland to resume his career in nature films.

If the coming of sound in the late 1920s had brought new life to Australian newsreels, then World War II brought them a maturity. From early in the war, *Cinesound Review* and *Australian Movietone News* made effective use of footage shot by cameramen working for the Department of Information (DOI) Film Division, formed in August 1940 some months after the DOI had sent its first combat cameraman, Damien Parer, to Palestine. While Cinesound focused largely on the war effort at home, Movietone, which had access to more overseas footage, was better able to place Australia's war effort in an international context. Both reels emphasised the human side of war, whether it was the Australian front-line forces, the women who moved into the wartime work force, or the visiting American troops who transformed Australian cities from late 1941. By mid-1942, an average of 90 per cent of stories from both reels dealt with some aspect of the war.

Propaganda content led the newsreels to express a stronger viewpoint, and a number of the Cinesound items worked hard to combat wartime complacency. Of these, the best-known was the 1942 Cinesound full-reel special *Kokoda Front Line*, featuring footage shot by the DOI's Damien Parer of Australian action against the Japanese along New Guinea's Kokoda Trail. The issue included a personal appearance by Parer, who contrasted the desperation of front-line New Guinea with the happy-go-lucky attitude of Australians back home. This heart-felt piece, along with editor Terry Banks' masterly combination of the Kokoda footage with other Parer material, helped *Kokoda Front Line* win an Academy Award as Best Documentary.

Overall supervision of the wartime *Cinesound Review* was by Ken G. Hall, who also directed a number of the approximately one hundred informational and propaganda shorts commissioned from independent producers by the DOI. Among the most impressive are the recruiting film *100 000 Cobbers* (1942) and two dramatised films, *I Had a Son* (1943) and *Return Journey* (1944), which prepared audiences for the loss of loved ones in action. The best-known wartime documentary made at Movietone was *Jungle Patrol* (Tom Gurr, 1944), for which cameramen Bill Carty and J. W. Trerise covered the Australian campaign in New Guinea's Finistere Range. Elsewhere, one of the most poignant of the propaganda films was Charles Chauvel's *While There is Still Time* (1943), which cautioned against industrial absenteeism. Such films gave not only directors such as Chauvel and Hall an opportunity to refine their skills, but also actors like Chips Rafferty and Peter Finch, both of whom give striking performances in this one.

Due to investor caution and film stock shortages, Chauvel's *The Rats of Tobruk* (1944) was the only major Australian-produced feature made and released between 1942 and 1945.[15] It was also the only wartime feature to depict the fighting exploits of Australians during the war, and Chauvel took great care to ensure the authenticity of the tale of his three heroes (Rafferty, Finch and Grant Taylor) in the Middle East and New Guinea. The result, however, is uneven, with too much emphasis on re-created battles at the expense of character. Although widely admired, the film did not approach the box-office results of *Forty Thousand Horsemen*.

The only other feature about Australia's war effort conceived during World War II was *The Overlanders* (1946), directed and written by Harry Watt for Ealing Studios. Watt based his story on an actual event: an overland drive of 100 000 cattle from the Northern Territory to coastal Queensland in 1942, when Japanese invasion appeared imminent. This film perfectly articulates the essence of national character, personified, as in *Forty Thousand Horsemen*, by Chips Rafferty's character. It also turns the fears of its droving team into a microcosm of broader national attitudes, and Watt's strong documentary approach breathes new life into such time-honoured traditions as cattle stampedes and water shortages. *The Overlanders* enjoyed major international success, and this persuaded Ealing to set up a full-time Australian unit at the old Pagewood studios in Sydney.

A wartime surge in Australian box-office takings gave local film-makers hope that their feature film industry would follow suit. Late in the war, Ken G. Hall was filming *Smithy* (1946) for Columbia Pictures, and a new director, Eric Porter, was embarking on a family drama called *A Son is Born* (1946). There were plans for at least

three other features in 1946–47, but, due to soon evident problems, none entered production.[16]

Smithy, financed by Columbia's earnings frozen in Australia during the war, has as its highlight the 1928 Pacific flight of famed Australian aviator Sir Charles Kingsford Smith. The film went into production with the advantage of a £53 000 budget—more than twice that of the most expensive of the 1930s Cinesound features—and Hall later recalled that for the first time in his life, 'There would be no restricting the story line because we could not afford it.'[17]

Smithy's central theme is one of pioneering zeal in opposition to apathy and conservatism. The choice of subject was a bid for the American market, and much is made in the film of the 1928 flight meaning 'as much to Uncle Sam as it does to Australia'. In terms of its technical demands, especially in the use of re-created flight scenes intercut with back projection and miniatures, *Smithy* shows Hall and his Cinesound team at the height of their abilities. But the early part of the film is handicapped by being too concerned with events rather than motivation. Hall's resolve not to make the post-Pacific flight story seem anticlimactic had something to do with this, and indeed the film develops more soul after the flight when it explores the psychology of Smithy's middle age and his determination to break an England-to-Australia flying record. There is an effective sense of loss and anguish, a mood carried over from certain of Hall's wartime propaganda shorts, especially *I Had a Son*.

Despite *Smithy*'s good returns in Australia and the US (where it was released as *Pacific Adventure*), Columbia boss Harry Cohn informed Hall he did not want his company to invest in further Australian films. For a while, Hall took solace in hopes of revived feature production under Cinesound, but in the late 1940s a series of badly-timed events made this look very unlikely.

The first of them, the British Rank Organisation's March 1946 half-purchase of Greater Union, initially appeared to promise big things. In late 1946, Hall visited England to discuss co-production plans with Rank and Ealing, but, by the time he returned to Australia, Greater Union's Norman Rydge was worried about over-stretching his company's resources. One of the reasons was that Charles Chauvel's *Sons of Matthew*, in which Greater Union had invested, had by now gone over schedule and over budget.

In April 1947, these doubts were compounded when the British government, in an effort to combat Hollywood, announced that it would tax 75 per cent of the earnings of all imported films. News of the proposal was enough for Greater Union to terminate Cinesound's co-production plans. When the tax was lifted a short while later, neither Rank nor Greater Union (which had experienced a postwar decline in box-office takings) was in a position to consider relaunching the joint venture. In the mind of Norman Rydge, theatres running a guaranteed supply of imported films could return money faster and more safely than local productions.[18]

Greater Union's decision not to invest in any further

Top: Bluey Donkin (Grant Taylor), Peter Linton (Peter Finch) and Milo Trent (Chips Rafferty). Charles Chauvel's *The Rats of Tobruk* (1944). Bottom: Charles Kingsford Smith (Ron Randell), second from left, and P. G. Taylor (played by Taylor), are interviewed in Ken G. Hall's *Smithy* (1946).

Cathy McAllister (Wendy Gibb) nurses Shane (Michael Pate), watched by Barney (Ken Wayne). Charles Chauvel's *Sons of Matthew* (1949).

features was a bitter blow not only for Ken G. Hall but also for the entire industry. Instead of the expected upturn in feature production, only six entirely Australian-produced features were released in the years 1946 to 1949, and the entire 1950s decade brought only 13. In contrast, the 1930s decade had seen the release of 52 Australian features, the 1920s no less than 100 such films, and the 1910–19 period around 160. The commercial viability which Ken G. Hall had so amply demonstrated at Cinesound in the 1930s was allowed to evaporate. Investors generally stopped thinking of Australian features at all.

Greater Union's co-investor in Chauvel's *Sons of Matthew* (1949) was the Australian branch of Universal Pictures. Herc McIntyre, as Universal's local managing director, proved to be the closest distribution ally Australian producers were to have for several decades.

Much of *Sons of Matthew* covers the pioneering work of the five sons and two daughters of one Matthew O'Riordan in mountainous south Queensland. The scenes of exploration, land clearing and farm development convey an infectious sense of adventure, and Chauvel's staging of a bushfire and a cyclone are among the best work he ever did. In overall terms, the family saga integrates well with Chauvel's rousing evocation of Australian landscape, but at times the canvas is just too broad, leaving the central conflict between two of the brothers to appear like an ingredient that had strayed from another film.

Unlike Ken G. Hall, who would have mixed studio with location footage, Chauvel had shot virtually all his *Sons of Matthew* exteriors on location, and most of those on the inaccessible Lamington Plateau. The film eventually moved into profit, but the fact that its budget had spiralled up to £120 000 (aided by an 18-month schedule) removed whatever willingness Norman Rydge had left to involve Greater Union in further production.

Among those discouraged by Rydge's attitude was Ealing, which had refurbished the Pagewood studios in the hope of attracting a co-production partner. Matters were not improved in 1951 when the federal Capital Issues Board forbade the formation of new film production companies with capital over £10 000. But somehow Ealing forged ahead to make two historical epics, *Eureka Stockade* (Harry Watt, 1949) and *Bitter Springs* (Ralph Smart, 1950), before announcing in 1952 that it would withdraw from Australian production.

Ealing had at least established a precedent for overseas companies filming in Australia and, as the 1950s progressed, so did the number of visiting productions. *Wherever She Goes* (1950), Michael Gordon's charming biopic of pianist Eileen Joyce, was followed in 1952 by Twentieth Century-Fox's misguided colonial opus, *Kangaroo* (Lewis Milestone), and in 1957 Rank embarked on an undistinguished remake of *Robbery Under Arms* (Jack Lee). Standing quite apart from the rest is *The Sundowners* (1960), directed by Fred Zinnemann for Warner Bros. Despite Zinnemann's tendency to keep intercutting the story with shots of cute Australian fauna,

it compares well with *The Overlanders* as an overseas-backed film that exactly distils a sense of Australian character.

The best Australian feature of the 1950s was Cecil Holmes' *Three in One* (1957). The film originated with Holmes' being approached by author Frank Hardy, who wanted to invest in a film adaptation of his own short story, 'The Load of Wood'. Securing further finance, Holmes proceeded to follow Hardy's story with two more, 'Joe Wilson's Mates', adapted from a Henry Lawson story, and 'The City', an original by Ralph Peterson. All had something to say about how Australian mateship could help people through times of economic adversity.

In 'Joe Wilson's Mates', scripted by Rex Rienits, there is an emphasis on solidarity as a group of bush workers organise a funeral for a total stranger when they discover he was a union man. It takes time to explore its characters, including a swagman, an actor and mourners who get drunk en route to the burial. The characters owe much to the bush legends created by the nationalist literature of the 1880s and 1890s, but they also show the strong influence of the 1953 folk musical *Reedy River*, which had an 1890s setting and a union theme. With its casual sense of humour and interpolation of folk songs, 'Joe Wilson's Mates' creates its own myth-making, supported admirably by Ross Wood's camerawork.

More engaging in a conventional sense is 'The Load of Wood', again scripted by Rex Rienits and set in a small country town during the 1930s Depression. The story presents the most militant confrontation in *Three in One* between the haves and the have-nots, the former represented by a stingy landowner (Keith Howard) and the latter by Darkie (Jock Levy), a relief worker who steals and distributes timber to the town's unemployed during a bitingly cold winter. Holmes sustains well the suspense of the theft, intercutting between Darkie and a mate hacking at the tree and the owner's dawning realisation that something is amiss, then capping it all with the terrified thieves coasting downhill through ghostly trees when their truck has refused to start.

'The City', the third story in *Three in One*, has a contemporary setting. Where the first two had have a background of known periods of economic turmoil, 'The City' is set in a time that most Australians were expected to believe was one of prosperity. There had been a recession in the early 1950s, and 'The City' tells how the high cost of housing has caused a young couple to delay their marriage. Following an argument, the couple split to roam the city at night, encountering a series of characters who help to throw their plight into positive relief.

If 'Joe Wilson's Mates' and 'The Load of Wood' echo some of the folk qualities Holmes admired from earlier Australian films, then 'The City' shows the influence of postwar Italian neo-realism. For this reason and because of its left-wing commitment, *Three in One* was a groundbreaking film and very different to the majority made in Australia that decade. When it screened at the Edinburgh Film Festival in 1956, *Sight and Sound* reported:

Tommy (Tommy Trinder) and Charlie (Nicky Yardley) in Ralph Smart's *Bitter Springs* (1950).

Venneker (Peter Ustinov) leads the pack in Fred Zinnemann's *The Sundowners* (1960).

Customer (Pat Martin) and Salesgirl (Joan Landor) in Cecil Holmes' *Three in One* (1957).

"Ça", said a French critic sitting beside me, *"C'est du cinéma!"* And certainly *Three in One* (as perhaps only John Heyer's *Back of Beyond* has really done before) suggests that Australian film-makers have at hand the kind of material from which a 'living cinema', rooted in a particular scene and a way of life, might be created.[19]

Although it sold abroad and was highly regarded at further international film festivals, *Three in One* failed to obtain a release on the domestic market. Only half its budget was returned, and Cecil Holmes—like Noel Monkman and others before him—found himself resuming a career in documentaries.

Much more conventional in his choice of material was director Lee Robinson, who was able to raise money for five features between 1953 and 1958. The redoubtable Chips Rafferty served as star and co-producer on most

of these films, and with Robinson embarked on *The Phantom Stockman* (1953) and *King of the Coral Sea* (1954), primarily for overseas B-film distribution. Although their actors were not usually given much of a chance to display their talents, the strength of the Rafferty-Robinson features lay in the use of exotic Australian backgrounds.

Exotica was pushed a step further with the New Guinea setting of the adventure tale *Walk into Paradise* (1956), the first of three films the Robinson–Rafferty interests were to co-produce with French companies. Robinson co-directed with Marcel Pagliero, and it is the most impressive film he made, keeping up the action and good characterisation as well as making vivid use of locations.

Charles Chauvel's final feature, *Jedda* (1955), like two of the Rafferty-Robinson films, was shot in inland Australia, but the results are far more spectacular. A love story between two full-blood Aborigines, *Jedda* tells of a

Marbuck (Robert Tudawali) holds Jedda (Ngarla Kunoth) in Charles Chauvel's *Jedda* (1955).

young woman (Ngarla Kunoth) who, having been raised from infancy as a white, is abducted and taken on a journey into wild mountain country by a tribal black (Robert Tudawali). While some of the drama is over-cooked, there is no denying the powerful absorption of Kunoth and Tudawali in their roles, and the way in which Chauvel and his cameraman, Carl Kayser (working in colour), interpret their Northern Territory locales. Chauvel had this film state his belief that Aborigines should not be expected to blindly follow all the conventions of white society, and *Jedda* was the first Australian feature in which leading black characters were actually played by black people. Indeed, as Colin Johnson wrote in 1987, 'It is to Chauvel's credit, or perhaps in spite of Chauvel, that the only dignified Aboriginal male lead [Tudawali] that has been allowed to exist in films made by white directors in Australia, is in *Jedda*.'[20]

Jedda was the last feature made by an Australian director whose career dated from the pre-sound era. But far from having no successors, Chauvel was being followed by people such as John Heyer, John Kingsford Smith and Ron Maslyn Williams, who were making their mark with postwar documentaries, some of them feature-length.

John Heyer, along with Lee Robinson and others, had been employed by the Film Division of the Department of Information, reconstituted under a new Australian National Film Board just after the war. At least two of

The mail truck in John Heyer's *The Back of Beyond* (1954).

Heyer's DOI films, *Journey of a Nation* (1947) and *The Valley is Ours* (1948), persuasively express hope for a better postwar world, with the first urging standardisation of Australia's railway gauges and the second looking at the work of soldier settlers in the Murray River valley. For the Shell Film Unit in 1954, Heyer made *The Back of Beyond*, a dramatised feature-length documentary which looks at life along the 500 kilometre Birdsville Track of Central Australia by covering the fortnightly trip along its length by mailman Tom Kruse. As *The Overlanders* had done, Heyer used inland people and landscapes to capture the essence of Australian character. Five years before, the same objective had been achieved, although in a fairly different way, by John Kingsford Smith with *The Inlanders* (1949), produced for the Australian Inland Mission.

Other notable directors in the early days of the DOI Film Division included Hugh McInnes, who provided excellent records of the lives of workers in *The Canecutters* (1948) and *The Steelworker* (1949), and Colin Dean, who adroitly used dramatised situations to educate against public service stupefaction in *A Matter of Manners* (1951), and to urge the use of modern farming methods in *Capacity Smith* (1951). The least typical DOI film of the period is Ron Maslyn Williams' 64-minute *Mike and Stefani* (1952), which had the aim of countering public criticism that selection procedures for non-British migrants were not sufficiently rigorous. Filmed mostly in Bavaria during 1949–50, it records the story of a Ukrainian couple, Mycola and Stefani, who had been separated during the war and reunited in a refugee camp before applying for resettlement in Australia.

Mycola and Stefani in Ron Maslyn Williams' *Mike and Stefani* (1952).

While *Mike and Stefani* consists mostly of authentic re-enactment, the crucial scene of the couple's selection interview was filmed as it actually happened. The immigration officer in the scene followed instructions to make the process look as hard as possible and it was the resulting official unease which helped confine *Mike and Stefani*'s distribution to government film libraries within Australia.

More palatable to official taste was *The Queen in Australia* (1954), produced by the Film Division's producer-in-chief, Stanley Hawes. The country's first feature-length colour film, it focuses on the ways in which countless thousands assembled to pay euphoric tribute to the recently crowned monarch as she toured the nation. Looked at today, *The Queen in Australia* shows a parochial Australia, still highly 'Anglo-centric' before the

first postwar wave of European migrants had had time to make itself seen and heard.

There is a world of change between *The Queen in Australia* and *From the Tropics to the Snow* (Richard Mason and Jack Lee) made exactly ten years later by the same film division, now called the Commonwealth Film Unit. An irreverent send-up of government travelogues and the process of bureaucratic film-making, *From the Tropics to the Snow* indicates that radically new values were on the way for both Australian society and its films.

Other films which both experimented with style and had public impact include *Concerto for Orchestra* (Robert Parker, 1965) and *The Gallery* (Philip Mark Law, 1970), while *Desert People* (Ian Dunlop, 1967), *One Man's Road* (Bob Kingsbury, 1967), *The Pictures that Moved* (Alan Anderson, 1968) and *Bullocky* (Richard Mitchell, 1969)

37

took new directions in exploring Australian life and heritage.

The international success of *Desert People* made Ian Dunlop one of the few Australian film-makers known abroad until the feature film revival of the 1970s. Running 52 minutes, *Desert People* was adapted from the three-hour *People of the Australian Western Desert* series which in 1965 had recorded the daily life of two nomadic Aboriginal families living in that region.[21] Besides running for many weeks in Australian city cinemas, *Desert People* received acclaim in Europe, and in Paris was screened repeatedly to enthusiastic audiences. After one of the screenings at the Cinémathèque Française, *Le Monde* reported: 'Australian film-maker Ian Dunlop has here achieved a prodigious film, which for nearly an hour held the audience breathless.'[22]

Some anticipation of this change of style had appeared immediately postwar with a new strand of ideologically committed documentary. The forerunner was Joris Ivens' *Indonesia Calling* (1946), which re-created recent events when Australian seamen and waterside workers refused to man Dutch ships carrying arms and ammunition for the newly-proclaimed republic of Indonesia. Produced for the Waterfront Unions of Australia, *Indonesia Calling* was to influence the establishment in the early 1950s of the Waterside Workers Federation (WWF) Film Unit. A similarly motivated film, less well known but smoother in approach, is *Coal Dust* (1947), directed by Edmund Allison for the NSW Miners' Federation. Its strong, sometimes shocking, images show the effects of the 'dusting' and premature ageing of miners, and it urged the NSW government to ensure that mine owners install greater protective measures.

Each of the WWF Film Unit films was jointly directed by Keith Gow, Jock Levy and Norma Disher. Between 1952 and 1958, the WWF Film Unit produced a dozen documentaries which expressed a left-wing viewpoint on such issues as waterfront working conditions, union solidarity and housing shortages. The most accomplished is *The Hungry Miles* (1955), a plea for unity among waterfront workers which ambitiously re-creates the history of labour relations on the Sydney waterfront from the 1930s Depression onward. The Unit deployed hundreds of labourers and veterans to re-create Depression-era poverty, scuffles for job tickets and battles with police. The style of *The Hungry Miles* and the subsequent *November Victory* (1955) shows the influence of the Russian filmmakers Eisenstein and Pudovkin, and with *Not Only the Need* (1957) the Unit tackled the housing industry crisis which had provided the background to 'The City' segment of *Three in One*.

Most of the WWF films were shot on 16mm at a time when the format had increasing use among documentary producers. In fact, the low cost of 16mm helped encourage a new boom in sponsored documentaries, particularly those intended for educational or industrial in-house use. A total of 610 sponsored short films were made in Australia in 1961–62, a period which brought the release of only one local feature.

Much of the inertia in the feature industry was due to the fact that the long-serving federal government of Sir Robert Menzies was prepared to do nothing to help producers break America's financial and cultural domination of film in Australia. But by the early 1960s, nonetheless, an influential minority of politicians was becoming concerned by the fact that the American domination of local cinemas was being repeated by the country's television stations. The first of these, Sydney's Ten, had gone to air in September 1956.

Following representation from the Australian Film Producers Association, the Postmaster-General had in January 1961 imposed a ruling that all television commercials be of Australian origin, and this was clearly of help to a number of film-makers. But infinitely more was needed for the feature film industry. Urged on by producer interests, the federal senate in November 1962 appointed a Select Committee to inquire into ways in which Australian films for television could be encouraged. The resulting report—known as the Vincent Report—summarised the film industry's dilemma thus: 'This country has already demonstrated that it can make world quality films and export them and the only reason why it did not continue to do so is that the industry was left unprotected and squeezed out of business by an overseas industry which was heavily protected in its own country.'[23]

The Vincent Report suggested a widespread programme of government aid for the local film industry, including a budget loan scheme, tax concessions and tax incentives. But the recommendations of the Report, presented to the senate in late 1963, were never put into effect, even though they did create a wide awareness of the need for government support.

Developments from this point on were considerably helped by the Australian public's new and deeper appreciation of the arts. Greater emphasis was placed on the question of national identity, and this was given some focus in the late 1950s and early 1960s by the publication of books such as *The Australian Legend* and *The Lucky Country*. Younger, would-be film-makers began to see a wider diversity of world cinema at the Melbourne and Sydney Film Festivals (established in the early 1950s), and an awareness grew of the contribution that film could make to national culture. Those who throughout the 1960s kept pushing for government aid for the film industry included documentary or television directors who were keen to move into features.

Also among the activists were those developing an Australian 'underground' (later known as 'alternative' or 'independent') cinema. Their films challenged the conservatism of Australian society, along with such specific issues as outdated film censorship and Australia's involvement in the Vietnam War. Separate styles of underground film were developed in Sydney and Melbourne, with the Sydney group taking its lead from the European avant-garde, and Melbourne from French New Wave cinema.

Throughout the 1960s, every sector of the film industry (save the mainstream distributors and exhibitors) energetically lobbied the federal government to act on

Graham 'Stork' Wallace (Bruce Spence) and Westy (Graeme Blundell). Tim Burstall's *Stork* (1971).

the recommendations of the Vincent Report. In 1967, Anthony Buckley, a member of the pressure group, the Australian Film Council, made *Forgotten Cinema*, which charts the rise and fall of the feature film industry, and this documentary impressed Prime Minister John Gorton, who in early 1969 made a promise of federal aid.

One important earlier move had been the establishment by Prime Minister Harold Holt in November 1967 of a federally-funded Australian Council of the Arts, which had a Film and Television Committee. In May 1969, events appeared to be gathering pace when the Committee recommended the encouragement of the film industry with the establishment of a federal film and television school, a film development corporation and an experimental film fund. Backed by persistent lobbying from film industry activists, these recommendations were accepted by Prime Minister Gorton, and all three initiatives were realised between 1970 and 1973.

The first film backed by the Experimental Film and Television Fund, *Or Forever Hold Your Peace* (Kit Guyatt and others, 1970), was a rousing *cinéma vérité* record of 36 hours in Sydney's massive anti-Vietnam War moratorium. In a way that few television news reports at the time did, it vividly emphasised the point that Australia's moratorium movement was not simply driven by hard-line radicals but involved ordinary citizens, who took the chance to voice their views through marches, demonstrations and draft-card burnings. In view of the growing number of politically-committed documentaries that followed, it was an appropriate kick-off for the new Fund.

The first feature to obtain government funding under the Australian Film Development Corporation was *Stockade* (Hans Pomeranz, 1971), based—like Ealing's 1949 *Eureka Stockade*—on events at the 1854 miners' rebellion at the Eureka Stockade in Ballarat, Victoria. Two other films which did considerably more to encourage investment back into Australian features were Tim Burstall's low-budget comedy *Stork* (1971) and Bruce Beresford's *The Adventures of Barry McKenzie* (1972).

Prior to the 1973 opening of the federally-backed Australian Film and Television School, one of the main training grounds for young film-makers had been the Commonwealth Film Unit. Producers and directors who had worked at the Unit in the 1960s included Peter Weir, Donald Crombie, Joan Long, Gil Brealey, Richard Mason, Anthony Buckley and Arch Nicholson, and many made films that reflected new styles and preoccupations with the medium. In 1971, the highlight of these developments was the CFU's feature-length, three-part film *Three to Go*.

Three to Go concerns the stories of three young people whose lives have reached a traumatic turning point. In Peter Weir's 'Michael', a young man is undecided about whether to stay with a cosy middle-class background or join a group of radicals. In 'Judy', directed by Brian Hannant, a teenage girl cuts her ties with a claustrophobic country town to seek a more vibrant life in the city; and in Oliver Howes' 'Toula', a young Greek girl incurs parental wrath by wanting to become less Greek and merge into a broader society. Of all the stories, the second and third create the greatest impact by looking at specific communities with a documentarist's eye. 'Toula' strikes the deepest chord because of the complexity of the girl's plight.

September 1972 brought the start of a fresh inquiry into the film and television industry, this time initiated by the federal Tariff Board. In their evidence, most filmmakers claimed that exhibition and distribution deals were too secretive and onerous on the producer, and some related how they had been able to avoid normal distribution costs by directly hiring venues to run their own films. There were calls for production subsidies and taxation incentives, and even a call for the 'reported restrictive trade practices' of the leading film trade companies to be investigated.

On 30 June 1973, the Tariff Board followed the producers' line in calling for radical government restructuring of Australia's film production, distribution and exhibition industries. Since the recently elected federal Labor government had introduced a wide range of political and social reforms, there were high hopes that the Tariff Board's suggestions would be implemented. But much to the chagrin of the producers, the only recommendation put into effect was the replacement of a highly criticised Australian Film Development Corporation with a new organisation. Legislation for this new body, the Australian Film Commission, was passed in March 1975.

Though most of the Tariff Board recommendations were officially overlooked, the film trade was now sufficiently aware of the political clout of Australian producers not to ignore the possibility of further government action. Also, compared to earlier times, local filmmakers were showing a far more sophisticated awareness of how the trade worked. There was talk of the trade and producers working together to 'build' local films, which in the past had usually suffered when compared to imported films arriving with proven box-office potential. Greater Union confirmed this improving situation, when it used *The Man from Hong Kong* (Brian Trenchard Smith, 1975) to resume investment in local features for the first time since 1949.

By the mid-1970s, Australian features were again proven money-earners. It was evident, nevertheless, that most of them needed an overseas market to return costs, and it was decided that producers and government should join forces to promote Australian films at the world's foremost cinema market place, the International Festival du Film, Cannes. Several Australian features, including Peter Weir's black comedy, *The Cars that Ate Paris*, had been well received at Cannes in 1974, and the following year the first-ever government-sponsored delegation was sent there to give an orchestrated marketing push to Australian films and television. By a happy coincidence, Ken Hannam's *Sunday Too Far Away* (1975) attracted bonus attention by being invited to screen as part of the high-profile Quinzaine des Réalisateurs (Directors' Fortnight).

Sunday Too Far Away was the start of a very confident 'new wave' of Australian cinema. It had made international critics think far more seriously about Australian

'Michael', Peter Weir's episode of *Three to Go* (1971).

films, and from here onwards the industry would be in a position to build on the reputation which *Sunday Too Far Away* had established. To some observers, local film-makers were now able to combine distinctive Australian ingredients with inspiration from not only American film traditions, but also from the European cinema to which the younger directors of the postwar generation had been exposed.

In the years ahead, many of the Australian feature film industry's long-term problems were to continue. Directors still faced many frustrating years between features, and government funding of films often see-sawed between the desire to create a financially viable industry, and the counter-desire for cultural advancement. Although the earlier industrial cycles were no longer as starkly defined, they could still reappear, motivated by factors such as the introduction or retardation of gener-

ous tax concessions to encourage industry investment.

What the Australian cinema did need was unflinching faith by investors and the ability of film-makers to sustain the interest of world markets. During the mid-to-late 1970s, with films like *Sunday Too Far Away, Picnic at Hanging Rock* (Peter Weir, 1975) and *The Devil's Playground* (Fred Schepisi, 1976), there was very good indication that this need would be fulfilled.

Acknowledgement

The author would like to express appreciation for recent research into pre-1914 Australian cinema generously provided by Chris Long. He would also like to acknowledge the help of Judy Adamson, Hugh McInnes and Clive Sowry, all of whom assisted with information and/or viewpoints during the preparation of this chapter.

Notes

1 *The Age*, Melbourne, 24 August 1986.
2 *The Bulletin*, 5 December 1986.
3 *The War Cry*, 22 September 1900.
4 Ibid, 18 August 1900.
5 This appears to have depended on projection speed. *The Bulletin* of 3 January 1907 quoted the duration of *The Story of the Kelly Gang* as around 40 minutes; *The New Zealand Times* of 13 May 1907 said it 'took nearly an hour to display'; and on 16 May 1907 *The Morning Herald* in Perth said it took 'considerably over an hour to pass completely across the light'.
6 I am indebted to the recent work by film historians Chris Long and Clive Sowry in establishing that Coates worked in this capacity on *The Story of the Kelly Gang*. Three of the references they have found to support this previously unknown connection are *Table Talk* (Melbourne), 3 January 1907; *The Bendigo Advertiser*, 21 January 1907; and *Stageland*, vol. 2, no. 7, 9 October 1907.
7 Rediscovery of footage from *The Story of the Kelly Gang* began in 1976 with the location of an individual series of frames in an Adelaide collection. Two minutes of unedited scenes (perhaps rejected takes) were found in 1978, and in 1981 the most complete indication of the finished film came with the finding of six minutes on a Melbourne tip. Just over half of that amount was able to be copied.
8 *Sunday Mail*, Sydney, 10 February 1907.
9 *Robbery Under Arms* and *For the Term of His Natural Life*, based on popular novels, were to be periodically remade throughout the ensuing history of Australian film. In the 1980s, they were adapted as television mini-series.
10 *The Lone Hand*, 20 March 1920.
11 Quoted in *Debates*, House of Representatives, 4 May 1928, p. 4688.
12 *Smith's Weekly*; article in the McDonagh sisters' scrapbook, held by Australia's National Film and Sound Archive.
13 *Everyones*, 13 July 1932.
14 Unidentified clipping from Ken G. Hall's scrapbook.
15 Lesser films of the period were an amateurish *A Yank in Australia* (Alf Goulding, 1942), a fairly stagey *Red Sky at Morning* (Hartney Arthur, 1944) and *Harvest Gold* (Mervyn Murphy, 1945), a reasonably well-made piece on mechanised farming.
16 These feature plans included 'Storm Hill', a timber drama to be directed by Eric Porter; a film by Rupert Kathner on the poet Adam Lindsay Gordon; and a talkie remake of the 1927 *Kid Stakes*.
17 Ken G. Hall, *Directed by Ken G. Hall*, Lansdowne Press, Melbourne, 1977, p. 172.
18 Sir Norman Rydge, interviewed by Hugh McInnes, 11 April 1978.
19 *Sight & Sound*, Autumn 1956.
20 Colin Johnson, 'Chauvel and the centering of the Aboriginal male in Australian film', *Continuum: An Australian Journal of the Media*, vol. 1, no. 1, 1987.
21 In 1967, Ian Dunlop returned to the region to make a further series of *People of the Australian Western Desert* films totalling three hours.
22 *Le Monde*, 4 March 1967.
23 Vincent Report, p. 26.

Top: Jimmie (Tommy Lewis) watches the Healys (Jane Harders and Tim Robertson) ride past. Fred Schepisi's *The Chant of Jimmie Blacksmith* (1978). Bottom: Barker (Richard Moir) in Ian Pringle's *The Plains of Heaven* (1982).

2
Formative landscapes

Ross Gibson

But the spirits have to be recognized to become real. They are not outside us, nor even entirely within, but flow back and forth between us and the objects we have made, the landscape we have shaped and move in. We have dreamed all these things in our deepest lives and they are ourselves. It is our self we are making out there. . .

David Malouf, *An Imaginary Life: A Novel*[1]

Mad Max once fought to police it. Nowadays, he is out there in it, simply subsisting. . .and changing according to its dictates. Picnickers seep into it, following the same path taken by countless innocents who have gone missing back of beyond. The man from Snowy River spurs his small and weedy beast in a race to master it.

In all these stories, the common denominator is the Australian landscape. It is a leitmotiv and an ubiquitous character. Its presence throughout the history of Australian film-making is such that the country has come to represent something much more than an environmental setting for local narratives.

In so many ways, the majority of Australian features have been *about* landscape. Think of all the films that have trudged so deliberately into the Never Never: *Journey Among Women* (Tom Cowan, 1977), *Long Weekend* (Colin Eggleston, 1979), *The Chant of Jimmie Blacksmith* (Fred Schepisi, 1978), *My Brilliant Career* (Gill Armstrong, 1979), *Gallipoli* (Peter Weir, 1981), *The Plains of Heaven* (Ian Pringle, 1982), *Razorback* (Russell Mulcahy, 1984), *Rikky and Pete* (Nadia Tass, 1988) and the 'Crocodile' Dundee films (Peter Faiman, 1986; John Cornell, 1988). Think also of the films that have clearly attempted to ring the changes on the landscape tradition: the Mad Max movies (George Miller, 1979 and 1981; George Miller and George Ogilvie, 1985), *Backlash* (Bill Bennett, 1986), *The Year My Voice Broke* (John Duigan, 1987) and *The Tale of Ruby Rose* (Roger Scholes, 1988), for examples. By featuring the land so emphatically in the stories, all these films stake out something more significant than decorative pictorialism. Knowingly or unknowingly, they are all engaging with the dominant mythology of white Australia. They are all partaking of the landscape-tradition which, for two hundred years, has been used by white Australians to promote a sense of the significance of European society in 'the Antipodes'.

In this chapter, I am not primarily concerned to pass judgement on films, to say this one gets it right, that one

gets lost. Rather, I want to understand why so many different film-makers, audiences and critics in Australia have been under the spell of some spirit of the land. Why this preoccupation with the natural environment? (It is too easy to say, 'Because it is there.') What can the cinematic rendition of the land tell one about Australian culture in general?

A trek toward some answers could light out from the territory of local art history. A cliché can be a point of departure: non-Aboriginal Australia is a young society, under-endowed with myths of 'belonging'. The country is still sparsely populated and meagrely historicised. Alienation and the fragility of culture have been the keynotes during two hundred years of white Australian images and stories. Every plot of Australian earth, every spike of spinifex, has not yet become a sign in the arbitrary system of meaning which is history—or rather, until recently, every plot outside city limits has tended to signify just one thing: homelessness. The connotations are variable, depending on the story, the teller and the listener: homelessness can mean destitution, and it can also mean freedom. But there is no denying the uniformity of the representation: to white sensibility, most of Australia has traditionally been construed as empty space devoid of inhabitants, architecture, agriculture and artefacts. The Australian landscape has not been incorporated into the European symbolic order, except as a motif of the 'extra-cultural', as a sublime structuring void louring over all Australian culture. Compare Terra Australis with England's 'green and pleasant land'. Every Old World hectare has been ridden over, written over and inscribed into an elaborate and all-engrossing national history. Unlike colonial cultures, England does not define itself with legends of arrival or choice in an environmental setting. Rather, English society perceives itself to be autochthonous: it appears to have grown out of the soil rather than planted itself there. Having no clear social memory of its beginnings, England simply *is*, in contrast to the colonial society, which *becomes*.

Virtually every region of England has been written into the 'sentence' of English history. East Anglia is not just arable land: it is also Constable country, habitable symbol of the pastoral dream. Cornwall connotes Celtic prehistory, where there was a beginning even before history, before the chance of political self-determination. Even the few regions like Dartmoor which do signify a certain predominance of nature over culture can actually be cited to emphasise how historicised the country has become: Dartmoor stands as the tiny exception that proves the rule about Britain's completely 'achieved' agriculture. Hampshire evokes maritime myth and history; the Midlands are 'about' industrialisation and transport; and so on in a national semiosis that is limited only littorally.

English people perceive themselves to be inhabiting a culture that covers the countryside. Australians, by contrast, seem to be neither here nor there. Extensive stretches of the continent remain practically unsurveyed, even as considerable expanses (such as Botany Bay, the 'Back of Bourke', Kelly Country, the Overflow, Van

Moira (Robyn Moas) in Tom Cowan's *Journey Among Women* (1977).

Danny (Noah Taylor) and Freya (Loene Carmen). John Duigan's *The Year My Voice Broke* (1987).

Jim Craig (Tom Burlinson) in George Miller's *The Man from Snowy River* (1982).

Diemen's Land, Snowy River) bear up under mythic connotations. To analyse the Australian landscape, one has to move constantly back and forth between questions of habitat and terms of hermeneutics, between referent and reference. In some respects, the continent is a symbolic terrain; but in others it seems comprehensible only as 'extra-systemic', preternaturally unmanageable or uncultural.

For a tract of country to be regarded as a landscape—that is, as part of an artistic discourse—the people utilising it need to feel in charge of it. The land has to become an object to their subjective dominion, unless it is meant to signify nothing but indomitability. The geography must have been domesticated (or at least regarded as such); it must have been rendered safe for human manipulation and consumption. Such is the state of the Old World, where millennia of agriculture have wrought the earth to human design, where there is no question that the territory referred to in a landscape image is already a cultural construct.

In white Australia, however, a different attitude has held sway. The idea of the intractability of Australian nature has been an essential part of the national ethos. It is a notion with its genesis in the ancient legends of the hellish antipodes; a notion promoted by the First Fleet annalists who detailed the anguish of a harrowed and perverse society's struggling to understand and subsist in a seemingly bizarre habitat; a notion certified by the nineteenth-century explorers whose diaries detail horrid deprivations in the central wastelands; a notion perpetuated to this day by the myriad legends of the bush, that mythic region of isolation, moral simplicity, homelessness and the terrible beauty of 'nature learning how to write'[2].

Not exclusively the field of indigenous natural forces, nor predominantly the domain of social organisation, the barely populated continent has been figured as a paradox—half-tamed yet essentially untamable, conceding social subsistence yet never allowing human dominance. Because it has been presented as so tantalising and so essentially unknowable-yet-lovable, the land has become the structural centre of the nation's myths of belonging. The image of the paradoxical region can be used to 'explain' so many of the inconsistencies of a colonial society. If the land can be presented as grand yet 'unreasonable', the society which has been grafted on to it can also be accepted as marvellous though flawed. Indeed, it can portray itself as marvellous because it has subsisted, with all its flaws, in this grand yet unreasonable habitat. It is the kind of myth which 'naturalises' a society's shortcomings and works to make them acceptable, indeed admirable.

As Hegel observed in his lectures on aesthetics, the history of any society entails a continuous process of shaping the environment to the community's needs even as the community adapts to the specifications of the environment:

Man realises himself through *practical* activity, since he has the impulse to express himself, and so again to

recognise himself, in things that are at first simply represented to himself as externally existent. He attains this by altering external things and impressing on them the stamp of his own inner nature, so that he rediscovers his own character in them. Man does this in order that he may profit by his freedom to break down the stubborn indifference of the external world to himself, and may enjoy in the countenance of nature only an outward embodiment of himself.[3]

Hegel's thesis seems especially pertinent to white Australian culture. It highlights the 'expressionist' aggression required of a parvenu society supplanting an autochthonous community and grafting other mentalities on to the place. Hegel's thesis enables one to think of the Australian environment as a developing social creation while never denying that the society is also to some contentious extent a 'natural' outgrowth of the habitat. In cinematic terms, it means that a movie screen which shows images of a landscape can be regarded both as the realist window on the existing world and as a canvas on which a created world can be presented.

During the 1970s and early 1980s, film-makers (encouraged in part by the 'culturally responsible' funding policies of the Australian Film Commission) were attempting to create a cohesive view of national character through the rendition of Australian landscape as if it were the one thing that all factions of the society held in common. Paradoxically, however, the same corpus of films was also, in effect, promoting the view that the land was definitively sublime and supra-social, that a society cannot make much of an impression on such a habitat—or, to approach it from another direction, non-Aboriginal film-makers have often attempted to read some innate Australianness in the landscape even as they have aimed to stamp their own inner natures on the external face of the continent.

Borrowing a notion from the rhetoric of Italian neo-realism, let us acknowledge 'that the place where we were born and where we have lived has contributed to making us different from one and other'[4]. In the case of Australia, which is such a diaspora of a society, the places of migrants' derivations are myriad. Accordingly, within the Australian community, the sense of factions' difference from one another is undeniable. But, of course, one encounters a paradox here: there is a sense also, within the logic of nationalism, of the adoptive society's unification. The colony is a diverse collection of ethnic and interest groups, but it is also unified by its shared 'rebirth' in the 'new' environment.

The landscape-cinema has asserted Australia's difference from the rest of the world, and it has also asserted the nation's singularity of constitution within its own boundaries. That is to say, there has been an attempt to portray 'us' as one people growing to maturity and confidence 'together'. Films such as *Sunday Too Far Away* (Ken Hannam, 1975), *Picnic at Hanging Rock* (Peter Weir, 1975), *The Man from Snowy River* (George Miller, 1982) and *We of the Never Never* (Igor Auzins, 1982) have said, 'Here is the key to our identity. . .Here are the myths

Mac (Tony Barry), Jeannie (Angela Punch McGregor) and Aeneas Gunn (Arthur Dignam). Igor Auzins' *We of the Never Never* (1982).

that we need.' They have been presented as 'generically Australian'.

Such stories (and images) work to rationalise dialectical oppositions: drought and flood, flood and fire, dearth and plenty, enormity and minimalism, attrition and creation, diversity and uniformity, savagery and morality, and, of course, nature and culture (which probably sums up all the foregoing). In such national myths, the landscape becomes the projective screen for a persistent national neurosis deriving from the fear and fascination of the preternatural continent. Because Australian stories have typically characterised the land in frontier terms as an awesome opponent, rather than in pastoral terms as a nurturing mother or a placid locale for the arbitrary organisation of social life, and since culture has not yet managed to subdue nature (or at least to convince people that it has), Australian art has tended, until quite recently, to be 'anachronistically' concerned with 'primitive' themes. Generally speaking, most of the influential Australian art in the twentieth century has barely been classifiable in terms of modernism (let alone post-

modernism), where culture self-referentially creates itself from the 'raw material' of extant culture rather than from nature.

Australian art has always been judged to be traditionally concerned with the primary process of turning nature into culture. Of course, resistant schools of artists and writers in Australia have been affiliated to internationalist modernism and post-modernism—indeed, in the second half of the 1980s the internationalist 'push' in the visual arts seems to be becoming irresistible—but throughout the past fifteen years of government support of the feature film industry the dictates of generic 'Australianism' have been pre-eminent.

John Hinde, in his evocative study, *Other People's Pictures*[5], contends that national cinemas arise at times of social crisis or turbulence, when there exists a 'seminal audience' which is in need of self-definition and self-congratulation. It could be argued that Australia in the 1970s, emerging as it was from more than two decades of conservative rule and economic stagnation, constituted a seminal audience and that the unifying myths of

A battle scene from Simon Wincer's *The Lighthorsemen* (1987).

nationalism were required and welcomed by a local population. This would clarify why the landscape cinema flourished so spectacularly until the early 1980s. It would also explain why the tables appeared to turn over the past five years, when local audiences have seemed less concerned with national definition and when a series of spectacular failures—*Burke & Wills* (Graeme Clifford, 1985), *The Lighthorsemen* (Simon Wincer, 1987), and *Razorback*, being examples—eroded the dependability of the genre. One of the paradoxes concerning the success of the landscape cinema of the 1970s was that it gave Australians a stronger sense of their significance in the international arena, thereby lessening the need for reassuring images and definitions of 'Australianness', thereby, in turn, dispersing the seminal audience which seems to have been so appreciative of the landscape cinema in the first place! In its very success, the landscape-cinema prefigured its demise, or at least its reconstitution.

However, until the change seemed to dawn on some film-makers and arts administrators in the early 1980s, the landscape myth was assumed to be as fertile as ever it had been over the past two hundred years. Australia could still be regarded as 'third world' at the same time as it was 'post-industrial'. This is to say, the nation seemed

to maintain its straightforward approach to culture: that art was the process of turning raw nature into first-degree culture. Sergei Eisenstein once wrote with regard to early-modernist Europe: 'At the intersection of Nature and Industry stands Art.'[6] Of the Old World in the 1980s, it might be said: 'Art is the industry of constructing new artefacts out of old signs that have already blotted out Nature.' There is no denying that Australia does seem 'different' in such terms. Given that the change has not yet been widely acknowledged in most Australian advertising, television, Top 40 music and sport, one could adapt Eisenstein's adage thus: 'After repeated collisions involving Nature and Industry, Art is scattered across the landscape, marking but never covering the continent.' The feeling is still quite strong that the land at our backs is primitive and is therefore a storehouse of some inexhaustible and ineffable Australianness. With the change on the way, but not yet overhead, it seems the Australian landscape is shimmering in the collective consciousness like a mirage, phasing in and out of focus as a sign at one moment and as pristine nature the next. Whereas an autochthonous society tends to celebrate creationist myths that thank God for the nation's inauguration, the colonial society has access to more secular myths about arrival and the struggle to establish communities. These myths come to be called history.

One might presume that because the arbitrary or even accidental beginnings of colonies are so well recorded, 'satellite' societies such as Australia would be less prone to the kind of essentialism which argues that a nation has been historically predestined to develop particular characteristics. However, paradoxically, while white Australia was slowly developing the autonomy to define itself not as a replica of the mother country, the colony strove to celebrate its peculiarly Australian qualities. And, of course, the most enduring aspect of Australian experience loomed almost limitless around the fledgling colony: the landscape would define the nation. In trying to differentiate itself from the Old World, Australian society began to define itself with essentialist myths of land. The specific qualities of the nation would grow from the land. The colony would gradually 'belong', it would eventually be 'in place' and it would cease to be a colony. So the story went.

Because it still seems that human beings have not cluttered the ground with their artefacts and connotations, the southern continent continues to spread out, in many minds, like the text of some divine and immanent (as opposed to social and arbitrary) system of native, *Australian* meaning. If you want the real Australia, look at the earth, not at the people or what they have produced (the erroneous implication here being that the landscape has not already been produced by social actions). The landscape seems to extend unsullied, as the handiwork solely of nature, inscribed and subscribed with innate messages. Quintessential Australia has not yet been prepared over by an alien Anglo-Saxon-Celtic culture. So the story goes.

All this reverence (obscuring the unspecified fear) of the landscape is clearly the *result of* an alienated society's experience around the ridges of a vast, unpopulated and speciously indomitable country. But what of the *effects*? The legends of the awesome land imply that the society cannot be seen to be directing the environment in its own interests (despite multi-nationals' advertisements celebrating their 'quiet achievements' in purportedly taming and rehabilitating the ecosystem at the same time as they reap profits from it).

The generically Australian story argues that society has no hope of stretching out to cover the unsubdued continent. Implicitly, if it is taken as given that the society *en masse* cannot make a mark on the land, then the next most comforting myth would have to be a story of heroic individualism, adaptability and ingenuity in the unwelcoming arena of national definition. The nation then becomes a motley gang of knockabout types, unified in the fact of their survival but not uniform or conformist according to rigid social schemes—a paradoxical nation, but a nation nonetheless. So the story goes, as in *Mad Max* (George Miller, 1979), *Crocodile Dundee*[7], *Rikky and Pete* and, indeed, in *Whatever Happened to Green Valley?* (1973), Peter Weir's sophisticated investigation of the Australian documentary and pastoral traditions

transplanted and hybridised in suburbia. The laconic, male, 'minimalist' hero hews a path for himself, communing with the spirit of the land, reading its messages, jotting down hints for survival, hoping for nothing more of society than a modicum of organisational support in his contestation with the emptiness. In the inhuman landscape, humanism prevails. The heroes' persistence in the legendary setting persuades us that the land is habitable, but only by a very special breed of people; in mythic terms, therefore, the nation is feasible, but only as a collection of extraordinary individuals.

Paradoxically, as Australian feature films of the past twenty years have configured this country of the mind, the majority of them have done so in realist terms rather than with a 'fantastic' sense of the mythic storytelling involved in the presentation of generic locationism. They have been more concerned with the dictates of the past than with the yet-to-be-created characteristics of the future, or even with the volatile flux of the present. Such complacency of imagination should come as no surprise, given the two dominant modes of film-making that have always prevailed in Australia: in the mainstream of feature film there has been the 'lower-budget' end of the Hollywood storytelling tradition—the 'classic realist text', if you like—and for six decades also there has been a consistent flow of government-sponsored documentaries, which (for 45 years at least) have been made in a house-style shaped by the precepts of a functional, documentary realism. All the other traditions of world cinema—for example, European avant garde experimentation and 'quality' narrative, surrealism and the more 'magical' genres of industrial cinema, such as the musical and the science-fiction fantasy—have played only minor roles in the history of cinema in Australia. Realism has been the orthodoxy, therefore. The paradox is that the *mythic* argument of so many of the landscape-films cannot logically be conducted through the techniques of realist representation. Take examples as wide-ranging as *Sunday Too Far Away*, *Gallipoli*, *Crocodile Dundee*, *Picnic at Hanging Rock*, and even *Rikky and Pete* with its deliberate emphasis on the *interest* (distressingly in excess of the narrative at most times) that we are meant to invest in the settings the characters trundle through.

The existence of the land in the image works to authenticate the actions of the figures in the landscape. The setting is definitive Australia; therefore, the actions and emotions elicited by such a setting must also be definitive. So the story goes. It would appear to be common sense.

Perhaps it is true that there is a vast and undeniable beauty backgrounding life in Australia. Perhaps it is a beauty that cannot really be comprehended and communicated within human systems. However, as soon as such geography is represented and dramatised within images, sounds and stories, it is no longer land. Rather, it is landscape; it has been translated and utilised as an element of myth, as a sign of supra-social Australianness. There is no such thing as a pristine landscape. There may be an *image* of the pristine (or of beauty, or of

Pete (Stephen Kearney) and Rikki (Nina Landis) in Nadia Tass' *Rikky and Pete* (1989).

innocence, etc.), but such a thing cannot mean anything outside of cultural systems. The landscape image might signify nature, but that is not to say it is nature. The very notion of nature is a cultural construct.

All these arguments about whether films can or cannot present natural truth or authenticity depend on the myth of veracity and trustworthiness that still clings to the institution of photography. The common-sense view that a photograph is an objective *analogon* of 'the real' also adheres to film appreciation, especially for a national audience which has been served very diligently by a documentary industry funded and distributed by government agencies.

This common-sense view of the trustworthiness of photography is problematic at best. For one thing, photography, like the notion of nature itself, is a cultural entity which is comprehensible and meaningful because it has long been ascribed uses within social systems such as journalism, law, art and science, all of which are arbitrary configurations of persuasion and argumentation. Secondly, and more specifically, in the case of cinematography, given the seriality of the motion picture, every image is located not just within culture generally but also within a specific accumulative flow which necessarily gives rise to some sort of meaning (even if the narrative ends up only being *about* incoherence). The photographic (and/or cinematographic) image is not the unmediated re-presentation of a portion of reality; it is a presentation, a newly created or arranged portion of the reality of the cultural world.

But the delusive common sense can prevail, particularly when a moving picture of a static, seemingly unartificed landscape is presented. It is tempting to regard the image as innocently witnessing all the facts about the setting, untouched, panoramically extensive, verified over time—simply photographed, objectively true. (It is worth recalling, here, the oft-repeated observation that the French word for the lens is *l'objectif*.) But to believe in the transparency of the cinematographic landscape would be to ignore the significance of so many aesthetic variables. What was the time of day? Was the camera pointed toward the sun or away from it? Were human beings included in the scene? What were they doing? What lens was used? Was there any camera movement? What was the duration of the shot? What was happening on the soundtrack? How did the landscape sequence fit into the overall pattern of the narrative so far? The list could go on. Each of these factors has meaning.

Evidently, the fact that the land cannot 'act' on cue does not render its filmic representation any less prone to manipulation. The presented image of a landscape is necessarily a sign. And in the Australian setting it has customarily been construed as a sign of nature (that is, as a sign that is not a sign) rather than as a sign of a sign. It is this strange 'negative capability' that is currently undergoing a change in Australian cinema. If people begin to imagine their environment differently (not just as 'land'), the national mythology will necessarily alter. And that means that people will start to think differently. Then, if you lived in this country, you'd have to ask this question:

Father (Michael Blakemore) and son (Leaf Nowland) in Michael Blakemore's *A Personal History of the Australian Surf: Being the Confessions of a Straight Poofter* (1981).

What would you like to be thinking?

If you lived in this country, one thing you would probably think about is the beach. *A Personal History of the Australian Surf: Being the Confessions of a Straight Poofter* (Michael Blakemore, 1981) is, in part, a meditation on this place in the mind and heart. It may not seem logical, at first, to include this whimsical essay-film in an article on landscape-cinema. After all, the film is about the ritual of turning one's back on the land. *A Personal History* is a relaxed celebration of *release* from demands for self-definition and constrained behaviour. What better locale than the beach for such a holiday from the pressures of identification? Here, the population can shed all outward signs of social placement—you can bask and play like a benevolent animal . . . like some kind of tropical seal, perhaps. The surf is just out of reach of the land. The surf, therefore, can represent a haven from the pressures of socialisation as it is organised through so many national myths of landscape. However, there is a para-

George Miller's *Mad Max 2* (1981).

dox lurking in this notion: because so many Australians choose to strip down toward anonymity on the beach and in the surf, this ceremony of normlessness becomes a definitive national characteristic! What is more, it is a ceremony that can be attributed directly to the overbearing influence of the landscape tradition. The day in the surf is so desirable because everyone has to return to the land when the sun goes down. The regulating influence of the land figures in this 'unregulated' behaviour. If even leisure is determined by mythology, you might feel inclined to ask how you could take charge of such story-telling so that your life is organised in your best interests rather than in terms of outmoded or impedimentary values.

From the early 1980s on, most films that relied successfully (critically and financially) on the impact of the pictorial qualities of the landscape posed such a question, implicitly if not explicitly. They did so with a sense of self-deprecation and with a conscious intent to revise the old myths. Take *Mad Max, Mad Max 2*[8] (George Miller, 1981), *Mad Max Beyond Thunderdome* (George Miller and George Ogilvie, 1985) and *Crocodile Dundee* as examples. On the evidence of the massively favourable responses to these films, it seems audiences were no longer prepared to take the landscape myth entirely seriously. The films still required the environment to be the principal motif of the story, but gone was the earnest nationalistic investment in the land as the template of a national identity.

In *Crocodile Dundee*, the landscape looks and sounds like the *idea* of land; it looks like a sign. *Dundee*'s environment is a 'compliant' one, respectful of American nostalgia for the myth of the frontier; the outback and its laudable inhabitants are fashioned to this fable of recurrent American colonisations. The national environment represented in the film is thus fitted to a transnational economy. *Crocodile Dundee* becomes a lesson about being respectful of power, a cheerful parable about succeeding through *getting Americans to like us*.[9] If this ambition calls for a refiguring of the generic Australian landscape, the reconstitution of the myth could be achieved quickly enough, from the producers' point of view, because everyone (except maybe a large portion of the American audience) knows that the film is dealing with a sign and not a 'fact'.

Similarly, but differently, the comic-book aesthetic celebrated throughout the Mad Max trilogy works to pull the images of the environment out of the realist traditions of Australian cinema. It locates the land in a different system, a more *explicitly* fantastic, mythopoeic discourse. In any one part of the trilogy, the film and the audience both know that signs are manipulable and refutable. Most crucial, signs are not natural, no matter if they are signs of nature. Indeed, the Mad Max movies can be interpreted as a spectacularly irreverent and effective meditation on the possibilities of change in Australian society, generally, and in the landscape tradition more particularly. The stories take into account the undeniably complex interrelationships now existing in Australia between an orthodox, officially sanctioned national culture and the constantly mutating complex of images and ideas that comprises the international popular culture that is imported and consumed here with such enthusiasm. This is not to say that all popular culture in Australia has abandoned the more simple nationalist criteria. Cinema and television such as Kennedy Miller's is still more 'vanguard' than 'mainstream' in thematic and formal terms. But the popularity of Kennedy Miller product indicates that attitudes are beginning to alter, albeit slowly, across the breadth of the society that gets called 'Australia'.

A somewhat more obscure film that also bears witness to the change is Roger Scholes' *The Tale of Ruby Rose*, a parable which invests great significance in the influence of landscape on personality but which also refuses to offer a myth for an entire nation. On the contrary, *Ruby Rose* presents characters that can only be understood and appreciated as *marginal*, just as their defining environment must be viewed as emphatically *not* generic-Australian. Here is an Australian landscape story that can be comprehended as such only if the definitions of the landscape tradition are radically refigured. In this cinematic 'Australia', generically unAustralian types are taking shape in a generically unAustralian habitat. They are there. Either you deny them their classification as 'Australian', or you refigure the epithet 'Australian'.

It is arguable that *Ruby Rose is* the first 'peasant film' produced in this country. It refuses to commandeer Aboriginal dreaming to certify an indigenous sense of 'belonging', but it still presents a curiously 'native' kind of world view, principally through Ruby's idiosyncratic and elaborate mythology which enables her to understand and survive her 'life on the land'. The film presents a curiously half-convincing 'native' mentality. It is not *completely* convincing, I think, because the style of the film sometimes connotes 'European art movie' in its attempts *not* to connote generically Australian cinema. For example, the 'epic' helicopter establishing-shots tend to signify human alienation in an unforgiving backdrop. In such sequences the film seems to succumb to the pictorialism that *reifies* rather than *animates* a landscape. But in the majority of scenes involving daily life in the high country, *Ruby Rose* presumes the possibility of a knowledge of environment, personality, community and a spiritual world, all of which are inseparable one from the other. The film is not 'Aboriginal' (it is careful not to be so opportunist and simplistic), but it is 'peasant', somehow. To be precise, the film does not present life *on* the land; it attempts to portray a non-Aboriginal life *of* and *in* the land.

Bill Bennett's *Backlash* is an intriguing film to consider with regard to this idea of the possibilities of non-Aboriginal acknowledgement. The picaresque narrative and the improvisational performances of *Backlash* set it up as an 'exploration'. The story of two white law-enforcers' journey to a more 'indigenous' knowledge of justice, oppression and payback should constitute a radical interrogation of some of the myths that have guided white society for two hundred years. Indeed, it does this to some extent by virtue of its scepticism about the right-

Henry Rose (Chris Haywood) struggles with Bennett (Martyn Sanderson). Roger Scholes' *The Tale of Ruby Rose* (1988).

Trevor Darling (David Argue), Kath (Lydia Miller) and Nikki Iceton (Gia Carides). Bill Bennett's *Backlash* (1986).

eousness of a white Australian judiciary presiding in cases of Aboriginal 'transgression'. But as the white characters act out their alienation in the moral and geographical environment which the story leads them into, the narrative also falls problematically into several classic nationalist orthodoxies that have always run through the landscape tradition. For example, the Aboriginal woman becomes equated with spirit of place, when she seems 'instinctively' to know where the waterhole of salvation will be found in this tract of country that she can never have learned. The improvisatory trek into the landscape tradition succumbs in part to the idealism that has haunted Australian nationalism, as if there is a body of pre-existent *Australian* knowledge buried just a few feet down.

Ultimately, *Backlash* seems to sanction myths about the 'inevitable alienation' of white Australian society. But it is only fair to say that in the context of the film's release in the 'Bicentennial era', this particular 'failing' is negligible in comparison to the film's dramatisation of the morally complex legacy of retribution that will track white Australia until (and for a long while after) it negotiates a dignified settlement with the incumbents who were dispossessed during the invasion.

Non-Aboriginal society now appears to be in the process of rearranging the myths it requires for its self-definition. It is a breeze of change that has been refreshing factions of Australian film culture for decades. Consider, for example, *The Back of Beyond* (1954), John Heyer's mythopoeic celebration of the story-telling and adaptability of the Birdsville Track society, a 'community' which is simultaneously both singularly 'Australian' *and* as undefinable as the diaspora of all the races and cultures that have made a go of it along the track.

Nowadays, as more products of Australian culture are

John Heyer's *The Back of Beyond* (1954).

redefining many of the national orthodoxies, there seems to be a need for a definition of 'Australia' which welcomes a sense of international 'contamination' in its constitution. The audience for Australian cinema no longer seems to be 'seminal'. It is now perhaps more interested in the world rather than in boundaries that could theoretically separate the nation from the remainder of the international community. As the economic and cultural constitution of the society is currently 'internationalising' so radically, the requirements of the national myths are also altering. If you lived in this country, therefore, you'd keep coming back to this question: What would you like to be thinking?

Notes

1 David Malouf, *An Imaginary Life: A Novel*, G. Braziller, New York, 1978, p. 39.
2 Marcus Clarke, Preface in *The Poems of the Late Adam Lindsay Gordon*, Samuel Mullen, London 1887, pp. v–vi.
3 G. F. W. Hegel, translated by B. Bosanquet, in *Philosophies of Beauty*, E. F. Carritt (ed.), Clarendon Press, Oxford, 1931, pp. 161–2.
4 Giuseppe de Santis, 'Towards an Australian Landscape', in *Springtime in Italy: A Reader on Neo-Realism*, David Overbey (ed.), Talisman, London, 1978, p. 125.
5 John Hinde, *Other People's Pictures*, ABC, Sydney, 1980.
6 Sergei Eisenstein, *Film Form: Essays in Film Theory*, edited and translated by Jay Leyda, Harvest, New York, 1977, p. 46. (Originally published in 1949 by Harcourt, Brace, Jovanovich, Inc., New York.)
7 It is *"Crocodile" Dundee* in the US.
8 It is *The Road Warrior* in the US.
9 The author is indebted to Meaghan Morris' article on *Crocodile Dundee*, 'Tooth and claw: tales of survival, and *Crocodile Dundee*', *Art & Text*, no. 25, June–August, 1987, pp. 36–9.

The archetypical innocent abroad: Barry (Barry Crocker) arrives in London, watched by Aunt Edna (Barry Humphries). Bruce Beresford's *The Adventures of Barry McKenzie* (1972).

3
A cultural revolution

Phillip Adams

That great misnomer, China's Cultural Revolution, crushed the ideas and ideals of artists and intellectuals for about a decade. At its end there was, albeit briefly, an explosion of pent-up creativity, much of which was expressed in the cinema. Censored, exiled and brutalised, and also cut off from outside influences, surviving film-makers poured out their hearts in features combining formal innovation with romantic intensity.

Australia's cultural revolution lasted far longer than a mere ten years. For the best part of half a century, indigenous culture atrophied. Far from subsidising the arts, government saw its job as protecting us from its salacious and subversive influence. Federal and state authorities had, between them, established a system of censorship that Eastern Europe or Northern Ireland might have admired, bringing down the curtain on such innocuous films as *Jag är Nyfiken—Gul* (*I Am Curious Yellow*, Vilgot Sjöman, 1968) and banning the likes of D. H. Lawrence, James Baldwin and even Mary McCarthy. The vice squads of our metropolitan police forces, when not keeping a fatherly eye on prostitution, could be relied upon to leap on a visiting replica of Michelangelo's David to shroud its genitals, to lurk in theatres awaiting the first opportunity to arrest a visiting comedian (e.g., Lenny Bruce), or seize a local playwright (e.g., Alex Buzo) who had put foul language into actors' mouths.

Our enduring bulwark of conservatism, ardent anglophile and obsequious monarchist, Sir Robert Menzies, permitted himself occasional acts of artistic patronage by providing modest cheques to the odd writer—but only after the novelist had been thoroughly vetted by the Australian Security and Intelligence Organisation. If he or she turned out to have any left-wing connections, the grant was cancelled.

If there was one way to be an Australian artist, it lay in leaving Australia. Those fancying themselves as intellectual or cultural aspirants were well advised to take a P & O liner to London, just as young Americans would exile themselves in Paris. Oddly enough, one of the only organisations to encourage the indigenous artist was the tiny Australian Communist Party whose front organisations published radical books, maintained a literary journal and ran theatre and film groups. It was perhaps just as well that its influence was minimal as, inevitably, socialist–realist theologies were dominant. Any writer or artist who took liberties with form or ideology was likely to be cast into outer darkness.

So what Menzies did on the right was parodied by those on the left.

Things, consequently, were decidedly grim. In the 1960s, only four Australian plays were professionally produced. Four Australian plays in ten years! Our commercial theatres were committed to American musicals or British drawing-room comedies, while the repertory companies experimented with the likes of Arthur Miller and Tennessee Williams.

There was, of course, a fringe. Actors would hire church halls and produce a *Waiting for Godot* while would-be avant-gardists would buy a Bolex or Bailleau camera and make experimental films—or, rather, remake other people's experimental films. To the European or American eye, local efforts would have been all too familiar: here a little René Clair, there a little Andy Warhol. Though, to be fair, *It Droppeth as the Gentle Rain* (Bruce Beresford and Albie Thoms, 1963), in which Sydney is inundated with a vast shower of excrement, has a certain raw, antipodean energy.

At this stage of Australian cultural life, every major city had one cinema specialising in French films. When the French New Wave arrived, *we* were duly arrived and copies of *Cahiers du Cinéma* were handed around to be read with reverence. Simultaneously, we crowded into film festivals to watch forbidden fruit—features that, often as not, the general public was not permitted to see.

In the middle 1960s, some of us made our first underground features, works that were as conceptually clumsy as they were technically inept. Audiences were all but non-existent, so we looked at each other's.

The painters were, I recall, the first to establish themselves. Although Australia's population is among the most urbanised populations on earth, our painters started filling local galleries with depictions of the hinterland as dazzling as Van Gogh's were of Provence. Our cities were confronted by images of burning desert and convict mythology, a defiance echoed in the work of writers, particularly the novels of Patrick White (subsequently to become our first Nobel Laureate of Literature) and the poetry of Judith Wright. But such activity was anomalous in a country afflicted by what was well described as Australia's 'cultural cringe'. As a British colony with aspirations to become an American colony, we were perfectly happy to import our politics and our culture, to anchor our social structures in British precedent while enjoying the energies of American comics, movies, music and paperbacks.

By the late 1960s, however, Australians were becoming alarmed at the dominance of their economy by foreigners. Vast tracts of cattle country were, we learned, owned by wealthy Britishers or Texans, while more and more of our manufacturing industry was being swallowed up by Americans. Having 'sold the farm', we were now well on the way to selling the factory.

A moment of opportunity came for would-be artists, and particularly for those who dreamed of making films, when a Liberal prime minister, John Gorton, began to respond to concerns of foreign ownership. (Please remember that here in Australia 'Liberal' means 'Conservative'. Many would argue that Labor means 'Conservative', too, but with Liberals it is proudly stated, whereas Labor governments strenuously deny it and protest the urgent desire to redistribute wealth.) Gorton shocked the establishment, and his own party, by speaking out against the dominance of multi-national corporations and hinting that he was willing to do something about it.

John Gorton was by no means a cultured man. Indeed, he belonged to the proud tradition of Australian anti-intellectualism. Moreover, he was on public record as liking American Westerns. But a group of us was able to persuade him that foreign ownership of cinemas and foreign domination of feature films and television productions were just as ominous a portent as the dominance of public companies and the stock market. So three of us[1] were sent off on an odyssey: to gather ideas that might be employed to encourage local production.

On the trinity's return, I wrote a one-page report to Gorton which began with some tongue-in-cheek plagiarism: 'We hold these truths to be self-evident.' The report said that it was 'time for Australians to see their own landscape, hear their own voices, to dream their own dreams'. What followed was a modest proposal for government involvement in the film industry. It had to be modest, otherwise it would have been rejected. For while Gorton was sympathetic, he wasn't enthusiastic.

(We had come back from our trip deeply impressed with something that André Malraux had said: 'Make the prime minister the Minister for Film. That will ensure that you get the money out of Treasury and, unlike a junior minister, he'll be too busy to interfere.')

The initial proposal, which Gorton accepted without so much as a Cabinet discussion, involved the expenditure of little more than a hundred thousand dollars. A few years later, government subsidy to film production (through a generous, indeed, profligate system of taxation concessions) would run into hundreds of millions of dollars.

Most of the original government funding was put into a so-called Experimental Film Fund. Not that the products were particularly avant-garde. It was a sad fact that, in Australia, any piece of film was 'experimental', even the most banal documentary on a seeing-eye dog school. The Fund simply gave money away—a few hundred dollars to a teenage film-maker, a few thousand to someone in his or her early twenties. The film could be on any subject, for any audience. The Fund was simply a fishing expedition, a means of talent scouting.

The idea was that the best and brightest to emerge from experimental film work would be admitted to a new film school, where they would spend four or five years studying and forming themselves into ongoing creative groups. On graduation, they would then be backed up by a hypothetical Australian Film Development Corporation (AFDC) and helped to make features.

The idea we had put to Gorton was to have a small industry along Scandinavian lines. Of all the models, what we had seen in Stockholm seemed the most admirable. Those of us with the prime ministerial ear envisaged an Australian New Wave making low-budget features for the international film festival circuit, for the global intelligentsia who were watching Ingmar Bergman, François Truffaut and Satyajit Ray.

Before Gorton had time to legislate for the three stages (Experimental Film Fund, National Film School and AFDC), he suffered a coup d'état. Right-wingers in his party, aided and abetted by media barons, used the excuse of alleged sexual improprieties to remove him from office when, of course, their real concern was for his nationalistic economic policies. At the same time, they inadvertently encouraged the momentum that would lead to the first left-wing government in Australia for 25 years. The first, and the last.

Now our cultural revolution was truly over. Within minutes of election, Prime Minister Gough Whitlam had recognised China, withdrawn Australian troops from Vietnam and started pouring money into the arts. We got our film school and our AFDC while, through the Australia Council, Whitlam, behaving exactly the way Malraux had predicted, got the money flowing from Treasury. Whereas Gorton had been persuaded by anti-American rhetoric to include a film industry as a small item on a much larger agenda, Whitlam became an enthusiast. The nearest thing to an Australian renaissance man, he was determined to be the arts' Medici, but had no need to see it in anti-American terms. He was going to be a Great Australian Prime Minister and his Great Australia needed Great Australian Art. And of all the arts, film would be the most democratic and accessible.

(To his credit, whenever Prime Minister Whitlam was presiding at an event relating to our burgeoning film industry, making a major announcement or cutting another ribbon, he would insist that Gorton attend. Such bipartisan, ecumenical events are rare in Australian politics and emphasise that it was Gorton who was the film's progenitor, though Whitlam would be its most munificent benefactor.)

The plan succeeded beyond our wildest expectations. Out of the tiny investments in experimental film funding came early works by the likes of Fred Schepisi and Peter Weir, though they had no need to attend the film school[2] which was unveiled soon afterwards. The AFDC began investing in local features which, almost immediately, began attracting international acclaim and sizeable local audiences.

As with China's Cultural Revolution, Australia's had obviously resulted in a huge amount of pent-up pressure which, very quickly, was released. The films were, like those of the Chinese, intensely romantic and stylistically innocent, as they made desperate attempts to make up for lost time while reclaiming lost history.

In the 1920s and 1930s, there had been an Australian tradition of fairly earthy, energetic comedies with an emphasis on egalitarian values. Long before *Crocodile Dundee*[3] (Peter Faiman, 1986), there had been any number of films of rural innocents coming to big cities, or exporting their naivety to London. Thus, the first film of the New Wave to attract a large local audience—and the very first film to be wholly financed by the AFDC—was a *Candide*-style story of an innocent who goes abroad. Not to New York, as in *Crocodile Dundee*, but to Lon-

The arts-loving Prime Minister Gough Whitlam is embraced by Edna Everedge (Barry Humphries), while watched by wife Margaret. Bruce Beresford's *Barry McKenzie Holds His Own* (1974).

don. His name was Barry McKenzie (Barry Crocker), and he ricocheted through any number of misadventures involving British class and media. Fastidious Australian critics shuddered with distaste at the vulgarity of the enterprise (which I produced with Bruce Beresford directing[4]), but audiences enjoyed it enormously. For the first time in forty years, a local film was a major force at the box office.[5]

Yet to get the film released had been very difficult. When we had completed it, we found that the cinema chains refused to show it, even though the production had been wholly funded with government money. The oligopoly was largely owned by American and British interests and, as ever, they wanted their cinemas to be kept safe for British and US product. So *The Adventures of Barry McKenzie* (1972) had to be screened in the few fringe cinemas that were outside the system and, subsequently, starved for product.

Prior to the Gorton–Whitlam intercession, I had made other features that had to be screened in rental halls and church buildings.[6] Australian film-makers had become used to this sort of hostility from the cinemas and continued to 'four wall'[7] their own product for years. Fred Schepisi's *The Devil's Playground* (1976) was knocked back by the cinema chains, as were films like Ken Cameron's *Monkey Grip* (1982). To fight at the barricades in the late 1960s and early 1970s was to face the prospect of mortgaging a home to make a film and then of taking out a second mortgage to screen it.

The success of *The Adventures of Barry McKenzie* was more or less coincident with that of two other comparably vulgar comedies: *Stork* (Tim Burstall, 1971) and *Alvin Purple* (Burstall, 1973). While hardly attractive to film theorists or festival juries, they served to introduce the local audience to local film. Now it was possible for Peter Weir to make *Picnic at Hanging Rock* (1975); for Bruce

The troubled Brother Francine (Arthur Dignam) in Fred Schepisi's *The Devil's Playground* (1976).

Respectable Australian film-making: top: Laura (Susannah Fowle) in Bruce Beresford's *The Getting of Wisdom* (1977); bottom: Sybylla Melvyn (Judy Davis) and Aunt Helen (Wendy Hughes) in Gill Armstrong's *My Brilliant Career* (1979).

The liberal 1970s: Alvin Purple (Graeme Blundell) and friend in Tim Burstall's *Alvin Rides Again* (1973), top right, which helped spawn a television series, with Alvin and an amorous librarian (Peta Peter), top left; Felicity (Helen Hemingway) in the television series of *The Box*, bottom left, which spawned Paul Eddey's theatrical feature of 1975, with Tony Wild (Ken James) and Lee Whiteman (Paul Karo), bottom right.

Beresford to make *The Getting of Wisdom* (1977); for Gill Armstrong to do *My Brilliant Career* (1979). With work like this, film-making became respectable and Australian audiences began to feel very cosy indeed. The acceptance of Australian films, meanwhile, at least coincided with —and may have spearheaded—a wider acceptance of Australian arts. Suddenly local theatre was booming and there was a new confidence in our fiction writers.

Whitlam gloried in his role as the greatest patron of the arts in Australian history but, then, the link had been forged even before his election. Whitlam was elected on the campaign theme of 'It's Time', which came as a patriotic anthem sung, in television commercials, by a wide variety of Australian celebrities, with particular emphasis on television actors. And if things had been difficult for us in the film industry, they had been bloody impossible for people trying to earn a living in television drama, where the local industry was drowned in dumped American product. Seeing Whitlam as a potential saviour, the Australian artists had carried him shoulder-high into office and now he could claim to be a part of their growing success, both local and international.

Seeing the political benefits of associating with the arts, the premiers of Australia's states decided to get involved. The first was Premier Don Dunstan of South Australia, a man of considerable, almost excessive, artistic interests. Even before Whitlam had passed the necessary legislation to cement our plans for film, Dunstan asked me to visit him in Adelaide where, collectively, we cobbled together the South Australian Film Corporation, to ensure that his off-Broadway state would be a part of the coming boom.

It was beyond politics, or at least party politics. In almost every state, the incumbent premier decided to follow Dunstan's example. In Victoria, the conservative premier, Rupert Hamer, established the Victorian Film Corporation (later renamed Film Victoria), while in New South Wales Neville Wran, another Labor premier, legislated for his variant, the New South Wales Film Corporation. Tasmania and Queensland followed with differing structures. Only Western Australia couldn't quite make up its mind.

What did the politicians get out of it? Image, glamour, photo opportunities and, as Australian film began to excite international attention, the entrée card to high places. More than one Australian prime minister, arriving at the White House, found that all the president and first lady wanted to discuss was the latest, favourite Australian film.

And we began to detect what economists call 'value-added' factors. The tourism industry certainly benefited from the Australian film boom, while trade officials at foreign embassies discovered that feature films, of all things, were becoming a factor in trade negotiations. There was a well-known instance of a South American company, based in a country where Australia didn't enjoy diplomatic representation, doing a trade deal because the chief executive had liked *Picnic at Hanging Rock*.

With Gorton's ascendancy came the death of censor-

ship. It was like the Berlin Wall coming down. First a few shards, then everything.[8] From being one of the most repressive countries on earth, Australia became one of the most liberal. From banning esoteric novels, we suddenly had full frontal nudity in television soapies.

The early Australian features were, by and large, elegiac images of failure. The central character would almost invariably fail to achieve his ambition and would accommodate himself to being second-best. For reasons that no one has fully explained, we made perhaps a dozen films in which the hero was an anti-hero, a sort of virile Woody Allen. It became painfully obvious to some of us that, to succeed internationally, particularly in the US, our heroes would have to measure up to the time-honoured cinematic template. They would have to win the war, get the girl and rob the bank. No more passive victims of circumstances—it was time for *Mad Max* (George Miller, 1979).

Mad Max was a watershed, a film about a winner. Where his predecessors had been content with second-best, Max was to carve a very wide swathe. The success of *Mad Max* in the US and particularly in Japan gave the producers confidence. Thus, in the sequel[9], their hero became even more heroic, while the iconography borrowed heavily from the Samurai movies. All Australian film-makers learned the same lesson: gentle, anecdotal, faintly wistful films might win accolades from the gentle, wistful people that attend film festivals, but they wouldn't attract the mass audience.

So, now, the Australian film lost its innocence and headed for the big time.

If anything, the Australian film lobby was to prove too successful. From making a dozen films a year, we were soon making twenty. There is an old Chinese adage which holds that the worst thing that can happen is to have your prayers answered. We were to find this true when, after the fall of Whitlam and the return of the conservatives, bipartisan enthusiasm for film led to taxation incentives of unprecedented generosity. Instead of being a small, dedicated group of film-makers following some sort of Scandinavian model, we became an overactive, overgreedy enclave of people making too many films too quickly for too much money, with too much of an eye on overseas markets. The result was, by and large, a catastrophe, a shambles, which led to politicians and audiences alike losing their enthusiasm for our efforts.

So government and industry rethought their assumptions. While some of our best and brightest moved to Los Angeles to greater fame and further fortune, a struggling art form had become a major industry, in which the search for a national identity had all too quickly been marginalised.

But with our established directors living and working in the US, a new era of film-makers, far less romantic than their predecessors, far less concerned with nationalist iconography, is about to take their place.

In the cinemas, the audiences' love affair with Australian films seems to be over. Yes, there is the odd blockbuster, with a Paul Hogan recycling a reliable formula. But the desire to see an Australian feature

Jessie Rockatansky (Joanne Samuel) is pursued by Toecutter's gang. George Miller's *Mad Max* (1979).

film, in a cinema, has lost its glamour and urgency. We have, however, reclaimed our own television industry so that, in most categories, Australian programmes now dominate.

These days Australian quizzes have replaced American quizzes, Australian soaps American soaps. But it seems that the vast energy of the American dream machine, aided and abetted by the new technologies of globalism, ensures a future that belongs to Hollywood and that, once more, Australian films will be a novelty.

The film-makers or would-be film-makers who had fought at the barricades in the late 1960s and early 1970s, those ardent cultural nationalists, have started to sign Mephistophelean contracts with America, either moving there to further their careers or seeking to make the so-called 'mid-Pacific' films that find a ready US market.

Crocodile Dundee is, of course, the most remarkably successful case, in which a mythological creature, wearing a costume that would seem more at home on Harrison Ford in a Steven Spielberg adventure, arrives in New York as a Candide and leaves it as Rocky.

This is, of course, exactly what Hogan did in real life, if a film star's life can be described as real. He returned to Australia a multi-millionaire and promptly married his leading lady. In the film, in that plot which combines the fairy story with the *National Inquirer*, Paul Hogan expresses a collective fantasy for all Australians and, sadly, defines the terms of reference for too many people in the film industry.

Notes

1 Phillip Adams, Barry Jones (a cultural adviser to Gorton and later a federal Labor politician and minister) and Peter Coleman (a NSW Liberal parliamentarian). [ed.]
2 Australian Film and Television School, later the Australian Film Television & Radio School. [ed.]
3 It is *"Crocodile" Dundee* in the US. [ed.]
4 *The Adventures of Barry McKenzie*, 1972. [ed.]
5 *The Naked Bunyip* (John B. Murray, 1970) and *Stork* (Tim Burstall, 1971) were also very successful at the box office, but *The Adventures of Barry McKenzie*'s achievement was on a more extensive scale. [ed.]

Another innocent abroad: Mick 'Crocodile' Dundee (Paul Hogan) among some New York locals. Peter Faiman's *Crocodile Dundee* (1986).

6   Adams was executive producer on *The Naked Bunyip*, and co-produced and co-directed (with Brian Robinson) *Jack and Jill: A Postscript* (1970). [ed.]

7   To 'four wall' a film is to hire a cinema or hall in which to exhibit the film oneself. [ed.]

8   Unlike much of Europe, however, Australia has never allowed the legalised screening of sexually explicit material in cinemas, though a large mail-order business exists for X-rated videos. [ed.]

9   *Mad Max 2* (George Miller, 1981).

The Aboriginal (Gulpilil) leads Brother (Lucien John) and Girl (Jenny Agutter) across the outback in Nicolas Roeg's *Walkabout* (1971).

4

Australian cinema in the 1970s and 1980s

Scott Murray

It is a difficult task undertaking a critical review of Australian cinema over the past two decades, for several reasons. One is to find a perspective that is fair to the many accomplishments but does not overrate them compared to those from elsewhere around the world. A second difficulty, having been a participant in the renaissance as a writer-director, is to fairly judge the work of others without wishing to be seen to push one approach to cinema in preference to another.[1]

What can unequivocally be said is that it has been a remarkable experience for any Australian who lived through the cinematically barren 1950s and 1960s to finally have an indigenous film industry. What always seemed impossible became real. Better yet, several directors, technicians and actors of world note appeared and, despite the inevitable highs and lows, there have been glimmers of real hope that Australia's cinema culture would become seen as an internationally important one.

At the same time, the finest Australian films lag behind the best from around the world. It has been a too rare occurrence for a critic's Top Ten films of any year to include even one Australian film (though decreasingly so). So the question has to be asked: Is Australia's cinema really good enough, or has the enthusiasm at seeing an industry reborn coloured critical judgement?

The vacuum

Before attempting to answer that question, it is worth looking briefly at two contradictory forces in Australia, an understanding of which is arguably key to any appreciation of the national cinema.

First, Australians rarely like anything which differs from their perception of the norm. This results in a perpetuation of the mundane, the unchallenging. Those who break away and achieve something original are seen as a threat to the status quo. They must be ridiculed and undermined to the point where they retreat back into the 'comfortable' den of mediocrity.

Contradicting this insidious impulse is the fact that Australians almost never make any effort to actually stop people being different: verbal abuse is usually as far as it goes. Thus, for example, while homosexuals are

verbally treated with derision, very few Australians will march against them or mobilise political forces in an attempt to suppress their activities.

The best demonstration of this laissez faire approach came in the early 1950s at the height of the Cold War when anti-communist sentiment ran high. Believing it could capitalise on this, the very popular Liberal government of the time tried to outlaw the Communist Party by referendum. But the move was defeated. One cannot imagine many other countries having voted similarly at that time.[2]

This combination of ridicule and indifference has made the role of the Australian artist quite unique. For film-makers to get anywhere, they must overcome the sense of disapproval and battle it out alone and in silence (money is often the only salve). If a good film *does* get made, it is a singular victory in an intellectual and cultural vacuum.

In Italy, France and other countries, artists and intellectuals are valued. The languages of these countries even have words and forms of address which acknowledge warmly the important role such people have in society. Significantly, Australia does not.

But governments, fortunately, don't always reflect mass apathy. Australia has been extremely fortunate in having had a succession of federal and state governments committed to an Australian film industry. Without their financial support, there would have been no need for this chapter to be written. And as the 1990s continue to prove to be a financial testing time, that government support remains the primary lifeblood. Every country needs the cultural input of a film industry—Australia more than most—and one hopes that successive governments will feel the same.

Films of the 1970s

As with all indigenous industries, there are considerable pressures on local production from foreign cultures. Australia is in the particularly difficult situation of being only one of several English-speaking countries. Its films have been in direct competition with those from the dominant American industry and, to an ever decreasing extent, the British. Whereas most countries have to some extent a captive home market (because of language), Australia is not that fortunate. One result was that, in the five decades after the short burst of activity in the 1910s, Australian cinemas were overrun by American and English films.

This foreign dominance was damaging in many ways, the most crucial being the adoption of foreign cultural modes and the lack of any cinematic exploration of Australia's complex national identity by local film-makers. Whatever interest audiences might have had in seeing indigenous subjects, that had to be 'satisfied' by the odd foreign film which used Australia as a location for their variably authentic stories, such as *The Sundowners* (Fred Zinnemann, 1960) and *They're a Weird Mob* (Michael Powell, 1966).

This trend continued into the early 1970s with, among

John Grant (Gary Bond) at Tiboonda station. Ted Kotcheff's *"Wake in Fright"* (1971).

many lesser examples, Tony Richardson's *Ned Kelly* (1970), Nicolas Roeg's *Walkabout* (1971) and Ted Kotcheff's *"Wake in Fright"* (1971).

Richardson's film is of interest primarily because it recounts one of the iconographic stories of white Australian history. But it was galling to many to have it made by the English, and starring as the Australian bushranger the singularly inappropriate Mick Jagger (who never jettisons his rock persona). Richardson also seemed to take little interest in historical accuracy and was heavily criticised for his 'dilettantish' view.[3]

The Roeg and Kotcheff films stand at the other extreme. As fine as any films made in Australia, they are classic examples of how foreign eyes can see and understand local issues with a clarity often unimagined at home. Roeg responded to the beauty and poetry in a landscape many Australians took for granted as cruel and ugly, and lovingly captured its rich colours and textures. Unlike

many Australian DOPs who, frightened by the harsh light, filter it out of existence, Roeg's camera found a perfect harmony.[4] Equally important, Roeg also found connections between the Aboriginal inhabitants and the white occupiers that went beyond the usual clichés of racial delineation.

As for Kotcheff, he told a story of the dark side of Australian mateship, that curious bonding between men which both protects and destroys. First evidenced in the convict days when men outnumbered women five to one, mateship has often since degenerated into a fearful retreat from the 'unknowable' sexuality of women into a comforting haze of alcohol. Worse, it leads to the insidious desire to drag everyone down to its own level by making people conform to the same patterns of behaviour.

This is best revealed in the scene where the schoolteacher, John Grant (Gary Bond), has just been driven a great distance across dusty roads by an aged Aussie. The driver looks across at Grant and says:

'Come and have a drink, mate.'
'No, thanks.'
'Come and have a drink.'
'No . . .'
'It'll only take a minute. Come on, come and have a drink with me.'
'Look, mate, I've given up drinking for a while.'
'What's wrong with you, you bastard? Why won't you come and have a drink with me? I just brought you 50 miles and you won't drink with me. What's wrong with you?'
'What's the matter with you people, eh? You sponge on you, you burn your house down, murder your wife, rape your child. That's all right. But not have a drink with you, a flaming, bloody drink, that's a criminal offence, that's the end of the bloody world.'
'You're mad, you bastard!'

How typical of Australia that Grant's bitingly accurate critique of mateship should be met by mindless insult and a blunt refusal to even consider its veracity.

Now while many Australians have always been aware of this status quo, no one had put it that honestly on film. But Kotcheff did and twenty-two years on it is still the toughest film about the destructive male bondings within Australian society.[5] That Kotcheff ventured from afar (Canada) and filmed here was not, as many first saw it, a cultural invasion, but rather a victory—and not only for the cinema.

First indigenous steps

As Roeg, Kotcheff and other visitors were leaving their marks, local film-makers kept trying to make theirs. They faced various problems, not least of which was a distribution circuit with little-to-no interest in showing locally-made films. Not only were foreign movies cheaper to handle (and thus more profitable), but they were all the local audiences had become used to seeing.

This would have mattered less if there had been in place a way of helping Australian film-makers finance films and reach an audience. But despite innumerable government inquiries and reports, it was not until the end of the 1960s that the Australian government provided support through the Australian Film Development Corporation (later restructured as the Australian Film Commission).

The establishment of this film-funding body was a direct challenge to the distribution-exhibition nexus, which held to the view, supported by a surprising number of commentators, that Australians had no desire or need for local product. That view had been seemingly reinforced by the poor commercial results of Tim Burstall's 1969 feature, *Two Thousand Weeks*.

The film that subsequently turned the situation round more than any other was *The Naked Bunyip* (1970), directed by John B. Murray, the executive producer of *Two Thousand Weeks*. His 136-minute documentary

about Australian attitudes to sex was made expressly to find out if Australians could be enticed into the cinema to watch indigenous films. The gamble paid off and the film was a big commercial success in the city areas (though less so when tested in the outlying country regions).

The film, while ostensibly a documentary, also contains a fictional thread, centred on a sex researcher (Graeme Blundell) who interviews the famous and unknown, and links the various sections. In his character and approach to situations there is a strong comedic element, which helped make the often controversial material palatable to an audience only then emerging from a highly conservative era.

By openly dealing with human sexuality, *The Naked Bunyip* also prefigured the first genre or style[6] to take a foothold in the 1970s: the sex comedy.

Sex comedies

Given the rapidly liberating climate of the time, it is not surprising that sex comedies represented the first wave of the Australian renaissance. Censorship had just been loosened and the 18-and-overs were given for the first time an 'R' rating for adult films. Distributors had great success with the nude frolics of films such as *Bedroom Mazurka* (John Hilbard, 1970) and the relative explicitness of pseudo sex documentaries from Scandinavia (hardcore was and still is banned in cinemas[7]).

Local film-makers sought to cash in on this market and made their own sex comedies. They were full of nudity but often surprisingly short in fornication. Sex was invariably treated with humour and there was little clinical exploration of the Scandinavian kind. In that sense, Australia's sex films owed more to the British tradition of show and giggle, though without quite the same level of prurient smuttiness. Sex was not dirty but life affirming, even if treated in a somewhat childish way.

The first sex comedy of note was *Alvin Purple* (Tim Burstall, 1973), which mixes full nudity with double entendres and bursts of slapstick. Alvin (Graeme Blundell), the otherwise unexceptional lead character[8], finds himself irresistibly attractive to women, leading to much clothes coming off and mattress squeaking. The aim was for audiences to identify with an 'ordinary' guy who 'got lucky', rather than to idolise a hero-stud. Then, according to the perverse traditions of this genre, the film opts for a moralistic ending where purity and virginal women are honoured above sexual freedom.

Assailed by the critics but loved by audiences, *Alvin Purple* became the first Australian blockbuster of the 1970s and, in real money terms, is still one of the country's greatest local hits.

Other lightweight sex comedies soon followed: *Number 96* (Peter Bernardos, 1974), *The Box* (Paul Eddey, 1975), *Plugg* (Terry Bourke, 1975), *Fantasm* (Richard Bruce [Richard Franklin], 1976), et al. There was also the odd 'documentary', such as *An Essay on Pornography* (Christopher Carey, 1973), *The Love Epidemic* (Brian Trenchard-Smith[9], 1975) and *Australia After Dark* (John D. Lamond, 1975). The best made of either style is

Top: Market Researcher (Graeme Blundell) outside Melbourne's VD clinic. John B. Murray's *The Naked Bunyip* (1970). Left: Sarah Gardiner (Eileen Chapman) in Tim Burstall's *Two Thousand Weeks* (1969).

Top: Alvin (Graeme Blundell) and Kinky Lady (Shara Berriman). Tim Burstall's *Alvin Purple* (1973). Bottom: a successful heterosexual relationship: Miles (Christopher Milne) and Felicity Robinson (Glory Annen) in John D. Lamond's *Felicity* (1979).

Felicity (John D. Lamond, 1979), a basically competent example of the 'first-love' style.

Brian McFarlane is typical of most Australian critics when he writes intemperately:

All these films. . .are witless, sexist, and shoddy, catering to the lowest and commonest of denominators. Presumably every national cinema, at least where censorship permits, has its squalid underbelly. . .[10]

However, not only is *Felicity*, for one, not 'shoddy', but why should soft sex films be moralistically linked to 'the lowest and commonest of denominators'? Meaghan Morris is much more to the point when she writes:

Felicity. . .take[s] up a positively pedagogical tone, emphasizing the desirability of a tolerant and understanding attitude to sex. . .[It] ends with a hymn to the virtues of a fusion of love and sex at the centre of a liberated life.

Felicity, interestingly, is the only [Australian] narrative film [up till 1980] to point to a sexuality free of conflict and antagonism of interests between men and women. . .[11]

Along with the sex comedies, many other films took advantage of the freeing of sexual attitudes to include scenes of lovemaking and nudity, such as the political student drama, *Demonstrator* (Warwick Freeman, 1971), the four-part look at relationships, *Libido* (John B. Murray, Tim Burstall, Fred A. Schepisi, David Baker, 1973), and the detective thriller, *Scobie Malone* (Terry Ohlsson, 1975).

Another is Tim Burstall's *Petersen* (1974), which stands apart for several reasons. Written by playwright David Williamson, the film is a fairly searching analysis of lost ambitions and class differences, and the destructiveness of undirected sexuality.

Petersen (Jack Thompson) is a working-class electrician who has a sexual affair with a university lecturer, Patricia (Wendy Hughes). The intensity of the relationship appears to overcome their intellectual and class differences. But when Patricia decides to leave for Oxford, the chasm between their true aspirations is brutally exposed. Petersen rapes Patricia, then drunkenly incites some policemen to bash him up. His intellectual and social hopes shattered, Petersen returns to his class role, one made bearable by his typically Australian sense of self-deprecation and humour.

Seen by many at the time as excessive and crude (as was *"Wake in Fright"*), *Petersen* remains one of the few Australian films to boldly address sexual relationships and to link sex roles with the class structure.

Most of the other sexually frank films, however, were not so thought-provoking, and the style proved relatively short lived. People seemed to tire of the mix of bare bodies and corny jokes, and overseas the market for tame sex films faltered in the face of heavier demands.

Looking back at them today, these films have an oddly naive quality. More important, and without wishing to overrate them, they have a vitality and freshness missing from much of the tepid Australian cinema of the 1980s.

Many viewers would have happily exchanged a little genteel taste for the cruder energies of the past. And while obviously exploitationist (but what cinema isn't?), the earlier films do make a revealing contrast with dominant genres that followed.

For example, American cinema in the 1980s often set up naked bodies as objects to be abused and mutilated, to be pierced violently by knives and cut apart by chain saws. In the much more innocent Australian cinema of the early 1970s, bodies, male and female, were seen as objects of delight, their free sexuality intending to inspire pleasure on and off the screen. Peculiar that the Calvinist attacks should have been so much stronger back then.

Ocker comedies

Parallel with the sex comedy was another energetic strain of comedy films, this one based on the cruder aspects of Australian behaviour. They have since come to be known as the 'ocker' comedies.

Film academic Sam Rhodie, an advocate of this style, has defined such films as projecting

not a nostalgic rural Australian beauty, but the vulgarity, philistinism and energy of an urban contemporary Australia. These [are] not the distanced and distancing vignettes of the past, a parade of Australians buttoned up in costume, but vicious, zany comedies of the present.[12]

Ocker films enjoyed a great following at the start of the 1970s revival, in part because they dealt lovingly with aspects of the Australian character that the British-based values of the middle class viewed as contemptuous. These included swearing and coarse language, drunkenness, an obsession with bodily functions, beery mateship and the accompanying derision of women, anti-intellectualism, and a violation of custom and ethnic/religious belief.

In the rampant nationalism of the early renascence, these elements were seized upon because of their very Australianness. What differentiated us from others was no longer an embarrassment but a source of pride. This was particularly true of anything that challenged or put down the values of Australia's scorned colonial rulers, the English.

The first ocker film of the modern cycle was arguably the 1966 *They're a Weird Mob*, directed by Michael Powell and written by Emeric Pressburger (under the pseudonym of Richard Imrie). Adapted from the Australian novel by Nino Culotta (i.e., Frank O'Grady), it is a comedy about an Italian immigrant's coming face to face with peculiarly Australian ways of life. Though lambasted by the critics, many of whom felt the film would harm Australia's image abroad, local audiences were entertained by the humorous caricaturing of an Australianness so rarely depicted in cinema.

As for 1970s cinema, there are moments of ocker behaviour in *The Naked Bunyip*, but the first feature to really celebrate it was Tim Burstall's *Stork* (1971). It begins with Stork (Bruce Spence) getting himself sacked for anti-corporate and -social behaviour (this is meant to

Petersen (Jack Thomson) in Tim Burstall's *Petersen* (1974).

Top: Nino Culotta (Walter Chiari) in Michael Powell's *They're a Weird Mob* (1966). Bottom: Barry McKenzie (Barry Crocker), right, protects his assets in Bruce Beresford's *Barry McKenzie Holds His Own* (1974).

be a good thing), then observes his rather elemental relationships with several others in a crowded house. Much emphasis is placed on crude language, drunken loutishness and tasteless party tricks (such as pretending a smoked oyster stuck up the nose is mucus, and then eating it).

The most popular of the ocker comedies was released the next year: Bruce Beresford's debut feature, *The Adventures of Barry McKenzie* (1972). It reverses and retells Michael Powell's tale of the innocent abroad by dispatching a naive Aussie on a visit to London. (This theme would be reworked again 14 years later in Peter Faiman's *Crocodile Dundee*[13], New York substituting for London, and in 1993 by Yahoo Serious in *Reckless Kelly*, Hollywood being the foreign place.)

In *The Adventures of Barry McKenzie*, the brash and vulgar behaviour of 'Bazza'[14] (Barry Crocker) contrasts sharply with, as the film has it, the hypocrisies of genteel Englishness (with bondage and kink seemingly behind every Englishman's door). The film glorifies Bazza's ocker behaviour, from the spraying of beer over innocent bystanders to the vomiting on a psychiatrist's head. The latter makes a stark contrast with the scene in Kotcheff's *"Wake in Fright"* where the drunken school teacher throws up while attempting loveless sex. Beresford goes for a meaningless (and unfunny) laugh; Kotcheff crystallinely portrays an unpalatable truth about many Australian men's attitude to (and inabilities regarding) sex and women.

The first Bazza film was followed by a second, *Barry McKenzie Holds His Own* (Bruce Beresford, 1974), and many others which use ocker elements, such as *Petersen*, *Sunday Too Far Away* (Ken Hannam, 1975) and *Don's Party* (Beresford, 1976). Television also mined ockerism in such shows as *Number 96* and *The Box*, both of which had spin-off features. In the 1980s, the exuberance had subdued a little and can be seen in the false 'naturalism' of programmes such as *Neighbours* and *Home and Away*.

Tom O'Regan argues in *The Australian Screen* that sex comedies such as *Alvin Purple* are also part of the ocker style.[15] But while *Alvin Purple* and the others have moments of ockerist behaviour, the true precedents are the soft British sex comedies typified by *Secrets of a Door-to-Door Salesman* (Wolf Rilla, 1973). It is one in a 'series' of films about ordinary men (window-washers, etc.) who find themselves seduced by all manner of women, and who behave in predictably caricatured ways.

Critic Meaghan Morris has argued that the use of stereotypes and generalisation in the ocker comedies

> bond[s] things together, although in an oddly ambiguous way. There is a process of holding figures up to be surveyed and identified, which places them at a distance, and virtually calls upon the audience to play anthropologist to their own culture. At the same time, however, the shared recognition of the typical feeds a sense that a unity and identity of some kind actually exists.[16]

But does that distancing actually occur? Certainly, the raucous way audiences reacted to ocker films suggests

otherwise. It is also highly arguable that many Australians, with their deep-seated anti-intellectualism, ever thought hard enough about these films' content to even remotely approach being anthropological. Rather, the ocker films were generally savoured by those who uncritically responded to the comic behaviour displayed in them. It is not dissimilar to the way Americans unthinkingly react to the visceral pleasures of a revenge action film. *The Adventures of Barry McKenzie* is as unlikely to invite a dispassionate analysis of ockerism among audiences as *Lethal Weapon* (Richard Donner, 1987) is to encourage a thoughtful appraisal of the American gun culture.

Whatever its merits, though, this ockerist elevation of the uncouth was short lived; people soon tired of the antics and were dulled by a comic vein that quickly ran out of ideas. The main benefit of the ocker comedies was that they helped convince distributors that Australians would go and see locally-made films. Increasingly, the distribution-exhibition chains began to take the Australian cinema seriously and began investing in local production. Village Roadshow (under the Hexagon banner) had led the charge with several sex comedies, but the other chains, particularly Greater Union, chose to back what would become the dominant genre for the rest of the 1970s.

The period film

The period film in Australia has been typified by Graeme Turner as

> a particular sub-genre: films set in the past, foregrounding their Australianness through the re-creation of history and representations of the landscape; lyrically and beautifully shot; and employing aesthetic mannerisms such as a fondness for long, atmospheric shots, an avoidance of action or sustained conflict, and the use of slow motion to infer significance.[17]

That is a fair summary of the perception of many (though the lack of action and conflict is arguably not as deliberate as Turner implies and the use of slow motion is not that common). One immediately thinks of films such as *Picnic at Hanging Rock* (Peter Weir, 1975), *Sunday Too Far Away*, *The Devil's Playground* (Fred Schepisi, 1976) and *My Brilliant Career* (Gill Armstrong[18], 1979).

The boom in this style of film was largely occasioned by the political changes that came late in the 1960s. As Brian McFarlane has written, 'The late 1960s witnessed a stirring of new life in Australia after the long, comfortably affluent sleep of the [Sir Robert] Menzies-led Liberal Government (1949–66)'[19] and its Liberal successors. In 1972, the left-wing Labor government of Gough Whitlam swept to power and with it an almost frantic desire to sweep away the last vestiges of British colonialism and culture, and oversee the forced birth of a uniquely Australian one. As well, there was the long-overdue rebellion against many American influences and

Jimmie (Tommy Lewis), right, prepares to sweep up as the whites 'shear the rams'. Fred Schepisi's *The Chant of Jimmie Blacksmith* (1978).

values (Australia's sheepish following of America into Vietnam being increasingly challenged).

In this time of (re-)emergent nationalism, many film-makers felt the desire to come to terms with the country's (usually white) roots. But unsure about what actually constituted Australianness, film-makers headed for the predigested opinions of others. Instead of writing original stories, they raided library shelves for anything that was remotely filmable, resulting in many less-than-inspiring novels making it to the screen.

One reason for this timid approach was that Australia has very little white history (less than two hundred years by 1970), and much of it concerns a very small number of people who were predominantly of one class. What written records there are of the early white days are fairly dry accounts of a convict and colonial past. To forge anything original would have meant an intense study of dusty records and a synthesis of years of minimalist history into a summation few felt capable of making. It was simply easier to use what already existed.

As for a visual record of Australian history, there was even less. Nearly all the early buildings had been pulled down and the first colonial paintings were done by Europeans unable or unwilling to accurately reproduce what they saw (Australian bush became English pastorale). While there have been significant periods since of painting in Australia, such as the Heidelberg School, the output until recently was relatively small. So, when film-makers visually researched earlier times, these few paintings were consulted over and over again. There is one painting in particular, Tom Roberts' *Shearing the Rams*, which has been so often recreated in films that it now represents the cliché image of shearing (a sad fate for an important work of art).

Arthur Trenbow (Corin Redgrave) and Radio Announcer (John Chance) in Michael Thornhill's *Between Wars* (1974).

This borrowing from the extant can be seen most particularly in the depiction of the outback landscape. It is a place where few Australians live and not many visit, so it was not surprising that when film-makers ventured out there in the 1970s they created images based on those already well-known from photography and newsreels. Not being part of their lives, the landscape and lives they filmed were manufactured ones. They had little connection with the realities out there and, inevitably, soap-opera formulations came to fill in the gaps left by lack of a knowledge truly learnt.

With all but a few directors prepared to create their own visions, it was not surprising that a visual staleness set in. This may well have been a factor in the declining interest audiences had for period films and re-creations of times past.

The Films

Many critics start the period film cycle in 1975 with Peter Weir's *Picnic at Hanging Rock*, but there were encouraging signs in the years preceding it.

In 1969, English director Tony Richardson had filmed *Ned Kelly*, and in 1971 came Peter Maxwell's *Country Town*, a spin-off from a television soapie, and Hans Pomeranz's barely distributed *Stockade*, a musical about a goldfield rebellion in 1854. The latter two generated little interest. What did, though not with the public, was Michael Thornhill's *Between Wars* (1974). It is one of the few Australian films of ideas. Scripted by novelist Frank Moorhouse, it boldly charts various political and philosophical debates of the years between the two world wars, largely as seen through the eyes of psychiatrist Edward Trenbow (Corin Redgrave). Unlike most of the period films to follow, it is an original, presenting a confronting view of an Australia wallowing in complacency. It borrows not from the predetermined experiences of others, but sees things afresh, never afraid to take a point of view.

The breakthrough with the public came a year later with Ken Hannam's *Sunday Too Far Away*, at its best a superb evocation of 1950s outback life. It humorously and touchingly details the mateship between shearers, in scenes of the men at work[20], and at rest, which is largely

Arthur Black (Peter Cummins) and Foley (Jack Thompson) prepare to shear the rams. Ken Hannam's *Sunday Too Far Away* (1975).

made up of drinking beer, insulting and assaulting the cook, and telling tall yarns. The spirit of friendship is seen almost exclusively from a positive light, suggesting that at heart the good Aussie cares about, and will come to the aid of, his mates. It also hints at the darker side of mateship in the rubbishing of those whose views on life differ (such as the youth who writes to a girl!), but the film suggests this is good humoured and essentially harmless.

Where the film does, perhaps unconsciously, see difficulties is in the relationships between men and women: like many films to follow, men are shown as happiest with each other. A woman's presence tempts men from the true and hallowed into a minefield of emotional traps. *Sunday Too Far Away* in fact falls apart dramatically

when Sheila (Lisa Peers) enters and Foley (Jack Thompson) falls in love.

Few have written about it, but Australia's films of mateship iconise a platonic homosexual bond between men—and this in a country which on the surface is homophobic. It is all too easy to think of films about positive mateship, but try thinking of Australian films which show a happy sexual relationship between a man and a woman as its central story. The near absence of any, plus the plethora of those charting the deleterious side, is a telling indication of how these relationships are perceived in Australia. (Howard Rubie's *The Settlement*, 1984, is one notable exception.)

Sunday Too Far Away's interests, though, are wider than merely this aspect. It effectively evokes an outback

Breakfast at Appleyard College in Peter Weir's *Picnic at Hanging Rock* (1975).

landscape with a controlled edge of romanticism, and also is rare for Australian film in linking people's happiness with the need for political struggle. The shearers' uncertainly going on strike at the end is not the powerful climax the film-makers would have hoped, but at least they chose an ending that does not kowtow to the insidiously 'neat' endings of much American cinema.

Two months later came *Picnic at Hanging Rock*, which set box-office records and delighted the critics. Its success would give the period film the injection of life that would propel it well into the 1980s.

Today the film is no less striking than in 1975, and it is still one of the finest Australian films of the revival. Though the film does lessen its grip a little towards the rather truncated end, the first hour is mesmeric.

Weir opens with many of the staples of an Australian period film: unknowable, unconquerable landscape; striking images and design; an obsession with the objects of another time; a gentle pace that defies conventional narrative drive; and a dream-like quality that draws one into a foreign world. Weir does this all very knowingly, exaggerating for effect and taking the film beyond historical recreation and into the surreal.

Weir conjures an aura of purity and light that lessens away to darkness[21], in parallel to the doom-like effects the disappearances on Hanging Rock have on all concerned. And it is those disappearances which provide the film with its continuing intrigue. The film plays with several possibilities, but none is more persuasive than the others. In fact, a Melbourne writer, Yvonne Rousseau, has written a particularly witty book which convincingly posits nine explanations[22]; this author had previously described several more[23], as have others[24].

More important from an Australian point of view, *Picnic at Hanging Rock* signalled the arrival of its first major director of the 1970s. Weir had made the intriguing *The Cars that Ate Paris* in 1974, but it does not have the confident mastery of *Picnic at Hanging Rock*. Weir was now someone who not only knew what he wanted to achieve, but also how to do it boldly.

Other period films of interest include Donald Crombie's *Caddie* (1976), a gentle and carefully observed story of a deserted wife and her children in the 1930s depression. It attracted special attention not only because of its craftsmanship and fine performances, but because, contrary to most films of the time, it focuses on a woman.

David Bracefeld (John Waters) leads the tribe in Tim Burstall's *A Faithful Narrative of the Capture, Sufferings and Miraculous Escape of Eliza Fraser* (1976).

Ted (Jack Thompson) and Caddie (Helen Morse) in Donald Crombie's *Caddie* (1976).

It is not an obviously feminist work in the way that Gill Armstrong's *My Brilliant Career* is, but it does succeed (where *Career* does not) in convincingly locating a story of independence won within a romantic cinematic tradition.

Another period film with a central heroine is *A Faithful Narrative of the Capture, Sufferings and Miraculous Escape of Eliza Fraser* (Tim Burstall, 1976), a drama largely set on the North Queensland island where the real Mrs Fraser was wrecked in 1836. Some critics, notably Tom Ryan[25], have posited intriguing readings of the film, but to most it is a less than engaging historical yarn with its many attempts at humour rather badly fumbled. It is also yet another film to include the now tiresome bashing of Australia's former colonial masters.

In stark contrast is Fred Schepisi's *The Chant of Jimmie Blacksmith* (1978), the boldest film of this period. Based on the acclaimed novel by Thomas Keneally, it is an uncompromising and uncomforting look at the subjugation of Aborigines in a country now ruled by whites. Specifically, it tells of one Aborigine, Jimmie Blacksmith (Tommy Lewis), who tries to become part of white society, willingly adapting to its ways and rules. But despite his subservience and courage, he is not accepted and with his half-brother he erupts in a moment of mayhem, killing several whites. He is then tracked down (with black help) and executed.

Up to this film, the early white treatment of Aborigines had not been a concern of the renascent cinema (and still largely isn't[26]). For white Australians, it is was a difficult issue. On the one hand, there was the desire to correct the errors of the past; on the other, there was a questioning of why whites should be made to feel guilt about the sins of long-dead generations.

As well, there was the heated issue of whether films about Aborigines should be made only by blacks. This mirrored the debate a decade earlier in the US about William Styron's *The Confessions of Nat Turner*. A book on that subject quotes historian Herbert Aptheker as saying: 'History's potency is mighty. The oppressed need it for identity and inspiration; oppressors for justification, rationalization and legitimacy.'[27] Now while that view is relevant to Aborigines coming out from under the yoke of white rule, just as it was for white Australians escaping British rule, its simplistic divisioning became a means of inhibiting debate.

Obviously, the easiest way to deal with the dilemma was to avoid it. And generally that was what Australian film-makers did, encouraged into disinterest by the knowledge that the topic was almost certainly uncommercial (one state film commission even had an unstated policy of not investing in any film which had Aboriginal characters).

With hindsight, it was inevitable that the person to challenge this state of affairs should be Fred Schepisi. He is a determined, individualistic film-maker uncowed by cinematic or box-office trends. He had a passion for the story and, against great odds, got it made.

At times, that very passion gets in the way (for many audiences, Schepisi is too confronting in his depiction of the violence), but passion, flawed or otherwise, is the very thing the Australian cinema most needs. When many Australian directors seemingly treat film-making as just a job, not a craft[28], Schepisi's bold effort should have been applauded. Instead, this being Australia, he was largely savaged. Thomas Keneally was most perceptive when he said,

> Schepisi did a heroic thing with this in a country that. . .almost congenitally values mediocrity. He said, 'I'm going to make one of the best ten movies since World War II.' Now, if there is anything wrong with Australia—which, as we all know, is God's own country—it is that there aren't enough people around saying, 'I'm going to make one of the best.'. . .Schepisi said that and people didn't like him. But he did produce a grand flawed film, a fine film.[29]

Other important films of the 1970s, but which address a more recent past, include Schepisi's earlier *The Devil's Playground* and *Newsfront* (Phil Noyce, 1978). The first is a starkly told tale of a boy's coming of age in a Catholic seminary. Based in part on Schepisi's own experiences, the film centres on Tom (Simon Burke) and his struggles to adapt to a spiritual life. He is not only troubled by a sexuality he is taught must be suppressed (holy water is suggested at one point as an aid in curbing masturbation), but also by the subjugation of all personal freedoms to the dictates of a rigid and often stultifying religious bureaucracy.

It is a pity Schepisi cut the film slightly just before its release, because the longer version included a telling moment where Tom, having 'escaped' from the seminary, stands outside a country store and looks in at a rack of magazines. Among them, Tom notices, is a men's magazine; free though he is, the magazine (and other yearned-

Jimmie (Tommy Lewis) leads wife Gilda (Angela Punch) home in *The Chant of Jimmie Blacksmith*.

Tom (Simon Burke) in Fred Schepisi's *The Devil's Playground* (1976).

Newscameramen Len Maguire (Bill Hunter) and Chris Hewitt (Chris Haywood). Phillip Noyce's *Newsfront* (1978).

for aspects of life) are still forbidden him. He is only partially along the road to manhood.[30]

The Devil's Playground is intelligently directed, avoiding most first-film indulgences. With just one feature, Schepisi confidently joined the ranks, alongside Weir and Beresford, of major Australian directors of the 1970s.

Quite different is *Newsfront*, an entertaining and warmly received tribute to the newsreel cameramen of the 1940s and 1950s. While never wholly successful in its examination of aspects of Australianness, it lingers longer in many a memory than most Australian films. One reason is the crisp dialogue and precise sense of character.

Cameraman Len (a brilliant Bill Hunter) is a somewhat stubborn and naive Aussie, loyal to his company and strengthened by a reserve of social conscience. His brother, Frank (Gerard Kennedy), in contrast, is prepared to abandon Australian shores for the temptations of Hollywood. This is seen as a very bad thing, yet it is precisely what the film's director, Phillip Noyce, did himself some years later. Now while that may be amusingly ironical, there is little irony in the film's moralistic siding with Len.

Take the scene where Frank returns to Australia and has dinner with Len and two friends. Unquestionably, it is one of the greatest in Australian cinema, the dialogue ricocheting with wit. But it is hard not to feel that here Len is a tragic figure. When Frank suggests that his hotel-owning buddy must have arranged for 'The Road to Gundagai' to be played in his honour, Len's response of 'Wacko' is very funny. But it is also pathetic. Len's self-indulgent sense of superiority and his refusal to consider notions outside his own narrow range (foreign in particular) could be argued to be a major factor in what limits this country.

Noyce, however, attempts no such perspective. Whereas he is happy to take pot-shots at a right-wing priest and a repressed Catholic wife, Len is accorded deferential treatment. This is most tellingly revealed in Noyce's only marginal examination of how Len and his newsreel mates were responsible for almost the only cinematic images Australians had of their country. Instead of taking an objective approach to their work, they knowingly practised a form of propaganda no less disingenuous than that of politicians. People were invariably shown springing to the aid of neighbours in a country where everyone has the same values, Christian and social. Subservience to a foreign monarch was never questioned, nor the merits of large construction projects in fragile environmental areas, workers forever soldiering on for the nation's good. Ethnicity was the butt of bad jokes, and so on.

Noyce does include the odd brief moment of personal conscience (a verbal to-do over a controversial line of commentary; furrowed expressions at management requests for more quaint 'Australianness'), but the myth-making went on. Len is no more a conveyor of the truth than the 'sold-out' Frank, whom he so smugly puts down.

The same year came *The Irishman* (Don Crombie), which, with *The Mango Tree* (Kevin Dobson, 1977), is seen as representing the beginning of the period film's

Jamie Carr (Christopher Pate), Man (Jonathan Hardy) and Professor (Robert Helpmann) in Kevin Dobson's *The Mango Tree* (1977).

demise. Both films have the obligatory obsession with period decoration and rather thin narrative lines (which the latter tries to bolster with a rather unconvincing strain of melodrama).

The Irishman is not a difficult film to watch (beautiful images, fine performances), but its story of struggle in the timber lands is only fitfully engaging. Compared with the cinematic catastrophes of the 1980s, however, it has been unfairly targeted as a critical whipping horse.

Then, just as everyone was convinced the genre had been played out, came Gill Armstrong's *My Brilliant Career*. This story of a young woman writer's personal and creative growth in the 1890s closely parallels the musical struggles of the girl in Bruce Beresford's earlier *The Getting of Wisdom* (1977).

This author is at odds with most Australian critics who, like Brian McFarlane, argue that:

My Brilliant Career is a tougher, less compromising film than *The Getting of Wisdom*. . .The [former] film's sense of relationships is. . .reassuringly firm-minded. The feeling between Harry (Sam Neill) and Sybylla

Paddy Doolan (Michael Craig), Jenny Doolan (Robyn Nevin) and Grandpa Doolan (Andrew Maguire) in Donald Crombie's *The Irishman* (1978).

(Judy Davis) deepens satisfyingly from the first meeting which has a tension that's comic and sexual to when, half-reluctantly, she dismisses him.

Much will probably be made of [novelist] Miles Franklin's 'feminism' here. . ., but the film's strength is less to be found in a proselytizing approach to a cause than its sympathetic understanding of a character and a personality struggling to assert itself.[31]

Rather, like Pauline Kael, this writer finds the romantic story within *My Brilliant Career* somewhat silly. As Kael says:

The subject matter is rather bizarre because what we are seeing is Sybylla teasing a man all the way through – a poor girl winning a rich man—then, after all this very sexual teasing, when he finally proposes, she is infuriated and tells us that wasn't what she meant at all.

Somehow the audience didn't pay that much attention to the odd feminine logic of it or to the curious phenomenon of a woman who is going off to become a writer not wanting to become involved in human and sexual relations, because that doesn't make a lot of sense. She seemed to think that she could only become an artist if she became a hermit, which is generally the last way to do it.[32]

As well, Harry is portrayed as such a wonderful man, one can't imagine that he would be at all restrictive of Sybylla's literary ambitions, or her desire for occasional solitude. It is as if Armstrong's insistence that a woman can be complete without a man has stood in the way of narrative believability.

Armstrong has said that she tried to keep modern feminist ideology from intruding into this 1890s story, but it is always a presence and can be seen disadvantageously in moments of uncharacteristic behaviour and in

Sybylla Melvyn (Judy Davis), the hermit writer, in Gill Armstrong's *My Brilliant Career* (1979).

the brittle edge to Judy Davis' spirited but mannered performance.

However, the feeling of most critics is summed up by Kael when she adds that it is 'a fine piece of film-making' and that 'it is very unusual to see a first film that is that assured'.

Despite the success of *My Brilliant Career*, however, the period film did not remain in favour. Increasingly, newspaper reviewers turned against it and scathingly attacked the staleness that had set in[33] and the lack of desire by film-makers to tackle modern issues. The latter criticism is hard to take seriously: how, after all, is it possible to make a film without the film-maker's consciousness of the time profoundly influencing the result? (Cf Borges' 'Paul Ménard, author of the *Quixote*'.[34]) As well, many film-makers deliberately used the past to talk about the

present in what they felt was a more palatable manner. As a film about a woman attempting to find herself, *My Brilliant Career* is no less relevant than the contemporary *Puberty Blues* (Bruce Beresford, 1981) or the only slightly backward-looking *Monkey Grip* (Ken Cameron, 1982).

Take in particular the case of *Picnic at Hanging Rock*. It is based on a novel, itself inspired (as the book acknowledges) by the disappearance of several schoolgirls on Hanging Rock in 1900. But there was no disappearance; author Joan Lindsay merely added that textual disingenuity for heightened drama. The book then sets up several possible explanations for the disappearances, some of which the film toys with, others it ignores. Now, Weir made his version at a time when much of the science fiction of his youth had become fact. He could thus

conjure in his film possibilities Joan Lindsay could not
have conceived of when she wrote the book (1957), and
which were quite beyond the thinking of anyone in 1900.
In that sense alone, it is a film of and about 1975; the
clothes and carriages have not altered that.

The critics of the period film also failed to countenance the fact that audiences preferred historical dramas
and showed little enthusiasm for realist works about urban
poverty and the like. (As the period film waned, so did
the box-office takings on Australian films.) But the criticism stung and the first of many sectionalisations began
to appear within the film industry.

One was the construction of the notion of the government or 'AFC genre' of film-making by writers Sue
Dermody and Liz Jacka[35], among others. As if to explain
away the perceived plethora of films which did not tackle
'modern' issues, the AFC was indirectly held up to blame.
It wasn't the film-makers' fault, it was that of the government film-funding bureaucracy.

However, this view remains, despite three books, un-
proven and relies in part on the notion of directors as
whimps unable to stand up to overpowering State forces.
But even the most cursory glance of cinema history reveals how film-makers in all political and social circumstances have proved able to make films that run against
the trend. Even if the AFC, acting on past box-office
results, did favour period films above others (and there
is no proof this is true), there have always been other
avenues open to film-makers. That so few chose to do
'modern' topics is an issue that should be raised with the
film-makers.

Other films of the 1970s

In most film industries, there is always a number of film-
makers whose work sits outside the usual categorisations.
Australia's is no different. There are quite a few directors in Australia who are labelled 'independent' because
their films are not self-professedly part of the commercial mainstream. Some critics go so far as to rate these
films as the true renaissance.

First, the word 'independent' is a misnomer as most of
these film-makers make totally government-subsidised
films. They are supported in other ways too as film asses-
sors and guest film-school lecturers, even having short
stints as bureaucrats at government film bodies. Some
within the mainstream industry are highly critical of those
existing on government beneficence, but many directors
worldwide have grown to cinematic maturity in such an
environment.

At the same time, some of those controlling government sponsorship have been accused of favouritism and
it is hard not to query why some film-makers are forgiven one bad film after another, while several directors
of talent are left ignored on the sidelines. But of what
country is this not also true?

In the early 1970s, those film-makers labelled as 'alternative' included Esben Storm, who made *27 A* (1974), a
grimly realistic tale of an aged alcoholic in a society that
cares little for its old and lonely. Though the film was

Lou (Gary Waddell) helps give Gerry (Carol Porter) another
hit in Bert Deling's incendiary *Pure S...* (1976).

much admired, Storm did not make another feature until
In Search of Anna (1979), the story of a man's search for
a lost love.

Also on the 'edge' of the industry is Bert Deling, who
began with *Dalmas* (1973) and in 1976 released *Pure
S...*[36], a film about a night in the life of some junkies as
they search for their next hit. Criticised by many for
advocating drug use, it remains one of the liveliest films
of the revival, even if the frenetic pace is sometimes
forced.

Another low-budget film of enormous energy is the
perversely funny study of entropy, *Yackity Yack* (1974),
made by Canadian film lecturer Dave Jones. Shot in a
concrete basement, this spiky black comedy about chickens, nudity and political revolution, to name only a few
of its many elements, typifies for many the idiosyncratic
pleasures of 'fringe' film-making.

Other directors who explored that penumbra include

Nigel Buesst (*Bonjour Balwyn*, 1971), Tom Cowan (*The Office Picnic*, 1972; *Promised Woman*, 1976; and *Journey Among Women*, 1977), Jim Sharman (*Summer of Secrets*, 1976) and Albie Thoms (*Sunshine City*, 1973, and *Palm Beach*, 1980). But the director who would become best known, and one of the most government-assisted[37], is Dutch-born Paul Cox.

A former photographer, Cox began with a series of short films which created considerable interest at film-makers' co-operatives and festival screenings, in part because his work was so strikingly visual. The best of these early films is the brilliant *Island* (1975), a hand-held 8mm voyage through a shadow-filled Greek island. (Cox would revisit the territory as part of his same-titled 1989 feature, as well as use similar techniques in most of his features.)

Cox's first feature was *Illuminations* (1976), an exploration of, as Cox calls it, 'the potential of the mind'[38]. He is concerned with how 'people always try to imitate life instead of inventing life'. For many, the film was poetic but inaccessible, so Cox's next feature, *Inside Looking Out* (1977), assumed a more conventional approach to film-making. This story of emotional undercurrents in the crisis of crisscrossing relationships shows Cox attempting what most Australian film-makers shy from: an analysis of the conventions and hypocrisies of modern sexual relationships. But after a series of shorts which had almost no dialogue, Cox seemed uneasy with the rendering and recording of speech. While he quite rightly wishes to fight against the bland American tradition of cliché phraseology, his characters' philosophical and poetic speeches (even when not written by Cox) sometimes have a risible, portentous ring. As well, and no doubt catalysed by this unease, Cox can be extremely mannerist in his camerawork, the 'drunken' zigzagging in the dinner scene being the most criticised example.

Two years later came *Kostas*, which addresses the ghettoisation of migrants within Australia by focusing on a love affair between a middle-class Australian, Carol (Wendy Hughes), and a Greek-born taxi-driver, Kostas (Takis Emmanuel). Some critics, such as Rod Bishop and Fiona Mackie, are very critical of the migrant aspects, arguing that *Kostas* caricatures

> the stigma of cultural difference and the pressures on the margins between cultures. . .The formal, old-fashioned passion of Kostas. . .for. . .Carol. . .comes across as a stereotype, while the situation gives a smug perspective on the unassailability of the barriers of class and culture. . .Since he is not above his station, the romance gains our blessings and the bulk of working-class Greeks are thereby obliquely put down. . .[39]

Presumably, Cox, an immigrant himself, had the intention of showing how the stark contrasts between life at home and in adopted Australia cause migrants to retreat within and find strength in the traditions they were brought up with, however incongruous they may be in the new country.

Kostas is of particular interest for its generally successful depiction of Kostas and Carol's relationship; they look as if they are in love and the cliché of the last-minute airport reunion is quite effective. (Compare it to the similar scene in *Boulevard of Broken Dreams*, Pino Amenta, 1988, which is devoid of similar feeling.)

Also concerned with the shifting nature of relationships is John Duigan. His second feature, *The Trespassers* (1976), is an intense look at infidelity (albeit rather arch) and his next, *Mouth to Mouth* (1978), is a wonderfully vibrant study of two teenage couples who live homeless lives on the fringes of Australian suburban life. It is one of the finer relationship films of the 1970s and immediately suggested Duigan as one of the country's more sensitive directors. Unfortunately, he followed it up with *Dimboola* (1979), a lame comedy about a marriage celebration in the country, and one had to wait to the mid-1980s for his next films of note.

Other regarded films include John Power's warmly nostalgic but minor-key *The Picture Show Man* (1977); Michael Thornhill's *The FJ Holden* (1977), seen by many as one of the few convincing attempts at portraying Australian working-class life; Richard Franklin's *Patrick* (1978), a quite effective attempt at genre film-making; Simon Wincer's first film, *Snapshot* (1979), a middle-of-the-road thriller with a fine debut performance from Sigrid Thornton; and Tim Burstall's *The Last of the Knucklemen* (1979), which melds skilfully moments of genuine Aussie humour with an incisive look at mateship.

That same year also saw the release of the film which stands apart from, and in fact towers above, most other films made by Australians during the decade.

Mad Max

Previously a medic (which has led some writers to append a 'Dr' to distinguish him from the similarly-named director of *The Man from Snowy River*, 1982), George Miller made a couple of short films, including the witty spoof on cinema gore, *Violence in the Cinema. . .Part One* (1972). But nothing could prepare one for the impact of his first feature.

Shot for the little money he and producer Byron Kennedy could raise privately (this was not the sort of film on which to expect government support[40]), *Mad Max*'s production is legendary for the widespread rumours about the director's 'incompetence'. Nothing could have been further from the truth, for *Mad Max* is brilliantly conceived and directed, and the first great visceral film made by an Australian at home.

Miller understands totally his genre and plays joyfully with its traditions. Believing that images tell more powerfully a story than do words, he pares dialogue to the minimum and constructs sequences around camera moves and intercutting. Instead of the pedestrian action scenes then expected in local films, Miller's are exhilarating and explosive. He also avoids the false sentimentality that taints most American films of this style, and the film retains a chilling edge (leading some commentators, including Phillip Adams, to call for its banning). The violence *is* frightening, particularly at the end with

Life at the window: top left: Gabi (Gabriella Trsek) and Tony (Tony Llewellyn-Jones) in Paul Cox's *Illuminations* (1976); bottom left: Elizabeth (Briony Behets) in Cox's *Inside Looking Out* (1977); top right: the Babysitter (Juliet Backsai) covers herself with shaving cream in Cox's *Inside Looking Out*; bottom right: Carol (Wendy Hughes) and Kostas (Takis Emmanuel) in Cox's *Kostas* (1979).

Max Rockatansky (Mel Gibson) and Jim Goose (Steve Bisley) in George Miller's *Mad Max* (1979).

the extremely tough option given the man chained to a soon-to-be-exploding wreck.

Miller's film also has a message embedded in its dark action: this country's insane and deadly road culture. Many Australians like to use their cars as lethal weapons, and there is an aggression on the roads unlike that found elsewhere (as well as a bloodthirsty approach to, and obsession with, motor accidents on the television news[41]). Out of that, Miller fashioned an ethos of the future.

Disturbing and iconoclastic, *Mad Max* came out of the wasteland of much Australian 1970s cinema, just as did its central hero, Max Rockatansky (Mel Gibson). The director would not have wanted it any other way.

The 1980s (and beyond. . .)

The story of the Australian cinema in the 1980s is significantly different to that of the preceding ten years. Local audiences became increasingly disinterested with indigenous films and sought more the mainstream pleasures of the American cinema. It became clear that, instead of having permanently become part of Australian life and culture, locally-made films were merely seen as a fad.

Realising that Australian ticket sales could no longer support local production costs, many film-makers began tailoring their films for the American market. One method was to use internationally known actors; another was to abandon the preoccupations with Australianness and make films which more closely followed American genre models. So was born what became disparagingly known as the 'mid-Pacific film'.

Paralleling this increasingly 'world' view were the dramatic changes to film financing that took place in the early 1980s. Most important was the 1981 amendment to division 10BA of the *Income Tax Assessment Act*, which meant investment in films certified by the government as being Australian received substantial tax benefits. Thus, instead of film-makers applying to the film bodies such as the Australian Film Commission for much of the budget, producers were now able to easily raise tax dollars on the basis of a minimum 15 per cent pre-sale (usually from a foreign distributor). Overnight, the control over what films were made shifted from the government bodies to the investment brokers, most of whom had no experience of, or real interest in, the cinema.

The most dramatic effect of 10BA was a production increase from the 1970s average of 16 features a year to 45 by 1985–86. There was an accompanying boom in tele-features and mini-series, both of which were instrumental in (momentarily) helping break the cultural stranglehold American product had on local television. And by decade's end, the figures were startling: 227 features, 78 tele-features, 70 mini-series and 521 documentaries financed through 10BA.[42]

Parallel with the production escalation was the emergence of many new film-makers. Of the 66 features made from 10BA's introduction to June 1985, 33 were by first-time directors. That represents a 50 per cent average, as compared to 38 per cent in the preceding two-and-a-half years. While the increase is less than usually assumed, it is still significant, especially given the sense of stagnation felt by many at the end of the 1970s.

Whether this new blood added significantly to the industry's standing is much debated. Some, like leading producer Hal McElroy, feel that 10BA gave 'lots of opportunities and [I] hoped, along with everybody else, that these opportunities would produce a Second Wave of actors, writers, directors, etc. But sadly they didn't.'[43]

Others view things differently. In a 1990 interview in *Cinema Papers*, noted French critic Michel Ciment cited among his most admired Australian films works by 1980s newcomers Jane Campion, this author and Bill Bennett.[44] As Ciment points out, he had only limited access to Australian films and other critics might wish to add the names of Yahoo Serious, John Hillcoat, Nadia Tass, Richard Lowenstein and Ian Pringle. (In the early 1990s, one could add Jocelyn Moorhouse, Ray Argall, Baz Luhrmann and John Ruane.)

There are also several key Australian films made under 10BA by first-time directors whose careers have not always continued or been as successful: *The Settlement* (Howard Rubie, 1984), *Moving Out* (Michael Pattinson, 1983), *Annie's Coming Out* (Gil Brealey, 1984), *Bliss* (Ray Lawrence, 1985) and *Fran* (Glenda Hambly, 1985), among others. There are also the directors of the nation's two biggest hits of the 1980s, Peter Faiman (*Crocodile Dundee*, 1986) and John Cornell (*"Crocodile" Dundee II*, 1988).

On the negative side, 10BA led to a major escalation of costs because of the competing demands on a limited number of technicians and name actors. Unions also fought for and won restrictive and expensive trade practices, for which the industry has continued to pay. For instance, it is now inconceivable that a film such as Peter Greenaway's *Prospero's Books* (1991), which cost but £1.2 million, could be made for an even remotely similar figure in Australia. Union rates and work practices render such a hope impossible. Yet, *Prospero's Books* is exactly the kind of low-budget fringe–mainstream film that ought to be attempted in Australia.

Then, there was the divisive issue of bringing in overseas actors to star in Australian films. To obtain a good (usually American) pre-sale, producers needed to have at least one marketable name. It doesn't matter how good an Australian actor is, how well regarded or loved he or she is in the home territory, it is how valued the name is in America which counts. And that means starring in a film that has made good money in the US for which the actor can be perceived to be at least partially responsible. The only Australian actors who qualified were Mel Gibson, Paul Hogan and Bryan Brown, followed by (on smaller-budget films) Judy Davis, Jack Thompson, Sam Neill and Colin Friels. Some attempts were made to bring other Australian actors to world recognition, but Kennedy Miller's successful teaming with Nicole Kidman is probably the only case were a production house helped create a 'star'.[45]

Most contingent on the industry's future, though, was the government's increasing alarm at the amount of money being 'lost' from Treasury through the 10BA tax benefits.[46] In response, it whittled down the 10BA provision, making it increasingly less attractive to investors. This resulted in a dramatic drop in feature production, from the 45 feature films in 1985–86 to only 21 in 1988–89. (The decline was equally significant with tele-features and mini-series.) Predictions of doom and gloom swept the industry and many saw a return to the cinematically barren years of the 1950s and 1960s (the early 1990s partially proving them right).

With things soured at home and abroad, the industry sought a quick solution. After examining various financing mechanisms, the government established in 1988 the Australian Film Finance Corporation, a quasi film bank. The basic funding scenario was that a producer had to raise at least 30 (now 40) per cent of the budget through private investment and then apply to the FFC for the remainder. The FFC's decision would be based on whether its investment could be recouped from the unsold territories.

The most obvious criticism was that the FFC represented a return to the one-door policies of the Australian Film Development Corporation and Australian Film Commission. Pity the poor film-maker who got on the wrong side of the controlling bureaucrats. The FFC countered that its decisions were deal driven and did not take into account aesthetic or personnel considerations. Well, while that may in principle avoid the potential for

96

favouritism, film-making never has been, and never should be, solely a bookkeeping exercise. What makes the best cinema great is clearly something else.

In a sense, the FFC has partly admitted this by establishing a series of Film Funds (there have been four so far), each totally financing up to five low-budget films. Known widely as the 'chook raffle', the results have been varied at best, though Mark Joffe's *Spotswood* (1992) and Gillian Armstrong's *The Last Days of Chez Nous* (1992) are both Film Fund successes.

However, as the recessions and depressions of the late 1980s and early 1990s show little sign of abatement, the FFC stands as one of the two major hopes for a continuing and, hopefully, valuable Australian film industry.

The other hope is the Australian Film Commission's foray into funding low-budget features, supported by Film Victoria, which has injected much new talent and enthusiasm into the industry.

The Films

Thrillers

A main staple of the 10BA era was the thriller. There had been a few made in the 1970s, but nothing could prepare for the ensuing flood. Many would never make it to the cinema, quickly heading to the video shelves, if that. Of those theatrically released, very few are of critical interest. Though some have incidental pleasures, it is difficult to think of many scenes of genuine tension or fright.

The decade began typically with John Lamond's *Nightmares* (1980), which assumes that a few tracking shots down dim corridors and the odd splash of blood are enough to satisfy audience expectations. Better crafted is Simon Wincer's *Harlequin* (1980), an updating of aspects of the Rasputin story which aims to be more mysterious than thrilling. While not convincingly worked through, the placement of a Harlequin character with magical powers within a drama of political intrigue did create enough moments of interest to suggest better things ahead for its director.

The next few years offered little better, the most applauded being Claude Whatham's *Hoodwink* (1981), notable mainly for John Hargreaves' performance as a prisoner pretending to be blind to help engineer an escape.

Roadgames (1981) is the third feature of director Richard Franklin, and was eagerly awaited after the critical success of *Patrick*. It is boldly conceived—a duel between a truck driver and an unseen pursuer across Australia's epically flat Nullarbor Desert—but it lacks any real frisson. Franklin knows and loves the thriller genre far better than most Australian directors, but he has perhaps yet to fully realise his talents.[47]

Then there is *Crosstalk* (1982), a film on which the original director, Keith Salvat, was sacked by the very producer he had hired. The first assistant director, Mark Egerton, took over amid understandable acrimony. The result is a rather unashamed remake of *Rear Window* (Alfred Hitchcock, 1956) which, while never really thrilling or scary, is more than fitfully engaging.

Another genre was the political thriller, the three most noted examples being *The Killing of Angel Street* (Don Crombie, 1981), *Heatwave* (Phillip Noyce, 1982) and *The Year of Living Dangerously* (Peter Weir, 1982). In each, the tension derives from a growing realisation of dark forces at work behind the facades of modern life.

Angel Street and *Heatwave* are both concerned with Sydney land developers prepared to do anything for a deal. Both are based in part on the actual disappearance of a journalist who was about to expose the collusion between developers and government.

Regrettably, each film is somewhat simplistic, reducing complex issues to a them-and-us mode, all right perhaps for a stylish *film noir* but inappropriate for films pretending to an objective analysis of an environmental and social issue. To Noyce's credit, he does work overtime trying to invest his story with unease, and endlessly moves his camera in and out of a stylised recreation of inner Sydney. Unfortunately, his characters remain caricatures and the stylishness suffers from artifice.

Weir's film is much more convincing and, though not particularly acclaimed at the time, stands as one of the better Australian films of the early 1980s.

Mel Gibson is Guy Hamilton, an Australian journalist caught in Indonesia during the end of Sukarno's regime, when a failed left-wing coup saw the right-wing party of Suharto sweep to power. Based on C. J. Koch's novel, the film convincingly recreates a particular time and place. Weir's use of the camera is particularly effective in evoking an eerie mood where violence can suddenly, inexplicably erupt, and Maurice Jarre's music keeps the film moving when David Williamson's somewhat expository script becomes a little bogged down.

The relationship between Guy and Jill (Sigourney Weaver) also works rather well, in that the actors make their characters look convincingly in love. But what is quite bizarre is Weir's casting of a woman (Linda Hunt) as the Chinese cameraman Billy Kwan. What was written as a struggle between two men for Jill's love becomes a weird triangle where Billy's protestations of heterosexual love have a decidedly lesbian ambience. This mitigates drastically the intended tension.[48]

That said, the other thriller aspects work well and the film has considerable narrative drive. While not always successful, it is an engaging cinematic experience.

Of a similar style, but only sporadically interesting, is John Duigan's *Far East* (1982), a modern reworking of *Casablanca* (Michael Curtiz, 1942), set in an undefined Asian country (that looks and feels like The Philippines). The film rarely generates any tension, and the love story between former lovers Jo (Helen Morse), now married, and Morgan (Bryan Brown) is flat. However, the film does evidence Duigan's continuing interest in locating his stories within a specific political atmosphere, in such a way that politics is not just talked about but is seen to directly affect people's lives (usually for the worse).

Thrillers of a more conventional kind include Russell Mulcahy's *Razorback* (1984), which sees him move uncertainly from his origins in rock videos to a visually overblown tale of a wild pig; *The Empty Beach* (1985), a

Kate Dean (Judy Davis) and Stephen West (Richard Moir) in Phillip Noyce's *Heatwave* (1982).

Guy Hamilton (Mel Gibson), a journalist in Indonesia during Suharto's rise to power. Peter Weir's *The Year of Living Dangerously* (1982).

Nikki Iceton (Gia Carides) escorts Kath (Lydia Miller) back to justice in Bill Bennett's *Backlash* (1986).

listless detective yarn from director Chris Thomson; Mark Joffe's *Grievous Bodily Harm* (1988), which goes for a *Miami Vice*-like stylishness but fails; and Ben Lewin's *Georgia* (1989), which has Judy Davis play two roles in a rather silly piece of hokum. There is also the work of the stolidly workmanlike Brian Trenchard Smith, with films such as *Dead-end Drive-in* (1986), with its self-explanatory title.

These singled-out films may read like a list of major disappointments, but, with a few exceptions, they are among the best thrillers made in Australia. What they do demonstrate is how unsuited Australians directors have so far shown themselves to be in inventively approaching the genre.

An interesting exception is Bill Bennett's *Backlash*

(1986), a disturbing journey across Australia as two white police (David Argue and Gia Carides) escort an Aboriginal woman (Lydia Miller) back for trial. The tension comes from the shifting relationships within the group and from their being tracked by a *gidaicha*[49] man (Brian Syron). Bennett also has his actors largely improvise their lines and, while that provides the odd awkwardness, the very experimentation adds to the film's claustrophobic tension.

Better yet, Bennett and director of photography Tony Wilson effectively use slightly wide-angle lenses to evoke a forbidding landscape that allows no refuge—for the whites in particular. While not always quite worked through, *Backlash* is one of the more original films of the late 1980s. Unfortunately, Bennett's next two features

Walter (Ralph Schicha) threatens wife Christine (Kerry Mack) and child (Gabrielle Barraket) in Frank Shields' *Hostage: The Christine Maresch Story* (1983).

do not evidence the same promise (the theatrically unreleased *Dear Cardholder* and *Jilted*), though his two television docu-dramas (*Malpractice* and *Mortgage*) show him back in striking, if somewhat hypertense, form.

Two other thrillers of interest are Frank Shields' *Hostage: The Christine Maresch Story* (1983) and *The Surfer* (1988). The first is the account of an Australian girl's mistreatment at the hands of her German husband who turns out to be a member of a neo-Nazi organisation. Based on a true story, it is efficiently directed, with good performances and an eye for visual detail. The latter is the key virtue of *The Surfer*, where in the first third Shields' visual style (much hand-held camerawork) keeps one attentive, even if the plot-line doesn't. Unfortunately, the film's drive dissipates once the characters hit the road. However, in both films Shields shows himself to be a director well aware of how films don't have to rely on words for meaning or structure, something too little appreciated in the dialogue-bound Australian cinema.

The last Australian thriller of the 1980s was Phillip Noyce's *Dead Calm* (1989), an adaptation of the Charles Williams novel Orson Welles filmed in 1966 as *The Deep*, but which remains unseen.

Noyce's film is always striking to look out (all deep focus and crisp light, finely composed), but rarely is it thrilling. Mostly, this is because Noyce cannot convincingly work up enough tense situations between the three characters (and dog) on a boat far out at sea. While the limited cast and locale obviously create difficulties, they are not insurmountable, as Roman Polanski proved with *Nóz w Wodzie* (*Knife in the Water*, 1962). Here, the main

error of judgement is to have Ingram (Sam Neill) away on a second boat for much of the picture, where the drama over whether he drowns or not in the flooded hull is less than involving. The film would have been much better suited by his presence on the main boat, thus unsettling the audience over whom might be the unseen presence behind a door or tiptoeing creakily down the steps.[50]

Many people do not share this writer's reservations, however, and found the film quite gripping. And, to Noyce's credit, he is a film-maker who *directs*, informing his images and performances with meaning. The stylishness is sometimes forced and a little showy, but he is one of the few Australian directors to conceive a visual style and then pursue it (here aided brilliantly by director of photography Dean Semler).

One of the best of all the thrillers, in terms of sheer tension and excitement, is Stephen Hopkins' *Dangerous Game* (1991). While this film might pass largely unnoticed in the US, where there are many films as competent as this, *Dangerous Game* is an Australian standout. The setting, a closed department store where five kids are trapped with a psychotic cop, is both claustrophobic and highly atmospheric. Production designer Igor Nay's department store set is grand and elaborate, and director of photography Peter Levy cleverly adds to the terror by playing with many a shade and shadow on the walls of this vast Gothic building.

Terrific fun to watch, the film was made as a calling card for Hollywood—and successfully so, for Hopkins and Levy have made two films there since.

Action–adventure

Coupled with the plethora of thrillers were the action-adventure dramas. The decade's first was Ian Barry's *The Chain Reaction* (1980), an unconvincing excursion into genre (with a tale of nuclear dirty business) greatly enlivened by some brilliant second-unit direction by George Miller.

The next year saw *Race for the Yankee Zephyr* (David Hemmings, 1981), which wastes a potentially interesting plot about recovering gold lost during the Pacific War with some rather listless direction and rather silly scripting. What it does attempt, and partially achieves, is the sort of amorphous big-budget look typical of films such as *The Eagle Has Landed* (John Sturges, 1976) and *The Cassandra Crossing* (George Pan Cosmatos, 1977).

In a similar vein is Colin Eggleston's *Sky Pirates* (1986). This parodic reworking of elements of the Indiana Jones films is fast paced, light-hearted and sometimes amusing. The direction is not particularly accomplished and too many actors bring too little to their oft underwritten parts, but the film has a quirky appeal and an energy too rarely seen in Australian cinema. Even more unusual, it revels in its knowing use of genre.

The film's biggest problem is the lack of a budget big enough to achieve all it sets out to do. To compensate, the film often sends itself up (cheap sets become part of its jokey tone) and the thinness of some action sequences

John (Sam Neill) and Rae Ingram (Nicole Kidman) in Phillip Noyce's *Dead Calm* (1989).

Murphy (Steven Grives), the deranged cop, in Stephen Hopkins' *Dangerous Game* (1991).

O'Reilly (Bill Hunter), Melanie (Meredith Phillips) and Harris (John Hargreaves) in Colin Eggleston's *Sky Pirates* (1986).

is partially disguised with comedic touches (a man thrown from a moving truck rolls into an electric fence, with sparkling results). The film is also notable for continuing the Australian cinematic and literary tradition of equating authority with corruption and evil, the stern commanding officer, Savage (Max Phipps), being revealed as a quasi Nazi with dreams of world domination. He is defeated, needless to say, by an Aussie adventurer of Lacedaemonian temperament.

More rewarding still is *Goodbye Paradise* (Carl Schultz, 1983), one of the most underrated films of the revival. This wittily scripted film (Bob Ellis, Denny Lawrence) takes a droll look at a right-wing coup in Queensland, Australia's northernmost state and its most reactionary. (Given the subsequent errant behaviour of one state

premier, such a scenario became less far-fetched than it first appeared.)

Ray Barrett, a great Australian actor, has the part of his life as the boozy journalist on the trail of dark deeds. Backed up with an often hilarious voice-over (itself a clever pastiche of the kind often spoken by Robert Mitchum's characters), Mike Stacey stumbles his way into the coup and ends up wandering disorientatedly through the battle zone where the forces of freedom finally prevail.

Most critics feel the film loses itself towards the rather hysterical end. This writer couldn't disagree more: what *Goodbye Paradise* does is that it takes an idea and boldly pushes it beyond the safe and into a poetic hyper-realism. It has the absolute courage of its convictions and bursts

Mike Stacey (Ray Barrett), right, meets Richard Quiney (Guy Doleman), an old friend, as a coup develops in Carl Schultz's *Goodbye Paradise* (1983).

free into a glorious explosion of ideas and light, managing to neatly wrap up a narrative in the approved genre way yet inject it with emotional power not artificially arrived at, but earnt. (Mike's musing about the destroyed crop of rhubarb somehow defining the positive side of the human spirit ranks as one of the finest and most powerful moments in all Australian cinema.) If only in this country of cinematic caution others had the same desire to take that extra step.

Boldness is certainly not lacking in *The Man from Snowy River* (George Miller, 1982) or its sequel, *The Man from Snowy River II* (Geoff Burrowes, 1988). Though propelled by the weakest and most contrived of plotlines, these films nevertheless delight in and celebrate the filmic experience, with their dazzling and obsessional recording of horses in motion. The climactic ride in the first is as visceral an experience as can be found outside the work of the other George Miller. (Igor Auzins' *The Coolangatta Gold*, 1984, attempts a similar result with its story of surfside athletes, but ends up as little more than colour and noise.)

Two other horse films of note are Simon Wincer's *Phar Lap* (1983) and *The Lighthorsemen* (1987). The first is a warmly sentimental story of Australia's (actually New Zealand's) greatest racehorse. A hero of the working class (it won its many races during the Depression against great odds), Phar Lap has often been touted as symbolising positive aspects of the Australian spirit. Wincer, showing a solid understanding of the Phar Lap legend, and his craft, makes a moving film that generally sidesteps the worst excesses of the 'battler' syndrome.

The Lighthorsemen is a re-creation of the heroic deeds of Australia's mounted lighthorse during the World War I in Turkey (also seen in Charles Chauvel's 1940 classic, *Forty Thousand Horsemen*). Largely reviled at the time, Wincer's film shows again his absolute mastery in shooting equine stories.

Where he is unsure is in dealing with the love story (it is stilted and arch), and the expository scenes are a bit perfunctory. But in visual storytelling he is quite striking. This is never better seen than in the scene where an Australian soldier drifts silently towards death,

Love in the High Country: Jessica (Sigrid Thornton) and Jim Craig (Tom Burlinson). George Miller's *The Man from Snowy River* (1982).

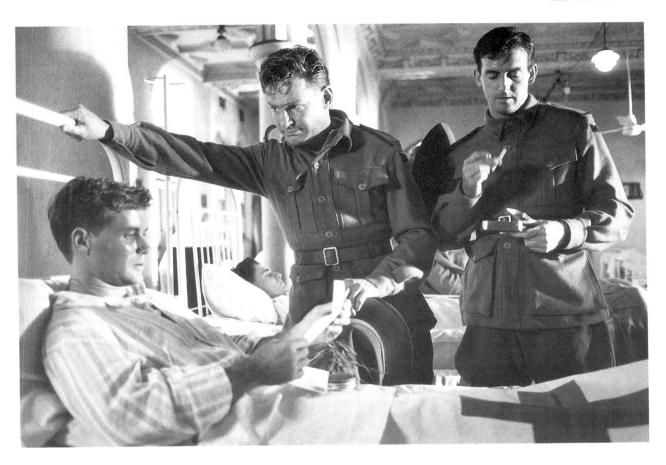

Frank (Gary Sweet) reads a letter from his ex-girlfriend brought by Tas (John Walton) and Chiller (Tim McKenzie). Simon Wincer's *The Lighthorsemen* (1987).

Matthew Quigley (Tom Selleck) and the gun for which he claims to have little need. Simon Wincer's *Quigley* (1991).

heartbroken at his girlfriend's abandonment of him for another. The slow camera movement forward cuts to a similarly paced crane shot of a tented lighthorsemen's camp at dusk.

After considerable success in the US, Wincer returned to Australia to make *Quigley*[51] (1991), a tall and intermittently amusing tale about an American gunman (Tom Selleck) who is brought to Australia to kill Aborigines, but who turns against his English master (Alan Rickman) to defend the preyed-upon. On release, the film was ridiculed by much of the Australian press, many critics being upset by the notion of an American saving the Aborigines.

What the critics also failed to notice was that David Eggby's photography of the outback was the most strikingly brilliant since Nicolas Roeg's in *Walkabout*, that Wincer's use of lenses, deep focus and cutting shows a craft level superior to that of most other Australian directors. While acknowledging the script is precariously thin (like many a good Western's), there still ought to

have been exhilaration at the freshness and majesty of the locations, at the stylish positioning of figures in a landscape, at the way Eggby etches his rich palette with every nuance of colour and texture in a towering rock face.

The critics were much kinder to the Australian–New Zealand co-production *The Navigator: A Medieval Odyssey* (Vincent Ward, 1988). Ward had shown himself a highly individualist director with his earlier *Vigil* (1984), but it is on a much more modest (and rougher) scale than *The Navigator*, with its bold tale of men tunnelling through the earth from a plague-ridden Cumbria of 1348 to an Auckland in the late twentieth century. Ward has an extremely striking visual style (albeit a little too derivative of Andrei Tarkovski's), but his scripts require leaps of faith some may not be prepared to take.

As for the best action–adventure film, that is indisputably *Mad Max 2*[52] (1981), the finest feature made by an Australian director on home territory. Whereas *Mad Max* works essentially as an action–adventure, its sequel

A battle in Vincent Ward's *The Navigator: A Medieval Odyssey* (1988).

is more concerned with aspects of mythology, established at the very start with a stirring montage (itself prefiguring the opening signature of the company's many and excellent television mini-series[53]). The purpose of the montage is to turn Max (Mel Gibson) from hero to icon, Miller delighting in the low-angled track forward, the mists of destruction swirling around this lone figure and a voice-over speaking of Max's coming out of the wasteland.

Max, the quintessential loner, is physically and emotionally tested in *Mad Max 2* when he is inexorably drawn into the lives of the owners of the world's last oil reserves. They are constantly under siege from the evil Humungus (Kjell Nilsson), and Max, despite his best survival instincts, is caught in the middle.

Using all he has learnt from the work of Joseph Campbell, most particularly *The Hero With a Thousand Faces*[54] (which argues that the most powerful stories are those common to most cultures: e.g., the 'superman' myth), Miller creates a tale in which each scene tingles

with frissons of other stories, other primeval legends. There is, for example, the familial tugs on Max made by the Feral Child (Emil Minty), who seeks a father. But Max must overcome such sentiment for his role in legend is that of mythic loner: emotional ties would only tarnish his powers.

Miller's images of civilisation in decay are extraordinarily potent and have, in fact, become the currency of the many films since which have tackled similar themes. Always, too, there is the joyous sense of a film-maker at home with, and in wondrous control of, his material.

The next sequel, *Mad Max Beyond Thunderdome* (George Miller and George Ogilvie, 1985), was for many a disappointment, but it is in fact Miller's favourite.[55] Whereas the preceding two were made well within the film-makers' gifts, Miller feels this extends beyond them —if it falls short, it has the honour of attempting the most.

Re-viewing the film years later helps clarify Miller's opinion, for it is the boldness of the design that dazzles

Feral Child (Emile Minty) and Max (Mel Gibson). George Miller's *Mad Max 2* (1981).

(mythic storytelling refined to an even more elemental level, but with a visual style that is hyper-realist compared to its more staid predecessors).

Sometimes, however, Miller and Ogilvie's handling of material is a little overworked. The below-ground sequences, for example, take a clever idea but dull it with the relentlessness of its visualisation (and also a matter-of-factness in some of the direction and acting, as when the dwarf is lowered into the pig excrement—it is not at all horrifying). Yet, given the odd lapse (and the children-of-the-crack sequence, while full of resonance, lacks narrative drive), there is still much in *Mad Max Beyond Thunderdome* which is on a far higher plane than that of other Australian film-makers. For example, there is the shot near the end where Max struggles to pick himself off the ground as the plane taking the children to freedom swoops overhead. Given how Miller has already iconised Max with low-angle tracks forward, this image of a man subjugating himself for the good of others, of a loner putting himself second to an ideal, is extremely powerful.

Finally, one should note David Peoples' *The Salute of*

the Jugger (1989), a curious 'evolution' of the Max cycle. An American-financed production made in Australia with some local cast and crew, it is one of the best-written and -directed films of the revival, with brilliant production design from John Stoddart and, yet again, excellent photography from David Eggby.

The time is the future, a post-apocalyptic wasteland straight out of *Mad Max Beyond Thunderdome*, with its poverty-stricken desert towns and horrendous underground cities where the rich and privileged live on one level, and the rest below. For the survivors of this wasteland, the only interest is The Game, an extremely violent derivative of rugby.

Clearly influenced by the sort of stories retold and analysed by Campbell, the film's heroic journey is of an outsider, Sallow (Rutger Hauer), who must return to the site of his defeat and win a victory that benefits others, not himself. While others bask in glory, Sallow is again cast into the wasteland, unforgiven, where he will continue to play The Game till totally blind and all life drained from him. That is his fate, to be the best yet known only through the stories that will continue to be told.

Max (Mel Gibson), Astro Pilot (Bruce Spence) and children prepare to flee in George Miller and George Ogilvie's *Mad Max Beyond Thunderdome* (1985).

Hated by those few critics who saw it, *The Salute of the Jugger* is a genuine undiscovered gem of the Australian cinema.[56]

Comedies

The most successful style of Australian cinema at the box office in the 1980s was comedy, with the two 'Crocodile' Dundee films, *Malcolm* (Nadia Tass, 1986) and Yahoo Serious' *Young Einstein* (1988).

Crocodile Dundee and *"Crocodile" Dundee II* are in some ways action–adventures, though it is for the comedy (and actor Paul Hogan) that they will be remembered. The first takes a seemingly innocent bush Aussie and deposits him in New York where his goodness and naivety overcome several evils of the modern world. Surprising for an Australian film, the romantic aspects also work quite well, particularly in the humorous and

tender last scene, which is a (probably unintentional) reworking in a New York subway of the boat-docking scene in Leo McCarey's *Love Affair* (1939).

The second film eschews what works in the first for an unconvincing and contrived plot about Colombian drug dealers. There is absolutely no surprise or interest in Dundee's outsmarting them. Worse, director John Cornell is unable to get more than one good laugh (the snake gag) from the way Dundee goes about it. Still, overseas audiences reacted by making it even more profitable than the first.

As already mentioned, both films make for an interesting comparison with *The Adventures of Barry McKenzie*. Most particularly, they show how approaches to the story of a naive Aussie abroad have changed over the years. *Barry McKenzie* deliberately and aggressively celebrates aspects of ockerism and makes no concessions to foreign audiences or those of tenderer sensibilities. On the other hand, the two 'Crocodile' Dundee films

Mick 'Crocodile' Dundee (Paul Hogan) and Sue Charlton (Linda Kozlowski). Peter Faiman's *Crocodile Dundee* (1986).

celebrate a calmer Australianness and are carefully aimed at world (particularly American) audiences. They selectively use language to suggest an exoticism about Australians, but do so in a context whereby foreigners can still understand everything that's going on (strange expressions are often explained through dialogue). At their worst, particularly the sequel, the 'Crocodile' Dundee films come across as tourist films selling Antipodean exotica to the uninformed.

As for the respective heroes, they could not be more different: Bazza is a vulgar, unintelligent, loud-mouthed boor, but Dundee is a cool, controlled, astute bushie able to be a hero in any setting. He is an advertisement of Australian bush male; Bazza is an embarrassment who today might be kept out of view.

In 1993 came another variation still on the innocent abroad: Yahoo Serious' *Reckless Kelly*. Here Serious plays a modern-day bank robber who goes to Hollywood to find the money to save his wilderness island from a sinister banker who wants to sell it off to the Japanese. In a brilliant comic invention, Serious has the island towed away from Australia for relocation in Tokyo Harbour.

Given the propensity of Japanese developers to buy Australian land for developments at which Australians are not always welcome, Serious' conceit has the crisp sting of a political cartoon by Nicholson or Tandberg. (Serious also has a painter's eye which gives his comic-book imagery a sharpness and detail many other directors of comic-book movies, such as Warren Beatty, have failed to evidence.)

Some have found the jokes a little thin and Serious' performance rather flat, but this is a film of relevant, largely undiscussed ideas about Australian society in the 1990s. If these very ideas are tossed aside too quickly, too superficially, at least Serious stands out from the pack by actually raising them. He may not be Australia's best comic director, but he is shaping up as one of the most forthright and topical.

Previous to *Reckless Kelly*, Serious had made *Young Einstein*, which is imbued with great energy and whimsy.

Serious places a lot of emphasis on slapstick, and he has a very adept way of moving his limber body. But the film tends to be very repetitive and, to this viewer at least, rather unfunny. And while the incessant rock

Top: Ned Kelly (Yahoo Serious) outside the Glenrowan Hotel & Video Rental. Yahoo Serious' *Reckless Kelly* (1993). Bottom: Albert Einstein (Yahoo Serious) creates the perfect surfboard in Yahoo Serious' *Young Einstein* (1988).

Malcolm (Colin Friels) in Nadia Tass' *Malcolm* (1986).

soundtrack and the gestures to 'relevant' issues are commercially astute, they are rather laboriously handled.

But whatever criticisms one may have of either film, there can be no dispute that Serious is a talent with the all-too-rare gift of making films people want to see.

Another with this gift is Nadia Tass, whose first film has the unlikely hero of Malcolm (Colin Friels), a misfit in society who finds a kind of self-worth as a criminal's offsider. *Malcolm* represents a decidedly personal taste in comedy (and regrettably not this writer's), but director Nadia Tass and writer-cameraman David Parker accurately judged audience reaction, making the film a surprise hit.

Tass and Parker were not so fortunate with their next, *Rikky and Pete* (1988), which found little favour with critics or audiences. It is a comedy without wit, reworking the quirkier aspects of *Malcolm* to uninspired effect (the zany inventions and splitable car replaced by an unwieldy and unamusing drilling horse).

Much more to public taste was *The Big Steal* (1990), a reworking of the young-love romances made in England

in the 1960s. Here, a schoolboy (Ben Mendelsohn) lies to his would-be girlfriend (Claudia Karvan), then goes to extraordinary lengths to cover his tracks. In the process, he is ripped off by a used-car salesman (Steve Bisley), upon whom he enacts a tricky (and unconvincing[57]) revenge.

To many newspaper reviewers, it is a charming comedy about eccentric characters, made with pace and flair. But such enthusiasm is difficult to share. The film is tepidly lit, carelessly directed (several actors looking to have received little instruction), and the much-praised charm is rather transparently applied. The characterisations are often offensive (particularly the parents'), derived as they are from the realms of the revenge fantasy. The used-car salesman, for example, after losing out to the boy and facing many indignities, is caught by the police while wearing ladies underwear. In their search for a gag, the film-makers show themselves prepared to adopt somewhat belittling strategies.[58]

The same can be said of aspects of John Ruane's *Death in Brunswick* (1991), a black comedy about a morally

Carl (Sam Neill) and Sophie (Zoë Carides). John Ruane's *Death in Brunswick* (1991).

Harry Reynolds (Bryan Brown), the likeable rogue in Michael Jenkins' *Sweet Talker* (1991).

adrift man, Carl Fitzgerald (Sam Neill), who goes from cook to near murderer of his mother.[59] Ruane bases his comedy on revenge aspects, as when Carl gets off on feeding people pizzas made of mouse droppings and worse. (This is a marked change from Ruane's gentle, sensitively-observed short features, *Queensland*, 1976, and *Feathers*, 1987.)

Then, too, there is Jocelyn Moorhouse's very black *Proof* (1991), discussed later, which gets its humour from the cruellest games of sexual and emotional manipulation, much of it vented against a blind man.

What *Proof*, *Death in Brunswick* and *The Big Steal* have in common is a wish to outrage (a moved ashtray, a stomped corpse, a sexual humiliation). There are moments of very cruel satire, several of which appear to have no other purpose than to hurt. It is quite different from the deliberate offensiveness of some the late 1960s and early 1970s film-making, where behind it lay an attempt to criticise aspects of a stifling bourgeois code. The 1990s versions, in contrast, appeal to a rather black cynicism.

However, this approach proved relatively successful in Australia, which must say something about the tastes of local audiences and of these film-makers' ability to read the market.

As for the other comedies, there is sadly little to stimulate the imagination, though some critics support Jacki[60] McKimmie's *Australian Dream* (1987), a send-up of the great Aussie barbecue, and Barry Peak's comedy sci-fi, *As Time Goes By* (1988). Also welcomed was the virtual demise of the ocker comedy, though both *Les Patterson Saves the World* (George Miller, 1987) and *Haydn Keenan's Pandemonium* (Haydn Keenan, 1988) energetically fought out the title for the film of most dubious taste. The latter has a scene in which a woman vitamises a recently-aborted foetus to use on her skin as a face pack. Perhaps Keenan is attempting a comment here about female obsession with physical beauty, but, if he is, it is not sufficiently focused.

As for *Les Patterson*, the grotesquely crude Les (Barry Humphries) attempts to thwart a plot whereby Arab terrorists are exporting lavatory seats impregnated with a fatal virus. In many ways the film arrived a decade too late: the venereal qualities of the virus have very unfunny connotations of AIDS, and the boorish, beer-swilling antics of Les hark back to a time when such behaviour was seen to be more amusing.

In complete contrast is the mildly charming *Sweet Talker* (Michael Jenkins, 1991), with Bryan Brown as a shyster who cons a town into thinking he has found the lost-for-centuries mahogany ship. The moral resurrection of this likeable rogue is all too predictable, as is the 'surprise' ending, but there is some light-hearted fun and the film's sunny tone never evaporates.

But the comedy for which the early 1990s will always be remembered is Baz Luhrmann's *Strictly Ballroom* (1992), his high-glitz, high-camp tribute to American dancing movies of the 1940s. Energetically directed and

115

Scott Hastings (Paul Mercurio) and Liz Holt (Gia Carides) in Baz Luhrmann's *Strictly Ballroom* (1992).

with a near fatal obsession for genre cliché, Luhrmann's film enticed from the suburbs thousands who go to see films most infrequently and, even more rarely, Australian ones.

Period films

The period film was a less dominant style in the 1980s. The decade began auspiciously enough with *'Breaker' Morant* (Bruce Beresford, 1980), which is a gripping courtroom drama about the trial of Australians tried for war crimes in the Boer War. With its obvious and deliberate parallels to the Vietnam conflict, *'Breaker' Morant* is a fine example of a period film's ability to address modern issues in a 'deflected' way.

While Beresford crisply handles the courtroom scenes,

it is a pity he felt the need to 'open' out the drama with overexplicit flashbacks (a fault to be found in many Australian films, including Stephen Wallace's *Blood Oath*, 1990). One also despairs at the anti-British sentiment in the film, so uncritically used.

What Beresford does achieve, and which helps make *'Breaker' Morant* one of the best films of the renaissance, is an extraordinarily high standard of performance. Edward Woodward, in particular, is magnificent as Morant, and his line about having already seen the world when offered a chance of escape is probably the most heart-renderingly delivered in all Australian cinema. It is also the overall brilliance of the performances that ensures the quietly-told ending, where two defendants (including Morant) are shot, is extremely moving.

Tim Burstall tried a war re-creation, too, in *Attack*

Lieutenant Peter Handcock (Bryan Brown). Bruce Beresford's *'Breaker' Morant* (1980).

Force Z (1982). This World War II drama is a workman-like film, and is notable mostly for its young cast, which includes Mel Gibson, Sam Neill, John Waters and Chris Haywood.

The effects of this war are also dealt with in Michael Jenkins' *Rebel* (1985), about American soldiers in Sydney on leave; Philippe Mora's *Death of a Soldier* (1986), where an American GI murders a Melbourne prostitute and is later executed; and Sophia Turkiewicz's *Silver City* (1984), about the emigration of Europe's homeless to Australia at war's end.

Arguably, the most praised of all the 1980s war films is Peter Weir's *Gallipoli* (1981). This account of innocent young Australians sent thousands of miles to fight in a foreign war raises several key aspects of the national character. One is the way its citizens view defeat as somehow more defining of character than victory. The second is how the innocence of Australians has been perverted by corrupt European (usually British) pragmatism.

What is disappointing about *Gallipoli*, for all its visual polish and fine performances, is that Weir rarely challenges or interprets the accepted wisdoms of the event.

The film is a homage to lost innocence that relies on sentimentality rather than rigour and which makes predictable mileage out of anti-British feelings still strong in Australia. This would matter less if *Gallipoli* were the first Australian film to take that position; but it isn't.

Outback period films were also popular with film-makers (though not at the box office). In 1982, Igor Auzins made the big-budget *We of the Never Never*, about a city woman's coming to terms with life on a remote cattle station. Hampered by an underwritten script, the film is memorable for its stunning use of light (captured by the late Gary Hansen) and an evocative score from Peter Best. It is also a classic example of how film-making pyrotechnics (all cranes through lone trees and helicopter shots across wild landscapes) can not only overpower a thin narrative line but work effectively against the feeling of isolation the film should have evoked.

We of the Never Never does, however, address the role of Aboriginal jackeroos, who had an invaluable but separate place on the outer edge of an Anglo-Saxon-Celtic society that few whites at the time had any desire to change.

Other period films to tackle the Aboriginal issue include *Manganinnie* (John Honey, 1980), about an Aboriginal woman and a white girl caught up in historical events which challenge their notions of homeland and family. There is also *The Fringe Dwellers* (Bruce Beresford, 1986), which concerns the stifling societal pressures on a black girl living among her people on the fringe of white civilisation.

Graeme Clifford's *Burke & Wills*, released a year earlier, is a recounting of the attempt to cross Australia from south to north by two explorers who perished on the return journey. Where Clifford's film is unusual is in turning the failed expedition into a success, by having the explorers actually reach the northern coast. Perhaps Clifford's stay in America (where he was an editor of note and where he directed *Frances*, 1982) gave him a different perspective to the typically Australian celebration of failure. Needless to say, his upbeat conceit was roundly criticised by Australian reviewers.

In many ways the film is a brave attempt, but it is also rather too attenuated and is surprisingly let down by Russell Boyd's over-filtered photography (it is as if this usually masterful director of photography is fighting unsuccessfully to tame the harsh light).

This story was also filmed the same year as the rather unfunny comedy, *Wills & Burke* (Bob Weis).

The most common type of period film in the 1980s concerned first love. The one to find greatest success at the box office was John Duigan's *The Year My Voice Broke* (1987), which was largely seen as a nostalgic account of a teenage boy's coming of age in a small country town. Shot in the amber dusk light and backed by the striking (but singularly inappropriate) music of Vaughan Williams[61], this sensitive film does render tenderly moments of experiences past. However, it is in the film's second half, when the style becomes more gothic, that the film really excels. Duigan abandons the elegiac to mount an attack on the restrictive pressures on Australian

Archy (Mark Lee) and Frank (Mel Gibson). Peter Weir's *Gallipoli* (1981).

William John Wills (Nigel Havers) and Robert O'Hara Burke (Jack Thompson). Graeme Clifford's *Burke & Wills* (1985).

Danny (Noah Taylor), right, and girls at a dance. John Duigan's *The Year My Voice Broke* (1987).

society which desire to quash all that is different, outside the norm. In this case, it is a free sexuality that was felt to have no place in the conservative country Australia of the late 1950s. Unable to understand a 'promiscuous' woman's sexual drive, the locals label her mentally unstable. And when tragedy engulfs her, there is no remorse among the townsfolk, only a wish to banish the episode from collective memory so as to enable a worry-free time at the pub.

Flirting, John Duigan's 1991 sequel, is unfortunately not up to the same standard, and is a fairly routine account of boarding-school life and several teenagers' growing awareness of their sexuality. The masters and many of the schoolchildren (particularly Nicole Kidman's rich bitch) are disappointingly caricatured, and the relationship between Danny (Noah Taylor) and a black girl (Thandie Newton) never goes anywhere interesting. The fact that her father is a Kenyan diplomat presumably locates her within a social–political framework (as is usual with Duigan's work), but it is only superficially relevant.

George Ogilvie's *The Place at the Coast* (1987) is about a girl's coming of age, but, despite worthy intentions, it

never really convinces and the script is too melodramatic in an uncritical way. Worse is *The Delinquents* (Chris Thomson, 1989), which tackles the teen film with seemingly little understanding of the genre. There is also this writer's *Devil in the Flesh* (1989), an Australianisation of Raymond Radiguet's famous novel, *Le Diable au Corps*, written in 1921 when Radiguet was only 18.

Outside the norm of Australian period films are several idiosyncratic films. One is *The Pirate Movie* (Ken Annakin, 1982), which symbolises for many the archetypical mid-Pacific disaster. Produced by Australian Ted Hamilton, who had had some television success in the US, it is a curious blend of Gilbert and Sullivan and soft modern pop. It is all rather silly, but rather less disastrous than most critics claim. For one, it has an energy many Australian films conspicuously lack, and the music is somewhat more adept than that found, say, in Gillian Armstrong's musical, *Star Struck* (1982).

Another unusual film for Australia is *Sumner Locke Elliott's Careful He Might Hear You* (Carl Schultz, 1983), a highly-regarded melodrama about a custody battle between two aunts (Robyn Nevin and Wendy Hughes) for a young boy, P.S. (Nicholas Gledhill). As in many of

Vanessa (Wendy Hughes) and her chauffeur (Steve Fyfield). Carl Schultz's *Sumner Locke Elliott's Careful He Might Hear You* (1983).

isms of Wendy Hughes. As well, there is the director of photography's attempts at recreating the lighting styles of the great Hollywood melodramas which fall noticeably short.

Much more in the realist mode, and far surer of where it is headed, is *The Tale of Ruby Rose* (Roger Scholes, 1988), the account of poor landfolk trying to survive in a bleak Tasmania of 1932. Spectacularly shot under extremely difficult conditions, the film marries the story of a woman's rebirth with a dramatic journey across an inhospitable but extremely beautiful landscape. Some critics complained of a sentimentality tincturing the later scenes, but most felt it part of a noticeable return to form for the Australian cinema in the late 1980s.

Sexuality and relationships

Australian film-makers have never been at ease examining human sexuality. Even at the height of the sex comedies in the 1970s, there was often evident a touch of embarrassment. So, in the face of increasing feminist criticism, many male directors took the soft option and avoided dealing with the subject. This failure of nerve was precisely pinpointed by François Truffaut in 1977:

> There is much pressure today to conform to a certain political line. And you have to resist it. You can't complain about Hollywood producers trying to make films with a happy ending, and then have socialists insist that people make films with a positive ending. Or a feminist ending.
>
> Servility is unforgivable, especially in the cinema, where it's glaringly obvious when someone injects into a film some fashionable ideas that he's just reproducing and not actually feeling.
>
> You can't make films to please other people. . .Being natural is the most important thing of all.[62]

If only Australian film-makers had shown some of Truffaut's fortitude. But the sad truth is that very few Australian films of the 1980s seriously tackle sexual relationships between men and women. In fact, if asked to name some, most critics struggle to come up with a scant few. This is particularly true of films which see sexuality and heterosexual relationships in a positive light. Some directors charted the miseries of affairs gone sour, but the reverse was barely addressed. As Meaghan Morris wrote in 1980 (and it is still largely true today):

> Australian cinema could scarcely be accused of promoting the virtues of life-long love and marriage. There is little or no glorification of full-blown love, for example, and none of the heightened respect for the eternal drama of the couple that defines the themes of so much European and American cinema. Instead, there is a fascination with group behaviour, and with relationships seen in the context of social institutions.[63]

Peter Weir's work is not atypical here. His first feature, *The Cars that Ate Paris*, has no heterosexual relationship of note and is set in a very male world. The only male-female relationships in *Picnic at Hanging Rock* are

the American films it so clearly wishes to resemble, the boy goes on a journey towards self-knowledge (wrapped up at the end with the all-too-neat device of P.S.'s learning and speaking his real name for the first time). While most critics praise its intelligent foray into American genre (comparing it to the work of Douglas Sirk and others), this author can find little evidence that the director and scriptwriter have a sure grasp of, or control over, the material.

But even if the script had better come to grips with Sumner Locke Elliott's novel (and, interestingly, no television or film adaptation of his writings has so far worked), there would still be the problem of acting styles which vary from the theatrics of Robyn Nevin to the awkward 'naturalism' of Peter Whitford, to the manner-

Henry (Chris Haywood) and Ruby Rose (Melita Jurisic). Roger Scholes' *The Tale of Ruby Rose* (1988).

platonic and the girls are presented as pretty but sexless, happiest, it seems, in each other's company. Their world is so devoid of sex, of physicality, that when the doctor mentions that one of the 'disappeared' girls is no longer wearing her petticoat one assumes this is because it made easier her climbing of the rock. Weir does not want or invite the audience to imagine anything sexual. In *The Last Wave* (1977), the husband and wife are separate from each other in spirit and desire, and drift increasingly apart. The same is true of Weir's married couples in *The Plumber* (tele-feature, 1979), which has the added threat of rape, and *The Mosquito Coast* (1986). *The Year of Living Dangerously* has the unsettling reverberations from the previously-mentioned casting of a woman for a man, and the once promising affair between Guy and Jill, although resolved 'happily', loses conviction. *Gallipoli* is all happy mateship and no women. In *Witness* (1985), there is the potential for a positive heterosexual relationship, but for no convincing reason the man backs away.[64] Then, most striking of all, there is *Dead Poets Society*, with its all-boys world. As with *Picnic*, Weir again iconises youth, Neal (Robert Sean Leonard) in particular; Weir's

photographing Neal with naked chest and 'laurel' wreath inevitably reminds one of how boys were objects of adoration in earlier Greek times. As for the film's one marriage, that is shown as such a monstrous perversion as to contribute significantly to Neal's suicide.

Finally, one has *Green Card* (1991), where Weir abandons the finalising conventions of the screwball genre in preference for a ending where Georges (Gérard Depardieu) and Brontë (Andie McDowell) are separated. Instead of the usual kiss and fade-out, Weir has the couple declare love for each other at the very moment Georges is being arrested and then deported. There is no indication he will be back or that Brontë is off to Paris (other than for an end-credits song about everything being all right, but whose perspective does that represent?). The important thing is Weir doesn't *show* everything being all right: while they may have found each other on some emotional/spiritual plane, Weir closes with an image of an unbedded couple's being physically pulled apart.

Brontë is also another of Weir's long list of unsexual lead women (can anyone imagine Brontë bedding her vegetarian boyfriend?). There are the virginal schoolgirls,

Rachel (Kelly McGillis) and John (Harrison Ford). Peter Weir's *Witness* (1985).

ethereal Diane de Portiers (Helen Morse) and frigid Miss McGraw (Vivean Gray) in *Picnic at Hanging Rock* (1975); the sexless Annie Burton (Olivia Hamnett) in *The Last Wave*; the neglected and neurotic Jill Cowper (Judy Morris) in *The Plumber*; and so on. Two exceptions are Jill Bryant (Sigourney Weaver) in *The Year of Living Dangerously* and Rachel Lapp (Kelly McGillis) in *Witness*, though Rachel's is a restrained Christian sexuality and she fails to excite her man enough to stay (as the film sees it).

What can be read from all this, whether intended or not, is that male-female relationships are dangerous or doomed, particularly on a sexual level. It may be all right to feel for others on an ethereal, platonic level, but (hetero)sexuality tends to interfere. This is a depressingly Australian view of human relationships.

As for Bruce Beresford, most of his films only marginally (if that) address male-female sexuality, but, when they do, he is often ill-at-ease. The one exception is the tenderly conceived *Tender Mercies* (1983), with its cautious optimism towards the relationship between Rosa (Tess Harper) and the emotionally tentative Mac (Robert Duvall). Of his more recent films, *King David* (1985) has a view of sexuality that is best described as silly. Then there is his section of *Aria* (various directors, 1987), where the nude scene is one of the more awkwardly handled in cinema (why the stilted, choreographed hiding of male genitalia?). As for *Her Alibi* (1988), it is a passionless and unsensuous love story, doubly surprising given Beresford's casting of a male sex symbol (Tom Selleck) and a world-famous glamour model (Paulina Porizkova). Then there is *Driving Miss Daisy* (1989), where the male-female relationship is completely platonic. As well, the reminder at the end that the chauffeur is not only married but has children makes one do a double take.

More recently, one has *Black Robe* (1992), an Australia-Canada co-production. Based on the novel by Brian Moore, it is a visually lavish account of a Jesuit

Annuka (Sandrine Holt) and Daniel (Aden Young) in Bruce Beresford's *Black Robe* (1992).

priest's journey into the wilds of seventeenth-century Quebec to convert the Algonquin Indians.

While sincerely made, it fails to make the spiritual trials of Laforgue (Lothaire Bluteau) meaningfully felt. Laforgue remains but a vague, shadowy character on the edge of what might have been an epic narrative.

In part, the fault lies with Moore, whose screen adaptation is a bowdlerisation of the original: where are the sights and sounds of defecation and sex, the visceral clash between faith and violence? The book explicitly describes sexual activity, and Laforgue's reactions, as when he spies Daniel and Chomina, carry a powerful sense of inner struggle. Moore writes:

> He watched as [Chomina] raised herself up and then. . .her head moved down to [Daniel's] loins. In all his celebate dreams [Laforgue] had never imagined such a thing. . .he began to jerk furiously until his semen spurted, spilling onto the ground.[65]

Compare that with the scene in Beresford's film, where Laforgue meekly watches the fully clothed couple wrestle on the ground. Laforgue's watchful gaze carries none of the above complexity and reduces the struggle with his own sexuality (the life blood of Moore's tale) to an irrelevance. Beresford's prudery may be consistent with his other work, but it quite disempowers *Black Robe*.

Beresford has since made *Rich in Love* (1992).

Take now George Miller's work. In *Mad Max*, the young wife (Joanne Samuel) takes a swim at a deserted beach miles from anyone, but (as others have commented) she still wears her bathers (no Lawrencean contact with nature here). Soon after, she and her offspring are murdered. Max then spends the rest of the film (and its two sequels) exhibiting no interest in women or sex. There is a momentary possibility in *Mad Max 2* that Warrior Woman (Virginia Hey) might be a worthy companion for Max (not that he shows any interest), but she is soon killed off. Max also backs away from adopting the lone Feral Child (Emil Minty). He wants to be alone, and what little contact or friendship he has is with males such as Gyro Captain (Bruce Spence). It is true that Miller is following genre traditions here, but the fact is he freely chose this genre in the first place.

There are also his first American films: an episode in *Twilight Zone: The Movie* (1983)—nothing romantic there—and *The Witches of Eastwick* (1987), which is hardly a paean to male-female love and sex.

But little more than one year after the above comments were published in the French edition of this book, along comes *Lorenzo's Oil* (1992), which, among many things, is a tribute to an all-conquering love between a man and a woman. While primarily a story of parental love and sacrifice, it is also the tale of the marriage of Augusto (Nick Nolte) and Michaela Odone (Susan Sarandon) tested beyond what any marriage should be. And yet, a pure love survives and grows. In one stroke, Miller has dashed a reading of his earlier work and triumphantly stands as *the* Australian director to record

heterosexual (and parental) love at its noblest.

At the opposite end of the spectrum, with by far the darkest views of male-female relationships, are the women directors. Gillian Armstrong's *My Brilliant Career* and *Hightide* (1987) both highlight women who prefer to live without men, seeing them as an inhibiting force. The latter film also has the woman sidestepping her maternal role and suppressing feelings for her abandoned daughter. *The Last Days of Chez Nous* (1992) shows the disintegration of one relationship and the birth of another. But Armstrong ends with its resolution up in the air, and with so little feeling evidenced between JP (Bruno Ganz) and Vicki (Kerry Fox) that in no way can the film be seen as celebratory of heterosexual togetherness.

Of her American films, *Mrs. Soffell* (1984) shows a bizarre relationship between a minister's wife and a criminal which ends with death, while *The Fires Within* (1991) goes for a happy (and somewhat unconvincing) resolution of lovers reunited.

As for Glenda Hambly's *Fran*, it shows a lone woman battling to survive with her children and having a perversely distrustful attitude towards men. Solrun Hoaas' *Aya* (1991) charts the breakdown of a marriage between an Australian soldier and a Japanese war bride. Then there is Jackie McKimmie's *Waiting* (1991), which is filled with whimpish men, sisterly togetherness and a sense that women probably can get on just fine without the inferior sex's interfering.

Much darker is Ann Turner's *Celia* (1989), which takes a bleak view of male-female relationships (and parental ones) in the highly conservative years of the 1950s. What is most unsettling is the clichéd way Turner equates frustrated male desire with a dobbing-in mentality and her simplistic setting up of women as a calming, humanist force in the face of male extremism (this in a country where countless polls since federation have shown women to be more conservative and reactionary than men).

That said, *Celia* has several qualities that make it one of the more thought-provoking films of the 1980s. Intriguingly scripted, if rather unsurely directed, it sets a human drama within an important political setting: the ostracisation, if not persecution, of communists in the late 1950s. Turner makes it a very dark time indeed, where no neighbour can be trusted and each innocent remark might be used for ill. And in this uncertain time, a girl of unusual spirit loses sense of the difference between reality and storytelling to quite drastic effect; de Sade's view of children as polymorphous perverts is most relevant here. Turner presents Celia's descent into 'evil', which is bizarrely and unconvincingly accepted by her mother, as not only the result of a child's inability to understand why the offspring of communists are no longer suitable as playmates, but also of her father's quite schizophrenic approach to child-rearing.

An equally dark view of male-female relationships can be seen in Jocelyn Moorhouse's much applauded debut, *Proof* (1991). Her characters are not only extremely unlikeable, they also play the cruellest games of manipulation and betrayal. Some have found the placing of

Augusto Odone (Nick Nolte), Lorenzo (Zack O'Malley Greenburg) and Michaela (Susan Sarandon). George Miller's *Lorenzo's Oil* (1992).

Beth (Lisa Harrow), Vicki (Kerry Fox) and Annie (Miranda Otto). Gillian Armstrong's *The Last Days of Chez Nous* (1992).

The dark childhood games of Ann Turner's *Celia* (1989).

Martin (Hugo Weaving) is put upon by Celia (Genevieve Picot) in Jocelyn Moorhouse's *Proof* (1991).

obstacles in the path of a blind man amusing, but this viewer was merely chilled.

One would like to read Moorhouse's depiction of the housekeeper, Celia (Genevieve Picot), as a sympathetic study in sexual obsession, but Picot so overplays Celia's downside that the housekeeper is too easily written off as a monster. As well, and most odd of all, Moorhouse posits no believable reason for Celia's fixation with Martin (Hugo Weaving). This has led critics to toss up all sorts of explanations, and some to argue the film's very openness is evidence of its worth.

When asked recently to explain what Celia sees in Martin, Moorhouse replied, 'That he's a man, that he's handsome.'[66] But this view is not supported by the film itself: Celia's photographs capture Martin's existence, his presence, but what indication is there that they also capture Celia's sense of physical beauty equals desire?

Moorhouse also says:

I don't see Genevieve as plain—I think she's gorgeous—so I dressed her down. She has this wonderful smouldering beauty that I wanted audiences to discover. Luckily, a lot of people do think she's really beautiful and they almost indignantly say, "How dare you! What's she doing as a housekeeper?", as if housekeepers can't be beautiful. It's a good effect because I wanted them to think Martin is stupid for treating her like a monster, because she's not. He's turned her into one by his cruelty.[67]

That reduces to: Martin is stupid because (unlike the audience) he doesn't realise that Celia/Picot is beautiful. Again, nothing in the film backs up this view, though Moorhouse keeps to it when she says of the scene where Martin sacks Celia, 'this [is] the first time that they actually [treat] each other like human beings. He even acknowledges that she has exceptional breasts.'[68]

The curious thing about this perspective, especially from a woman director, is that the film ends up feeling misogynist. Why should a woman be judged by her physical appearance?

Compare this to Paul Schrader's *The Comfort of Strangers* (1990), where Schrader explores the dangers of society's iconisation of physical beauty, analysing all too chillingly what it is in the human psyche that makes one obsessed by beauty. Moorhouse, however, is not interested in criticising the tyranny of the beauty myth, for she also says of the heroine in *Jane Eyre* that 'Jane is a plain but incredibly fascinating woman'.[69]

What can be said with certainty about *Proof* is that Moorhouse's characters love to play nasty power games in an uncaring world of distrust and betrayal, broken marriages and loveless sex. Whichever way one looks at it, or tries to explain it, the portrayal of human sexuality is bleak indeed.

As for the work of New Zealander Jane Campion, it has offered little hope either for personal relationships, be they as depicted by the disturbed and lifeless affair of Kay (Karen Colson) and Louis (Tom Lycos) in *Sweetie* (1989), the break-up of friendship in *2 Friends*

(tele-feature, 1986), the tortured story of loner Janet Frame in *An Angel at My Table* (mini-series, 1990) and the melodramatic passions and violence of *The Piano* (1993). Then there are Campion's various short films, which cover the deadeningness of family life (*Peel*, 1982), incest (*A Girl's Own Story*, 1983) and sexual harassment at work, which results in suicide (*After Hours*, 1984).

At *Sweetie*'s end, Campion does suggest the birth of a new kind of relationship, one based on lessons hard learnt, but disturbingly it only seems possible at the cost of someone's life. *The Piano*, too, ends on a note of hope, with Ada (Holly Hunter) and Baines (Harvey Keitel) together in a new land and with a new piano. But this still-uncertain sense of renewal comes, again, only at the expense of a life-endangering act, Ada's husband chopping off one of her fingers. As well, Ada's new lover is the very man who forced sexual power games upon her.

The Piano has other puzzlements. The biggest for those not caught up in the film's dramatics (and most clearly are) is that too little is explained and some is unconvincing, such as Flora (Anna Paquin) delivering Ada's love token to her step-father, rather than the intended Baines. It is arguable that Flora is exacting revenge on Ada from having her locked out of a love session in Baines' house, but Flora seems hardly peeved at the time and has shown no significant resentment since. As well, Flora has shown no empathy with Stewart (Sam Neill) and to go to him with something she, at the very least, suspects will cause trouble is unbelievable. Her act is little more than a plot device to catalyse the drama, indirectly catapulting Flora alongside Ann Turner's Celia as one of the cinema's more unpredictable and perverse young harbingers of doom.

Equally, Stewart's attacking Ada with an axe seems contradicted by all one has been shown of him before. Stewart is a relatively sensitive and weak 1850s male, albeit one hideously repressed sexually and with a very basic view of ownership (symbolised by those land stakes he so endlessly carries around in his little bag). His uncharacteristic act of violence is an example of how Campion sees that even in the heart of the most gentle of men there is a violent, cruel life force that will stop at nothing to exercise control.

Where Campion is more successful, as in all her films, is in creating and sustaining a beguiling visual universe. She has not always been well helped of late by her DOPs (in *The Piano*, the exposures and colour saturation vary greatly, and there is the distracting graininess and flat lighting), but her compositional eye is precise and her placing and choreography of characters loaded with meaning. Campion's growing assurance as a craftswoman has seen her rise to being an international director of real note, and acclaim, her future work anticipated in a way few Australians' ever has.

In her best work, Campion does approach Vladimir Nabokov's notion of great art appealing 'to that secret depth of the human soul where the shadows of other worlds pass like shadows of nameless and soundless ships'.[70] But sometimes, as in moments of *An Angel*

Ada (Holly Hunter) in Jane Campion's *The Piano* (1993).

Dawn (Genevieve Lemon) and Kay (Karen Colston). Jane Campion's black look at relationships, *Sweetie* (1989).

at My Table and *The Piano*, artifice intrudes (the predictable physical casting and stylistic obsessions; the scripting ellipses and ornamentalism, such as the metal finger). In reviewing *An Angel at My Table*, *New York*'s David Denby wrote:

> Jane Campion has made a plain and dry movie from the rapturously lyrical autobiography of New Zealand writer Janet Frame...Campion revels in the joke that this awkward, unprepossessing woman, diagnosed as a schizophrenic and subjected to electroshock therapy, could emerge as a major writer, but she emphasizes

the shyness so much that we never see the aggressive intelligence, the sensibility, the taste—whatever it was that made Frame a writer. Campion appears to love victimization more than art.[71]

Of course, Campion and these other singled-out directors are by no means alone in not more often offering positive examples of male-female relationships. In part, their work reflects Australian attitudes. Australian males are shown as happiest when among themselves, and especially in places (like pubs) where women are few or not allowed. The sex act is often performed by them when drunk, a car bonnet (*The FJ Holden*, etc.) or scrap

Janet (Alexia Keogh) in class. Jane Campion's *An Angel at My Table* (1990).

of scrubby land (*"Wake in Fright"*, et al.) just as good as a bed. The advantage for the male of being drunk is that he doesn't have to communicate with the female afterwards. For him, sex is a need that has to be got out of the way when nature calls; it is not a desired ideal, except perhaps of romantic schoolboys who know no better. This helps push Australian women to the sidelines of male society, unwanted for true companionship, their contribution to society, or for their intellectual and artistic gifts.

This dark view is taken to extremes in *Shame* (Steve Jodrell, 1988), where seemingly every man is portrayed as a rapist or a wimp. Sexual molestation is encouraged by fathers who think their sons are entitled to some fun, forgiven by mothers who blame the victims and call them 'sluts', and protected by townspeople who wish to preserve the beloved status quo.

All this is powerful and relevant, but after little more than half-an-hour the film abandons its serious purpose for genre clichés. It descends into absurdist behaviour (the rich woman's trying to buy a rape victim's silence with an offer of new clothes is ludicrous) and into uncontrolled melodrama, which relies on the creaky conventions of the thriller genre to keep the plot moving (such as leaving the victim in an unchecked police station on the night of rampage).[72]

There are moments of precise observation, as when most of the town's girls back away from the teenage boys after the rapes become more public. Quickly grabbing the chance, two younger girls move in, perhaps

133

Sergeant Wal Cuddy (Peter Aanensen) muscles Danny Fiske (David Franklin) on the night of violence in Steve Jodrell's *Shame* (1988).

excited by the aura of excitable 'masculinity'. But such moments are rare and the film succumbs to the crudest of visceral appeals. At the end, for example, the woman lawyer goes up to one of the arrested boys and slugs him. Dazed, he makes an ineffectual open-handed swipe at her, to which she responds with a sharp kick to the groin and a vicious and near-successful attempt at strangling him. For a long time, the citizens and the police stand by, doing nothing.

Some critics have argued this ending condones violence, as if the legal 'nicety' of a presumption of innocence is a hindrance to a true justice only brutality can achieve. It is hard to disagree, for the tone of the film at this point is clearly behind that black leather boot as it thuds into the male genitals.

In stark contrast is Howard Rubie's much under-valued *The Settlement* (1984). While it too depicts towns-folk in violent protest against forms of sexual behaviour, here the setting is the 1950s and the set-upons are three itinerant workers who choose to live in a *ménage à trois*: Kearney (Bill Kerr), Martin (John Jarratt) and Joycie (Lorna Lesley).

What is unusual is that Rubie and scriptwriter Ted Roberts have the trio refuse to split up in accord with community pressures. They walk off into the future together, a future glimpsed briefly at the close where they are making a living in the side-show business—successfully this time. Quite clearly, Rubie and Roberts are arguing that the threesome's very success (all have been

losers before) is because they are living their lives exactly as they wish, not as others may demand. This is a stirring and most welcome message.

The same can be said for Ray Lawrence's *Bliss*, which has one of the finest romantic resolutions in Australian cinema, not only for seeing a romance through to a happy ending, but for the imaginativeness of the reconciliation.

Harry Joy (Barry Otto), an advertising whiz, suffers a heart attack and is 'dead' for four minutes. While re-evaluating his life, he falls for Honey Barbara (Helen Jones), a hippy prostitute from a country valley. But Harry's appalling and avaricious family fights back. He is committed to an asylum and blackmailed into returning to his wife. Honey Barbara angrily leaves.

Finally free of asylum, family and cancer-ridden city, Harry starts life anew in the bush. But Honey Barbara, still angry, ignores him. Harry waits, writing a love letter that takes eight years to be sent: trees that first must grow before her bees can savour its delicious scent and sweeten her honey. Tasting her unexpectedly glorious honey, Honey Barbara walks through the forest to Harry and says, 'I'm not going to spend the rest of my life hating you.'[73]

Other films of the 1980s which attempt to tell a happy tale of male-female relationships include Bruce Beresford's *Puberty Blues* which ends with the film's teenage girls' 'finding themselves', but through an image of them breaking into the previously male domain of surfing (why is aping men deemed somehow worthy?), and Michael

THE 1970s AND 1980s

Robertson's *The Best of Friends* (1982), which deals awkwardly with the question of whether women and men can be just good friends, ending with a sudden marriage as the answer.

There is also the romantic confection of John D. Lamond's *Breakfast in Paris* (1982), the Snowy River and 'Crocodile' Dundee films, and *The Delinquents*. *The Man from Snowy River* ends with Jim Craig (Tom Burlinson) saying he is coming back for his horses and 'what else is mine', while looking at Jessica (Sigrid Thornton). He finally does in the sequel, but, after a combined build-up of nearly three hours, the film-makers cut from the lovers' riding to the hut of their wedding night to the next morning. Sex, it seems, has no place being discussed or dealt with in the high country.

But if that avoidance is merely coy, the 'Crocodile' Dundee films take it to a new level. At the end of the first, Dundee has won the girl ('won' is how the film sees it). However, the whole of the sequel avoids the very issue of their sexual relationship, and even tries to tell the audience they haven't slept together. Bizarre indeed in any cinema but Australia's. (It is revealing that in a recent history of eroticism in the cinema, only one Australian film, *Devil in the Flesh*, was included.[74])

One director with a serious interest in tackling human relationships is Paul Cox. His *Lonely Hearts* (1982) is a touching story of two loners whose romantic lives have almost passed them by. Warmly played by Norman Kaye and Wendy Hughes, the tentative, would-be lovers shuffle tentatively towards a happiness previously thought outside their range of experiences. Family pressures and outdated views of obligation make attempts at romance difficult and lead to the inevitable, frightened escape back into the safeness of solitude. The reconciliatory ending is not quite convincing, but the film is rich in nuance and imbued with a warmth emanating from the characters themselves, easily making it Cox's finest film. It was also the first time he and a scriptwriter (here John Clarke) found the right tone of voice in the dialogue.

Some writers have bracketed *Lonely Hearts* with Cox's next two films, *Man of Flowers* (1983) and *My First Wife* (1984), as an unofficial trilogy. While that stretches the usual concept a little far, *Man of Flowers* in particular does feed off ideas within its predecessor. In the former, Peter (Norman Kaye) is a fiftyish bachelor with an interest in amateur dramatics whose inadequate and infrequent sexual contacts with women include an unconsummated encounter at home with a prostitute. In *Man of Flowers*, there is Charles (Norman Kaye), a loner who lives in a shut-off world of music, his only connection with members of the opposite sex being to pay one to undress in front of him (after which, in an unintentionally funny scene, he sublimates his arousal by pounding a church's organ). But whereas *Lonely Hearts* has a clear perspective on its characters' fumbling attempts at love, *Man of Flowers* is lost among the bric-a-brac of set decoration and the deadening overlay of opera excerpts.

At one point, Charles elaborately murders the boyfriend of the 'stripper', but Cox provides no convincing rhyme or reason. (Charles doesn't like his paintings?)

Part of the narrative confusion probably stems from the fact that the film started out as a sex film (there are glimpses of naked girls in a swimming pool and in bed which perhaps owe some connection to earlier intentions). However, quite early on in production, Cox changed course and began reworking familiar material. The result of this strange birth is Cox's messiest and least interesting film (though others, such as David Stratton, think it his finest).

The disappointment was fortunately short-lived, for *My First Wife*, from a craft point of view, is Cox's most assured work. He and editor Tim Lewis create beautiful rhythms with the cutting, and the photography (one long pan excepted) is firmly at the service of his story of a heated custody dispute. John Hargreaves and Wendy Hughes are generally believable as the separating couple, though Hughes has the unenviable task of playing the unsympathetic character. She is shown as unfaithful right at the start, effectively and deliberating inviting the audience to turn against her. Her claims for their daughter fall on deaf ears, and her errant behaviour hardly wins friends.

Though one was not to know it at the time, this directing an audience to react to a character in a specific way, based on a brief and unchallenged moment of caricature, would become an increasing trademark, and flaw, of Cox's work to follow.

However, if one puts aside this bias (and that requires great effort), *My First Wife* is an at-times cogent argument for men's rights in marital disputes. Too often young children are seen as a mother's natural 'possession' (especially if a girl), and Cox's film pleads for a rethink.

Cox's next relationship films were *Cactus* (1986), about a blind girl's finding love, and *Island* (1989), where three women find friendship and forms of rebirth on a Greek island. Neither is a major work, each hampered by overly precious dialogue about the meaning of life and death. (In between, Cox made the documentary, *Vincent: The Life and Death of Vincent van Gogh*, 1987.) Cox has since made the disappointing *Golden Braid* and *A Woman's Tale* (both 1991), *The Nun and the Bandit* (1993) and *Exile*; as his stories become more miniaturist (fetishism and life's end), the film-making becomes more bland, even clumsy.

A Woman's Tale, in particular, also continues Cox's reliance on stereotypes. He takes cheap and nasty swipes at, among others, some gay Frenchmen (recalling the evil Frenchman in *Island*) and an uncaring family. When the daughter of a dead old soldier says at the funeral, 'We saw him every Christmas day', and Martha (Sheila Florance) self-importantly replies, 'That was the only day we didn't see him', Cox is revealing all too clearly his black-and-white, moralistic view of things. For someone who so often proclaims his own (and his work's) humanity, this cold-hearted caricaturing reveals a puzzling interregnum.

The other director who shares some ground with Cox, not only for his interest in human relationships but the effects of European cinematic and artistic culture on his work, is Ian Pringle. His first feature, *The Plains of Heaven* (1982), is a Wendersesque story of two men

135

AUSTRALIAN CINEMA

Top left: Peter (Norman Kaye) and Patricia (Wendy Hughes) in Paul Cox's *Lonely Hearts* (1982). Bottom left: David (Chris Haywood) and Lisa (Alyson Best) in Cox's *Man of Flowers* (1983). Top right: Bernard (Chris Haywood) and Terese (Gosia Dobrowolska) in Cox's *Golden Braid* (1991). Bottom right: Martha (Sheila Florance) and Anna (Gosia Dobrowolska) in Cox's *A Woman's Tale* (1991).

136

Mary (Jo Kennedy) and David (Richard Moir). Ian Pringle's *Wrong World* (1986).

working in a kind of self-imposed exile in the mountains, one trying to live in tune with the environment, the other overwhelmed by it.

Wrong World (1986), set in a bleak, night-shrouded Melbourne and the mysterious twilight world of Bolivia, is remarkable for its intense portrait of a world on the edge. Mary (Jo Kennedy) and David (Richard Moir), like most of Pringle's characters, feel alienated within the cold, materialist world, where relationships are often transient moments of shared directionlessness. His characters are literally and emotionally homeless.

Pringle is a romanticist working with a nihilistic palette and there is usually a movement forward to emotional expansion. In *Wrong World*, as Rod Bishop has pointed out, David and Mary's

> relationship, made necessary by a mutual desire to escape the institution, is instinctively testy and suspicious; they behave like threatened, feral animals, despite their individually-felt desires for warmth and affection. . . Their intimacy grows, but the affection is checked by one unstated condition: their eventual, unavoidable separation.[75]

Marred only by an intrusive voice-over, *Wrong World* is one of the genuinely underrated Australian films of the 1980s.

After *The Prisoner of St Petersburg* (1990), which Pringle completed in Berlin in 1988, Pringle made, in France and North Africa, *Isabelle Eberhardt* (1992), about the pioneering explorer.

Also influenced by European aesthetics is *The Coca-Cola Kid* (1985), a film which, contrary to the Australian norm, delights in human sexuality, both in its existence and its cinematic representation. It also sees itself convincingly through to an upbeat ending of man, woman and child forming a family (rather like in *Tender Mercies*). But it was made by a Yugoslavian director, Dušan Makavejev.

Devil in the Flesh is another film to depict sexuality and male-female relationships. Unlike many films about first love, however, the film attempts an unromanticised and detached examination of an immature boy's new-found sexuality. Delighting in his sexuality, but emotionally unable to cope, the boy leads himself and others towards tragedy. But unlike the book's bleak Victorian end[76], the film opts for a bitter-sweet finale, whereby the

137

Marthe (Katia Caballero) and Paul (Keith Smith) in Scott Murray's *Devil in the Flesh* (1989).

woman is contentedly back with a loving and understanding husband and the boy has progressed towards an
emotional maturity.

Rolando Caputo writes in *Cinema Papers*:

> This is a film of visual exactitude, the world in micro-
> cosm—nothing exceeds the immediate environment of
> the lovers. . .narrative form stripped to its essence. At
> all times, the camera keeps its proper distance from
> the action, respecting the intimacy of the lovers'
> thoughts. The film avoids, at all costs, attempts at
> psychological intrusion: at no time is a banal explana-
> tion of the characters' behaviour laid out for the audi-
> ence. In turn, much is left to the audience members'
> interpretation and their respective moral viewpoints.
> Such refinement of style results in a work which I would

call classicism in a minor key (though it is imbued at
times with the modernism of mid-period Chabrol).[77]

Social realist films

As other writers have detailed elsewhere in this book,
Australia has one of the finest documentary traditions in
the world. Given the cross-pollenisations of a small film
industry, it was inevitable that the documentary tradition
would influence styles of feature film-making. As well,
the best material on television was usually in the social-
realist mode. Together they informed a strain of realist
film-making that is still at work today: *Fran*, *The Fringe
Dwellers* and *Candy Regentag* (aka *Kiss the Night*, James
Ricketson, 1989). Elements of it are even seen in the

Michael (Sam Neill) and Lindy Chamberlain (Meryl Streep) watch Michael on the news in Fred Schepisi's *Evil Angels* (1988).

historical films with an obsession for period accuracy, screenplays that simplistically go through the storytelling motions without flourish or inventive twists, and an acting style that is bogged down in a realist mode. Orson Welles' maxim about film needing to be true, rather than real, has not taken root in Australia.

An exception is Fred Schepisi's *Evil Angels* (aka *A Cry in the Dark*, 1988), the study of a major Australian criminal case: the disappearance of the baby of Lindy and Michael Chamberlain at the base of Ayer's Rock. Based on a brilliant, best-selling book by John Bryson, *Evil Angels* is an attack on the hasty judgement of ordinary Australians and journalists. In a dense cloud of prejudice ('She looks guilty'), a miscarriage of justice occurred. It took eight years to correct it, Bryson's book being a significant contributor.

The underside of *Evil Angels* is very dark indeed, Schepisi scathingly attacking the Australian public's rush to judgement. Because the Chamberlains did not conform to the Australian 'norm' (they were Seventh Day Adventists), they refused to play the media game of looking distressed in public and they took photos of where their

child had disappeared), they were remorselessly criticised. As Schepisi says,

I was astounded by the passion and vehemence with which people held their opinions. Even very intelligent people would have a rational argument, examine the facts, and despite everything would end up saying, 'She did it.'[78]

Evil Angels is the more telling for the realist technique Schepisi employs (a cross between home movies and cinéma-vérité) which takes little heed of the narrative patternings of mainstream American cinema. Instead of keeping the audience in doubt over the characters' guilt, he opted to make a film which stresses the difference between the public perception and the private reality.

Other social realist films of note are Gil Brealey's *Annie's Coming Out*, a powerful retelling of a woman's attempts to free someone wrongly thought to be intellectually disabled from an insensitive religious bureaucracy; the aforementioned *Fran*; and Bill Bennett's first feature, *A Street to Die* (1985), about a soldier's unsuccessful attempts at adjusting to life after Vietnam.

Steve (Frankie J. Holden) and Gary (Ben Mendelsohn). Ray Argall's *Return Home* (1990).

Then, too, there is the work of Richard Lowenstein, with his fine recreation of working-class life and struggle, *Strikebound* (1984), and his highly-underated *Dogs in Space* (1987), with its surrealist tinge.

One film to incorporate aspects of the social-realist style within a sensitively detailed story of familial relationships is Ray Argall's *Return Home* (1990). It is the story of one man's coming to terms with his past, and the responsibility and rewards of family love.

Noel (Dennis Coard), in his late thirties, is a successful insurance broker in Melbourne who returns home one summer to the Adelaide suburb of his childhood. There, he stays with his elder brother, Steve (Frankie J. Holden), and his family. Steve is a motor mechanic with a real love for his job, but both he and his ideals are on borrowed time in an era of franchised consumerism.

Argall sets up this tale (of the negative forces of progress held tentatively at bay by one man's inherent goodness) as a metaphor for Australian society today. It is simply but effectively directed (Argall cuts and tracks only when he really needs to), with a subtle and affecting screenplay, and an understated level of performance rare in Australian film.[79]

Others who have boldly examined the working-class society of today are such 1990s film-makers as Leo Berkeley, Aleksi Vellis and Geoffrey Wright. *Holidays on the River Yarra* (Berkeley, 1991) and *Nirvana Street Murder* (Vellis, 1991) have their origins in social realist cinema, though both could be equally categorised as post-modern comedies. They have a catch-it-on-the-run quality and the acting, while stylised to a degree, aims to be ordinary and real (as opposed to bourgeois theatrical).

The world of *Romper Stomper* (Wright, 1992) is far darker, even 'scrungier'. A frenetic, surprise box-office hit about a gang of neo-Nazis, the film caused heated debate about the film's politics and the difficulty in determining the director's attitude to his characters' racism. Most illuminating is the closing scene where a busload of Asians watches two 'dick-headed' Aussies fight to the death on the beach below. While there is a quite relevant irony at work here, Wright has shot the bus (from a very low-angle) so that its arrival is totally ominous (it has the forceful, invasive presence of a military tank). Here, Wright's perspective is all too clear.

What renders this highly visceral (and noisy) work less than satisfying is the crudeness of much of the *mise en*

Top: Eddie (Craig Adams) and Mick (Luke Elliot). Leo Berkeley's *Holidays on the River Yarra* (1991).
Bottom: Boady (Mark Little). Aleksi Vellis' *Nirvana Street Murder* (1991).

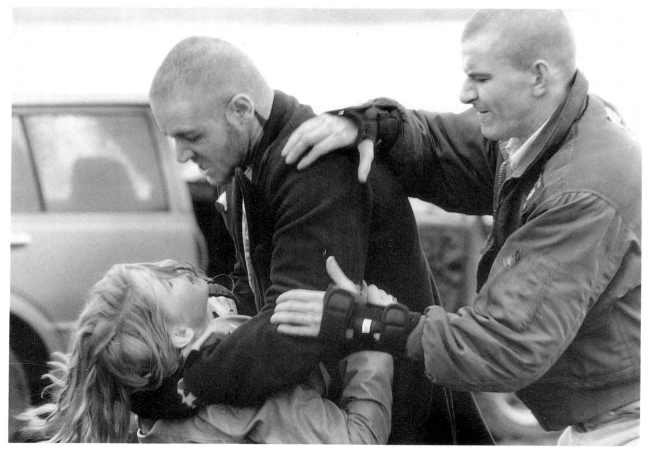

Gabe (Jacqueline McKenzie), Hando (Russell Crowe) and Davey (Daniel Pollock). Geoffrey Wright's *Romper Stomper* (1992).

scène (the opening fight in the tunnel is a staccato array of mismatched shots), over-obvious lighting and a reliance on the worst excesses of *Miami Vice* (the sub-plot with the father is not the least disturbing but obvious from his first appearance and quite silly in its resolution). Like many films on the alternative fringe, the film also takes a very 'I want to be part of the proletariat' stance (not in Wright's case, but in many others this is a pretension of firmly middle-class directors).

Finally, there is Dennis O'Rourke's *The Good Woman of Bangkok* (1992), a part-documentary, part-*cinéma vérité* look at Aoi (Yagwalak Chonchanakun), a Bangkok prostitute. After a broken marriage, O'Rourke visited Thailand and became interested not only in the relationship between Western client and Thai prostitute, but between himself as a man and a film-maker. So began the genesis of this extremely powerful film, one of the most brutally revealing and personal works of the Australian cinema.

Whatever O'Rourke may state in interviews about his relationship with Aoi[80], the film itself takes a parallel and interrelated course. Apart from a brief glimpse in a rear-view mirror, O'Rourke is not physically sighted, but his voice-over questions and his moral presence codify every frame.

O'Rourke is not always as honest or as up-front as he ought to be (he, for example, never shows Aoi with another client, a strange act of prurience on his part), but everything he does and doesn't do is revealing of himself. In some ways, then, the film is ultimately more about O'Rourke than Aoi, but the memories one carries away, and which never cease to haunt, are of a girl lost in a world not of her making:

I don't know what's love. What I love, I don't know. I want love but I know me. Me is no good. No people can love me. I don't have anything good. . .only bad. Who can love me? No. Say love me, I don't believe. Because I know me. I know me. . .I cannot give.[81]

Aoi (Yagwalak Chonchanakun) in Dennis O'Rourke's *The Good Woman of Bangkok* (1992).

A summary

So, it comes time to re-pose that original question: Is Australia's cinema really good enough, or has the enthusiasm at seeing an industry reborn coloured critical judgement?

Well, the best is certainly of world standard, and some of the directors (particularly George Miller) are among the world's finest.[82] And while Australia has only 0.3 per cent of the world's population, by any fair account it contributes far more than its share of internationally significant film-making. If its film-makers have not *consistently* reached the high levels of the best European cinema, one should bear in mind that Australia's is a relatively young film culture, with very little cinematic heritage and expertise to draw on. For a country that in the 1950s and 1960s had virtually no feature-film industry, the turnaround is both dramatic and worthy of celebration.

However, that is not enough, because the vast majority of Australian cinema is mediocre. Far too many directors approach their work with little passion or innovation, without any sense of a personal vision or cinematic style. Rarely do they take hold of the material and breathe life into it; rather, they cautiously and routinely transfer the written page to the screen, often oblivious to the merits or otherwise of the original script. In short, they are neutral transferers.

Bruce Beresford is an obvious example: give him a good screenplay (for '*Breaker' Morant*, *Driving Miss Daisy*) and he makes a fine film, preserving all that was good and even improving on it; give him one that's flawed (for *Side by Side*, 1973, or *King David*) and he seems unable to reshape it into something better. Many foreign directors could have made something of the *Her Alibi* script, but arguably very few Australian. They are too timid and too unversed in genre patterning to know where to turn. To them, the overriding challenge is merely to get everything centred in frame and vaguely in focus, a tendency picked up in the pressured environment of television, where many work. Others make a living from commercials, which may help explain why their features often have well-crafted moments but fail as complete narratives.

Most of the films these directors make are pitched uneasily in the no-man's-land between art-house cinema

143

and the commercial mainstream. They live up to the potential of neither and satisfy few. Yes, these films have their incidental pleasures (pretty images, calm narratives, sensitive moments), and they did help initiate critical interest at the start of the revival. But in the past decade that spotlight has increasingly narrowed onto the work of the genuine *auteurs*, such as Miller and Campion. The time has come for the Australian cinema to deliver much, much more . . .

And, yet, as soon as these words are written along come new films, new directors, new hopes. There is much to be proud of, much to look forward to. In some respects, Australia may have the film industry it deserves; in others, it is far more special—and precious.

Notes

1 The author also admits to a slight apprehension at writing, sometimes critically, about the work of fellow film-makers. Whereas many film cultures have a long tradition of film-maker-critics, and would encourage an undertaking such as this, Australia is not one of them. As well, the Centre Georges Pompidou's brief for this chapter was that it be concerned primarily with thematic issues. As such, and given space restrictions, this account is much less concerned with the images, cutting and sounds of cinema than the author would like.

2 This view is gentler than the one expressed in *Celia* (Ann Turner, 1989), which portrays Australia as an actively intolerant and rather frightening place in the 1950s. (See discussion later in main text.)

3 Quite unfairly, too. Richardson was unfortunate in being here at a time when there was still a blinkered adherence to the notion that historical films should accurately follow the 'facts'.

4 The very moment Roeg arrived here by plane, he was asked the then predictable question of what he thought about Australia. 'Two stops overexposed' was his reply.

5 *Shame* (Steve Jodrell, 1988) attempts a similarly bold view of Australian mateship, among other things, but loses dramatic power in its increasingly uncritical use of melodrama.

6 'Genre' and 'style' are used rather interchangeably in Australian criticism, in part because there are so few Australian films which knowingly fit the exigencies of 'genre'.

7 There exists a booming business in mail-order X-rated material, which must be first approved by the Commonwealth Film Censor. Films and videos are still banned.

8 In some comedic ways, Alvin is a variation of, and expansion on, the character Blundell played in *The Naked Bunyip*.

9 The name is sometimes unhyphenated.

10 Brian McFarlane, *Australian Cinema 1970–1985*, William Heinemann Australia, Melbourne, 1987, p. 123. McFarlane's 'all' refers specifically to *Felicity*, *The ABC of Love and Sex Australia Style* (John D. Lamond, 1978), *Fantasm, Fantasm Comes Again* (Eric Ram [Colin Eggleston], 1977) and *Australia After Dark*.

11 Meaghan Morris, 'Personal Relationships and Sexuality', in *The New Australian Cinema*, Scott Murray (ed.), Thomas Nelson Australia and Cinema Papers, Melbourne, 1980, p. 138.

12 Sam Rhodie, '*Gallipoli* as World Camera Fodder', *Arena*, No. 60, 1982, p. 39.

13 It is *"Crocodile" Dundee* outside Australia. The sequel, *"Crocodile" Dundee II* (John Cornell, 1988), reverses the journey of Mick 'Crocodile' Dundee (Paul Hogan), sending him back from New York to the Australian outback.

14 Australians invariably refuse to call each other by their correct names. If the name can't be easily lengthened or shortened ('Bazza' for 'Barry', 'Brucie' for 'Bruce', etc.), a descriptive nickname is used ('Shorty', 'Lofty', etc.). While many find such a practice amusing, it is yet another way in which Australians marginalise individuality and drag people down to the same level.

15 Tom O'Regan, 'Cinema Oz: The Ocker Films', *The Australian Screen*, Albert Moran and Tom O'Regan (eds), Penguin, Melbourne, 1989, p. 76.

16 Morris, op. cit., p. 146.

17 Graeme Turner, 'Art Directing History: The Period Film', *The Australian Screen*, op. cit., p. 100.

18 Gill Armstrong would credit herself as Gillian Armstrong on her subsequent features.

19 McFarlane, op. cit., p. 19.

20 The aforementioned Tom Roberts painting is restaged in one of the shearing shed sequences.

21 Where *Picnic at Hanging Rock* iconises then undermines the world of schoolgirls, in *Dead Poets Society* (1989) Weir takes a similar approach with the world of male youth.

22 Yvonne Rousseau, *The Murders of Hanging Rock*, Scribe Publishers, Melbourne, 1980.

23 Scott Murray, '*Picnic at Hanging Rock*', *Cinema Papers*, No. 7, Nov.–Dec. 1975, pp. 264–5.

24 Debate ignited again in 1988 when the 'missing' last chapter of Joan Lindsay's original novel was published (in *The Secret of Hanging Rock*, introduced by John Taylor and with a commentary by Yvonne Rousseau, Angus & Robertson Publishers, Sydney, 1987). Its explanation of events (time dimensions) is perhaps one of the least appealing, but it did lead some writers to claim that this explanation must be seen as the correct one. Such a view is blind to the fact that any possibility that can convincingly be read from a film or book has a justified place in debate. It is quite probable that some of the most intriguing cinematic explanations were not in the mind of Weir or screenwriter Cliff Green. There is also little doubt that the open-endedness of the film was a major factor in the film's phenomenal and lasting success.

25 Tom Ryan, 'Historical Films', in *The New Australian Cinema*, op. cit., pp. 115–19.

26 The same was largely true of representations of the modern-day treatment of Aborigines, though things are changing with such films as *Blackfellas* (James Ricketson, 1993) and *Deadly* (Esben Storm, 1992), both made by whites. As well, Tracey Moffatt has just completed the first feature to be directed by an Aborigine, *Bedevil*.

27 Quoted in *William Styron's Nat Turner: Ten Black Writers Respond*, John Henrik Clarke (ed.), Beacon Press, Boston, 1968, p. vii.

28 Too few Australian directors are at the forefront in terms of knowledge about their craft. It can be difficult steering Australian directors away from dull talk about where they got the idea and cast from, and how much the film cost, to a discussion about the use of lenses, editing and sound. In fact, at a recent conference on sound in film, one of Australia's leading sound editors commented resignedly that only on two films (out of the many he had worked on) had the director taken an interest or shown any expertise.

29 Quote taken from an interview with Keneally conducted for *Australian Movies to the World* (Gordon Glenn and Scott Murray, 1983), a two-hour television documentary on aspects of the Australian cinema, and published in David White, *Australian Movies to the World: The International*

Success of Australian Films Since 1970, Fontana Australia, Sydney, and Cinema Papers, Melbourne, 1984, p. 57.

30 The closing shots of Tom in the car do carry some sense of this, but the very explicitness of the referred to moment gave the film, to this viewer at least, a more focused and powerful ending.

31 McFarlane, 'My Brilliant Career', Cinema Papers, No. 23, Sept.–Oct. 1979, p. 565.

32 Quote take from an interview with Kael conducted for Australian Movies to the World and reprinted in White, op. cit., pp. 65–6.

33 In part, this staleness was the result of the Australian Film Commission's having continued to back directors whose work had seriously dropped off in quality by decade's end. An industry is made vibrant by the strength of its emergent talent, but, after the first new wave (typified by Phillip Noyce and Gill Armstrong), things went relatively quiet and the established directors continued to hold sway.

34 Included in Labyrinths, Selected Stories and Other Writings, Donald A. Yates and James E. Iroy (eds), New Directions, New York, 1964.

35 Cf Susan Dermody and Elizabeth Jacka, The Screening of Australia Volume 2: Anatomy of a National Cinema, Currency Press, Sydney, 1988, and The Imaginary Industry: Australian Film in the Late '80s, Susan Dermody and Elizabeth Jacka (eds), AFTRS Publications, Sydney, 1988.

36 The film was to be called 'Pure Shit', but the Commonwealth Censor objected to the title and the film was released with the revised title.

37 Cox sees it differently. In an article by French critic Max Tessier, Cox claims 'the Australian Film Commission has always given me a hard time and has always tried not to send my films abroad.' Cox adds that he is so fed up with the philistinism of Australia that he wants to leave. The point is, Cox has received support from government of a level and over a period unimaginable in most countries. His recent Golden Braid (1991), for example, was totally cash-funded by the AFC and Film Victoria, and was actively promoted around the world by the AFC. His next film, A Woman's Tale (1991), was mostly FFC-financed and again AFC-supported at festivals and markets. This has been followed by The Nun and the Bandit and Exile, both majority funded by the FFC.

38 This and the subsequent quote are from 'Making Silence Speak: Interview with Paul Cox', interview by Tom Ryan, Cinema Papers, No. 13, July 1977, p. 19.

39 Rod Bishop and Fiona Mackie, 'Loneliness and Alienation', in The New Australian Cinema, op. cit., pp. 157–8.

40 This was apparently never tested and one can never be too sure of how government bodies will react.

41 Whereas the television news in many countries enthusiastically covers cultural events and achievements, Australia's almost always does not, preferring to concentrate on images of car crashes and murder victims. Even a bus wreck in the Andes is considered more newsworthy than Australians reaping rewards (and awards) for their work around the world. (The Nine Network in Melbourne placed news of Jane Campion's co-winning the Palme d'Or for The Piano last before the sports reports on its prime-time news.) That a television news, such as France's, reports on film, even down to informing the public about upcoming theatrical releases, is inconceivable in Australia.

42 Source: Get the Picture, Peta Spear (ed.), Australian Film Commission, Sydney, 1989.

43 'Hal and Jim McElroy', interview by Scott Murray, Cinema Papers, No. 79, May 1990, p. 14.

44 'Michel Ciment', interview by Rolando Caputo, Cinema Papers, No. 78, March 1990, p. 65.

45 Kidman starred in the Kennedy Miller miniseries Vietnam (John Duigan, Chris Noonan, 1987) to great effect. Since then a miniseries was written for her (Bangkok Hilton, Ken Cameron, 1989), plus roles in features such as Dead Calm (Phillip Noyce, 1989) and Flirting (John Duigan, 1991). So unusual was her nurturing that women's magazines ran stories about writer–producer Terry Hayes' 'platonic' interest in her talents.

46 Little is actually 'lost', however, as the AFC has consistently argued, for a great deal of a film's budget is paid to individuals and companies that have to pay taxes in Australia on those earnings.

47 This is in no way meant to denigrate Franklin's work. Rather, he seems one of those directors whose skill improves the more he works. This is far less common than it seems; many, if not most, directors do their best work in their first three films. A perfect example of the Franklin type is Alfred Hitchcock, who took some twenty features till he got it fully right.

48 Lest their be any criticism of having been wise after the event, let it be said this author saw and wrote about the film before its commercial release and before some of the press had picked up on the odd casting. The opening credits, too, deliberately blurred the issue of Hunt's sex by turning 'Linda' into an 'L'. What the film could not disguise were her very female gestures and walk, let alone her voice.

49 A gidaicha man is 'a human agent of death' in Aboriginal folklore. See Sean Maynard, 'Black (and White) Images: Aborigines and Film', in The Australian Screen, op. cit., p. 227.

50 A case in point is when Rae (Nicole Kidman) fires her spear gun through a wooden door at what she thinks, and Noyce wants the audience to think, is Hughie (Billy Zane). But there are far too many minutes of the film left for it to be, which means the blood seeping under the door must come from the only other living presence on the boat: the dog. There is, then, no surprise when the door swings open to reveal all.

51 It is Quigley Down Under outside Australia.

52 In the US it is The Road Warrior.

53 The Dismissal (George Miller, Phillip Noyce, George Ogilvie, Carl Shultz [sic], John Power, 1983), Bodyline (Carl Schultz, George Ogilvie, Denny Lawrence, Lex Marinos, 1984), The Cowra Breakout (Phillip Noyce, Ken Cameron, 1985), Vietnam, The Dirtwater Dynasty (Michael Jenkins, John Power, 1988) and Bangkok Hilton.

54 Joseph Campbell, The Hero Has a Thousand Faces, The Bollingen Series XVII, Pantheon Books, New York, 1949.

55 Conversation with this author, 1988.

56 This section is based on a review published in Cinema Papers, No. 92, April 1993, p. 53.

57 The time taken to replace engines is unconvincingly short. It is also surprising Tass makes so little of the sequence: there is no joy in a mechanic's skilled use of tools, of building up a montage that is a paean to craftspeople at work.

58 Apparently, the gag was thought up by actor Steve Bisley, but Tass must take the bouquets/brickbats for having accepted it.

59 Regrettably, the film takes a similar soft option as in Martin Scorsese's Cape Fear (1991), when the river washes away Cady (Robert De Niro) just before Bowden (Nick Nolte) can smash in his head with a rock, thereby removing Bowden from the moral/legal quandary. In Death in Brunswick, Mrs Fitzgerald (Yvonne Lawley) has a heart attack just before she drinks the cup of tea that will bump her off, thus saving Carl from actually committing a murder.

60 Jacki McKimmie would add an 'e' to her first name on her subsequent films.

61 The very tone and spirit of Vaughan Williams' music is English pastorale, which has no relevance in a film set in and prescribed by the Australian landscape. Just because *The Lark Ascending* is emotional music does not make it appropriate. Sadly, this approach to music is all too common, Paul Cox with his unconnected use of European opera being another example. There is also the problem that, whereas composers write music which fits exactly the filmic moment, borrowed bits of classical music do not, and have to be mixed in and out at quite unjustified moments to suit the scene, causing disturbing results for caring ears.

62 'Truffaut: *L'homme qui aimait les femmes*—A Thematic Reading', article and interview by Jan Dawson, *Cinema Papers*, No. 15, January 1978, p. 208. The order of the paragraphs has been changed slightly to suit readability here. The text is a translation from French.

63 Morris, op. cit., p. 135.

64 There is dialogue along the lines of 'I belong in New York and you belong here', but they are mere words: Weir does not sufficiently make one feel those differences, does not make one believe their living together is impossible.

65 Brian Moore, *Black Robe: A Novel*, E. P. Dutton, New York, 1985, pp. 55–6.

66 'Jocelyn Moorhouse: The Gift of *Proof*', interview by Jan Epstein, *Cinema Papers*, No. 85, November 1991, p. 8.

67 ibid., p. 10.

68 ibid., pp. 10–11.

69 ibid., p. 10.

70 From Vladimir Nabokov, *Nikolay Gogol*, New Directions, Norfolk, Connecticut, 1944, quoted in Brian Boyd, *Vladimir Nabokov: The American Years*, Chatto & Windus, London, 1991, p. 57.

71 *New York*, 10 June 1991, p. 77.

72 A telling contrast is with Arthur Penn's *The Chase*, made 22 years earlier, which is a fine example of how one can intelligently combine elements of gothic melodrama with percipient social criticism.

73 This section is based on an entry in *Australian Film 1978–1992: A Survey of Theatrical Features*, Scott Murray (ed.), Oxford University Press, in association with the Australian Film Commission and Cinema Papers, Melbourne, 1993.

74 Jacques Zimmer's *Le Cinéma Érotique*, Editions J'ai lu, Paris, 1988. This is from memory as the only known copy in Australia was recently destroyed in a house fire.

75 Rod Bishop, 'Wrong World', *Cinema Papers*, No. 56, March 1986, p. 69.

76 In the novel, Marthe dies, weakened from childbirth and the walk in the rain from hotel to hotel. (Raymond Radiguet, *Le Diable au Corps*, Bernard Grasset Editeur, Paris, 1923.)

77 '*Devil in the Flesh*', a review by Rolando Caputo, *Cinema Papers*, No. 71, January 1989, pp. 54–5.

78 'The Making of *Evil Angels*', interview with Fred Schepisi by Philippa Hawker, *Cinema Papers*, No. 70, p. 9.

79 Much of the comment on *Return Home* is based on a section in 'Ray Argall: Return Home', article and interview by Scott Murray, *Cinema Papers*, No. 78, March 1990, p. 29.

80 'Dennis O'Rourke and *The Good Woman of Bangkok*', an interview by Andrew L. Urban, *Cinema Papers*, No. 84, August 1991, pp. 4–13.

81 ibid., p. 12.

82 It has been said that George Miller is the only Australian director to influence foreign film-making styles (Steven Spielberg's *Hook*, 1991, even has explicit hommages to Miller). But one can now add Jane Campion's name because Paul Brickman's *Men Don't Leave* (1991) seems in moments quite specifically influenced by certain Campion aesthetics. As well, there is the case of the recent French tele-feature adaptation of Radiguet's *Devil in the Flesh*, which stylistically owes much, to say the least, to the Australian version made four years earlier.

Watched by several African children, Lorenzo (Zack O'Malley Greenburg) and Omouri (Maduka Steady) fly a kite. George Miller's *Lorenzo's Oil* (1992).

5

AUSTRALIAN DIRECTORS OVERSEAS 1970–1992

Scott Murray

From the time writer–director John Farrow jumped ship in California in the late 1920s[1], Australia has had an extraordinary tradition of exporting talent overseas.

Along with the many successful directors in the US, there have been the heralded directors of photography. Not only did Robert Krasker and Dean Semler win Academy Awards (for *The Third Man*, 1949, and *Dances with Wolves*, 1990, respectively), others have found prominence overseas, such as John Seale, Russell Boyd, Don McAlpine, Andrew de Groot, Peter James, David Eggby and Geoff Burton.

The same is true of some Australian actors, from Errol Flynn to Bryan Brown, Judy Davis and American-born Mel Gibson. Then there are the composers (such as Brian May), art directors (Academy Award-winning Luciana Arrighi), writers and technicians.

For such a small population as Australia's, the number and talent of those who have found success overseas is quite remarkable. Sadly, it is also a reflection of the extreme difficulty of finding back home sufficiently sustainable work, financially and aesthetically.

At the same time, to many Hollywood is the nirvana of film-making, where work is highly paid and the finished films more likely to find wide distribution. That directors also have to give up degrees of aesthetic control is a price most have been prepared to pay.[2]

On the other hand, there is a small band of film-makers more interested in being part of European cinema.[3] Paul Cox, Rolf de Heer, Ben Lewin and Ian Pringle are notable examples. As well, there are several new Australian directors whose work suggests an affinity with European cinematic culture, such as New Zealand-born Jane Campion and Ray Argall.

Hollywood

Of those Australians to work recently in America, the most successful are George Miller, Peter Weir, Bruce Beresford, Fred Schepisi, Phillip Noyce and Roger Donaldson. They all are, or have been for a time, what the Americans like to term 'A' directors.

George Miller has made only two full features in the US, *The Witches of Eastwick* (1987) and *Lorenzo's Oil*[4] (1992), having first contributed to the portmanteau *Twilight Zone: The Movie* (1983). In Miller's frenetic episode ('Nightmare at 20,000 ft'), a paranoid passenger 'sees' a monster sitting on the wing of an aeroplane during a fierce storm. It is brilliantly and crisply directed, and far outshines the other efforts (by Joe Dante, John Landis and Steven Spielberg). Whereas Miller is happy to use state-of-the-art effects, he never, like the others, loses the focus of his eerie tale.

In some stylistic ways, this episode prefigures *The Witches of Eastwick* with its marriage of the storytelling skills of the Mad Max films with the pyrotechnics of Hollywood special-effects cinema. Often dazzling to the eye, *The Witches of Eastwick* is a technical triumph. But it is of more minor narrative interest, with Michael Cristofer's script a Hollywoodian trivialisation of an intriguing novel. John Updike's story about middle-aged women realising that the onset of age denies them their dreams, and that fading sexuality alienates the sexes, is here denied full resonance by youthful, pretty casting and a nervousness about equating women with primeval forces.

The film-makers (including, apparently, Miller's insistent producers, Peter Guber and Jon Peters) have replaced nuance with 'burlesque demonology'[5]. Several of the 'big' moments are exercises in excess (the cherry-pip vomit being a much noted example) and the acting, while playful, sometimes becomes overly hammy. Where the film works is when Miller's *mise en scène* fashions something iconoclastic from the thinness of the concept, as with the windblown journey to and entry of the church by Daryl Van Horne (Jack Nicholson), and his subsequent vociferation on women.

The Witches of Eastwick was not a happy experience for Miller[6], and he took a long sabatical as director before returning to the US for *Lorenzo's Oil* in 1992. Not only is it his masterpiece, but it is also the finest film made by an Australian.

When told Lorenzo (Zack O'Malley Greenburg) has ALD and two years at most to live, Augusto (Nick Nolte) and Michaela Odone (Susan Sarandon) try every specialist doctor in the hope of some breakthrough. But the experimental therapies are intrusive failures. Refusing to give up, the Odones begin their own search for a cure, wading through all the relevant medical literature they can find, though neither has any medical training. The result is the breakthrough use of oleic oil and erucic acid in stopping those with the disease from degenerating further.

But Miller's film is much more than a reconstruction of two people's fight to save a son and of an extraordinarily brave boy's will to live. It is also about true nobility of spirit, about individuals who question and challenge, who sidestep self-pity and despair and move forward heroically. They stand alongside all those individuals

149

Valentine (John Lithgow) prepares to 'take out' his ghastly apparition in George Miller's episode of *Twilight Zone: The Movie* (1983).

Plain, middle-aged women reworked Hollywood style: Sukie (Michelle Pfeiffer), Alexandra (Cher) and Jane (Susan Sarandon). George Miller's *The Witches of Eastwick* (1987).

Kumar (Bembol Rocco) and Guy (Mel Gibson) in Peter Weir's study of clashing cultures, *The Year of Living Dangerously* (1982).

throughout history who have refused to accept conventional wisdom and searched for their own truth.

In his film, Miller not only extols individuality, but also ethnicity. Miller is arguing that all specialness is to be valued, as must be the very struggle to be oneself. This is made quite explicit when having be called arrogant, Augusto explains that the Latin root for the word is 'arogare', meaning 'to claim for oneself'.

On several occasions, Miller captures visually the enormity of this struggle. The most dramatic is when the Odones go to the library for the first time to begin their studies. The camera climbs and twists up a wall and ceiling to reveal the massiveness of the library and its reference collection. The daunting task facing these individuals is clear.

This cinematic command is indicative of how *Lorenzo's Oil* is the work of a master film-maker at the height of his powers.[7]

Given Miller's universal approach to film-making in Australia, his success in the US comes as little surprise. Peter Weir is a perhaps different case, as his best early films (such as *Picnic at Hanging Rock*, 1975) have a far greater affinity with European cinema and its attendant sensibilities. Of the then major Australian directors, he seemed the one most suited to working in France or Italy. But, instead, Weir went to America.

In retrospect, Weir's last Australian film, *The Year of Living Dangerously* (1982), is a crossover: not only was it officially an Australia-US co-production (at least at Cannes in 1983), it used American (Sigourney Weaver, Linda Hunt) and international (Maurice Jarre) elements, and employed a narrative style more traditionally Hollywoodian. It is a 'bigger' film than his others, in its canvas and its scope. It tackles the political realities of Australia's closest neighbour, Indonesia, something ignored by most local film-makers. In other words, it steps aside to observe and place Australia in a wider, more world context.

Weir followed up with *Witness* (1985), which brought traditional Australian/European directing techniques—calm pace, lack of interest in manufacturing false dramatic peaks and valleys—to the story of cross-cultural

Culture clash: Samuel (Lukas Haas), an Amish boy, and John Book (Harrison Ford), a big city cop. Peter Weir's *Witness* (1985).

love in an Amish community of America. In that sense, it follows on from the cross-cultural relationships and affairs of *Living Dangerously*, but in *Witness* the story is set very much in, and only about, one society: America's. It is also another in Weir's examinations of individuals fending for themselves in 'foreign' societies or cultures: here, a Philadelphian policeman in a timeless Amish community.

Weir tackled a similar theme with his next film, *The Mosquito Coast* (1986), where a family uproots from middle America and heads south to a wild coastal region of Central America. Again, there is a clash of cultures, of philosophies both political and familial. But Weir's grasp of the entire narrative falters, as it did in *The Cars that Ate Paris* (1974) and *The Last Wave* (1977). For one, Allie Fox (Harrison Ford) is shown to be too nutty and unlikeable at the start for his increasing insanity to have much dramatic effect. For another, the range and detail of Allie's rantings numb rather than focus.[8]

Despite these flaws, the film is of interest for its snatches of well-crafted moments, a bold visual style and River Phoenix's fine performance. From a new director,

The Mosquito Coast would be heralded as proof of a major new talent. Certainly its serious-minded critique of materialistic American values stands it apart from much contemporary cinema.

Weir's most applauded success is *Dead Poets Society* (1989), again about a clash between political ideologies. A teacher, John Keating (Robin Williams), returns to his old school to bring freshness to stale methodologies, to encourage emotional birth instead of conservative replicationism. But for all its outwardly noble intents, for this viewer it is (with *Green Card*, 1991) Weir's least successful film. For one, Williams is inappropriately cast as Keating, unable to speak poetry with enough conviction or verve to imaginably inspire anyone. If only Kevin Kline had been cast, for whom one imagines the role could have been written (cf the pantheon speech on the Brooklyn Bridge in Alan J. Pakula's *Sophie's Choice*, 1982).

More puzzling still is Weir's handling of the narrative subtext which reads as an apology for McCarthyism. Under a minimal amount of authoritarian pressure (a

153

Top: saying goodbye to America: Allie (Harrison Ford), Mother (Helen Mirren), Charlie (River Phoenix), April (Hilary Gordon), Jerry (Jadrien Steele) and Clover (Rebecca Gordon). Peter Weir's *The Mosquito Coast* (1986). Bottom: John Keating attempts to inspire a class of American schoolboys in Peter Weir's *Dead Poets Society* (1989).

A Frenchman in New York: Georges (Gérard Depardieu). Peter Weir's *Green Card* (1991).

wrinkled brow, a proffered pen), Weir's schoolboys weaken and sign a false declaration which destroys an innocent man's career. Weir fails to make one believe the boys have gone through a *real* moral dilemma and their capitulations are staggeringly quick. In short, they are weak, confused and conservative boys who put their own well-being above principle. This may well be an accurate portrayal of some youth, and Weir's asking an audience to be a little sympathetic to their plight is understandable. But he goes much further by trying to make the audience feel proud of them—and merely because they stand on their desks in a weak and altogether too late tribute.

Interestingly, Weir shies away from showing the boys actually sign the false document: such an image could turn the audience against these youths. In contrast, and on the evidence of such films as *If. . . .* (Lindsay Anderson, 1969), it is fair to assume that many English and French directors would have chosen a different ending, one where

the boys showed real courage and principle, refused to sign and were expelled. Conscience and individuality would have been lauded, and McCarthyite pressure not posited as an excuse for inexcusable action.

Finally, one has the recent *Green Card*, which again places an individual, the French Georges (Gérard Depardieu), in a foreign environment: New York. But that is really only a subtext to Weir's interest in a screwball-genre treatment of the relationship between Georges and Brontë (Andie McDowell). While Depardieu has some fine moments, the film is hampered by a thin script, some inappropriate casting (the bit players let fly with theatrical cliché) and some uninvolving direction.

Another Australian to head to Hollywood in the early 1980s was Bruce Beresford. First up he made the tenderly observed *Tender Mercies* (1983), which was followed (in the US) by *King David* (1985), *Crimes of the Heart* (1986), *Her Alibi* (1988), *Driving Miss Daisy* (1989) and *Rich in Love* (1992).

155

Mac Sledge (Robert Duvall) and stepson Sonny (Allan Hubbard). Bruce Beresford's *Tender Mercies* (1983).

Daisy (Jessica Tandy), second from right, in her synagogue. Bruce Beresford's *Driving Miss Daisy* (1989).

Barbarosa (Willie Nelson) in Fred Schepisi's *Barbarosa* (1982).

Beresford's American work is unpredictable. There is the *Tender Mercies* and *Driving Miss Daisy* type of film (gently paced and sensitive, calmly and astutely recorded) and the major misfires, such as *King David*, one of the least credible and creditable of biblical dramas, and *Her Alibi*, which is so lifeless and so unloving of its genre as to question why its director ever wanted to make it.

This inconsistency parallels Beresford's career in Australia, from the peak of *'Breaker' Morant* (1980) to the misjudgement of *The Fringe Dwellers* (1986). As mentioned in the previous chapter, it seems that Beresford is one of those directors whose standard of work is directly related to the quality of the script. Give him a good one and he handles it carefully and intelligently, never imposing a personal or eclectic style to the detriment of the inherent tone. This makes him a very solid choice as director on a good project. On one with a flawed script, however, Beresford has so far seemed unable to ignite it dramatically.

At the same time, there is much in Beresford's direction that surpasses what could have been expected of most top American directors. He encourages performance (not mere words) to command meaning and the ending of *Driving Miss Daisy* is a model of restraint, with his conceit (of a superimposed image of the car's driving away) proving a marvellously delicate and affecting touch.

Beresford has also worked recently outside the US, with *Mister Johnson* (Kenya, 1990) and the Australia-Canada co-production *Black Robe* (1992), made in Quebec.

As for Fred Schepisi, he has been quite candid about why he left Australia:

I came to America for a number of complex reasons, not the least of which was to get paid. I put a lot of my own money and my company's money into *The Chant of Jimmie Blacksmith* [1978] and *The Devil's Playground* [1976] and you just can't afford to keep doing that unless you get it back in a large way.

I also came to test myself in what I consider the hotbed of international filmmaking. . .I wanted to get into the kitchen, and get amongst the heat and get in the pressure cooker, test myself and hone myself in various areas.[9]

But the early days were not easy for Schepisi, with the desired projects not making it through to production ('Meet Me at the Melba') or being taken over by others (Michael Apted on *Raggedy Man*).

Schepisi's first American film was *Barbarosa* (1982), a Western written by Bill Whitliff, who would later receive acclaim for his script of *Lonesome Dove* (mini-series, Simon Wincer, 1989). *Barbarosa* gained some critical following, particularly from *The New Yorker* critic Pauline Kael, who praised Schepisi for his innovative use of the genre, calling it 'the best Western that's been done here for perhaps the past five or ten years'[10]. But it was not a commercial success.

Schepisi's next film, *Iceman* (1984), also proved quiet at the box office. It is a strange project. Essentially a B-movie about a frozen Neanderthal man's coming back to life, it is directed by Schepisi with great seriousness, as if beneath the essential hokiness of the tale lie profound truths about man's condition.

Still, the opening and closing sequences are superb, Schepisi dramatically capturing figures and movement in frozen wastelands. It is a pity the idiosyncratic cutting through 90-degree angles, and from extreme wide-shots to extreme close-ups, set up frissons the rest of the film doesn't deliver.

Sidestepping genre altogether, Schepisi next made *Plenty* (1985), arguably his finest film. It is a carefully told, largely faithful reworking of David Hare's darkly etched play about a woman's dramatic and often tragic movement through English postwar history. It is a beautifully acted film (Schepisi's often are), even if the wondrous Meryl Streep acts her part rather than exists it (leading some to pine for Kate Nelligan, for whom the play was written and is in part about).

Schepisi and Hare have muted some of the play's original sting, which both applauds and condemns this woman's drive for independence, even at the risk of losing (male-determined) sanity. But the film is crisply conceived, and the fine English prose of the dialogue reverberates joyously with meaning and spirit.

Roxanne (1986) is a jeu d'esprit, based on Rostand's brilliant verse play, *Cyrano de Bergerac*. Schepisi creates a loving sense of small-town camaraderie and he keeps the tone warm and frothy. But beneath the surface a dark side bubbles that one feels could have more percipiently made its presence felt by the end.

It is curious that of Schepisi's nine features till the end of the decade, *Roxanne* is the only love story in the

A woman's movement through post-war history: Susan Traherne (Meryl Streep) and Mick (Sting) in Fred Schepisi's *Plenty* (1985).

Barley (Sean Connery) and Katya (Michelle Pfeiffer). Fred Schepisi's *The Russia House* (1991).

traditional sense. Marriage, when mentioned in his other work, seems repressive and deceit-laden, and male-female relationships usually do not play all that much a part (*Plenty* excepted). It is therefore curious that the one film where he has a conventionally happy romantic ending should involve totally rewriting Rostand's sagaciously tragic one. More puzzling, there is nothing in the characterisation of Roxanne (Daryl Hannah) which convinces one that she would want a shared sexual life with the Cyrano character, C. D. Bales (Steve Martin). Yet again it is a case of a Hollywood imposing the upbeat ending for presumed (and here considerable) commercial gain.

After the success of *Roxanne*, Schepisi returned to Australia to direct *Evil Angels* (1988). Then it was off to Moscow and Europe for *The Russia House* (1991). *The Russia House* is an exception to the above in that it is a traditionally Hollywood love story where the lovers overcome great odds to be joyously joined together in the last shot (which Schepisi surprisingly step-prints; look how much more effective the shot is when reprised at the end of the credits at normal speed). While there are some fine moments in the film, especially between Barley (Sean Connery) and Katya (Michelle Pfeiffer), the original story is not one of Le Carré's finest (compare it with the vastly superior *Moscow Rules* by Australian Robert Moss). Schepisi's judicious and loving use of Russian locations cannot totally make up for the narrative elisions.

After *The Russia House*, Schepisi made *Mr Baseball* (1992) in Japan, which had poor reviews in the US and is unreleased in Australia. He has since shot *Six Degrees of Separation*, based on the John Guare play. In many senses, this is an important film for Schepisi, who battled long to make it.

Another not exactly beloved at present by the critics is Phillip Noyce, whose *Patriot Games* (1992) received the most savage review in recent memory from the usually reticent *Variety*. Still, the film made money and Noyce quickly moved on to *Sliver* (1993), a big-budget thriller with Sharon Stone, the hottest actress in Hollywood today (even if her talent is somewhat overlooked).

Noyce's first film in the US, *Blind Fury* (1989), met with considerably less success. An action genre piece about a blind swordsman, it has found few supporters, save Adrian Martin who finds it 'a model of pure textual movement: a circulation of plot devices and bits of spectacular events into highs and lows, clinches and clichés'.[11]

The last of the 'A' directors is Roger Donaldson, who was born in Australia but left for New Zealand when 19 (and apparently prefers to be known as a New Zealander). There he established a career as a director of commercials. Later, he began making films, including the political thriller *Sleeping Dogs* (1977) and an off-centred road movie, *Smash Palace* (1981).

After finding some success at home, Donaldson went to the US, where he made *The Bounty* (1984), which was to have been filmed in New Zealand by David Lean. This large-scale film is rather routine and lacks the eccentric charms and star personae of the Frank Lloyd and

Nick (Rutger Hauer), the blind swordsman, in Phillip Noyce's *Blind Fury* (1989).

Lewis Milestone versions (*Mutiny on the Bounty*, 1935 and 1962).

Three years later, Donaldson made the hugely successful, but critically uninteresting, *Cocktail* (1987). Both it and *The Bounty* have Australian actors in lead roles: Mel Gibson and Bryan Brown (whose part was truncated and partially re-shot after he was found to overshadow Tom Cruise at the test screenings).

Donaldson's four other American films are the little-seen-but-admired *Marie* (1985), *No Way Out* (1987), *Cadillac Man* (1990) and *White Sands* (1992). *No Way Out* is a relatively successful updating of Kenneth Fearing's *The Big Clock*. While Donaldson's film is tricksy and shallow compared to John Farrow's 1948 version (the characters are mostly cut-outs and the film's treatment of the homosexual fall guy is unpleasant[12]), it does have great energy and drive (aided by the many well-crafted chase sequences). Competently directed in the standard Hollywood manner, it suggests Donaldson as a worthy director-for-hire.

The same can be said of *Cadillac Man*, about a simple man foolishly holding a car yard to ransom. The film's origins as a play are all too clear and Donaldson fails to smooth out or make tenable the bizarre stylistic changes within its structure. But it is well acted (particularly by

Jack Ryan (Harrison Ford) rushes to protect wife Cathy (Anne Archer) and daughter Sally (Thora Birch). Phillip Noyce's *Patriot Games* (1992).

Joey O'Brien (Robin Williams) in Roger Donaldson's *Cadillac Man* (1990).

Susan (Sean Young) and Tom (Kevin Costner) in *No Way Out* (1987). Roger Donaldson's reworking of Kenneth Fearing's *The Big Clock*.

a great Tim Robbins) and the ending is not without poignance. It certainly maintained Donaldson's reputation as a director to watch.

But that changed abruptly with *White Sands*, a tensionless thriller about drug dealings and false identities. Shot in exotic locations with the requisite big-budget gloss, the film doesn't deserve the critical wrath it sparked (it is no worse than hundreds like it). All the same, the very limpness suggests Donaldson was ill-at-ease with this genre outing.

Also successful in the US is Simon Wincer. His first American films were the charming fairytale, *D.A.R.Y.L.* (1985), and the tele-feature, *The Girl Who Spelled Freedom* (1986). After directing the racing mini-series *Blue Grass* in 1988, he did *Lonesome Dove* (1989), his finest work so far.

Brilliantly adapted from Larry McMurtry's novel by Bill Whitliff, *Lonesome Dove* is the sort of large-scale television that does justice to a classic novel the way conventional-length features cannot. McMurtry's is an epic story, and the mini-series captures that, balancing

skilfully the narrative scope with careful delineation of characters. Wincer extracts fine performances from all (even from television actors who had never promised so much), and as a piece of directorial craft it is quite outstanding, Wincer composing and cutting in a clear and astute way. Not even by the far-off end has a sense of stylistic repetition set in. As well, he knows when to remain straightforward, as in the death scene of Gus (Robert Duvall). With *Lorenzo's Oil*, this is the best work done by an Australian in the US in recent times.

Wincer came back to Australia to make the Tom Selleck 'Western', *Quigley*[13] (1991), before returning to the US, where he now lives, for *Harley Davidson and the Marlboro Man* (1992). It is Wincer's first misstep in some time.

Essentially a Western set in the near-present (1996, for some unexplained reason), the film is a return to the buddy-buddy films of the 1970s, a caper where two itinerant friends team up to do good but run afoul of the bad guys (who wear black Kevlon versions of Sergio Leone's brown ankle-length coats). Though these mates finally win through, all their friends are dead and personal relationships are ruptured (except for their own). In fact, their parting at the end is the film's one moment of genuine emotion. In that sense, the film is typical of many Australian films about non-sexual homosexual-like relationships (cf Ray Argall's *Return Home*, 1990, Jocelyn Moorhouse's *Proof*, 1991, et al.).

The biggest problem with *Harley Davidson* is a script which is nothing but a loose assembly of clichéd dialogue (one knows what is to be said well before the characters do) and situations. The actors, too, particularly Mickey Rourke, are listless. Only the energetic and visual use of locations, plus a few good action scenes, suggest a director of real note is at work here.

Wincer has since directed an episode of *Young Indiana Jones* (1992) for George Lucas and the much-acclaimed *Free Willy* (1993).

Another Australian director living and working in the US is Philippe Mora. His credits include *The Beast Within* (1982), *A Breed Apart* (1984), *The Howling: Part 2: Your Sister is a Werewolf* (1984) and *Communion* (1988). Of these, this author has only seen *The Howling: Part 2*, and its Australian cousin, *Howling III: The Marsupials* (1986), neither of which is of much interest, except as parodies of genre film-making. David Stratton does not share this view, finding *Howling III: The Marsupials* 'engagingly preposterous. . .full of wonderfully wacky characters and situations. . .a good antidote to more serious, and less successful, horror films'[14]. Some reviewers in America have also been supportive of *Communion*, as was the case with *Death of a Soldier* (1986) in Australia.

At the time of writing, Mora was set to embark on a $30 million film on Hitler, returning him thematically to his early documentary, and greatest success, *Swastika* (UK, 1973).

Richard Franklin, who in the 1970s and 1980s was Australia's most consistent director of thrillers, has had a varied career in the US. *Psycho II* (1983), his first American film, is lively and cinematically witty and, unlike most sequels, bears comparison with the original. The

Gus McCrae (Robert Duvall) and Lorena Wood (Diane Lane) in Simon Wincer's *Lonesome Dove* (1989).

Harley Davidson (Mickey Rourke) and Marlboro (Don Johnson). Simon Wincer's *Harley Davidson and the Marlboro Man* (1992).

166

Michael MacCleary (Paul Clemens) is possessed by an unknown force in Philippe Mora's *The Beast Within* (1982).

Norman Bates (Anthony Perkins) in Richard Franklin's *Psycho II* (1983).

Rollie (Bryan Brown) surprises his girlfriend, Brady (Rachel Ticotin) in Richard Franklin's *F/X2* (1991).

espionage thriller *Cloak and Dagger* (1984), a remake of Fritz Lang's 1946 original, is considered by many to be his most successful, whereas *Link* (1986), about connections between man and ape, suffered cruelly from post-production interference. Then after an aborted attempt to make a film on boxer Les Darcy back in Australia, Franklin returned to the US to make another sequel, *F/X2* (1991), with Australian actor Bryan Brown. Franklin is also responsible for the fine opening episode of television's *Beauty and the Beast*.

Also working in the thriller-adventure mode, but with a sci-fi twist, is Russell Mulcahy. In 1986, he directed the British-US *Highlander*, which, despite good box office and a cult following in France, generated little excitement elsewhere. It is a stylistically overblown film (as is Mulcahy's want), the script is tired and the performances (especially the wooden Christophe Lambert's[15]) weak. Mulcahy has since directed another sequel (*Highlander II: The Quickening*, Argentina, 1991), but it is no improvement, replacing the mythic elements of the first with tedious displays of mechanistic violence. Mulcahy has also made *Ricochet* (1991) and *Blue Ice* (1993), and has finished *The Real McCoy*.

Critically, John Duigan has fared slightly better. His one completed American film, *Romero* (1989), was made in Mexico and is about the murder of Salvadoran Archbishop Romero (Raul Julia). While some have found it an oddly passionless film, given the violent political and social events it portrays, it has been well received by several critics.

Since then, Duigan made *Wide Sargasso Sea* (1992) from the novel by Jean Rhys.

Of the Australian women directors to work in the US are Gillian Armstrong, Nadia Tass and Lyndall Hobbs.

Armstrong's first American film, *Mrs. Soffel* (1984), is perhaps her least successful. The material is dramatically undercut by some flat direction, and Diane Keaton never convinces as a minister's wife in the 1900s. Armstrong's next film, *The Fires Within* (1991), sidestepped a theatrical release in Australia and went straight to video. It is not one of her finer efforts, and Armstrong has laid much of the blame on her female producers whom she feels were too weak to stand up to the Hollywood patriarchy.

Whereas Armstrong once led the push by Australian women directors in Hollywood, Nadia Tass may take over the mantle. Her filmic style is the most American of all her compatriots and she is the one who will probably have there the greatest success. Certainly her first American film, the Martin Short comedy *Pure Luck* (1991), has proved itself suited to American tastes by bringing in respectable box-office receipts. However, at present Tass seems to be content working on Australian projects, such as the mini-series *Stark* (1993), and developing the film studios she and partner David Parker bought in Melbourne.

Lyndall Hobbs has made only one feature, *Back to the Beach* (1987), a tribute to the beach movies of the 1950s. Hobbs captures some of the wholesome cheeriness of the originals, and casting Frankie Avalon and Annette Funicello as the parents is amusing, but the gaiety soon pales and the thin concept becomes tiresome.

Other Australians to work in the US include Graeme Clifford (*Frances*, 1982; *Gleaming the Cube*, 1989; *Ruby Cairo*, 1992), George Miller (*A Mom for Christmas*, 1990, and several other tele-features), Carl Schultz (*The Seventh Sign*, 1988), Peter Faiman (*Dutch* (aka *Driving Me Crazy*), 1991 and *FernGully: The Last Rainforest*, 1992, producer) and Geoff Burrowes (*Run*, 1991).

169

Ramirez (Sean Connery) approaches Heather (Beatie Edney) and Connor (Christopher Lambert) in Russell Mulcahy's *Highlander* (1986).

Salvadoran Archbishop Romero (Raul Julia), centre, tries to enter his church with supporters. John Duigan's *Romero* (Mexico, 1989).

Jack Biddle (Matthew Mondine), Ed Biddle (Mel Gibson) and Kate Soffel (Diane Keaton). Gillian Armstrong's *Mrs. Soffel* (1984).

Campanella (Danny Glover) and Proctor (Martyn Short) in Nadia Tass' *Pure Luck* (1991).

Eva (Eva Sitta) and Janis (Chris Haywood). Paul Cox's *Island* (1989).

Europe

Few Australian feature directors have so far ventured to Europe. One is Dutch-born Paul Cox, who returned to his homeland for *Vincent: The Life and Death of Vincent van Gogh* (1987), a partially dramatised documentary about Van Gogh based on his letters to his brother. An art-house success in the US, *Vincent* is a return in some ways to Cox's short film, *Island* (1975). There is a similar playing with light, of step-printing hand-held tracking shots down narrow streets, of repeating images and playing with memories. Cox succeeds in avoiding almost all the clichés of 'art documentaries', except for the odd moment of word equals image, and for those who connect well with its stylisation it is a joyous bursting forth of colour and emotion.

Where some part ways with the film is over the insistent soundtrack of John Hurt's reading of excerpts from Van Gogh's letters. There is barely a frame of silence and the delivery is mannered, to say the least. The result can be quite stifling.

Cox returned to Europe with *Island* (1989), shot in Greece with a cast from Sri Lanka, Greece and Australia. Using the notion of an island as a psychic healing zone, Cox interweaves the lives of three women attempting to correct traumas from their pasts. Generally regarded as the poorest of Cox's features, it is hampered by a very underwritten script (several characters, such as Norman Kaye's, make literally no sense) and acting that ranges from the wooden (Eva Sitta's) to the gargantuanly theatrical (Irene Papas'). Most disappointing is a visual flatness.

What can be said for *Island*, however, is that it is at least an example of an Australian film-maker's attempting to consider foreign cultures and ideologies, and the way the East influences the West through a higher spirituality. It certainly is the work of someone who is not bound by notions of Australianness and who sees film as a universal language.

Another director to work in Europe is Ian Pringle, who made *Wrong World* (1986) partly in South America, *The Prisoner of St Petersburg* (1990) in Berlin and *Isabelle Eberhardt* (1992) in Africa and Europe. Whereas Cox belongs to a traditional European culture, Pringle is more a post-modernist internationalist. His films are essentially nihilistic, and see culture and society in decay. While all his films are marred by a sense of not having fully come together, he is one film-maker whose single-mindedness

Jack (Noah Taylor), Elena (Solveig Dommartin) and Johanna (Katja Teichmann). Ian Pringle's *The Prisoner of St Petersburg* (1990).

Slimen (Tcheky Karyo) and Isabelle Eberhardt (Mathilda May). Ian Pringle's *Isabelle Eberhardt* (1992).

and sensitivity suggest he may make a film of real importance in the future.

In *The Prisoner of St Petersburg*, Pringle's typically angst-ridden protagonist is Jack (Noah Taylor), adrift in Berlin and haunted by the ghosts of great Russian literature. Shot in stark black and white (by Ray Argall), the film is sometimes awkward (the change from 'Russian' and German to English reveals a grating archness in the dialogue), and only Nadja Teichman among his actors is up to the difficult tasks asked of them. But, like Pringle's other films, it must be acknowledged for its attempt at portraying a psychic landscape and for treating seriously characters the rest of the Australian cinema largely ignores.

Isabelle Eberhardt is a much criticised film, but in many ways it is a positive artistic step for Pringle and, despite its rather obvious failings, is one of the better European-style films made by an Australian.

Several critics have complained about the script's unexplaining, cryptic nature, but what Pringle has bravely

tried to do is make a film in the style of a French miniaturist biography, such as Roland Barthes' pacesetting work on Michelet. The very essence is reductionism, where all factual detail that does not precisely define a subject's state of mind or perspective is ruthlessly discarded.

The problem with the film equivalent is the demands placed on the lead actor and, sadly, Mathilda May fails almost completely. She is so modern in manner, so shallow in spirit, that her performance (for which Pringle must also take responsibility) all but scuttles the film.

What makes it worth watching, and deserving of praise, is the visual style. This is a film with barely a frame out of place, where a director has found a precise equivalent for the minimalist biographer's cryptic prose. Sometimes the *mise en scène* is a little lethargic, but the film is always a joy to watch, with its gloriously etched shades and shadows, its dark skies and white sunshine.

Vincent Ward, the New Zealand-born director, has a strong European involvement in his new feature, *Map*

176

Albertine (Anne Parillaud) and Avik (Jason Scott Lee). Vincent Ward's *Map of the Human Heart* (1993).

of the Human Heart (1993). A UK-Australia-French-Canada co-production, it was shot in the remote Artic, as well as Montréal and London.

George Miller has also ventured to Europe, for the little-seen *The Aviator* (Yugoslavia, 1985) and the much more successful *The NeverEnding Story II: The Next Chapter* (Germany, 1990). But Miller's skills and interests are, in the best sense, those of the everyman (best seen in the winningly sentimental children's film, *Bushfire Moon*, 1987) and his work is not tied to any nationality or culture.

As for other directors, Dutch-born Rolf de Heer, director of *Incident at Raven's Gate* (1989), which some critics admire, made *Dingo* (1992) as a French–Australia co-production. This story of cultural interchange between Anglo-American Billy Cross (Miles Davis) and Australian John Anderson (Colin Friels) also contrasts the jazz world with suburbia, and Paris with outback Australia.

There is also the new Ben Lewin film, *The Favor, the Watch and the Very Big Fish* (1992), made in France, and

Jane Campion's *The Piano* (1993), which was shot in New Zealand with French money. Of all the new directors, Campion is probably the one the Europeans most wish to be involved with.

Europe seems at this stage to be an increasingly important arena for Australian directors. Not only does the low-key style of much direction and the emphasis on character suit a more European approach, American pre-sales are drying up and increasingly Australian producers are having to look to Europe for some financing. Despite superficial compatibilities with America, there are also strong historical and cultural grounds for why Europe may prove a happier and more worthwhile partner than Hollywood. Certainly there is reason for hope.

Notes

1 For an account of John Farrow's life and career, see this author's article on Farrow published in *Cinema Papers*, No. 77, January 1990, pp. 32–52.
2 And this is not just restricted to important matters such as lack of final cut. The Directors Guild of America recently won an arbitration dispute stopping Sean Penn from taking a 'writer–director' credit on *Indian Runner* (1991) instead of the DGA-approved 'written and directed by'.
3 France, for example, is an auteurist culture where a film-maker's moral rights are protected by law.
4 Miller considers *Lorenzo's Oil* to be an Australian film. Both carry the pre-credit: 'A Kennedy Miller film'.
5 A term used by Louise Sweet in her review of the film in *Monthly Film Bulletin*, Vol. 54, No. 644, September 1987, p. 265.
6 See '*Lorenzo's Oil*: A Manual for Courageous Human Conduct', an interview with George Miller by Scott Murray, *Cinema Papers*, No. 92, April 1993, pp. 60, 62.
7 Based in part on Murray's introduction to '*Lorenzo's Oil*: A Manual for Courageous Human Conduct', op. cit., pp. 5–7.
8 Even scriptwriter Paul Schrader has criticised the casting of Ford, whose part was originally written for Jack Nicholson. Schrader feels it required Nicholson's 'reptilian charm' to keep the character likeable, something Ford never does. See *Schrader on Schrader & Other Writings*, Kevin Jackson (ed.), Faber and Faber, London, 1990, p. 128.
9 From a filmed interview with Schepisi in *Australian Movies to the World* (Gordon Glenn and Scott Murray, 1983). Also quoted in *Australian Movies to the World: The International Success of Australian Films since 1970*, David White, Fontana Australia, Sydney, and Cinema Papers, Melbourne, 1984, p. 129.
10 *Australian Movies to the World: The International Success of Australian Films since 1970*, p. 131.
11 Adrian Martin, 'Blind Fury', *Cinema Papers*, No. 76, November 1989, p. 63.
12 Compare with how Farrow non-judgementally handles the homosexuality of Steve Hagen (George Macready) in *The Big Clock*.
13 It is *Quigley Down Under* in the US.
14 See David Stratton, *The Avocado Plantation: Boom and Bust in the Australian Film Industry*, Pan Macmillan Publishers, Sydney, 1990, pp. 303–4.
15 The credits on the English version adds an 'r' to his first name. Surprisingly, the sequel, *Highlander II: The Quickening*, then drops it.

John Heyer's *This Valley is Ours* (1948).

6
The documentary

Megan McMurchy

Documentary film-making represents the most enduring strand of production running through the history of the Australian cinema. It provides a rich record of Australian social and political life which fills in many of the holes left in the portrait of Australia constructed by its feature films.

Although documentaries usually occupy a subordinate position relative to feature films, it is possible to argue that, had it not been for the stable continuum of documentary production activity and support for the film industry infrastructure during the barren years of the 1950s and 1960s, there would have been little foundation on which to build the renascent feature industry.

Looked at in the long view, and taking a rather broad definition of 'documentary', it is possible to see the history of documentary film-making in Australia represented by a continuous line of *government* documentary production intersected by discontinuous strands of *independent* documentary production (with the latter encompassing varieties of both political and commercial documentary-making).

Government documentary production

Ever since 1911, when the Commonwealth government appointed its first full-time cameraman, government film-making has been assigned the dual roles of promoting Australia's national image overseas (to encourage trade and migration) and of promoting within Australia the project of 'nation-building'.

As government priorities changed during different eras, so did the location of administrative responsibility for the government's film production unit, which was known after 1921 as the Cinema and Photographic Branch (or simply the Cinema Branch). Throughout the 1920s and 1930s, its staple product was documentary shorts—'scenics' and 'industrials'—which were screened widely in Australian cinemas as feature film supports (such as the 76-part series *Know Your Own Country*). With few exceptions, the documentaries were prosaic and conventional, delivering a strictly official account of life in Australia and ignoring what life was really like for most Australians during the Great Depression (when Australia suffered an unemployment rate second only to Germany's).

World War II created an urgent new propaganda function for film and a Film Division was established within the Department of Information (DOI) in 1942.

That same year, the first official Australian team of war correspondents, led by Captain Frank Hurley and including cameraman Damien Parer and director-producer Ron Maslyn Williams, was sent to the Middle East. The footage shot by official war photographers was made available to the two Australian newsreel services, Australian Movietone News and Cinesound Review, which also periodically compiled special editions. One such documentary, *Kokoda Front Line* (1942), was screened widely in Britain and the US, and became the first Australian film to win an Academy Award.

Several other events during the war were to have a vital effect on the future of government documentary production. In April 1940, John Grierson, founder of the British documentary movement, visited Australia. Grierson had established the National Film Board of Canada (NFBC) the previous year and brought with him a zeal for documentary as a medium capable of effecting social reform. His proposals for a body similar to the NFBC in Australia were initially ignored, but in 1945 the Australian National Film Board (ANFB) was set up.

Under producer-in-chief Stanley Hawes, a Grierson protégé who remained head of government film production until 1970, the DOI's Film Division entered a period of production during which, for a short time[1], the creative powers of its talented bank of people meshed with the ANFB's prescribed social purposes to produce a body of distinguished films. Despite political, aesthetic and religious differences amongst these film-makers[2], the documentaries they produced seemed to share a common vision of their postwar world, and together they initiated the first great era of Australian documentary-making.

Most of these films strongly reflected the then widespread belief in the advent of a 'new social order', and celebrated the striving of the Australian people to bring into existence a productive nation hewn from conditions of natural adversity. John Heyer's *The Valley is Ours* (1948) represents an apotheosis of this strand of documentary. A portrait of the Murray River valley and the people and industries supported by the huge river system, Heyer's film is patterned by an incantatory narration which builds and subsides with the river flow, carried along on a litany of names, numbers, distances, tonnages and cash values of produce—everything swept up into the effort to develop the land, the river and its resources. Labour is the unifying force which bonds Australians into one people and renders nature productive.

The period of postwar reconstruction, and the economic development that took place during the 1950s, saw an unprecedented expansion of manufacturing industry, the undertaking of massive civil engineering projects and the absorption of 1.3 million European migrants into a population that began the decade at eight million.

Along with the many poetic expressions of this nation-building ethos, the ANFB also produced several experiments in dramatised documentary, such as *Mike and Stefani* (Ron Maslyn Williams, 1952). But with the departure of innovative film-makers like John Heyer, and

Ron Maslyn Williams' *Mike and Stefani* (1952).

the increasing dominance of Stanley Hawes[3], these early impulses mostly congealed into bland conformism by the mid-1950s.

At the national level, the pressures of the Cold War, the deadening effects of a seventeen-year reign by the conservative (and royalist) Prime Minister Sir Robert Menzies, the complacency produced by the achievement of full employment and the smothering of Aboriginal and migrant problems under the blanket rhetoric of 'assimilation' contributed to an official climate in which non-conformist views were excluded from the government film production house.

The abolition of the DOI in 1950 and the transfer of the Film Division to the Department of the Interior's News and Information Bureau (with the ANFB having already been relegated to token status) maintained the Film Division's exposure to hostile indifference and petty interference by its bureaucratic masters. Hawes was obliged to spend much of his energies defending the Film

Division (known after 1956 as the Commonwealth Film Unit, or CFU) from such attacks. He nevertheless managed to introduce a 'nursery system' which brought in bright, well-educated production assistants and, by the mid-1960s, a spark of something less conservative began to show through again in CFU productions.

From the Tropics to the Snow (1964) is often identified as the film which best typified the new mood at the CFU. Co-directors Richard Mason and Jack Lee, with tongues in cheek, parodied the conformist pressures they were so familiar with by producing two films-within-a-film: one wittily caricaturing the CFU's 'old style' film full of bland cliché, the other suggesting a new style based on 'poetic integrity', artistry and experimentation. Undoubtedly a ground-breaking film at the time, viewed in retrospect it fails to escape its anodyne institutional mission (to present another comprehensive round-up of Australian tourist icons) and is completely lacking any hint of what was really going on across the country: the birth of 'mod'

Richard Mason and Jack Lee's *From the Tropics to the Snow* (1964).

youth culture, Aboriginal 'freedom rides' into racist out-back towns, lock-outs of miners in Mt Isa and the controversial introduction of army conscription.

It was left to the other arm of government documentary-making, the Australian Broadcasting Commission (ABC), to begin tackling difficult contemporary subjects and explore the possibilities of a more spontaneous, candid style of film-making. By the mid-1960s, the ABC had begun to develop an Australian counterpart of the exciting television documentaries which had been pioneered at the BBC by film-makers such as Ken Loach, Peter Watkins and Ken Russell. This new era at the ABC was heralded by Cecil Holmes' *I, the Aboriginal* (1964), which won the Australian Film Institute's Gold Award. In the following year, Gian Carlo Manara's *Living on the Fringe* graphically portrayed inner-city poverty and the plight of Aborigines coming to the city in search of work.

Working on the BBC model, documentary-makers such as Tom Haydon, John Power, Michel Pearce and Ken Hannam were able to choose their own subjects and work with an unusual degree of freedom to make documentaries examining controversial contemporary issues. Then, in 1967, producer Tom Manefield returned from the BBC and persuaded the ABC to undertake a documentary series similar to the BBC's *Man Alive*, which it did in 1969 under the title *Chequer-board*. Employing a 'living camera' style and intrusive close-ups as a social probe, *Chequer-board* opened up issues such as homosexuality, divorce and personal relationships in a new and powerful way for television audiences. Although its initial, electrifying impact waned over time, *Chequer-board* continued to influence Australian documentary film-making over the years as its alumni moved onto other areas.

By the late 1960s, changes were on the way at the CFU, too. A talented body of film-makers, writers, editors and cameramen helped create a new style of government film-making that began to take greater creative

Gian Carlo Manara's *Living on the Fringe* (1965).

risks (Robert Parker's *Concerto for Orchestra*, 1965; Stefan Sargent's *The Change at Groote*, 1968; and Chris McGill's *The Line*, 1970; et al.). In 1965, Ian Dunlop commenced his massive *People of the Australian Western Desert* series. Filmed during two CFU trips to central Australia, which were sponsored by the Australian Institute of Aboriginal Studies, the full series of nineteen films documented the daily life and technology of the last Aboriginal families still living in the desert as hunter–gatherers before the Australian government's assimilation policy forced them from their traditional lands. Dunlop's films extended the earlier tradition of Australian ethnographic film-making initiated in 1901 by Professor Walter Baldwin Spencer and continued between 1926 and 1938 by the Board for Anthropological Research at the University of Adelaide.[4]

Dunlop's films did not endorse prevailing assimilationist notions, but even up until the early 1970s some other CFU documentaries did. An example is *Walking in the Sunshine, Walking in the Shadows* (Bob Kingsbury, 1971), which uncritically gives voice to well-intended white teachers whose mission is to undermine the traditional allegiances and lifestyles of the Aboriginal children in their charge.

In relation to immigration policy, too, CFU documentaries continued to serve the imperative of binding into 'one people' the tides of diverse ethnic populations which continued to flow into Australia during the late 1960s and early 1970s to meet the demand for labour. But the totalising mythology of a unified, homogenised nation was soon to disappear under the impact of the post-1968 political movements and the influence of a group of young film-makers who brought the ideas of the New Left and the 'counter-culture' with them to the government production house (renamed Film Australia in 1973 and transferred to the Department of the Media).

Unlike the postwar era, the 1970s permitted no unified vision for the country and its people. The young film-makers at Film Australia were alive to the realities of social inequity, discrimination and the divisive political

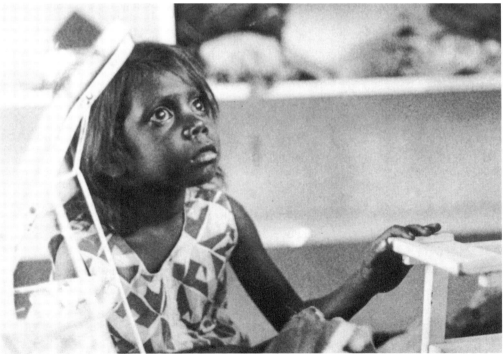

Top: Ian Dunlop's *People of the Australian Western Desert* (1966–1970). Bottom: Bob Kingsbury's *Walking in the Sunshine, Walking in the Shadows* (1971).

The Human Face of China (1979).

movements which had already activated the new generation of independent, political documentary-makers.

When *Chequer-board's* originator, Tom Manefield, moved to Film Australia in the mid-1970s, he encouraged these younger film-makers to apply a modified living-camera style in a series of short 'discussion-starter' documentaries about adolescence. This method of packaging a series of short documentaries, each embodying an aspect of a social issue or problem in the story of one particular individual, had been initiated by producer Suzanne Baker in the 1975 series *Putting a Face to an Issue* (1975), and has since remained a durable and successful documentary format for television and educational use.

Other documentaries employing an observational camera style and dealing with such social themes as women's liberation, Aboriginal issues, family relation-ships, alcoholism and drug addiction formed a prominent part of Film Australia's output during the late 1970s (Jane Oehr's *Stirring*, 1975; Bob Kingsbury's *Mr Symbol Man*, 1975; and Deborah Kingsland's *All in the Same Boat*, 1977; et al.).

A new kind of suburban anthropology was also being developed in films which took a hard look at everyday Australian institutions and communities (such as Peter Weir's *Whatever Happened to Green Valley?*, 1973). Documentaries on South Pacific nations also became increasingly prominent during this period (e.g., *Our Asian Neighbours*, 1971–75, and *The Human Face of China*, 1979).

By the end of the 1970s, however, Film Australia entered a period of declining staff morale and loss of direction that endured until the mid-1980s. Staffing and budget cutbacks, the loss of some of its best staff to the burgeoning feature-film industry, public controversies about several film projects and management upheavals contributed to this malaise. The federal government's decision in mid-1987 to establish Film Australia as an autonomous, government-owned business was greeted as an opportunity, finally, to steer the organisation in self-determined directions.

One of the strongest strands of documentary developed at Film Australia during this mid-1970s to mid-1980s period was its series of films on Aboriginal themes. As well as Ian Dunlop's continuing ethnographic work, there emerged another group of films on Aboriginal subjects which eschewed an ethnographic stance, making clear the films' political allegiance to the Aboriginal communities they document. They are a very far cry from the government-line films made about 'the Aboriginal problem' in the 1950s and 1960s.

More recently, young Aboriginal film-makers were given formal training opportunities at Film Australia and the outcome was two excellent documentaries on traditional and contemporary Aboriginal art by Michael Riley, *Boomalli* and *Dreamings* (both 1988).

Another government agency, the Australian Institute of Aboriginal Affairs, has also produced a large body of documentaries on Aboriginal themes since the establishment of its film unit in 1975. Employing such documentary-makers as Roger Sandall (*Coniston Muster*, 1972), Curtis Levy (*Sons of Namatjira*, 1975), Kim McKenzie (*Full Circle*, 1987) and David and Judith MacDougall (*Link-Up Diary*, 1987), the institute has produced films which reflect the cultural and political renewal that has arisen within Aboriginal communities since the 1970s.

In general, Film Australia's greater use of freelance directors and producers since the mid-1980s has encouraged the production of documentaries marked by a more personal style. And, like independent documentary-makers, Film Australia has increasingly turned to television sales as a means of offsetting rising production costs and securing substantial audiences. While establishing ties with the ABC and commercial broadcasters, it has also begun generating large-scale international documentary series, such as *Roads to Xanadu* (1989), John Merson's impressive study of the historical relationship between Chinese and Western technological development.

In this new climate, the ABC has also reinvigorated its in-house documentary production capacity. David Goldie's major exposé of the Australian prison system, *Out of Sight, Out of Mind* (1988), the outstanding wildlife series *Nature of Australia* (1989), the current series of feature documentaries produced for *Hindsight* and individual documentaries such as *The Devil You Know* (Jenny Brockie and Vascha Sidwell, 1990) indicate that the national broadcaster has returned to documentary production with serious intentions, influenced by contemporary developments in documentary style.

Independent documentary production

If the 'actuality' films which were the first products of the Australian film industry can be regarded as a primitive form of documentary, then it can be said that independent documentary in Australia has a lineage that extends back to the pioneering entrepreneurs who invented the Australian cinema: Maurice Sestier and Walter Barnett with their first recording of the Melbourne Cup, E. J. Thwaites and Robert W. Harvie, Mark Blow, the Salvation Army's Limelight Department, and Millard Johnson and William Gibson.[5]

When cinema was still a novelty in the 1890s, people were magnetically drawn by moving representations of 'the real'. Even well into the 1920s, travelling photographers could still attract crowds in a country town by simply screening a locally filmed reel showing shopfronts, workplaces and faces the audience recognised.

By the early 1910s, more exotic subjects were required to hold the attention of city cinemagoers. T. J. West produced short actualities with titles such as *Sydney's Sirens of the Surf* (1911), *The Aboriginals of Victoria* (1911) and *Whale Hunting in Jervis Bay* (1913).[6]

The full potential of cinema as an incomparable medium for communicating exotic reality was exploited by the extraordinary photographer and cameraman Frank Hurley, who pioneered the Australian tradition of travel-adventure documentary. An inveterate adventurer and entrepreneur, he joined Douglas Mawson's Australian expedition to Antarctica in 1911 as official photographer, returning in 1915 with the British expedition of Ernest Shackleton. These trips resulted in his two most acclaimed documentaries, *Home of the Blizzard* (1913) and *In the Grip of the Polar Ice* (1917).

Hurley also filmed pioneering flights with aviator Ross Smith, and made *Pearls and Savages* (1921) in Papua and the Torres Strait Islands before touring it successfully throughout Australia. After making two melodramatic narrative feature films set in Papua, he made further trips to Antarctica with Mawson to produce *Siege of the South* in 1931.

Joining the Cinesound studio in the early 1930s, Hurley made travelogues, industrials and films of occasion. His flair for portentous imagery and rhetoric was put to full use in *A Nation is Built*, the 1938 official documentary for the 150th anniversary of Britain's colonisation of Australia.

Frances Birtles was another intrepid adventurer who documented his own travels for the screen, collaborating with Hurley in 1914 on the film *Into Australia's Unknown*, which records a motoring trip to the Northern Territory and the Gulf of Carpentaria.

Production of actuality and promotional shorts was maintained throughout the 1920s by companies such as Herschell Films, whose series of documentaries for the Made In Australia Council provide a fascinating portrait of bygone industrial processes in such films as *Sheep to Shop—Woollen Goods* and *Evolution of a Chocolate* (both from the early 1920s).

In the 1930s, commercial documentary-making was dominated by Cinesound. In addition to the films made by Ken G. Hall and Frank Hurley, independent documentary producers such as Stan Hawkins and Mel Nichols

John Merson's *Roads to Xanadu* (1989).

Frank Hurley's *Pearls and Savages* (1921).

The outback mailman and a stockman in John Heyer's *The Back of Beyond* (1954).

made industrial shorts and travelogues through the company.

In Melbourne, Frank Thring's Efftee Studio produced almost one hundred shorts between 1931 and 1934, including travelogues, filmed recordings of Australian vaudeville and stage acts, and natural history shorts produced by cinematographer Noel Monkman. In 1931, Monkman and Thring formed Australian Educational Films to produce Monkman's series of documentaries on the Great Barrier Reef.

Monkman made a further outstanding series of films on the natural history of tropical Queensland, which was grouped together as the *Australian Marvelogue* series (1932–33).[7] His nature films began a tradition in Australian documentary-making which continues strongly to the present time.

In Melbourne, Herschell Films continued prolific documentary production during the 1930s, much of it comprising industrial, nature and travelogue films sponsored by state government departments.

During the late 1930s, well after the worst years of the Depression, the earliest examples of left-wing political cinema began to emerge sporadically. *Take Notice*, made in 1939 by the Sydney Unity Film Group, is a semi-dramatised protest against unfair rent rises. Around the same time was *A Brief Survey of the Activities of the Brisbane City Mission* (1937), a documentary about the welfare activities of the mission, which provided tearooms for homeless men and emergency employment for 'needy mothers or single women'.

These atypical films presented a very different version of Australia to that being projected in the Cinema Branch's tireless enumeration of the nation's manufactured products, or Frank Hurley's boastful jingoism.

During World War II, independent film-making capacity was mobilised in support of the war effort.

Afterwards, documentaries settled into two decades of conventionality. Invariably, they employed a male 'voice of God' narrator to present a didactic or promotional message on behalf of the films' sponsors. The stifling conservatism of Australia during the 1950s is accurately reflected in most of these films whose main producers included Cinesound, the Shell Film Unit and John Kingsford Smith's Kingcroft Productions.

Only a few films emerged from these production companies which could equal those produced by the government's newly established ANFB. Of these, John Heyer's *The Back of Beyond* (1954) is unarguably the most outstanding. It broke new ground in Australian documentary-making. Going well beyond Stanley Hawes' formula for documentary which 'seeks the dramatic pattern in actuality'[8], Heyer created his own drama and poetry, and injected them into the landscape he was recording.

In total contrast to the conservatism of most sponsored documentaries, there emerged in the late 1940s a different strain of documentary, one with an avowedly left-wing political agenda. There was the work of the Realist Film Association and the Waterside Workers' Federation Film Unit, which between 1952 and 1958 produced a series of forceful agitprop documentaries on subjects such as pensions, affordable housing for industrial workers and bad working conditions in the waterfront and coalmining industries.

A major influence on this development had been the presence in Australia towards the end of the war of the distinguished Dutch documentarist Joris Ivens. With the clandestine participation of several Film Division employees, Ivens made *Indonesia Calling* (1946), which documents Australian trade union actions in solidarity with Indonesia's independence struggle against the Dutch.

The total collapse of the Australian feature film industry during the 1950s and 1960s thwarted what might otherwise have been a natural progression into feature production for several of the period's most gifted documentary-makers. Ron Maslyn Williams, John Heyer, Cecil Holmes—who had already experimented with dramatised documentary (Williams' *Mike and Stefani*, 1951), documentary-inflected drama (Holmes' *Three in One*, 1957), and a documentary which stretches towards poetic narrative (Heyer's *The Back of Beyond*)—accommodated themselves to the period's attenuated opportunities and continued producing documentaries throughout the 1960s.

During this period, little of interest emerged in the independent documentary field. Hundreds of short sponsored documentaries were produced by commercial production houses, many of them unbearably dull recruiting films for the banking and retailing industries, the army or nursing services.

One exuberant new development, however, was the series of surf movies[9] which were originated by Bob Evans in 1960 with *Surf Trek to Hawaii*, and continued with his *To Ride a White Horse* (1967), George Greenough's *The Coming of the Dawn* (1970), Albert Falzon's *Crystal Voyager* (1973) and Paul Witzig's *Rolling Home* (1974), among others. These enormously successful

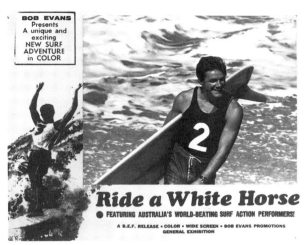

Bob Evans' *To Ride a White Horse* (1967).

documentaries may represent a unique Australian contribution to world cinema.

But the really significant development in Australian documentary during the 1970s was the emergence of a new wave of political film-makers concerned with the anti-war movement, women's liberation, the Aboriginal land rights movement, gay liberation and campaigns by other disadvantaged minorities.

This wave of political film-making had been preceded by the development of a vital and active film 'underground' in Sydney and Melbourne during the early 1960s. Co-operatives were formed in various cities and, although the founders' interests lay in experimental cinema, the co-ops were to become increasingly identified with political documentaries, especially during the late 1970s when feminist film-makers became a dominant force.

Among the first radical independent documentaries to be distributed by the co-ops were *Or Forever Hold Your Peace* (Kit Guyatt and others, 1970) and *Beginnings* (Rod Bishop, Gordon Glenn, Scott Murray and Andrew Pecze, 1971), both portraying mass demonstrations against the Vietnam War. While the latter was privately funded, the former was the first film to receive finance from the newly established Experimental Film Fund, which was to become the main source of funding for independent documentaries until it was replaced by the Australian Film Commission's Creative Development Fund in 1978.

Over the next ten years, there was an extraordinary upsurge in independent documentary production fuelled by the conjunction of liberal film financing policies and a growing body of politicised film-makers who adopted the documentary form as an efficient vehicle for promoting their radical views. Documentary had the natural advantage of rendering immediately visible and articulating what had remained suppressed and silent in the mass media.

One of the earliest key films was Alessandro Cavadini's

Dennis O'Rourke's *"Cannibal Tours"* (1988).

Top: Bob Connolly and Robin Anderson's *First Contact* (1982). Bottom: Bob Connolly and Robin Anderson's *Joe Leahy's Neighbours* (1988).

Ningla A-Na (1972), which captured the dramatic begin-nings of Aboriginal activism. This film initiated one of the most important continuing cycles of independent Australian documentaries. Evolving from an early phase in which white film-makers made films *about* Aboriginal issues, to a collaborative phase in which white film-makers worked *with* Aboriginal communities, this cycle has recently reached a new phase in which communities and individual Aboriginal film-makers have begun to initiate and produce their own film and video pro-grammes.

Several of the outstanding films were made by Cavadini with Carolyn Strachan: *Protected* (1976), *We Stop Here* (1978) and *Two Laws* (1981), the last being made with the Borroloola people of the Northern Territory. These films comprise a series of accounts of Aboriginal com-munities' histories of massacre, dispossession and in-stitutionalisation, and are particularly striking for moving beyond ethnography and 'testimonial' documentary to-wards a more formally innovative form grounded in community-based collaboration.

Other major films in this cycle have tended to be more conventional in form and include Michael Edols' *Lalai Dreamtime* (1976), Alec Morgan and Martha Ansara's *Robin Campbell—Old Fella Now* (1979), Essie Coffey's *My Survival as an Aboriginal* (1979) and Alec Morgan's *Lousy Little Sixpence* (1983).

Interestingly, the new documentaries from Aboriginal film-makers are generally far more daring and uncon-ventional in their approach, as seen with Lorraine Mafi-Williams' *Eelemarni: The Story of Leo and Leva* (1988), *Extinct But Going Home* (1989), by Rhonda Foster and Mick Barker, and Tracey Moffatt's *Moodeitj Yorgas/Solid Women* (1989).

Another important cycle of independent documenta-ries has taken as its focus the indigenous peoples of the South Pacific. These films concerned themselves with recording the complex changes to traditional cultures and economies in the post-colonial era. Dennis O'Rourke's films represent the most substantial contribution. Com-mencing with *Yumi Yet: Independence for Papua New Guinea* (1976), which celebrated Papua New Guinea's independence, his work has charted both the humorous and malign aspects of the meeting of Western and indig-enous cultures in the South Pacific in *Ileksen: Politics in Papua New Guinea* (1978), *Yap. . .How Did You Know We'd Like TV?* (1980), *The Sharkcallers of Kontu* (1982), *Half Life: A Parable of the Nuclear Age* (1985) and "*Cannibal Tours*" (1988).

Bob Connolly and Robin Anderson have also chosen New Guinea as the site for their investigations into the legacies of colonialism. In *First Contact* (1982), they made use of footage filmed in the early 1930s by Australian gold prospectors who had stumbled across peoples un-known to the outside world. In *Joe Leahy's Neighbours* (1988), they trace the historical fall-out of that en-counter in the relationship that now exists between the mixed-race son of one of the prospectors and the tribal people he dominates through his flair for western-style business.

In 1992, Connolly and Anderson released *Black Harvest,* which covers events five years on from *Joe Leahy's Neighbours.*

Moving further north in their geopolitical ambit are Gary Kildea's *Celso and Cora* (1983), about daily life among poor urban dwellers in The Philippines; Chris Nash and Maree Delofski's *Philippines, My Philippines* (1988), which examines the decline in human rights observance under the rule of Cory Aquino; Martha Ansara, Mavis Robertson and Dasha Ross' *Changing the Needle* (1982), which documents Vietnamese efforts to deal with the massive drug problem left over from the war; and Solrun Hoaas' exploration of expatriated Japanese culture in *Green Tea and Cherry Ripe* (1988).

The internationalism of contemporary Australian documentary-making is well illustrated in the work of David Bradbury, whose first two films dealt with the dramatic global careers of two Australians: television news cameraman Neil Davis in *Front Line* (1980) and controversial left-wing journalist Wilfred Burchett in *Public Enemy Number 1* (1981). His subsequent docu-mentaries switched focus to the politics of Central America, with *Nicaragua: No Pasaran* (1984), *Chile: Hasta Cuando?* (1985) and *South of the Border* (1988).

David Knaus' *Contradictions* (1988) and George Gittoes' *The Bullets of the Poets* (1987) are also con-cerned with aspects of Nicaragua's Sandinista revolution, while *Cry Havoc—Mozambique* (1987), by Fionna Douglas and Stephen Levitt, documents South Africa's efforts to destabilise Mozambique by sponsoring terror-ism. Frank Heimans (*Paradise Camp*, 1986) and Karin Altmann (*Raoul Wallenberg: Between the Lines*, 1985) made films dealing with the history of the Jewish Holo-caust.

In view of these well-developed strands of internation-ally-oriented documentary, it seems fair to comment that independent film-makers have generally been much less interested in documenting the diversity of cultures which has developed *within* Australia's shores since the mas-sive migration programme of the postwar era. With the exception of a few titles such as Fabio Cavadini and Suzie Walker's *Other Side of the Coin* (1979), Brian McKenzie's *Winter's Harvest* (1980), Gillian Coote's *Out of Dark-ness—Rithy's Story* (1984) and Anna Kannava's *Ten Years After—Ten Years Older* (1986), the reporting of Aus-tralia's extraordinary 200-year experiment in mass mi-gration has been left to Film Australia and the Special Broadcasting Service (SBS), with its long-running series of half-hour multicultural documentaries commissioned from independent film-makers, *Australian Mosaic.*

The other major strand of independent documentary since the early 1970s is comprised of feminist documen-taries. The Sydney Women's Film Group (SWFG) was formed in 1971, growing out of the Sydney women's lib-eration movement, which already had its own newspaper and pamphlet publishing group. Women's film produc-tion and distribution groups were also formed in Mel-bourne and other cities during the 1970s.

The earliest of the SWFG's documentaries were self-financed and made a virtue of its limited means, pre-

Top: Gary Kildea's *Celso and Cora* (1983). Bottom left: Martha Ansara, Mavis Robertson and Dasha Ross' *Changing the Needle* (1982). Bottom right: David Bradbury's *Nicaragua: No Pasaran* (1984).

Solrun Hoaas' *Green Tea and Cherry Ripe* (1988).

Brian McKenzie's *Winter's Harvest* (1980).

Megan McMurchy, Margot Nash, Margot Oliver and Jeni Thornley's *For Love of Money* (1983).

senting the facts about workplace discrimination and household drudgery in gritty black-and-white with little respect for conventional distinctions either between personal and political issues, or between documentary and drama form. *Home* (1973), *Women's Day 20c* (1973), *What's the Matter Sally?* (1974) and *Film for Discussion* (1974) struck a nerve with audiences and continued to circulate actively for many years.

By the late 1970s, feminist film-makers had successfully organised their own film-making workshops and a significant number of women was also emerging from the Australian Film Television & Radio School. Having already addressed the most obvious forms of institutionalised discrimination and abuse, feminists began turning to more subtle issues of gender construction and sexuality, producing a stream of films arguing for an extensive programme of social demands. Widely circulated documentaries of this period included *The Selling* of the *Female Image* (Carole Kostanich, 1977), *Size 10* (Susan Lambert and Sarah Gibson, 1978), *Birth at Home* (Barbara Chobocky, 1978), *Working Up* (Maureen McCarthy and Chris Warner, 1980) and *Mum's the Word* (Carole Kostanich, 1982).

Jeni Thornley's landmark *Maidens* (1978), a poetic family history which links feminist analysis to general social history, sparked off a series of documentaries which reinterpreted aspects of Australian history from a feminist perspective: *Bread and Dripping* (Wimins Film Collective, 1981), *For Love or Money* (Megan McMurchy, Margot Nash, Margot Oliver, Jeni Thornley, 1983) and *A Singular Woman* (Gillian Coote, 1985) to name just three.

All these films utilised the 'compilation documentary' form, combining archival footage and interviews to illustrate historical theses. This technique was employed increasingly during the 1980s as interest in the retrieval of certain 'hidden' histories became more widespread among independent documentary-makers.

Some of the films mentioned above also form part of the strand of labour-movement documentaries produced by independents. *The Bloodhouse* (Garry Lane, 1977), one of the earliest of these films, presents a critical history of Australia's largest company, BHP. This combative stance on behalf of workers was continued in *Know Your Friends, Know Your Enemies* (Peter Gray and Garry Lane, 1982), and in Tom Zubrycki's *cinéma vérité* films which document two major industrial confrontations, *Kemira: Diary of a Strike* (1984) and *Friends and Enemies* (1987). *Rocking the Foundations*, Pat Fiske's 1985 documentary about the role of a powerful Building Workers' Union in 'green banning' millions of dollars' worth of high-rise development in the early-to-mid 1970s, in defence of traditional inner-city workers' homes, is one of the most impressive labour-movement documentaries to have been produced thus far.

Documentaries treating environmental issues have been produced in modest quantities throughout the 1980s in relation to a series of particular preservation campaigns: *Give Trees a Chance* (Jenni Kendall, 1980), *A Voice for the Wilderness* (Christina Wilcox and Michael Balson,

Top: Pat Fiske's *Rocking the Foundations* (1985). Bottom: Fabio Cavadini and Mandy King's *We Come From the Land* (1988).

197

1983) and *We Come From the Land* (Fabio Cavadini and Mandy King, 1988). It is perhaps surprising that the heightened sense of global crisis in the late 1980s and early 1990s has not yet created a spate of new environmental films. Possibly the rapid appropriation of these issues by television has acted as a disincentive.

Another area where Australian independent documentary has given ground to television is that of the investigative documentary, where the resources and time required to research political cover-ups or corruption are obviously difficult for non-institutional film-makers to come by.

In 1983, Helen Grace made *Serious Undertakings*, a deftly abstract film about politics and the production of history, sexual difference and national identity. It was unlike any other documentary that had been produced in Australia and it made a profound impact on local film practice. Its influence can be felt in most of the experimental, essay-form documentaries that followed it: *Camera Natura* (Ross Gibson, 1985), *Landslides* (Sarah Gibson and Susan Lambert, 1986), *All That is Solid* (John Hughes, 1988) and *Universal Provider* (Mark Jackson and Mark Stiles, 1988). In many ways, it is in the area of 'experimental documentary' that Australian independents have created their most interesting work. Short films such as *Maximum Security* (Mark Stiles and the Prisoners' Action Group, 1978), *Behind Closed Doors* (Sarah Gibson and Susan Lambert, 1980) and *Making Biscuit* (Sharon Laura, 1987) use highly stylised imagery, together with 'documentary' soundtracks, to imaginatively deliver information about sensory deprivation in prison, domestic violence and factory labour.

A substantial strand of personal and contemplative documentary can also be identified within Australian independent documentary-making. Peter Tammer (*Journey to the End of the Night*, 1982), Brian McKenzie, (*The Last Day's Work*, 1986; *Kelvin and His Friends,* 1987) and David Perry (*Love and Work*, 1986) occupy this terrain. But possibly the most powerful work in this mode has been produced by long-time film experimentalists Arthur and Corinne Cantrill with *In This Life's Body* (1984), a deceptively simple account of Corinne's life and work, told almost entirely through assembled photographs, but with a cumulative impact that is quite overwhelming.

Among some younger independent documentary-makers, there is a strong tendency towards experimentation and playfulness with the documentary form. There is Maria Stratford's *Samba to Slow Fox* (1986), which gently and hilariously dissects the odd world of competitive ballroom dancing, and David Caesar's series of offbeat documentaries—*Shoppingtown* (1987), *Living Room* (1988) and *Bodywork* (1989)—the last being a ghoulishly funny documentary about people employed in the death business.

Among this group of irreverent new Australian documentaries, Mark Lewis' *Cane Toads: An Unnatural History* is notable for the outstanding commercial success it achieved during 1988–89. Made by an independent film-maker working on contract for the government production house, Film Australia, *Cane Toads* stands at a crossroads where the historical and structural boundaries between government-produced documentary, independent documentary and mainstream television documentary begin to blur.

In emulation of *bufo marinus*, its irrepressible amphibian subject, *Cane Toads* leaps beyond the conventions of documentary form, invading a stylistic terrain normally considered the preserve of fictional narrative cinema. Its use of subjective camera, dramatic music and a strategic mix of humour and horror transforms a standard wildlife documentary into exciting cinematic entertainment.

In the extent of its extraordinary success and its stylistic transgressions, *Cane Toads* stands as a unique phenomenon among contemporary Australian documentaries. But it is nevertheless possible to discern in the production and marketing strategies, which created both the film and its audiences, several elements which are common to a new stream of Australian documentaries: a deliberate blurring of the traditional factual/fictional divide; the use of highly stylised cinematography to enhance dramatic, entertainment or information effects; and a dominant orientation to television as the most effective medium for presentation of documentary.

Notes

1   Albert Moran, 'Nation building: the post-war documentary in Australia', in *Continuum: An Australian Journal of the Media*, vol. 1, no. 1, 1987, pp. 57–79.
2   Moran, op. cit., pp. 59–62.
3   Moran, op. cit., pp. 67–70.
4   Michael Leigh. 'Curiouser and curiouser', in *Back of Beyond: Discovering Australian Film and Television*, ed., Scott Murray, Australian Film Commission, Sydney, 1988, p. 84.
5   Graham Shirley in this volume, chapter 2.
6   Chris Long in *The Documentary Film In Australia*, eds Ross Lansell and Peter Beilby, Cinema Papers in association with Film Victoria, Melbourne, 1982, pp. 24, 25.
7   Chris Long, Ken Berryman in *Filmnews*, February 1990, pp. 8, 9; Andrew Pike & Ross Cooper, *Australian Film 1900–1977*, Oxford University Press, in association with the Australian Film Institute, Melbourne, 1980, p. 240.
8   Definition provided in full to this author by Film Australia historian Judy Adamson.
9   Ross Lansell, Kim Dalton in *The Documentary Film in Australia*, op. cit., pp. 43, 128.

Mark Lewis' *Cane Toads: An Unnatural History* (1988).

Belinda Chayko's *Swimming* (1990).

7
The short film

Adrian Martin

Swimming (Belinda Chayko, 1990) is one of the most striking of recent short Australian films. Existing on 16 mm, it is comprised mainly of small scenes of domestic life shot on video, as if by one of the characters in the fiction. These scenes are assembled in a deliberately fragmented, elliptical way, punctuated by violent 'glitch' edits and finally coming to seem like the ambiguous 'testament' or audiovisual document assembled by a young girl who has uncovered a terrible truth about her own family. The only interruption to the video imagery is provided by something else which is not, in the first place, 16mm footage—Super 8 shots mocked up as the 'home movie' format of an earlier historical moment.

The film is only eleven minutes long. By conventional narrative standards, it is not all that easy to follow. It is built up through inference, 'a web of visual cues'[1] and clues, slowly accumulating its sense through a kind of indirect narration. Things are not as laboriously spelt out for the spectator as in so many Australian film narratives (short or long) but rather is suggested, in a 'pointillistic' fashion. The title is a sombre pun which does double duty, referring not only to a mysterious death, but also the 'swimming' or drifting of sense in the work itself, quietly offering a meaning which seems to circle the film or hover just above it, a meaning which might evaporate if one froze the projector and interrogated the film for specifics at any given frame. Chayko remarks, tellingly, that 'it's a film about feeling, not about knowing'[2].

There is another sense in which this film 'swims': in its very ambiguity as a material, so-called 'filmic' object, given the nature of its images; that is, *Swimming* is clearly not a video, but can we say, with the same old certainty, that it is a film? The reason the film uses video to generate its material is of course not at all mysterious. In the line of those important mainstream films that have incorporated extensive use of video for key sequences— such as *The King of Comedy* (Martin Scorsese, 1983), *Prince of Darkness* (John Carpenter, 1987) and *Shocker* (Wes Craven, 1990)—*Swimming* grounds its video images in a diegetic motivation; they belong to the fiction. Yet it takes the 'disturbance' of video's eruption into the heart of a film—so palpable an unease in Scorsese's masterpiece—a little further still, by creating a film which is almost *all* video, completely invaded as it were by this 'other' medium, somewhat brutal and artless even in comparison to the inadvertent poetry of old Super 8

footage (which carries a poignant, expressive effect here as in many a Paul Cox feature).

But is it really a matter any more, in the 1990s, of one medium 'threatening', invading, incorporating another? Are there still the same rigid boundaries around the various media allowing such reveries of alien 'otherness'? For today, on the unstoppable capitalist terrains of technological production and market distribution, it seems that everything, ineluctably, is swimming—and that no medium or channel for expression is necessarily drowning. This swimming or drifting is having enormous effects on all sectors of film culture at once: on the relations between film and video, and between all the gauges of film itself (Super 8, 16, 35, 70mm); on the hitherto sacrosanct division between the short and the long film; and on the aesthetics of mainstream cinema vis-a-vis experimental art.

Consequently, a new strategy for surveying the short film in Australia is required of a critic who is at all sensitive to what's in the air. The old strategy—which has given Australian film culture its distinctive character for about 25 years—was openly polemical and territorial. One staked out one's ground with a claim to the strategic primacy, and the exotic specificity, of Super 8, or video art, or experimental film, or whatever, and then one railed against those other territories unfairly favoured through the cultural networks of subsidy, promotion and criticism. Some tensions are still very much in play—there will always be a 'mainstream' and its 'margin'—but much of the ground defining the old battles, or at least the terms in which they could be posed, is now fast turning into quicksand.

Swimming, although at this point in time a unique and exceptional film, is one that points towards a possible future, in all the dimensions that will be here discussed. Technologically, it marks the increasing intermingling, within any one work, of film (in its various gauges) and video, and of low tech with high tech. In the way it tells its story, it hints at a new kind of 'fast fiction' which may be increasingly understood and indeed demanded by a mass audience brought up on the audiovisual forms developed on television. And last, it is tempting to welcome the film as a kind of breakthrough for experimentation in a training institution—the Australian Film Television & Radio School (AFTRS)—characterised essentially by an aesthetic conservatism, a tendency to narrow creative options so as to better fit into the mainstream of the media industries.

Where are we swimming to? Before the utopian reverie, it might be helpful to review some of the constraints that have so far held the Australian short film in a fairly fixed place.

'No More Boring Shorts!'

Some years ago, the film-goers of Australia were regaled, at their favourite mainstream theatres, with a campaign announcing 'No More Boring Shorts!' The sorry result of this activism within the film exhibition sector was basically the removal of *all* shorts—not just the 'boring'

Laurie McInnes' *Palisade* (1987).

ones (meaning the sponsored documentaries on industry or wildlife that were provided as free fodder to exhibitors). It became virtually impossible, at that moment, to ever imagine seeing an interesting, challenging short film up against a 'big' film before a large, unprepared, unpredictable audience.

As in many other countries, the short film in Australia has had, for the most part, a marginal status, withheld from a general public trained only to be impatient or dismissive towards it. For a long time, government-sponsored television channels (such as the Australian Broadcasting Corporation) had the same 'filler' or 'fodder' approach to the use of short material as did the major cinema chains. Only in the past few years has a concerted push behind 'independent film' secured it an intermittent presence in certain 'specialised' slots on tele-

vision (such as the music video-oriented programme *Eat Carpet* on the multicultural channel SBS or, a few years back, the *First Take* series on the ABC), or as the entrée offering before the feature at certified art-house cinemas. One notes, however, that occasional, well-publicised programmes that are wholly comprised of a diversity of shorts—the annual graduate screenings of student work from the Swinburne Film and Television School in Melbourne, or a programme of women's films with a lot of awards behind it—are increasingly able to draw in large audiences.

Despite this welcome improvement in its cultural status, short film (and video) is in many regards still very limited and straitjacketed. Independent film is often a very constrictive category, taking in mainly only a certain 'well-made' form of comedy, drama or documentary, usually

Jane Campion's *A Girl's Own Story* (1983).

on 16mm. Content (a good 'subject' or topical social issue) tends to take precedence over any consideration of or exploration into film form, thus ruling out many kinds of experimental or radical art. Sure, some room is made for the occasional 'stylish' work that exploits to the hilt the once-off novelty of an innovative technique (like pixillation in the Cannes Palme d'Or winner *Palisade*, Laurie McInnes, 1987), or the brazenly 'eccentric', poetic vision of a Jane Campion (whose shorts are relatively well known outside Australia).

Ultimately, however, so-called independent film does not depart from a comfortable, well-contained circle of 'art cinema' possibilities. And what occurs within this circle always genuflects, in the last instance, to the 'norms' of narrative–representational–industrial (i.e., mainstream) cinema.

Short film is cast as a kind of 'playground' where people try things out, jazz things up a bit, experiment just a little, all in order to learn how to make films 'right', or at least manage them within a rather stable economy of form and content elements. It is still tacitly assumed by many, even those active within the sphere of independent film, that 'real' film-making is achieved and found only at feature-length level, and that the short film is, at best, a 'ladder up' to, a mere training ground for, working in features. Is it any wonder we might assume this, when virtually every major film festival, every popular and specialist publication, every historical textbook and every scrap of media promotion centres obsessively and unquestioningly on the feature film as the very definition of cinema itself?

Guerrilleros in the mist

An outsider to Australian film culture would probably not perceive straight away the radical extent of the separation between mainstream and self-professedly 'marginal' activity. Naturally, not all talented Australian film-makers 'come up' through one or other of the film schools to the feature industry. Indeed, at least in some quarters, it has functioned as a badge of authenticity *not* to be linked to institutions such as these.

Truly independent film-making in Australia has two essential, identifiable periods. The first belongs to the 1970s, the period of the film-makers' co-operatives, one in Sydney and another (not lasting as long) in Melbourne,

Jan Cornall and Mystery Carnage in Susan Lambert's *On Guard* (1983).

with a network of 'media resource'/workshop outfits in some of the other states. This was a diverse time, reflecting at one extreme an engagement with leftist/feminist political film-making, particularly documentary, and at the other an experimental practice that took its inspiration variously from romantic avant-garde traditions (Stan Brakhage, Gregory Markopoulos) and formalist/structuralist ones (Hollis Frampton, Peter Gidal). Many of the film-makers associated with the co-op scene have of course continued producing work past the 1970s: in the more agitprop camp, John Hughes (*All That is Solid*, 1988) and Susan Lambert and Sarah Gibson (*Behind Closed Doors*, 1980); in the more experimental camp, Arthur and Corinne Cantrill (*The Second Journey (To Uluru)*, 1981) and Michael Lee (*A Contemplation of the Cross*, 1989). With rare exceptions, most of the work of all the film-makers related to the co-ops had been on 16mm.

As the 1980s proceeded, many of these film-makers came around to exploring modes they were not in the first place associated with, and often with pleasing, startling results. Lambert made a feminist, action short-feature *(On Guard*, 1983) and later (with Gibson) the subjective, avant-garde exploration *Landslides* (1986) under the aegis of a Documentary Fellowship[3]; the

Cantrills made a detour from their highly formalist landscape studies and abstractions into autobiography with *In This Life's Body* (1984). And although some of the co-op figures did indeed eventually strike out with narrative features (such as Albie Thoms' *Palm Beach*, 1980; Monique Schwarz' *Pieta*, tele-feature, 1987; and Nigel Buesst's *Compo*, unreleased, 1989), this could never be construed as a wholesale 'career move'. For every mainstream film-maker such as Phillip Noyce *(Backroads*, 1977; *Heatwave*, 1982; *Dead Calm*, 1989), who is eulogised as having 'cut his teeth' on freewheeling co-op shorts on his way to becoming a big boy in the industry, there are a dozen others who have more or less made their permanent home in the independent scene, patching a life together through an unsteady combination of teaching, cultural work, grants for short film-making and the occasional crack at a more ambitious project.

The 1980s post-punk cultural milieu (in music, fashion, design, comics) gave rise to another kind of film 'scene' destined to slug it out with the former co-op movement: the Super 8 'new wave'. Rejecting political statement and art-world aestheticism alike, Super 8 film-makers of the early 1980s such as Mark Titmarsh, Jayne Stevenson and Paul Fletcher (like their counterparts in

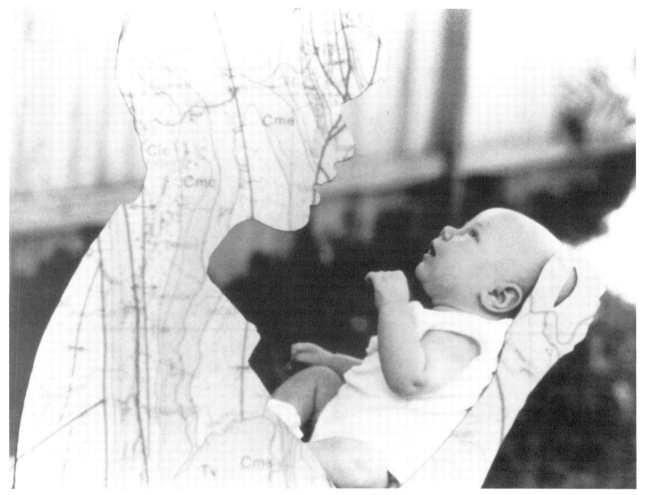

Susan Lambert and Sarah Gibson's *Landslides* (1986).

Europe and the US) made 'domestic', ephemeral, often quite raw short Super 8 films, and were championed by those film-makers who were the new exponents of a particularly aggressive 'pop' theory. A subsequent wave of Super 8 artists in the mid-1980s (including Chris Windmill, Anne-Marie Crawford [now Marie Craven] and Andrew Frost) developed a more refined aesthetic approach to the medium, but it never lost its 'underground' glamour of being 'easier' than 16mm, and proudly far away from the 35mm mainstream.

Nearing the end of the 1980s, there arose even further factional disputes, and separate new 'scenes' of cultural activity. Those involved with *video art* banded together to form the Australian Video Festival in Sydney, and asserted that the medium's 'specificity' had been de-

valued in relation to celluloid of whatever size. Another group in Melbourne formed the Modern Image Makers Association (MIMA), trying to keep strictly *experimental* work (film or video) visible in a film culture that was mainly honouring the safe 'middle ground' of independent production (documentaries and short narratives, many from the film schools).

Hitting the 1990s, however, all these *guerrilleros* of the short work found themselves in a mist. Despite all the rhetoric, and all the moves to preserve this 'species' or that of the short film/video, things started mutating all around. Under the influence of 'computer art', and new forms of image generation, former 'video artists' now declared themselves explorers of the 'time-based' or 'electronic media' arts, a heady mix of all the new

Corinne and Arthur Cantrill's *In This Life's Body* (1984).

technologies of film, video, sound, installation and performance. In the official organ of the Melbourne Super 8 Group, fans list (without explanation) such 16mm films as Frank Lovece's *Te Possino Ammazza* (1987) and Bill Mousoulis' *Between Us* (1989) among their favourite Super 8 works, presumably because they evidence the same lyric rawness or narrative minimalism once identified as the most sought-after 'Super 8 effects'. And everywhere, in the projects of particular artists, the gauges and media are being mixed up, relayed from production to post-production to form different 'machines' (as Deleuze and Guattari would say): Virginia Hilyard's *E. G.* (1990), blown up from Super 8 to 35mm via a special video process; and the compilation *Personal Ads* (1989), bringing diverse fragments of Super 8, 16mm and video to rest on a tape for late-night television broadcasting.

206

The Gentle Revolution

These developments are synchronous with signs in other countries, many of which show a surprising leapfrog of 1970s-style, independent 16mm practitioners right into the 1990s: in Britain, former 'structuralist–materialist' film-maker Malcolm Le Grice is now working with computer animation, while in the US maverick independent Jon Jost predicts that the form most amenable to the 'artist-outsider' will soon be

a combination of video/computer synthesis, done on home-level equipment such as the Super VHS, Beta ED, or video 8 formats interfaced with Amiga or Atari or the new generation Macintosh computers for graphics and music. These tools, utilized with the same iconoclastic mind-set that distinguishes the real independent, offer the same aesthetic elasticity and room for creative cost cutting that formerly made 16mm film such an advantageous format.[4]

Naturally, we are talking of much more here than mere technological adaptation. Even in the biggest mainstream releases, there are glimpses of an aesthetic mutation taking place with the increasing interface of film and video. In *I Love You to Death* (Lawrence Kasdan, 1990), an insert of a pizza which has been naturalistically thrown into the air in the previous shot shows a shot-on-video pizza matted into the 35mm frame; in *She-Devil* (Susan Seidelman, 1989), the heroine walks away from her exploding house, which is a back-projected video image. We are already far from Coppola's obvious and deliberately 'artificial' laboratory experiments incorporating video into film (*One From the Heart*, 1982). Today, it is not that the average moviegoer exactly either notices, or doesn't notice, these new moments of film-video mutation; he or she simply accepts unconsciously that the conventions of the screen have now been elasticised, incorporating video into the 'natural' plasticity and unreality of the image just as, once upon a time, colour or widescreen formats were incorporated. The same 'gentle revolution' (as Michel Chion calls it[5]) is happening with sound technology. After Dolby, 'surround sound' and Spectral recording, cinema soundtracks are starting to absorb the 'hyper-realistic' experiments in 'sampling' and computer treatments carried out in contemporary recorded music.

New technology brings its own cutthroat, exclusionary mechanism: the professional insistence on only 'high tech', and the restriction of access to this tech to already certified 'professionals'. Independent, short film/video (as Jost indicates) is still the place where 'low' and 'high' technology can be mixed up with impunity—that is, today, its 'edge', its reserve of strangeness and rawness. The mid-1980s genre of 'scratch' video, for instance, has developed anew with the capacity to create extremely sophisticated montages of 'found' images and sounds from television, video, records and tapes along with computer graphic input, all on affordable domestic equipment; see, for example, the tapes of Ross Harley (*Futuropolis Now*, 1990) and Peter Callas (*Neo Geo: An American Purchase*, 1990).

What is at stake in the increasing mutability of gauges and formats that is overtaking our audiovisual culture? Perhaps this: a gradual changeover in orientation from *theatrical* materials—writing scripts, building up characters with actors, constructing sets—to purely *sampled* ones, digitalised and recombined from a vast cultural audiovisual 'archive'. Already, 'animatronic' spectaculars such as *Who Framed Roger Rabbit* (Robert Zemeckis, 1988), *Beetlejuice* (Tim Burton, 1988) and *Gremlins 2* (Joe Dante, 1990) give us glimpses of what a 'synthetic' work of this sort might look, move and feel like. Commercial television, too, seems to be 'producing' less and less new images, while resifting and re-formatting its own archive ever more feverishly. Given this drift, it is possible that the students with the best artistic intuitions for tomorrow are those trained not 'theatrically' (as in the major film schools) but principally in the video editing suite, as can be witnessed in all the small colleges and art schools around Australia where students furiously 'treat' found material and fashion elaborate montages.

Fast Fiction

It has always been the case that short innovative work has 'pioneered' certain aesthetic explorations later appropriated (and sometimes 'cleaned up') by mainstream cinema, television advertising and music video. However, there is a special sense in which the short film/video is today directly signposting the possible future of our Western audiovisual culture, a future in which, perhaps, short works will no longer be regarded as (at best) 'sketches' for 'real' works, but consumed at large as full, complete and satisfying. More and more film-makers, whatever their position in the industry, are probably pondering the almost unthinkable question: Is the era of the feature film about to enter its death throes? In an advanced television age—in which even slow, stuffy old literature starts to occasionally package itself as 'fast fiction' for instant consumption—'movies' as we have known them are starting to take on (for some) the quaintness of relics from a bygone time: overlong, over-explanatory, too slow in getting from one high-point to the next.

Recently, two Australian film-makers (Philip Brophy and Aleksi Vellis) have stated in public their belief that 'real films'—feature films for mass consumption—are about to contract dramatically in their average running time from 90 to 120 minutes down to perhaps 40 to 50.[6] Their own films support this prediction in a vivid way. Brophy's 47-minute *Salt, Saliva, Sperm and Sweat* (1988) and Vellis' 75-minute *Nirvana Street Murder* (1991) are kinetic and spectacular, cramming virtually every screen moment with some striking event. They 'feel' like features to most viewers; indeed, the former ran for a season without anyone complaining at the box office that he/she had been cheated out of a 'real' film with a 'normal' running time. And although popular screenwriting manuals still preach the necessity of not placing undue narrative demands on an average audience—not overloading them with 'information'—we may well be approaching a widespread aesthetic of extraordinary narrative streamlining and condensation. There are early signs of this in other countries also: the move of American independent Mark Rappaport from 16 mm to video for *Postcards* (1990) has, for instance, drawn this remark from critic Jonathan Rosenbaum: 'video enriches his palette; the tape is only half an hour, but has the density of a feature'.[7]

This reverie is no doubt a little premature; it is unlikely we will see the sequel to a blockbuster like *Dick Tracy* (Warren Beatty, 1990) in a year or so shot on high-tech video and running for 45 minutes. Yet, as lovers of adventurous short film and video already well know, the experience of art (narrative or otherwise) is only artificially defined and constricted by convention's endless

The Man (Phillip Dean) plays with The Boy (Nicholas Hanigan) in Philip Brophy's *Salt, Saliva, Sperm and Sweat* (1988).

repetition. Ultimately, there is no good reason why popular films must be shot and preserved on celluloid, and run for set amounts of time. These may still be determinate material conditions on cultural production today, but time, money and technology are busy undoing them. All that really matters, for narrative as for spectacle, is that the viewer is made to experience a suitably aesthetic *form* (a variegated shape, a dynamic structure) and a *volume* (or 'density') of detail. Who knows more, for today and for tomorrow, about audiovisual form and volume than the practising explorers of short film and video?

As Australian film culture enters the 1990s, there is suddenly a great deal of renewed militancy around the 'cause' of the short film/video. New forms of distribution and exhibition for shorts are being explored—particularly the possibilities offered by the 'home video' market, which may well be more attune to the increased 'speeds' and emerging manners of post-modern audiovisual consump-

tion than either commercial or 'art' cinema operations. New festivals and events based almost solely around short works are springing up, such as MIMA's 'Experimenta' and the Sydney Super 8 Film Group's 'Matinaze', adding to the already existing Super 8 and video festivals. Just as significantly, current practices of film journalism, theory and criticism are coming under severe scrutiny for the ways in which they either summarily pigeonhole or completely ignore short work—an indictment of several generations of commentators who are unwilling and unable to 'engage in any critical way with work which moves beyond familiar forms and boundaries' (Jodi Brooks).[8]

More than ever, all the boundaries which once fenced off and regulated the flows of our audiovisual culture are in question. The time is fast disappearing when a 'short' —and already that word is starting to become inadequate, obsolete—meant a quaint little novelty item: a harmless animation, a quirky documentary, a flashy

Tracey Moffatt's *Night Cries: A Rural Tragedy* (1990).

dramatic or comic vignette. Whether we like it or not, we are swimming towards a future in which the short film/video will not be regarded as a 'miniature', a sketch or an anecdote, but something more akin to a *crystal*: an object with multiple surfaces and depths, creating resonances for a viewer and complexities of reading that extend far beyond the work's apparent 'size'. Those aficionados of the short form who already know and love works such as *Night Cries: A Rural Tragedy* (Tracey Moffatt, 1990), *Tales From Vienna Hoods* (Marcus Bergner, 1989) and *Viva* (Mark Titmarsh and Stephen Harrop, 1989) already have a fair idea of what this sparkling, crystalline future will be like.

Notes

1 Michael Hutak, 'Gems unseen', *Filmnews*, June 1990, p. 20.
2 Quoted in Philippa Hawker, 'Lifeworks in focus', *The Sunday Herald*, 22 July 90, p. 27.

3 The Documentary Fellowship scheme was one set up by the Australian Film Commission to allow the production of innovative documentaries made over a comparatively lengthy period without the necessity for an initial, scripted, pre-planned treatment of a subject. *All that Is Solid* was also made under this scheme.
4 Jon Jost, 'End of the Indies', *Film Comment*, January–February 1989, p. 45.
5 cf. Michel Chion, *La Toile Trouée*, Cahiers du cinéma, Paris, 1988.
6 Brophy discusses this in the interview 'Fantastic voyage', conducted by Tom Ryan, *Cinema Papers*, no. 71, January 1989. Vellis made his statement on the stage of the Melbourne Film Festival, 1990.
7 Jonathan Rosenbaum, 'Rotterdam: new director, old traditions', *Sight and Sound*, Spring 1990, p. 77.
8 Jodi Brooks, letter to editor, *Filmnews*, August 1990, p. 2.

Beer at night: Bob (Carl Stever) and Kevin (Paul Couzens). Michael Thornhill's *The FJ Holden* (1977).

8
Australia and the Australians

Debi Enker

I love a sunburnt country,
    A land of sweeping plains,
Of ragged mountain ranges,
    Of droughts and flooding rains,
I love her far horizons,
    I love her jewel sea,
Her beauty and her terror—
    The wide brown land for me!

'My Country', Dorothea Mackellar

Once, the image of Australia immortalised by the second stanza of Dorothea Mackellar's famous poem neatly summarised one view of this country and encapsulated its image abroad. Australia was perceived exclusively as a place of vast, open spaces, burnt brown by the relentless sun and characterised by a striking landscape rather than a culture.

From the other side of the planet, this immense continent seemed a remote British penal colony, sparsely populated by Anglo-Saxon-Celtic white settlers and dominated by its distinctive topography and exotic native wildlife. Those who imagined cities at all perceived them to be primitive places, overrun by kangaroos and home to tanned, beefy men who spent their days doing hard, physical work and their nights throwing cold beers down thirsty throats. Australia came to represent a final frontier for white settlement, an inhospitable, if visually impressive, no-man's land where reluctant pioneers carved out rudimentary existences at their peril.

In the past decade, one extensively reported local product has done much to alter that image. Successful and widely seen Australian soap operas—such as *Neighbours, Home and Away, A Country Practice* and *The Flying Doctors*—have created another image of the life in and nature of Australia. Without exception, the contemporary soap operas depict Australia as a white, middle-class, suburban society where characters live comfortably and casually in close-knit and supportive communities. This sunny, fictional Australia is a place of climatic and social warmth, and, to coin a popular phrase, an example of 'the lucky country'. There is no poverty and nearly everyone has a steady job, often in a respectable profession. People own their own houses, which are surrounded by neat, well-tended gardens and sit on orderly streets. It seems a steady, uniform and stable environment, a place where problems are transient and generally resolvable.

When the soap operas delve beneath these surfaces to reveal the dramas of everyday life, what they expose, despite themselves, is stability. In this television world, problems are rarely persistent and very rarely political. Characters are preoccupied with personal traumas: troubled marriages or romances, teenage frustrations, family conflicts, illnesses, accidents. It is an insulated white world, impervious to social, political or economic extremes: no poverty, no racial tensions, no natural disasters, no climatic extremes, no political upheavals. There is uniformity and equanimity, and, though these fictional communities are besieged by local problems, they remain essentially stable and supportive.

This television image of Australia, like the celebration of the wide brown land in Dorothea Mackellar's poem, is challenged and undermined by the Australian cinema. Less constrained by the imperative of soap opera to appeal to the broadest possible audience, Australian feature films reflect a more diverse, and often disturbing, image of 'the lucky country'. As a group, Australia's film-makers have probed the darker depths eschewed by the soap operas, though their inspiration, at least in one area, is comparable.

The suburban lifestyle that preoccupies television producers has also held its fascination for film-makers. This is hardly surprising as the vast majority of Australians live in cities, on the periphery of the vast, hot, open spaces that once characterised the entire country. The cinema's depiction of life in the city, or, more specifically, its sprawling suburbs, challenges the notion of a safe, supportive, nurturing haven insulated from major upheavals. Often, these communities are depicted not as close-knit but as utterly repressive bastions of intolerance, enclaves that eye outsiders with suspicion and demand conformity from their residents.

Suburban life in the Australian cinema is only rarely an existence in a rich emotional heartland. The predominant image is of a soulless brick wasteland, where characters are estranged from each other and the emotional coldness is chilling. Set in Sydney's western suburbs, traditionally a home of the working class, *The FJ Holden* (Michael Thornhill, 1977) presents the suburbs as a cultural and spiritual desert. It is a place where regular bouts with the bottle are the only antidote for lives without hope or direction.

Characters work in dispiriting, demeaning jobs and spend their leisure time at the local pub or the shopping mall. The environment offers no other possibilities for social activity. The young adults who are the focus of the film seem hollow, clearly unsatisfied yet oddly inert. They play out their ritualised mating games like passionless robots: men drunkenly initiate and women obediently comply. There is no visceral connection between the characters: they barely talk and, when they have sex, it is primitive and almost mechanical. Victims of their own reduced expectations of life's possibilities, they play out an empty imitation of life, numbed by alcohol and doomed to exist in an emotional wasteland.

Estranging city life: top left: Rob (Bryan Brown) and Lou (Judy Davis) in John Duigan's *Winter of Our Dreams* (1981); top right: Noni Hazlehurst (Fran), with Cynthia (Rosie Logie) and Tom (Travis Ward) in Glenda Hambly's *Fran* (1985); bottom left: Jeanie (Sonia Peat) and Carrie (Kim Krejus) in John Duigan's *Mouth to Mouth* (1978); bottom right: Colin Turner (Chris Haywood) and Lorraine Turner (Jennifer Cluff) in Bill Bennett's *A Street to Die* (1985).

Many other depictions of city life are similarly despairing. In two different films, set in different cities, John Duigan creates coldly inhospitable environments that alienate characters afflicted by lives of quiet desperation. From the homeless, disenfranchised Melbourne teenagers of *Mouth to Mouth* (1978) to the economically secure, middle-class couple in Sydney of *Winter of Our Dreams* (1981), society is depicted as an overwhelmingly oppressive opponent that eventually quashes the spirit or drives characters to desperation.

The sense of estrangement permeates films as disparate as *Fran* (Glenda Hambly, 1985), where a single mother in Perth struggles angrily for her survival, and *Sweetie* (Jane Campion, 1989), where a troubled family of virtual strangers individually, and unsuccessfully, make desperate bids at fulfilment, unable to help themselves or each other. In Bill Bennett's *A Street to Die* (1985), a community of Vietnam veterans lives in virtually identical houses on the neat streets common to the television soap operas, places where barbecues in the backyard are common, the sun seems to shine all the time and family holidays are taken at nearby beaches. But this is, quite literally, a sick community where the veterans, poisoned by their exposure to deadly defoliating chemicals sprayed during the war, are slowly dying. Though some degree of physical or psychological pain is apparent in each home, the families remain separate, divided, rather than united, in their common grief.

In Ann Turner's *Celia* (1989), the leafy streets of Melbourne are home to another community that is emotionally cold in spite of the ever-present sunshine. This is a community that reacts to new ideas with alarm and actively stifles dissenting voices, with disastrous consequences that are apparent long before the final, cathartic events. Here, as in many Australian films, the sexes are separated, except in childhood. Husbands and fathers habitually elect to spend their free time drinking at the pub with their mates while wives tend house and care for children. Newcomers are tentatively welcomed, until they demonstrate beliefs that conflict with those held by the residents. Then, they are shunned as a threat to stability.

In these films, the suburbs function as an emotional straitjacket, strangling any spirit of independence. Nonconformity is tantamount to breaking the law and is certainly seen to contravene the unspoken customs of the community. The suburbs virtually assume the sinister character of the repressive educational institutions depicted in *The Devil's Playground* (Fred Schepisi, 1976), *The Getting of Wisdom* (Bruce Beresford, 1977) and even in Peter Weir's American-made *Dead Poets Society* (1989). They are places that separate the sexes, actively stifle the spirit and exact a debilitating toll on those who challenge the prevailing order.

One of the very few films that evokes a suburban environment that people might actually aspire to live in is Ray Argall's *Return Home* (1990). Argall's affectionate and distinctively gentle depiction of an Adelaide family reveals an exquisite richness beneath the surfaces of everyday activity. Here, a slightly run-down and wholly unexceptional suburban home and an outdated garage

are transformed into wellsprings of regeneration. One lost son returns to his roots here in order to reassess his past and find the direction for his future. Another finds fulfilment by digging in, his inner strength consolidated by his family and the business that he refuses to surrender to changes that purport to be progress. Though there is frustration and conflict, the bonds of family offer a powerful support system and the individual, even if destined to stray, can ultimately find both a nurturing place to belong and a sense of emotional satisfaction. Battles for independence, both personal and professional, can be fought and won, and these battles make characters, their families and communities stronger and closer. Here, individuals can retain their inherent differences and still fit in. Yet *Return Home*, in both its celebration of suburban life and its representation of a community that accepts variations in human nature, is something of an exception, for the repression of the human spirit is a recurrent theme of Australian cinema. Though protagonists sometimes survive these pressures, even triumph over them, the compulsion to conform is clearly and consistently delineated, even in films as stylistically and narratively divergent as *Shame* (Steve Jodrell, 1988), *My Brilliant Career* (Gill Armstrong, 1979) and *2 Friends* (Jane Campion, tele-feature, 1986).

In purely geographic terms, the small towns and settlements of the outback seem far removed from these suburban centres. Yet there are striking similarities in the film-makers' perceptions of how these remote and isolated communities function. The social conventions and the implicit values travel from city to country with ease. Ted Kotcheff's *"Wake in Fright"* (1971) and Ken Hannam's *Sunday Too Far Away* (1975) present comparable accounts of aggressive, predominantly masculine societies. The uniquely Australian concept of mateship—highly cherished and exclusively male camaraderie—pervades all interaction, actively and robustly discouraging those who would be different. Here, a man who refuses to share a drink at the pub with his mates, or even his new-found acquaintances, is the object of ridicule; a man who doesn't drink beer at all is a social leper; a man devoted to his wife is a man to be mocked. Disagreements are automatically resolved by fists: the stronger fighter is the winner; might is right.

The pub once again serves as the focal point of community life, not a café or a corner store or a church but a place where men meet to relax and drown their sorrows together, separate from women. The women exist to serve, literally from behind the bar or sexually in relationships that are limited and come nowhere near the intensity of the emotional bonds shared by the men. The social and emotional separation of men and women, most clearly defined by the segregation of the pub, is a subject that permeates Australian films. In social situations, men and women are seen to gravitate to the security of their own sex.

There is a bond established between male characters that precludes women, or at least demotes them to a defined and secondary status. They can be servants or sexual partners, compliant wives or caring mothers, they

Cathartic events: Celia Carmichael (Rebecca Smart) in Ann Turner's *Celia* (1989).

A celebration of suburban life: Steve (Frankie J. Holden) and Judy (Micki Camilleri). Ray Argall's *Return Home* (1990).

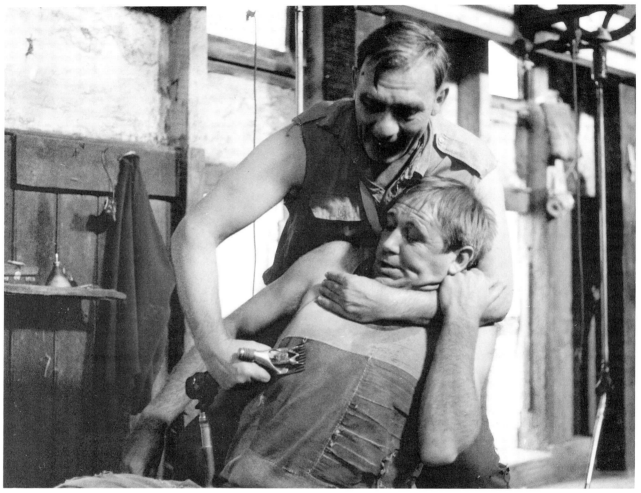

Masculine society: Tom West (Robert Bruning) and Basher (Jerry Thomas) in Ken Hannam's *Sunday Too Far Away* (1975).

may even pose a brief threat to male friendships, but, finally, they cannot join or penetrate the dominant male order, one that equally condemns the male characters to lives of emptiness. In the outback, as in the suburbs, there is a pervasive sense of hollow, ritualised behaviour, of conventions that can't be broken and of unfulfilling patterns of behaviour that are doomed to repetition.

The male characters exist in an oppressive cycle: hard physical work, hard drinking and hard gambling. They are seen as highly competitive: being the best fighter, fastest shearer, best shot with a gun or biggest drinker are prized titles. To be the most devoted father, most exciting lover, most respected intellectual or happiest husband is not a distinction to be coveted. Like the sub-urban communities, the outback settlements are seen as insular and limited, suspicious of outsiders and prone to putting newcomers through arduous initiation rites in

order to earn a place in the group. They are places that test and usually break the human spirit, condemning their inhabitants to lives of soulless conformity.

Because so many Australian films overtly or implicitly acknowledge the pressure to conform to the operative rules of community life, characters who refuse to abide by the conventions, or battle to break free of them, are often cast as heroes. Australians harbour a special affection for those who take up the good fight, whether they win or not. The willingness to meet life's challenges or injustices head-on, unflinchingly and with resolve, is so admired and deeply ingrained that the popular ver-nacular has coined a description to define the type: the Aussie battler. It is an expression firmly entrenched in the Australian vocabulary and an approach to life that is admired without reservation.

The combat undertaken by the Aussie battlers of

Females freeing social shackles: top left: Sybylla Melvyn (Judy Davis) in Gill Armstrong's *My Brilliant Career* (1979); top right: Caddie (Helen Morse) in Donald Crombie's *Caddie* (1976); bottom left: Teresa (Helen Buday) in Stephen Wallace's *For Love Alone* (1986); bottom right: Asta Cadell (Deborra-Lee Furness) in Steve Jodrell's *Shame* (1988).

the cinema covers a range of campaigns. Many struggle for honour and a 'fair go' (another common Australian expression). Some struggle for survival, some for emotional fulfilment and some battle the limitations and prejudices of the society. Generally, characters who wrestle to break free of social shackles are female as in *My Brilliant Career*, *Caddie* (Donald Crombie, 1976), *For Love Alone* (Stephen Wallace, 1986), *Shame* and the American-made *Mrs. Soffel* (Gillian Armstrong, 1984). But characters who refuse to acknowledge societal constraints at all are generally male.

The vast majority of Australian cinematic heroes, and certainly the definitive ones, are male. They are men who stand apart from the group, perhaps by virtue of their skills as horsemen or warriors, rarely by virtue of their prowess as lovers or their capacity as intellectuals. They are characters who live life instinctively, by their own codes of honour, whether or not these codes are common to the community that they inhabit.

The heroes of Australian cinema are cast from a mould fashioned by American Westerns. They are strong, silent types, men who prefer decisive action to words, stoics who rarely reveal their emotions, if ever. To look at the small group of prominent leading actors—Mel Gibson, Jack Thompson, Bryan Brown, Paul Hogan—is to get a clear picture of the type: physically strong, rugged, with chiselled features that suggest experience of the world, and a manner that warns 'Don't mess with me.' If they are seen to have humour, it is dry and cryptic. They are doers not talkers, fighters not lovers, individualists invariably admired by male characters who are less endowed. Australian films are implicitly suspicious of men who talk a lot and rarely present a male character who will discuss his feelings readily or with ease. Men need to be driven to crisis point to verbally air their thoughts, and alcohol, invariably beer, is seen as the tongue-loosener as well as a pain-killer. In what is perhaps a colonial distillation of Anglo-Saxon reserve, emotions are rarely discussed and frustrations are often revealed and resolved through violence, in an explosion of pain, as in *The Chant of Jimmie Blacksmith* (Fred Schepisi, 1978).

Characters who talk a lot, particularly male characters, are generally seen as weak, boastful, naive, untrustworthy or downright silly. Those who maintain a relatively silent composure with stoicism are tacitly admired. It is a notable contrast to the contemporary American cinema, for example, which relishes discussion of feelings, revelations of personal truths and self-analysis. Australian characters are uncomfortable with intimate talk, preferring decisive action to speak for them, much like the heroes of the Wild West.

Two of the Australian cinema's most popular heroes are the road warrior Max Rockatansky (Mel Gibson), of the Mad Max trilogy, and Mick 'Crocodile' Dundee (Paul Hogan). Max is an archetypal loner, a cowboy of the future. From the time his family is killed in *Mad Max* (George Miller, 1979), he is fated never to have a home and not even to belong to the makeshift communities of the post-apocalyptic world. He becomes a nomad, surviving on his wits and physical abilities. He can form a close, even dependent relationship with a child without becoming paternal. He meets his world on his own terms; confident of his skills without being arrogant, he is utterly self-reliant. He talks only when he must and then using only a few choice words.

While Max exists in an unmistakably action genre, and Mick Dundee in a primarily comedic one, Mick too is a decisive man of action, though one open to romance. The knife-wielding crocodile hunter embodies a range of positive traits and virtues cherished by Australian cinema and popular culture. Mick is calm and easygoing but he is also quick-witted. He might be unworldly but he is nobody's fool. He is fast and extremely capable with his fists when he needs to be, but he is also gentle and charming; he can drink anyone at his local pub under the table with ease.

Like Max, he is self-reliant, able to survive and thrive as easily in outback Australia as on the mean streets of Manhattan. He is a man of the working class, most comfortable with fellow workers but, when he is thrust into high society, he takes it in his stride, charming his associates with his lack of pretension. He is courteous and respectful, fiercely loyal to his friends and inspiring similar devotion from them. He has a sense of humour about life, never taking it too seriously yet never allowing its challenges to defeat him. Quick with a smile and confident without being proud, Mick is a prime example of all that Australian cinema cherishes in its heroes.

Though Mick finds true love with an American journalist, it has been quite sensibly argued that the 'Crocodile' Dundee films are as much about mateship as romance. Mick must fight to win the woman he loves—literally and extensively in *"Crocodile" Dundee II* (John Cornell, 1988)—but he values and relies upon the support system of his mates at the Walkabout Creek pub. The union of these two forces is neatly encapsulated in the final shot of *Crocodile Dundee*[1] (Peter Faiman, 1986), where Mick simultaneously embraces his love and clasps the hand of a nearby male in a triumphant assertion of the value of masculine teamwork.

The emphasis on male relationships and their centrality is no accident or aberration here. Stories of love and respect between men percolate through Australian cinema, which explores the bonds between men in a range of situations, from war to the workplace, and even through to the effect of male friendships on married life and heterosexual romance. It is interesting to note that even in a romantic comedy such as *Crocodile Dundee* male relationships remain crucial to the narrative.

Examining romantic relationships between men and women in Australian films is illuminating, if only as a guide to the film-makers' collective discomfort with heterosexual love stories and scepticism about the possibility for enduring passion. There is a striking absence of the grand passions that are intrinsic to, and characteristic of, French and American cinema.

The 'Crocodile' Dundee films are among the very few that allow their central couple a romantic happy ending. Yet in *"Crocodile" Dundee II*, where the relationship between Mick and Sue (Linda Kozlowski) has been well

Popular hero: Max (Mel Gibson) in George Miller and George Ogilvie's *Mad Max Beyond Thunderdome* (1985).

Popular hero II: Mick 'Crocodile' Dundee (Paul Hogan) in John Cornell's *"Crocodile" Dundee II* (1988).

established, Sue suggests that the relationship remains platonic. When a curious girlfriend questions Sue about Mick's prowess in bed, Sue responds that she too remains in the dark about Mick's talents as a lover because he is still sleeping (alone) on the floor. Perhaps she is just being sassy and evasive, protecting their privacy and guarding against public knowledge of their shared sexual bliss. Or perhaps—and it is equally plausible—this couple is still confined to the kissing stage, and sex, for an honourable man like Mick, could only follow marriage.

It is also possible that *"Crocodile" Dundee II* doesn't want to startle its target family audience with discussion or depiction of Mick and Sue's sex life. But whatever the reason, it is impossible to imagine a romantic liaison between consenting adults in European or American cinema that endures through two films and abstains from sex. Not even Superman was so restrained.

There is a popular Australian joke about men and sex that places both romance and mateship in a uniquely Australian context. It goes: Why do Australian men make lousy lovers? Because they are in a hurry to finish so that they can go to the pub and share details of the encounter with their mates. The underlying notion is that the value of the male friendship far outweighs the pleasure of the sexual experience, that men sharing a discussion of sex is at least as pleasurable as men and women doing it. Perhaps that is why Australian films have repeatedly examined bonds between men and shied away from love stories between men and women. Certainly there are very few films that depict a romantic relationship from the first flutter of attraction through to a blissfully happy ending for the couple. There is an entire cinematic vocabulary, now admittedly somewhat clichéd, that exists as shorthand for the existence of love, lust, passion, attraction, sensuality. There are eyes that meet across crowded rooms, couples dancing cheek to cheek, flirtations over candle-lit dinners. There are suitors who serenade their loved ones from beneath bedroom windows, lovers who send enough flowers to fill rooms, couples who walk hand in hand along beaches at sunset. There are tender moments where lovers share intimacy in a bathtub, and there are scenes of sexual pleasure and abandon in bedrooms.

One will rarely see such scenes in Australian films, not because film-makers are rejecting such clichés but because such relationships are rarely explored. Australian cinema seems sceptical about the capacity of love, and particularly passion, to endure. And even when it flickers for a while, it generally dies.

It is true that there are marriages that are depicted as unions of love and respect, where equal partners share lives of fulfilment. There are married couples who are seen as loving, sexually compatible and supportive, couples that regard the marriage vow of 'Till death do us part' as a fervent wish rather than a life sentence. These couples—in films such as *Return Home*, *A Street to Die*, *Malpractice* (tele-feature, Bill Bennett, 1989), *Dead Calm* (Phil Noyce, 1989) and *David Williamson's Emerald City* (Michael Jenkins, 1989)—draw strength from their union. They discuss their problems and share their fears. Certainly they experience trouble spots in their marriages, they face crises, conflict and obstacles that would drive lesser unions apart. But they ride out the rough patches together and, in spite of the tensions, the relationships endure. Their devotion is depicted within the framework of an under-lying solidity: only death can separate them.

These are, however, established relationships. These are couples that have had children and these are unions that have lasted long enough to establish a rhythm and balance. These are characters a long way beyond the longings and expectations of a first date.

Alas, when the Australian cinema depicts the early stages of love, that period when attraction is kindled and affairs are born, it is generally just the first stop on a journey that concludes with the demise of the relationship. There are very few lovers who walk hand in hand into the sunset at the end of a film and few films like *Crocodile Dundee* that end with a lovers' embrace.

Though the conclusions are often similar, the circumstances that drive lovers apart are varied. A married character who embarks on an extra-marital affair, as in

Extramarital affairs: top: Julian (Ivar Kants) and Nina (Gosia Dobrowolska) in Sophia Turkiewicz's *Silver City* (1984); bottom: Morgan Keefe (Bryan Brown) and Jo Reeves (Helen Morse) in John Duigan's *Far East* (1982).

Destructive passion: Anna (Saskia Post) and Sam (Michael Hutchence) in Richard Lowenstein's *Dogs in Space* (1987).

Unfinished Business (Bob Ellis, 1986), *Devil in the Flesh* (Scott Murray, 1989), *Silver City* (Sophia Turkiewicz, 1984) and *Far East* (John Duigan, 1982), will ultimately return to his or her spouse. While the motivations may vary dramatically, the affair becomes a brief fling, an experience that may have had its joys but is finally painful. The teenage passions that permeate the American cinema, and often end in a triumphant union of the young couple despite parental and peer pressure, in Australian films, such as *The Year My Voice Broke* (John Duigan, 1987), end with the disintegration of the couple.

Couples may be driven apart by social or political circumstances, as in *The Year of Living Dangerously* (Peter Weir, 1982), by their own inadequacies or by what is cast as the impossibility of their union. But they are repeatedly driven apart. Passion is often seen as obsessive and destructive, as in *Monkey Grip* (Ken Cameron, 1982) and *Dogs in Space* (Richard Lowenstein, 1987).

Interestingly, too, passion has been seen as something that may not bloom on barren Australian soil. If one accepts the notion of Australian society as fundamentally repressive, this is no great surprise. Two films that attempt to depict grand passion, *Far East* and *The Year of Living Dangerously*, are set in Asia. In both cases, the background is a turbulent political situation. Emotions are heightened and there is an element of danger. Here the westerners are thrust together, away from familiar circumstances and removed from the conventions that govern behaviour at home. But in *Far East*, the lovers are finally driven apart.

Perhaps Australians are natural sceptics where love and happy endings are concerned, more at ease with fighters than lovers, more comfortable with stories of male friendship than heterosexual—or overt homosexual—passion.

However, just as the despairing depiction of suburban

Tender romance: Patricia (Wendy Hughes) and Peter (Norman Kaye) in Paul Cox's *Lonely Hearts* (1982).

life has its exception with the gentle perspective of *Return Home* as the dissident voice, Paul Cox's gentle love story, *Lonely Hearts* (1982), is an exception in its romantic relationship. Cox's tender account of the unlikely union of two middle-aged and deliberately unglamorous characters is one of the very few films that charts a relationship from first meeting through to a conclusion that allows the couple to remain united. And it is worth noting that Cox is a film-maker of European birth.

Any attempt to draw a straight line through the themes and concerns of a national cinema is fraught with obstacles. There will always be points where the line needs to curve, where it meets exceptions that take it off on a different tangent. There are exceptions to all generalisations and hard-and-fast rules simply don't apply. To attempt a biopsy of the Australian cinema is to extract a sample that reveals the perceptions of a variety of hearts and minds. Though they might pulsate to comparable rhythms or gravitate to superficially similar themes, each has its own variations on a theme.

Efforts to generalise will invariably ignore or minimalise the exceptions and will disregard the nuances that give many films their distinctive nature. Two film-makers recording an identical situation will see it quite differently, though such subtleties fall by the wayside in the attempt to locate common themes. The ways that *Unfinished Business* and *Devil in the Flesh* evoke their ill-fated love affairs are radically different, though their endings are comparable. The heroes of *Mad Max* and *Crocodile Dundee* share some characteristics, though the films are quite dissimilar in style and subject. The suburban lives depicted in *Sweetie* and *The FJ Holden* are distinctive in their differences, though a sense of alienation is common to both films.

To try to X-ray the Australian cinema and generalise about it from a sample of films is, of course, to simplify and to reduce to common denominators, like shared themes and similar characters. But if this can be done, and bearing in mind the limitations of the approach, Australian cinema can be said to emphasise struggle and sacrifice, against the land itself and against the societies that the inhabitants have created for themselves. Characters are repeatedly alienated and driven apart, condemned to loneliness, or at the very least to being alone.

223

Top: Maureen (Michele Fawdon) and Geoff (John Clayton) in Bob Ellis' *Unfinished Business* (1986). Bottom: Paul Hansen (Keith Smith) and Marthe Foscari (Katia Caballero) in Scott Murray's *Devil in the Flesh* (1989).

In this context, the dearth of happily resolved love stories is entirely appropriate.

Mackellar's poem is a lyrical tribute to Australia. It celebrates the landscape in all its vast spaces and spectacular extremes. It embraces a rugged and distinctive natural beauty. Australia's film-makers have concentrated more on the spaces that separate people, on communities that stifle the spirit and circumstances that drive lovers apart. It is a much darker and despairing vision than that of a frontier paradise promising freedom and unlimited scope for fulfilment.

Note

1   It is *"Crocodile" Dundee* in the US.

Alvin Purple (Graeme Blundell) and Tina Donovan (Elli Maclure). Tim Burstall's *Alvin Purple* (1973).

9
Filmography: one hundred and fifty Australian films

Scott Murray, Raffaele Caputo and Claudine Thoridnet

A

The Adventures of Barry McKenzie

Bruce Beresford

Colour, 35mm, 114 mins, 1972

Longford Productions.

Producer: Phillip Adams.

Scriptwriters: Bruce Beresford, Barry Humphries. Based on comic strip written by Barry Humphries and drawn by Nicholas Garland.

Director of photography: Don McAlpine.

Production designer: John Stoddart.

Sound recordist: Tony Hide.

Editors: John Scott, William Anderson.

Composer: Peter Best.

Cast: Barry Crocker (Barry McKenzie), Barry Humphries (Aunt Edna; Hoot; Meyer de Lamphrey), Peter Cook (Dominic), Spike Milligan (Landlord), Dick Bentley (Detective), Dennis Price (Mr Gort), Julie Covington (Blanche), Avice Landon (Mrs Gort), Joan Bakewell (Herself), Paul Bertram (Curly).

This is the first of two films to be based on the Barry McKenzie character in the comic strip written by Barry Humphries. Here, Barry becomes the innocent abroad by going to visit London. Much of the humour comes from sending up the stultifying British class system and contrasting it with the crude antics of his Aussie mates in Earls Court and the pretensions of his Aunt Edna. The film is generally regarded as the first ocker comedy of the 1970s revival.

All for Gold (aka: Jumping the Claim)

Franklyn Barrett (?)

Black and white, 3000 ft, 1911

West's Pictures.

Scriptwriter: W. S. Percy.

Director of photography: Franklyn Barrett.

Cast: Herbert J. Bentley (Jack Cardigan), Hilliard Vox (Ralph Blackstone), Lilian Teece (Nora Fraser), Ronald McLeod (Bert Fraser), E. Melville (Warden), Walter Bastin (Jim Carey).

'A young Englishman, Jack Cardigan, strikes gold on his claim, and writes at once to share the news with his sweetheart, Nora. He entrusts the letter to a friend, Ralph Blackstone, who concocts a plan to murder Cardigan and take possession of the claim. He poisons Cardigan's drink and hurls his body into a river. . .[Nora] manages to arrive in time to expose Blackstone's treachery, and to find Jack Cardigan alive. . .'

Andrew Pike and Ross Cooper, *Australian Film 1900–1977: A Guide to Feature Film Production*, Oxford University Press in association with the Australian Film Institute, Melbourne, 1980, p. 35.

Alvin Purple

Tim Burstall

Colour, 35mm, 97 mins, 1973

Hexagon Productions.

Producer: Tim Burstall.

Scriptwriter: Alan Hopgood.

Director of photography: Robin Copping.

Production designer: Leslie Binns.

Sound recordist: John Phillips.

Editor: Edward McQueen-Mason.

Composer: Brian Cadd.

Cast: Graeme Blundell (Alvin Purple), Abigail (Girl in See-through), Lynette Curran (First Sugar Girl), Christine Amor (Peggy), Dina Mann (Shirley), Dennis Miller (Mr Horwood), Jill Forster (Mrs Horwood), Fred Parslow (Alvin's Father), Valerie Blake (Alvin's Mother), Alan Finney (Spike Dooley).

This celebration of male wish-fulfilment fantasies concerns a naive young male who finds himself the object of every woman's desire. The story follows him from his school days through various jobs as a waterbed salesman, sex therapist and, eventually, convent gardener.

Among the Hardwoods

Lacey Percival

Black and white, 16mm, 1936

Department of Commerce, Cinema Branch, Melbourne.

Director of photography: Burt Ive.

'Generally, the Cinema Branch films of the 1930s are straightforward and unmemorable, though notable exceptions include Lacey Percival's *Among the Hardwoods* (1936), shot by Bert Ive. This highly creative film used natural sound to the exclusion of dialogue in a romantic audiovisual portrait of the timber industry in Western Australia.'

Young Janet (Alexia Keogh), with her sister and brother. Jane Campion's *An Angel at My Table* (1990).

Chris Long, '1930s Australia: The Coming of Sound', in *The Documentary Film in Australia*, Ross Lansell and Peter Beilby (eds), Cinema Papers in association with Film Victoria, Melbourne, 1982, p. 33.

An Angel at My Table

Jane Campion

Colour, 35mm, 150 mins, 1990

Hibiscus Films in association with the New Zealand Film Commission.

Producer: Bridget Ikin.

Scriptwriter: Laura Jones. Based on the autobiographies of Janet Frame.

Director of photography: Stuart Dryburgh.

Production designer: Grant Major.

Sound recordist: Graham Morris.

Editor: Veronika Haussler.

Composer: Don McGlashan.

Cast: Kerry Fox (Janet), Alexia Keogh (Young Janet), Karen Fergusson (Teenage Janet), Iris Churn (Mum), Jessie Mune (Baby Janet), K. J. Wilson (Dad), Francesca Collins (Baby Jane), Melina Bernbecker (Myrtle), Andrew Binns (Bruddle), Glynis Angell (Isabel).

An Angel at My Table is based on the autobiographies of New Zealand author Janet Frame. The film, originally shot for television, traces the major portion of Frame's life, from early childhood, through internment in an asylum to her reaching literary fame in London.

Australia Calls

Raymond Longford

Black and white, 4000 ft, 1924

Commonwealth Immigration Office–British Empire Exhibition Commission.

Scriptwriter: Lottie Lyell.

Director of photography: Arthur Higgins.

Cast: Ernest Idiens.

The story, by two of *The Bulletin*'s regular contributors, vigorously expresses that magazine's xenophobia, and was a warning to apathetic Australians to beware of the Yellow Peril. Made for presentation in the Australian pavilion at the British Empire Exhibition in London in 1924.

B

Backlash

Bill Bennett

Colour, Super 16, 89 mins, 1986

Mermaid Beach Productions.

Producer: Bill Bennett.

Scriptwriter: Bill Bennett.

Dialogue: David Argue, Gia Carides, Lydia Miller, Brian Syron, Bill Bennett.

Director of photography: Tony Wilson.

[Production designer: not credited.]

Sound recordist: Leo Sullivan.

Editor: Denise Hunter.

Composers: Michael Atkinson, Michael Spicer.

Cast: David Argue (Trevor Darling), Gia Carides (Nikki Iceton), Lydia Miller (Kath), Brian Syron (The Executioner), Anne Smith (Publican's Wife), Don Smith (Publican), Jennifer Cluff (Waitress), George Skiadas (Cook), Mary Prentice (Motel Receptionist), John Lawrence (Property Owner).

A hardened, streetwise cop and a young female rookie take a prisoner back to a small desert town to stand trial. The prisoner is a beautiful black girl, charged with the murder of a bar-owner. They decide to take a short cut, but become stranded in the desert. Forced to live off the land, a bond grows between them all. Then they realise that someone, or something, has been following them.

The Back of Beyond

John Heyer

Black and white, 35mm, 66 mins, 1954 (shot 1952)

Shell Film Unit.

Producer: John Heyer.

Scriptwriters: John Heyer, Janet Heyer, Roland Robinson.

Director of photography: Ross Wood.

Sound recordists: Mervyn Murphy, John Heath.

Editor: John Heyer.

Composer: Sydney John Kay.

Narrator: Kevin Brennan.

Cast: Tom Kruse, William Henry Butler, Jack the Dogger, Old Joe the Rainmaker, the Oldfields of Etadinna, Bejah, Malcolm Arkaringa, the people of the Birdsville Track.

'This reconstruction of life on the Birdsville Track follows the daily work of Tom Kruse, an outback representative of the Royal Mail. Each fortnight he drives 300-odd miles through the desert in his old lorry to deliver supplies and mail to the few isolated settlements between Marree and Birdsville in central Australia.'

Pike and Cooper, *Australian Film 1900–1977*, p. 286.

Backroads

Phillip Noyce

Colour, 16mm, 61 mins, 1977

Backroads Productions.

Scriptwriters: John Emery, Phillip Noyce and cast.

Director of photography: Russell Boyd.

Sound recordist: Lloyd Carrick.

Editor: David Huggett.

Composer: Robert Murphy.

Cast: Gary Foley (Gary), Bill Hunter (Jack), Zac Martin (Joe), Terry Camilleri (Jean-Claude), Julie McGregor (Anna).

'Jack, a white vagrant, and Gary, a young Aboriginal, steal a 1962 Pontiac Parisienne and head off around the dusty roads of western New South Wales. They steal booze, rifles and fancy clothes, and pick up a trio of fellow-travellers...Although the action is redolent of the "road movie" genre, the film becomes, in the dialogues between Gary and Jack, an angry polemical statement about white responsibility for black poverty and destitution.'

Pike and Cooper, *Australian Film 1900–1977*, p. 395.

Between Wars

Michael Thornhill

Colour, 35mm, 101 mins, 1977

Edgecliff Films–McElroy & McElroy–T & M Films.

Producer: Michael Thornhill.

Scriptwriter: Frank Moorhouse.

Director of photography: Russell Boyd.

Production designer: Bill Hutchinson.

Sound recordist: Ken Hammond.

Editor: Max Lemon.

Composer: Adrian Ford.

Cast: Corin Redgrave (Dr Edward Trenbow), Judy Morris (Deborah Trenbow), Günter Meisner (Dr Karl Schneider), Arthur Dignam (Dr Peter Avante), Patricia Leehy (Marguerite), Jone Winchester (Deborah's Mother), Brian James (Deborah's Father), Reg Gillam (Trenbow's Father), Betty Lucas (Trenbow's Mother), Neil Fitzpatrick (Lance Backhouse).

Edward Trenbow, a young doctor in the Australian Army Medical Corps in World War I, works among victims of shell shock in an army hospital, where he meets a German prisoner-of-war, Dr Karl Schneider, who introduces him to the writings of Sigmund Freud. Trenbow develops an interest in psychiatry, still regarded with suspicion by the medical fraternity. So, to escape notoriety, Trenbow moves to a country practice. But conflict develops.

The Big Steal

Nadia Tass

Colour, 35mm, 99 mins, 1990

Dr Edward Trenbow (Corin Redgrave) and Deborah Trenbow (Judy Morris). Michael Thornhill's *Between Wars* (1977).

Doug (Mike Nikol), Lawyer (Robert Meldrum), Gordon Farkas (Steve Bisley) and George (Roy Edmunds). Nadia Tass' *The Big Steal* (1990).

Cascade Films.

Producers: David Parker, Nadia Tass.

Scriptwriter: David Parker. Additional scriptwriting: Max Dunn.

Script consultants: Bob Ellis, Andrew Knight, David Lander.

Director of photography: David Parker.

Production designer: Paddy Reardon.

Sound recordist: John Wilkinson.

Editor: Peter Carrodus.

Composer: Philip Judd.

Cast: Ben Mendelsohn (Danny Clark), Claudia Karvan (Joanna Johnson), Steve Bisley (Gordon Farkas), Marshall Napier (Mr Desmond Clark), Damon Herriman (Mark Jorgensen), Angelo D'Angelo (Vangeli Petrakis), Tim Robertson (Mr Desmond Johnson), Maggie King (Mrs Edith Clark), Sheryl Munks (Pam Schaeffer), Lise Rodgers (Mrs Johnson).

The story of a young man who buys a Jaguar to impress a young woman on their first date. The occasion turns out disastrously, but he and his mates engineer a revenge on a devious car salesman.

Bitter Springs

Ralph Smart

Black and white, 35mm, 86 mins, 1950

Ealing Studios.

Scriptwriters: W. P. Lipscomb, Monja Danischewsky. Based on the story by Ralph Smart.

Director of photography: George Heath.

Production designer: Charles Woolveridge.

Sound recordist: Hans Wetzel.

Editor: Bernard Gribble.

Music: Vaughan Williams.

Cast: Tommy Trinder (Tommy), Chips Rafferty (Wally King), Gordon Jackson (Mac), Jean Blue (Ma King), Michael Pate (Trooper), Charles Tingwell (John King), Nonnie Piper (Emma King), Nicky Yardley (Charlie), Henry Murdoch (Black Jack).

In the early 1900s, a pioneer family undertakes a 600-mile trek to the land in the outback South Australia that they have bought from the government. When they arrive, they clash with an Aboriginal tribe that depends for survival on the waterhole, now claimed by the settlers as their private property. One of the family is speared before a compromise is reached, and the Aborigines and settlers agree to work together to establish a profitable sheep station around the waterhole.

Black Robe

Bruce Beresford

Colour, 35mm, 100 mins, 1992

Alliance Communications and Samson Productions.

Producers: Robert Lantos, Stéphane Reichel, Sue Milliken.

Scriptwriter: Brian Moore. Based on his novel.

Director of photography: Peter James.

Production designer: Herbert Pinter.

Editor: Tim Wellburn.

Composer: Georges Delerue.

Sound recordists: Gary Wilkins; Henri Roux (France).

Cast: Lothaire Bluteau (Laforgue), Aden Young (Daniel), Sandrine Holt (Annuka), August Schellenberg (Chomina), Tantoo Cardinal (Chomina's Wife), Billy Two Rivers (Ougebmat), Lawrence Rayne (Neehatin), Harrisen Liu (Awondole), Wesley Côté (Oujita), Frank Wilson (Father Jerome).

The story of the journey of Father Laforgue in seventeenth-century Canada to convert the Indians.

Bliss

Ray Lawrence

Colour, 35mm, 115 mins (originally 135), 1985

Window III Productions and New South Wales Film Corporation.

Producer: Anthony Buckley.

Scriptwriters: Ray Lawrence, Peter Carey. Based on the novel by Peter Carey.

Director of photography: Paul Murphy.

Design consultant: Wendy Dickson.

Art director: Owen Paterson.

Sound recordist: Gary Wilkins.

Editor: Wayne Le Clos.

Composer: Peter Best.

Cast: Barry Otto (Harry Joy), Lynette Curran (Bettina Joy), Helen Jones (Honey Barbara), Gia Carides (Lucy Joy), Miles Buchanan (David Joy), Jeff Truman (Joel), Tim Robertson (Alex Duval), Bryan Marshall (Adrian Clunes), Jon Ewing (Aldo), Kerry Walker (Alice Dalton).

'The central character is Harry Joy, apparently happily married, a successful ad man and fond father. His unexpected death. . .is followed by his even more unexpected recovery. But he returns to a world where his wife is openly cheating on him with his business partner; his son is a drug pusher whose main ambition is to go to New York and join the Mafia; and his daughter is an addict who gives her brother sexual favours in return for free dope.'

David Stratton, 'A Matter of Life and Death: *Bliss*', *Cinema Papers*, November 1985, p. 65.

Blood Oath

Stephen Wallace

Colour, 35mm, 109 mins, 1990

Blood Oath Productions–Siege Productions–Village Roadshow.

Producers: Charles Waterstreet, Denis Whitburn and Brian Williams.

Scriptwriters: Denis Whitburn and Brian Williams.

Director of photography: Russell Boyd.

Production designer: Bernard Hides.

Harry Joy (Barry Otto). Ray Lawrence's *Bliss* (1985).

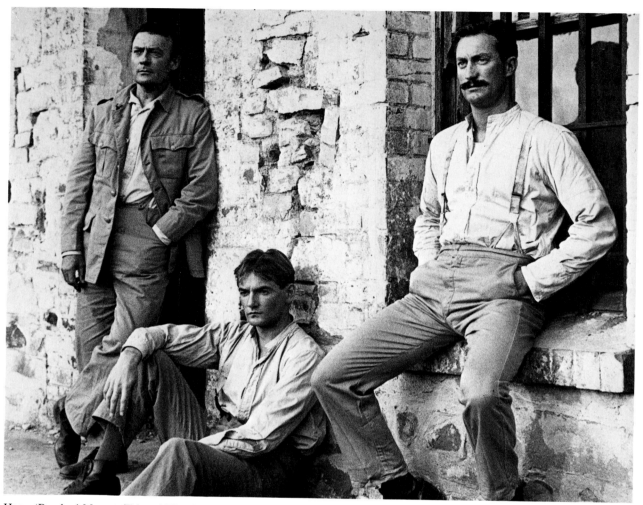

Harry 'Breaker' Morant (Edward Woodward), Lieutenant George Witton (Lewis Fitz-Gerald) and Lieutenant Peter Handcock (Bryan Brown). Bruce Beresford's *'Breaker' Morant* (1980).

Sound recordist: Ben Osmo.

Editor: Nick Beauman.

Cast: Bryan Brown (Captain Cooper), George Takei (Commander Takahasi), Nicholas Eadie (Keenan), John Clarke (Sheedy), John Polson (Jimmy Fenton), Noriaki Shioya (Hideo), Sokyu Fujita (Matsugae), Deborah Unger (Sister Littell), Russell Crowe (Lieutenant Corbet), Jason Donovan (Private Talbot).

Shortly after the surprise attack on Pearl Harbour, Japanese troops captured the Australian garrison on the little-known Dutch East Indies island of Ambon, 650 km north-west of Darwin. The Japanese established a POW camp which would be the scene of atrocities and genocide. Six hundred Australians entered Ambon Island POW camp; three years later, 120 were barely left alive. After the war, the Australian army held a war-crimes trial on the island. *Blood Oath* is the story of that trial.

'Breaker' Morant

Bruce Beresford

Colour, 35mm, 104 mins, 1980

South Australian Film Corporation; made with the assistance of the Australian Film Commision, the 7 Network and PACT Productions.

Producer: Matthew Carroll.

Scriptwriters: Jonathan Hardy, David Stevens, Bruce Beresford. Based on the play by Kenneth Ross.

Director of photography: Don McAlpine.

Production designer: David Copping.

Sound recordist: Gary Wilkins.

Editor: William Anderson.

Musical arranger: Phil Cuneen.

Cast: Edward Woodward (Harry 'Breaker' Morant), Jack Thompson (Major J. F. Thomas), John Waters (Captain Alfred Taylor), Bryan Brown (Lieutenant Peter Handcock), Charles Tingwell (Lieutenant-Colonel Denny), Terence Donovan (Captain Simon Hunt), Vincent Ball (Colonel Ian 'Johnny' Hamilton), Ray Meagher (Sergeant-Major Drummond), Chris Haywood (Corporal Sharp), Russell Kiefel (Christiaan Botha).

'Breaker' Morant is based on the famous Boer War incident in which three Australian soldiers were court-martialled (for the killing of a number of Boer prisoners) by the British army as political scapegoats and later executed.

The Breaking of the Drought

Franklyn Barrett
Black and white, 6 reels, 1920
Golden Wattle Film Syndicate.
Producer: Franklyn Barrett.

Scriptwriters: Jack North, Franklyn Barrett. Based on the play by Bland Holt.

Director of photography: Franklyn Barrett.

Cast: Trilby Clark (Marjorie Galloway), Dunstan Webb (Tom Wattleby), Charles Beetham (Jo Galloway), Marie La Varre (Olive Lorette), John Faulkner (Varsy Lyddleton), Rawdon Blandford (Gilbert Galloway), Nan Taylor (Mrs Galloway), Arthur Albert (Walter Flour), Ethel Henry (Molly Henderson).

'When the outback station of Wallaby is gripped by drought, the proud old owner, Jo Galloway, can do nothing to prevent the repossession of his land by the bank. In poverty, he moves to the city with his wife and daughter to stay with his son, Gilbert, only to learn that Gilbert has long been embezzling the family funds to lead a life of luxury and decadence. Many dramatic events follow, including a murder and a suicide, before the family can return, reunited, to the station, and the rain starts to fall once more.'

Pike and Cooper, *Australian Film 1900–1977*, p. 131.

Buddies

Arch Nicholson
Colour, 35mm, 97 mins, 1983
JD Productions.
Producer: John Dingwall.
Scriptwriter: John Dingwall.
Director of photography: David Eggby.
Production designer: Phillip Warner.
Editor: Martin Down.
Composer: Chris Neal.

Cast: Colin Friels (Mike), Harold Hopkins (Johnny), Kris McQuade (Stella), Bruce Spence (Ted), Dennis Miller (Andy),

Johnny (Harold Hopkins) and Mike (Colin Friels). Arch Nicholson's *Buddies* (1983).

Simon Chilvers (Alfred), Norman Kaye (George Spencer), Lisa Peers (Jennifer Spencer), Andrew Sharp (Peter), Dinah Shearing (Merle).

Buddies, written by *Sunday Too Far Away*'s John Dingwall, is set in the central Queensland gemfields around Emerald. It is the story of the conflict between the traditional pick-and-shovel fossickers and the bulldozer operators who use large-scale mechanisation to gouge sapphires out of the ground.

Burke & Wills

Graeme Clifford
Colour, 35mm, 140 mins, 1985
Hoyts–Edgley.
Producers: Graeme Clifford, John Sexton.
Scriptwriter: Michael Thomas.
Director of photography: Russell Boyd.
Production designer: Ross Major.
Sound recordist: Syd Butterworth.
Editor: Tim Wellburn.
Composer: Peter Sculthorpe.

Cast: Jack Thompson (Robert O'Hara Burke), Nigel Havers (William John Wills), Greta Scacchi (Julia Matthews), Matthew Fargher (John King), Ralph Cotterill (Charley Gray), Drew Forsythe (William Brahe), Chris Haywood (Tom McDonagh), Monroe Reimers (Dost Mahomet), Barry Hill (George Landellis).

Based on the true story of Burke and Wills' failed attempt to cross the Australian continent from south to north through the centre, this film turns their journey into a success by showing their reaching the Gulf of Carpentaria. But tragedy overtakes them on their way back.

C

Caddie

Donald Crombie

Colour, 35mm, 103 mins, 1976

Anthony Buckley Productions.

Producer: Anthony Buckley.

Scriptwriter: Joan Long. Based on the autobiography by 'Caddie'.

Director of photography: Peter James.

Production designer: Owen Williams.

Sound recordist: Des Bone.

Editor: Tim Wellburn.

Composer: Patrick Flynn.

Cast: Helen Morse (Caddie), Takis Emmanuel (Peter), Jack Thompson (Ted), Jacki Weaver (Josie), Melissa Jaffer (Leslie), Ron Blanchard (Bill), Drew Forsythe (Sonny), Kirrili Nolan (Esther), Lynette Curran (Maudie), June Salter (Mrs Marks), John Ewart (Paddy Reilly).

Based on the autobiography of a Sydney barmaid published pseudonymously in 1953, the film reconstructs her life between 1925 and 1932, after she leaves her adulterous husband to fend for herself and her small children. She falls in love with a Greek migrant, Peter, but their life together is disrupted when family obligations force him to return to Greece. In the depths of the Depression, Caddie's income is barely enough to live on, and she falls victim to malnutrition and nervous exhaustion. Help comes from a friendly 'rabbit-o' whose family shares its meagre lot with her until she is well again.

Cane Toads: An Unnatural History

Mark Lewis

Colour, 16mm, 46 mins, 1988

Film Australia.

Producer: Mark Lewis.

Scriptwriter: Mark Lewis.

Directors of photography: Jim Frazier, Wayne Taylor.

Editor: Lindsay Frazer.

Sound recordist: Rodney Simmons.

Documentary about the way cane toads are overtaking Queensland and moving south through New South Wales. The authorities consider them vermin, some line them up for target practice when driving the toad-strewn highways and others think of them as cute pets.

The Cars that Ate Paris

Peter Weir

Colour, 35mm, 91 mins, 1974

Salt Pan Films–Royce Smeal Film Productions.

Producers: Hal McElroy, Jim McElroy.

Scriptwriter: Peter Weir. Based on a story by Peter Weir, Keith Gow, Piers Davies.

Director of photography: John McLean.

Production designer: David Copping.

Sound recordist: Ken Hammond.

Editor: Wayne Le Clos.

Composer: Bruce Smeaton.

Cast: John Meillon (Mayor), Terry Camilleri (Arthur), Kevin Miles (Dr Midland), Rick Scully (George), Max Gillies (Metcalf), Danny Adcock (Policeman), Bruce Spence (Charlie), Kevin Golsby (Insurance Man), Chris Haywood (Daryl), Peter Armstrong (Gorman).

A sardonic exercise in Australian Gothic horror, *The Cars that Ate Paris* introduces an indecisive innocent, Arthur, who is a passenger in a car that crashes on a country road near the lonely town of Paris. Stranded in the town, Arthur gradually realises that the town's people make a living from car accidents and deliberately cause them. A climax comes when a fleet of monstrous vehicles, reconstituted from wrecked cars and driven by local delinquents, attacks the town and causes widespread destruction.

Celia

Ann Turner

Colour, 35mm, 102 mins, 1989

Seon Films.

Producers: Timothy White, Gordon Glenn.

Scriptwriter: Ann Turner.

Director of photography: Geoffrey Simpson.

Production designer: Peta Lawson.

Sound recordist: Lloyd Carrick.

Editor: Ken Sallows.

Composer: Chris Neal.

Cast: Rebecca Smart (Celia Carmichael), Nicholas Eadie (Ray Carmichael), Mary-Anne Fahey (Pat Carmichael), Victoria Longley (Alice Tanner), Margaret Ricketts (Granny), Alexander Hutchinson (Steve Tanner), Adrian Mitchell (Karl Tanner), Callie Gray (Meryl Tanner), Martin Sharman (Evan Tanner), Claire Couttie (Heather Goldman).

It is the start of the long summer holidays and Celia Carmichael turns nine years old. Her world is made up of best friends and arch enemies, storybook monsters and oaths of everlasting loyalty. Her closest friends are her Granny and her pet rabbit, Murgatroyd. Then one day, Granny dies. In the deep of the night, the monstrous Hobyahs start climbing the window. Celia's familiar world of backyards, blood brothers and blissful innocence is about to end.

Celso and Cora

Gary Kildea

Colour, 16mm, 109 mins, 1984

Arthur (Terry Camilleri) and Mayor (John Meillon). Peter Weir's *The Cars that Ate Paris* (1974).

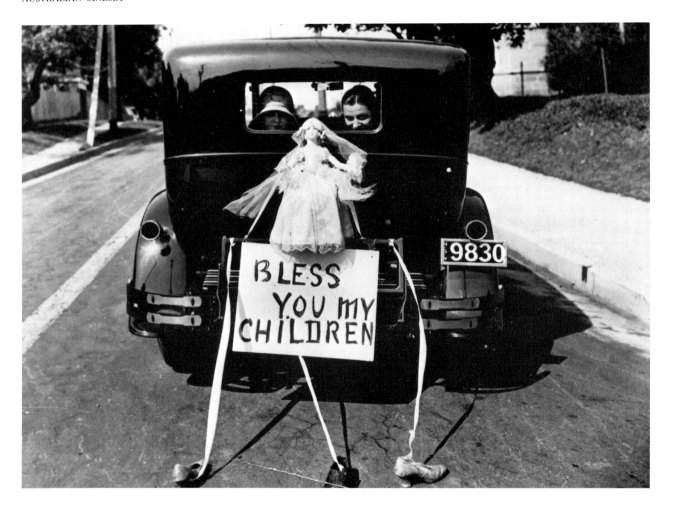

Paulette McDonagh's *The Cheaters* (1930).

Producer: Gary Kildea.

Scriptwriter: Gary Kildea.

Director of photography: Gary Kildea.

Editor: Gary Kildea.

Celso and Cora is a feature-length documentary about a young couple and their two children living in a squatter settlement in Manila. Cora and Celso make a living selling cigarettes at night outside a downtown hotel in defiance of city regulations. The film follows their lives over a three-month period, beginning with Cora's attempt to find a new room for the family after they have been evicted from their previous home. Later, Celso and Cora face a crisis in their own relationship aggravated by the stresses of their daily life.

The Chant of Jimmie Blacksmith

Fred Schepisi

Colour, 35mm, 120 mins, 1978

The Film House, Melbourne, Australia, with the assistance of the AFC, the Victorian Film Corporation and Hoyts Theatres Ltd.

Producer: Fred Schepisi.

Scriptwriter: Fred Schepisi. Based on the novel by Thomas Keneally.

Director of photography: Ian Baker.

Production designer: Wendy Dickson.

Sound recordist: Bob Allen.

Editor: Brian Kavanagh.

Composer: Bruce Smeaton.

Cast: Tommy Lewis (Jimmie), Freddy Reynolds (Mort), Ray Barrett (Farrell), Jack Thompson (Rev. Neville), Angela Punch (Gilda), Peter Carroll (McCready), Don Crosby (Newby), Elizabeth Alexander (Miss Graf), Peter Sumner (Dowie Stead).

Jimmie is a young half-caste Aborigine. Born at the turn of the century, he is torn between his Aboriginal roots and a desire to integrate into the colonial society. He works as a farmer and then police tracker, but disillusionment causes him to move on. Finally goaded by whites, he explodes, and leads his uncle and half-brother on a horrifying rampage.

The Cheaters

Paulette McDonagh

Black and white, 6000 ft, 1930

McDonagh Productions.

Scriptwriter: Paulette McDonagh.

Director of photography: Jack Fletcher.

Production designer: Phyllis McDonagh.

Cast: Marie Lorraine (Paula Marsh), Arthur Greenaway (Bill Marsh), John Faulkner (John Travers), Josef Bambach (Lee Travers), Nellie McNiven (Mrs Hugh Nash), Elaine de Chair (Louise Nash), Frank Hawthorne (Keith Manion), Leal Douglas (The Lady), Stanley Court (Jules Severie), Reg Quartley (Jan).

Bill Marsh, an embezzler, swears vengeance on a businessman, John Travers, who has turned him into the police. Twenty years pass, and Marsh emerges from gaol and establishes himself as the head of a powerful crime empire, with his daughter, Paula, serving as bait to attack wealthy victims. But Paula falls in love with Lee Travers, the adopted son of Marsh's old enemy, and begins to have doubts about her life of crime.

The Clinic

David Stevens

Colour, 35mm, 93 mins, 1983

The Film House & Generation Films.

Producers: Robert Le Tet, Bob Weis.

Scriptwriter: Greg Millin.

Director of photography: Ian Baker.

Production designer: Tracy Watt.

Sound recordist: John Rowley.

Editor: Edward McQueen-Mason.

Music director: Redmond Symons.

Cast: Chris Haywood (Dr Eric Linden), Simon Burke (Paul Armstrong), Gerda Nicolson (Linda), Rona McLeod (Dr Carol Young), Suzanne Roylance (Pattie), Veronica Lang (Nancy), Pat Evison (Alda), Max Bruch (Hassad), Gabrielle Hartley (Gillian), Jane Clifton (Sharon).

The Clinic is a comedy about a day spent in a clinic for the treatment of venereal disease and other sexual problems. It focuses on the four doctors, the ancillary staff, a medical student visiting for the day and a bevy of patients, perhaps a couple of dozen in all.

The Coca-Cola Kid

Dušan Makavejev

Colour, 35mm, 93 mins, 1985

Cinema Enterprises & David Roe.

Producer: David Roe.

Executive producer: Les Lithgow.

Co-producer: Sylvie le Clezio.

Scriptwriter: Frank Moorhouse. Based on short stories in *The Americans*, *Baby* and *The Electrical Experience* by Frank Moorhouse.

Director of photography: Dean Semler.

Production designer: Graham (Grace) Walker.

Editor: John Scott.

Sound recordist: Mark Lewis.

Composer: William Motzing.

Original songs: Tim Finn.

Cast: Eric Roberts (Becker), Greta Scacchi (Terri), Bill Kerr (T. George McDowell), Max Gillies (Frank), Kris McQuade (Juliana), Tony Barry (Bushman), Chris Haywood (Kim), Paul Chubb (Fred), David Slingsby (Waiter), Tim Finn (Philip).

Terri (Greta Scacchi) and Becker (Eric Roberts). Dušan Makavejev's *The Coca-Cola Kid* (1985).

Helen Davey (Nicole Kidman) and Colin Rogers (John Hargreaves). Michael Jenkins' *David Williamson's Emerald City* (1989).

Made in Australia by Yugoslavian director Dušan Makavejev, the film is a modern comedy about capitalism and the nuclear family. T. George McDowell, the soft-drink czar of a small country area, refuses to sell out to Coca-Cola and its perky American representative, Becker. When Becker pursues Terri, little knowing she is McDowell's daughter, tensions escalate. The film ends happily with a sense of personal growth in defiance of societal pressures.

Crocodile Dundee (US: "Crocodile" Dundee)

Peter Faiman

Colour, 35 mm, 102 mins, 1986

A Rimfire Films production.

Producer: John Cornell.

Line producer: Jane Scott.

Associate producer: Wayne Young.

Scriptwriters: Paul Hogan, Ken Shadie, John Cornell.

Director of photography: Russell Boyd.

Production designer: Graham (Grace) Walker.

Sound recordists: Gary Wilkins (Aust.); Bill Daly (US).

Editor: David Stiven.

Composer: Peter Best.

Cast: Paul Hogan (Mick 'Crocodile' Dundee), Linda Kozlowski (Sue Charlton), John Meillon (Walter Reilly), David Gulpilil (Neville Bell), Ritchie Singer (Con), Maggie Blinco (Ida), Steve Rackman (Don), Gerry Skilton (Nugget), Terry Gill (Duffy), Peter Turnbull (Trevor).

The story of a Northern Territory hunter, Mick 'Crocodile' Dundee, who, with his mate Wally, runs an outfit called 'Never Never Tours'. Following the publicity he receives for surviving a crocodile attack, he attracts the attention of hero-hunting, New York reporter Sue Charlton, who decides to take him to New York and turn him into a celebrity.

D

Dad and Dave Come to Town

Ken G. Hall

Black and white, 35mm, 97 mins, 1938

Cinesound Productions.

Producer: Ken G. Hall.

Scriptwriters: Frank Harvey, Bert Bailey. Based on a story by Ken G. Hall.

Director of photography: George Heath.

Production designer: Eric Thompson.

Sound recordist: Clive Cross.

Editor: William Shepherd.

Composer: Hamilton Webber.

Cast: Bert Bailey (Dad Rudd), Shirley Ann Richards (Jill), Fred MacDonald (Dave), Billy Rayes (Jim Bradley), Alec Kellaway (Entwistle), Sidney Wheeler (Pierre), Connie Martyn (Mum),

Ossie Wenban (Joe), Valerie Scanlan (Sarah), Muriel Ford (Myrtle).

In this third film of the Dad and Dave series, Dad inherits a women's fashion store in the city. When the family moves into town to take over, they find it difficult adapting to city ways. A rival also tries to put them out of business, but the Rudds win through, Dad returning to the country and his daughter staying to run the store.

Dangerous Game

Stephen Hopkins

Colour, 35mm, 98 mins, 1991

Quantum Films.

Producers: Judith West, Basil Appleby.

Scriptwriter: Peter West. Based on an original script by Michael Ralph. Additional material: Stephen Hopkins, Jon Ezrine.

Director of photography: Peter Levy.

Production designer: Igor Nay.

Sound recordist: Phillip Keros.

Editor: Tim Wellburn.

Composers: Les Gock, Steve Ball.

Cast: Miles Buchanan (David), Marcus Graham (Jack), Steven Grives (Murphy), Kathryn Walker (Kathryn), Sandie Lillingston (Ziggy), John Polson (Tony), Max Meldrum (History Tutor), Raquel Suarstzman (Girl No. 1), Kerry McKay (Girl No. 2), Robbie McGregor (Police Superintendent).

Five youths use a computer to help break into a closed department store, only to be trapped there by a deranged cop with vengeance on his mind.

David Williamson's Emerald City

Michael Jenkins

Colour, 35mm, 93 mins, 1989

Limelight Productions, in association with the New South Wales Film Corporation.

Producer: Joan Long.

Scriptwriter: David Williamson. Based on Williamson's play.

Director of photography: Paul Murphy.

Production designer: Owen Williams.

Sound recordist: Ben Osmo.

Editor: Neil Thumpston.

Composer: Chris Neal.

Cast: John Hargreaves (Colin Rogers), Robyn Nevin (Kate Rogers), Chris Haywood (Mike McCord), Nicole Kidman (Helen Davey), Ruth Cracknell (Elaine Ross), Dennis Miller (Malcolm Bennett), Ella Scott (Penny Rogers), Haydon Samuels (Sam Rogers) Nicholas Hammond (Ian Wall), Michelle Torres (Kath Mitchell).

Based on David Williamson's hit play, *Emerald City*, this is the story of a screenwriter, Colin, and his publisher wife, Kate, who

Rae Ingram (Nicole Kidman) and John Ingram (Sam Neill). Phillip Noyce's *Dead Calm* (1988).

Major Patrick Dannenberg (James Coburn) and Private Edward Leonski (Reb Brown). Philippe Mora's *Death of a Soldier* (1986).

move to Sydney and encounter a world of opportunists, hustlers and cynics. The film portrays the temptation of Colin and Kate, and their crises of conscience as they try to reconcile their desires with the integrity they thought they had.

Dead Calm

Phillip Noyce

Colour, 35mm, 95 mins, 1989 (mostly shot 1987)

Kennedy Miller.

Producers: Terry Hayes, Doug Mitchell, George Miller.

Scriptwriter: Terry Hayes. From the novel by Charles Williams.

Directors of photography: Dean Semler; Geoff Burton (opening sequence).

Production designer: Graham 'Grace' Walker.

Sound recordist: Ben Osmo.

Editor: Richard Francis-Bruce.

Composer: Graeme Revell.

Cast: Nicole Kidman (Rae Ingram), Sam Neill (John Ingram), Billy Zane (Hughie Warriner), Rod Mullinar (Russell Bellows), Joshua Tilden (Danny), George Shevtsov (Doctor), Michael Long (Specialist Doctor); Lisa Collins, Sharon Cook, Paula Hudson-Brinkley, Malinda Rutter (*Orpheus* Cruise Girls); Benji UD, AD (Dog).

Veteran sailor John Ingram joins his beautiful young wife, Rae, on the deck of their sailing yacht, *Saracen*, and finds the ocean mirror-flat, the air dead calm. Suddenly John and Rae's cruise is interrupted when they spot a dinghy being furiously rowed away from a large schooner lying some half-mile to starboard. The other ship, *Orpheus*, shows no sign of life. The sole occupant of the dinghy is Hughie Warriner, a frightened young American. Ingram rows out to the schooner and discovers that something ominous and horrifying has occurred on the *Orpheus*.

Death in Brunswick

John Ruane

Colour, 35mm, 100 mins, 1991

Meridian Films.

Producer: Timothy White.

Scriptwriters: John Ruane, Boyd Oxlade. Based on the novel by Boyd Oxlade.

Director of photography: Ellery Ryan.

Production designer: Chris Kennedy.

Sound recordist: Lloyd Carrick.

Editor: Neil Thumpston.

Composer: Philip Judd.

Cast: Sam Neill (Carl Fitzgerald), Zoë Carides (Sophie Papafagos), John Clarke (Dave), Yvonne Lawley (Mrs Fitzgerald), Nico Lathouris (Mustafa), Nicholas Papademetriou (Yanni Voulgaris), Boris Brkic (Laurie), Deborah Kennedy (June), Doris Younane (Carmen), Denis Moore (Catholic Priest).

Carl Fitzgerald, a middle-aged, hopeless and clumsy oaf, is dominated by his mother. He lives a mundane life in the inner-urban sprawl of Brunswick until he meets and falls for a teen-age Greek girl.

Death of a Soldier

Philippe Mora

Colour, 35mm, 105 mins, 1986

Suatu Film Management–A Scotti Brothers Picture.

Producers: David Hannay, William Nagle.

Scriptwriter: William Nagle.

Director of photography: Louis Irving.

Chainsaw Man (Chris Haywood) and party guests. Richard Lowenstein's *Dogs in Space* (1987).

Production designer: Geoff Richardson.

Sound recordist: Geoff White.

Editor: John Scott.

Composer: Allan Zavod.

Cast: James Coburn (Major Patrick Dannenberg), Reb Brown (Private Edward J. Leonski), Bill Hunter (Detective Sergeant Fred Adams), Maurie Fields (Detective Sergeant Ray Martin), Belinda Davey (Margot Saunders), Max Fairchild (Major William Fricks), Jon Sidney (General Douglas MacArthur), Michael Pate (Major General Richard Sutherland), Randall Berger (Private Anthony Gallo), John Cottone (Major General R. G. Marshall).

In Melbourne, during a 16-day period of the cold, bleak winter of 1942, three women are choked to death. It soon emerges that the murderer is one of the sixty thousand American soldiers stationed in Australia. To appease an Australian people and government increasingly at odds with the American presence, General MacArthur orders the killer be tried and executed under Australian law. And though Private Edward J. Leonski is clearly insane and suffering from Lepto Meningitis, the courts find him guilty and he is hanged.

Devil in the Flesh

Scott Murray

Colour, 35mm, 104 mins (Aust. version 99 mins), 1989 (shot 1985)

JCW Film Management Limited & World Film Alliance present a Collins Murray Production.

Producer: John B. Murray.

Scriptwriter: Scott Murray. Based on the novel *Le Diable au Corps* by Raymond Radiguet.

Director of photography: Andrew de Groot.

Production designer: Paddy Reardon.

Sound recordist: Laurie Robinson.

Editor: Tim Lewis.

Composer: Philippe Sarde.

Cast: Katia Caballero (Marthe Foscari), Keith Smith (Paul Hansen), John Morris (John Hansen), Jill Forster (Jill Hansen), Colin Duckworth (Pierre Fournier), Reine Lavoie (Madelaine Fournier), Jeremy Johnson (Simon Greene), Odile le Clezio (Simone), Louise Elvin (Artists' model), Luciano Martucci (Ermanno).

The story of a schoolboy, Paul Hansen, who enters into a passionate love affair with Marthe Foscari, the young French wife of an Italian immigrant interned by the Australian government soon after the outbreak of hostilities. The writer–director, Scott Murray, has transported Raymond Radiguet's famous French novel to the Australian environment of the early 1940s.

The Devil's Playground

Fred Schepisi

Colour, 35mm, 107 mins, 1976

The Film House.

Producer: Fred Schepisi.

Scriptwriter: Fred Schepisi.

Director of photography: Ian Baker.

Production designer: Trevor Ling.

Sound recordist: Don Connolly.

Editor: Brian Kavanagh.

Composer: Bruce Smeaton.

Cast: Arthur Dignam (Brother Francine), Nick Tate (Brother Victor), Simon Burke (Tom Allen), Charles McCallum (Brother Sebastian), John Frawley (Brother Celian), Jonathan Hardy (Brother Arnold), Gerry Duggan (Father Hanrahan), Peter Cox (Brother James), John Diedrich (Fitz), Thomas Keneally (Father Marshall).

Partially based on Schepisi's own upbringing, the film tells of a 13-year-old boy who is trying to find a balance between his natural desires and his attempts to conform to the strict regimen of the Catholic seminary where he is a pupil. His final resolve is to run away.

Dogs in Space

Richard Lowenstein

Colour, 35mm, 93 mins, 1987

An Entertainment Media & the Burrowes Film Group production.

Producer: Glenys Rowe.

Scriptwriter: Richard Lowenstein.

Director of photography: Andrew de Groot.

Production designer: Jody Borland.

Sound recordists: Dean Gawen, Stephen Vaughan.

Editor: Jill Bilcock.

Musical director: Ollie Olsen.

Cast: Michael Hutchence (Sam), Saskia Post (Anna), Nique Needles (Tim), Deanna Bond (The Girl), Tony Helou (Luchio), Chris Haywood (Chainsaw Man), Peter Walsh (Anthony), Laura Swanson (Clare), Adam Briscomb (Grant), Sharon Jessop (Leanne).

Dogs in Space is a fast and furious love story set amid the comedy, the chaos and crazy confusion of a typical inner-city shared household as the indulgent years of the 1970s give way to the harsher realities of life in the 1980s.

Don's Party

Bruce Beresford

Colour, 35mm, 90 mins, 1976

Double Head Productions.

Scriptwriter: David Williamson. Based on Williamson's play.

Director of photography: Don McAlpine.

Production designer: Rhoisin Harrison.

Sound recordist: Des Bone.

Composers: John Grayling, Leos Jan.

Editor: William Anderson.

Don (John Hargreaves), Mack (Graham Kennedy), Susan (Clare Binney), Mal (Ray Barrett) and Cooley (Harold Hopkins). Bruce Beresford's *Don's Party* (1976).

Yoram Gross' *Dot and the Kangaroo* (1977).

Cast: Ray Barrett (Mal), Clare Binney (Susan), Pat Bishop (Jenny), Graeme Blundell (Simon), Jeanie Drynan (Kath), John Gorton (Himself), John Hargreaves (Don), Harold Hopkins (Cooley), Graham Kennedy (Mack), Veronica Lang (Jody).

It is election night, 1969, and friends of Don and Kath arrive to celebrate the foregone conclusion of a Whitlam victory over Gorton. They intend to toast the eve of the social-democrat utopia with a laundry full of beer. Of the guests, only Simon and Jody are unenthusiastic about the prospect of a Labor government, and this produces the first hint of tension. The evening, the hilarity and the flirtation progress until the guests face the catastrophic fact that Labor is losing, whereupon a host of tensions surface.

Dot and the Kangaroo

Yoram Gross

Animated, colour, 80 mins, 1977

Yoram Gross Film Studio.

Scriptwriter: John Palmer. Based on the novel by Ethel Pedley.

Directors of photography: Frank Hammond, Graham Sharpe.

Art director: Sandra Gross.

Character design: Laurie Sharpe.

Editors: Rod Hay, Klaus Jaritz.

Composer: Bob Young.

Voices: Spike Milligan, Lola Brooks, Joan Bruce, Barbara Frawley, Peter Gwynne, Ron Haddrick, Ross Higgins, Richard Meikle, June Salter.

Dot, the little daughter of a settler in the Australian outback, loses her way in the bush. Terrified by the dark shadows and the unfamiliar sounds of the bush, she is soon befriended by a big kangaroo. Dot travels in the kangaroo's pouch on an adventure-packed journey. She meets many bush animals and birds. There is tension and excitement until, with the help of the bush creatures, Dot finally finds her home and the kangaroo returns to its natural environment.

E

Evil Angels (US: **A Cry in the Dark**)

Fred Schepisi

Colour, 35mm, 121 mins, 1988

Warner Bros presents a Cannon Entertainment Inc./Golan-Globus Production in association with Cinema Verity.

Producer: Verity Lambert.

Scriptwriters: Robert Caswell, Fred Schepisi. Based on the book by John Bryson.

Director of photography: Ian Baker.

Production designers: Wendy Dickson, George Liddle.

Sound recordists: Gary Wilkins.

Editor: Jill Bilcock.

Composer: Bruce Smeaton.

Cast: Meryl Streep (Lindy), Sam Neill (Michael), Maurie Fields (Barritt), Charles Tingwell (Justice Muirhead), Bruce Myles (Barker), Nick Tate (Charlwood), Sandy Gore (Joy Kuhl), Neil Fitzpatrick (Phillips), Dennis Miller (Sturgess), Dorothy Alison (Avis).

On a cool spring night in 1980, in the vast Australian outback, a baby disappears. Was tiny Azaria Chamberlain abducted as her distraught mother maintained, or did Lindy Chamberlain commit the most bizarre murder in Australia's history? Azaria's disappearance obsessed a nation and triggered a media witch hunt that lasted for half a decade. Azaria's body was never found, but her parents were tried—by rumour, suspicion and religious intolerance—and, in a court of law, Lindy was found guilty of murder.

F

Far East

John Duigan

Colour, 35mm, 102 mins, 1982

The dingo. Fred Schepisi's *Evil Angels* (1988).

Filmco Australia presents an Alfred Road Films Production.

Producer: Richard Mason.

Scriptwriter: John Duigan.

Director of photography: Brian Probyn.

Production designer: Ross Major.

Sound recordist: Peter Barker.

Editor: Henry Dangar.

Composer: Sharon Calcraft.

Cast: Bryan Brown (Morgan Keefe), Helen Morse (Jo Reeves), John Bell (Peter Reeves), Raina McKeon (Rosita Constanza), Henry Duval (Rodolfo De Cruz), Sinan Leong (Nene), Bill Hunter (Walker), John Clayton (Tony Alsop), Duc Sanh Lieu (Kip), Anna Rowena (Julia).

In this pastiche of *Casablanca* (Michael Curtiz, 1942), Peter Reeves, a journalist, takes his wife, Jo, to the Far East. There they meet Morgan Keefe, a tough and apparently amoral bar owner. Jo had once been Morgan's lover in Saigon. While Peter becomes passionately and dangerously involved with the local trade unionists, Jo and Morgan reignite their love.

The Far Paradise

Paulette McDonagh

Black and white, 7000 ft, 1928

MCD Productions.

Producer: Paulette McDonagh.

Scriptwriter: Paulette McDonagh.

Director of photography: Jack Fletcher.

Production designer: Phyllis McDonagh.

Cast: Marie Lorraine (Cherry Carson), Gaston Mervale (James Carson), Arthur McLaglen (Karl Rossi), John Faulkner (Howard Lawton), Paul Longuet (Peter Lawton), Arthur Clarke (Lee Farrar), Harry Halley (Brock).

'Unknown to Cherry Carson, her father is deeply involved in crime and is the subject of an investigation by the attorney-general, Howard Lawton. Cherry falls in love with Howard Lawton's son, Peter, but her father tries to disrupt the affair. Soon after, Carson goes into hiding, taking Cherry with him. A year later, Peter finds her selling flowers in a mountain tourist resort, struggling to support herself and her father, who has taken to drink.'

Pike and Cooper, *Australian Film 1900–1977*, p. 190.

The FJ Holden

Michael Thornhill

Colour, 35mm, 105 mins, 1977

F.J. Films.

Producer: Michael Thornhill.

Scriptwriters: Terry Larsen, Michael Thornhill.

Director of photography: David Gribble.

Production designers: Monte Fieguth, Lissa Coote.

Sound recordist: Don Connolly.

Editor: Max Lemon.

Composer: Jim Manzie.

Cast: Paul Couzens (Kevin), Eva Dickinson (Anne), Carl Stever (Bob), Gary Waddell (Deadlegs), Graham Rouse (Sergeant), Karlene Rogerson (Cheryl), Vicki Arkley (Chris), Robert Baxter (Senior Constable), Colin Yarwood (Brian), Sigrid Thornton (Wendy).

Kevin is an apprentice motor mechanic in the western suburbs of Sydney, who drives an FJ Holden. He and his best mate, Bob, spend most of their spare time driving around trying to pick up girls. Kevin meets Anne at the local pub and takes her to a posh restaurant to impress her. However, Kevin is out of place; he's much happier with his mates at a drag race. Despite his fondness for Anne, Kevin finds it difficult to sustain a mature relationship. When Anne throws him out of her house one day, Kevin turns up drunk at a party and causes a stir, but arrives home at dawn to find the police waiting.

Flirting

John Duigan

Colour, 35mm, 99 mins, 1991

Kennedy Miller.

Producers: George Miller, Doug Mitchell, Terry Hayes.

Scriptwriter: John Duigan.

Director of photography: Geoff Burton.

Production designer: Roger Ford.

Sound recordist: Ross Linton.

Editor: Robert Gibson.

Cast: Noah Taylor (Danny Embling), Thandie Newton (Thandiwe Adjewa), Nicole Kidman (Nicola Radcliffe), Bartholomew Rose ('Gilby' Fryer), Felix Nobis (Jock Blair), Josh Picker ('Backa' Bourke), Jeff Truman (Mr Morris Cutts),

Kevin (Paul Couzens). Michael Thornhill's *The FJ Holden* (1977).

Marshall Napier (Mr Rupert Elliott), John Dicks (Rev. Consti Nicholson), Kym Wilson (Melissa Miles), Naomi Watts (Janet Odgers).

In 1965, three years after the events of *The Year My Voice Broke*, 17-year-old Danny Embling boards at St Alban's College. Acting like a magnet is the nearby sister school of Circencester College, where Danny becomes involved with a Kenyan girl, Thandiwe.

For the Term of His Natural Life

Norman Dawn

Black and white, 10 000 ft, 1927

Australasian Films–Union Master World Pictures.

Producer: Norman Dawn.

Scriptwriter: Norman Dawn. Based on the novel by Marcus Clarke.

Directors of photography: Len Roos, William Trerise, Bert Cross.

Production designers: Norman Dawn, Dorothy Gordon, James Coleman.

Editors: Katherine Dawn, Mona Donaldson, Norman Dawn.

Cast: George Fisher (Rufus Dawes; John Rex), Eva Novak (Sylvia Vickers), Dunstan Webb (Maurice Frere), Jessica Harcourt (Sarah Purfoy), Arthur McLaglen (Gabbett), Katherine Dawn (Mrs Vickers), Gerald Kay Souper (Major Vickers), Marion Marcus Clarke (Lady Devine), Arthur Tauchert (Warder Troke), Beryl Gow (Sylvia Vickers as a Child).

'To protect his family's reputation, a young aristocrat accepts responsibility for a murder he did not commit, and under the name of Rufus Dawes is transported for life to the convict settlement of Van Diemen's Land. . .*For the Term of His Natural Life* stands as a landmark in the history of the production industry, although in narrative terms it offered nothing new. The story was well known to Australians and had been filmed twice before, in 1908 and 1911 (as *The Life of Rufus Dawes*), and the new film made no attempt to modify the mid-Victorian devices of the plot for a modern generation.'

Pike and Cooper, *Australian Film 1900–1977*, p. 179.

249

Thandiwe Adjewa (Thandie Newton), Melissa Miles (Kym Wilson) and Janet Odgers (Naomi Watts). John Duigan's *Flirting* (1991).

Norman Dawn's *For the Term of His Natural Life* (1927).

Forty Thousand Horsemen

Charles Chauvel

Black and white, 35mm, 101 mins, 1940

Famous Feature Films.

Producer: Charles Chauvel.

Scriptwriter: Charles and Elsa Chauvel (from a story by Charles Chauvel and E. V. Timms).

Director of photography: George Heath.

Editor: William Shepherd.

Production designers: Eric Thompson, J. Alan Kenyon.

Sound recordists: Arthur Smith, Clive Cross.

Composer: Lindley Evans.

Cast: Grant Taylor (Red Gallagher), Betty Bryant (Juliet Rouget), Chips Rafferty (Jim), Pat Twohill (Larry), Harvey Adams (Von Hausen) Eric Reiman (Von Schiller), Joe Valli (Scotty), Albert C. Winn (Sheik Abu), Kenneth Brampton (German Officer), John Fleeting (Captain Gordon), Harry Abdy (Paul Rouget).

Intended as 'a message of inspiration for a new generation of soldiers', the film narrates the heroic work of the Anzacs in the Sinai Desert campaign in World War I. The film follows the exploits of three brave Anzacs in the Light Horse: Red, Larry and their gangling, comic mate, Jim.

Fran

Glenda Hambly

Colour, 16mm, 94 mins, 1985

Barron Films.

Producer: David Rapsey.

Scriptwriter: Glenda Hambly.

Director of photography: Jan Kenny.

Production designer: Theo Mathews.

Sound recordist: Kim Lord.

Editor: Tai Tang Thein.

Composer: Greg Schultz.

Cast: Noni Hazlehurst (Fran), Annie Byron (Marge), Alan Fletcher (Jeff), Narelle Simpson (Lisa), Travis Ward (Tom), Rosie Logie (Cynthia), Danny Adcock (Ray), Steve Jodrell (Michael Butlin), Penny Brown (Sally Aspinal), Faith Clayton (Waigani Supervisor).

Fran is a contemporary drama of a mother whose need for a man's attention strongly conflicts with her need to love and care for her young children. Her unorthodox lifestyle, her emotional insecurity and her apparent promiscuity bring her into direct confrontation with the Department of Welfare. A ward of the state as a child, Fran hates and fears the Welfare Department's involvement in her own family and begins a pitched battle with it.

The Fringe Dwellers

Bruce Beresford

Colour, 35mm, 98 mins, 1986

Fran (Noni Hazlehurst). Glenda Hambly's *Fran* (1985).

Fringe Dwellers Productions in association with Ozfilm Limited.

Producer: Sue Milliken.

Scriptwriters: Bruce Beresford, Rhoisin Beresford. Based on the novel by Nene Gare.

Director of photography: Don McAlpine.

Production designer: Herbert Pinter.

Sound recordist: Max Bowring.

Editor: Tim Wellburn.

Composer: George Dreyfus.

Cast: Kristina Nehm (Trilby Comeaway), Justine Saunders (Mollie Comeaway), Bob Maza (Joe Comeaway), Kylie Belling (Noonah Comeaway), Denis Walker (Bartie Comeaway), Ernie Dingo (Phil), Malcolm Silva (Charlie), Marlene Bell (Hannah), Michelle Torres (Audrena), Michele Miles (Blanchie).

Based on Nene Gare's period novel, the film is set in contemporary Australia. It is the story of an Aboriginal family, the Comeaways, and their proud and exuberant daughter, Trilby. She is set on escaping the wretched conditions of the fringe camp in which her family lives. She and her sister, Noonah, coax their parents into moving to a Housing Commission home in town. Patronised by the whites, they miss the bonding and support of their own community, cannot pay the rent and eventually face eviction.

Mollie Comeaway (Justine Saunders) and Joe Comeaway (Bob Maza). Bruce Beresford's *The Fringe Dwellers* (1986).

Jack (Bill Kerr) and Archy (Mark Lee). Peter Weir's *Gallipoli* (1981).

Frog Dreaming

Brian Trenchard-Smith	
Colour, 35mm, 93 mins, 1986	
UAA Films presents a Middle Reef Production.	
Producer: Barbi Taylor.	
Scriptwriter: Everett DeRoche.	
Director of photography: John McLean.	
Production designer: Jon Dowding.	
Sound recordist: Mark Lewis.	
Editor: Brian Kavanagh.	
Composer: Brian May.	

Cast: Henry Thomas (Cody), Tony Barry (Gaza), Rachel Friend (Wendy), Tamsin West (Jane), John Ewart (Ricketts), Dennis Miller (Mr Cannon), Katy Manning (Mrs Cannon), Dempsey Knight (Charlie Pride), Chris Gregory (Wheatley), Mark Knight (Henry).

Fourteen-year-old Cody is an unabashed adventurer. On an idyllic picnic outing, he discovers an eerie body of water that appears on no map. Cody reckons this place is 'frog dreaming', a taboo area which, according to the local Aborigines, is inhabited by a terror called 'Donkegin'. Despite parental disapproval, Cody and his mates begin the adventure of a lifetime. In the near tragedy of the conclusion, he comes of age.

G

Gallipoli

Peter Weir	
Colour, 35mm, 105 mins, 1981	
Robert Stigwood–Rupert Murdoch for Associated R & R Films.	
Producers: Robert Stigwood, Patricia Lovell.	
Scriptwriter: David Williamson. Based on a story by Peter Weir.	
Director of photography: Russell Boyd.	

Design co-ordinator: Wendy Weir.

Art director: Herbert Pinter.

Sound recordist: Don Connolly.

Editor: William Anderson.

Additional music: Brian May.

Cast: Mel Gibson (Frank Dunne), Mark Lee (Archy), Bill Hunter (Major Barton), Robert Grubb (Billy), Bill Kerr (Jack), John Morris (Col. Robinson), Harold Baigent (Camel Driver), Tim McKenzie (Barney), David Argue (Snowy), Harold Hopkins (Les McCann).

Peter Weir's film deals with the horrors of World War I, particularly the tragic Gallipoli campaign against the Turks, which is seen through the eyes of Archy and Frank. These two farm boys meet and become buddies at a provincial track competition; from there on, their lives intertwine as they join the swashbuckling light cavalry and take part in the bloodbath that wiped out tens of thousands of soldiers.

The Getting of Wisdom

Bruce Beresford

Colour, 35mm, 100 mins, 1977

Southern Cross Films.

Producer: Phillip Adams.

Scriptwriter: Eleanor Witcombe. Based on the novel by Henry Handel Richardson.

Director of photography: Don McAlpine.

Production designer: John Stoddart.

Sound recordists: Des Bone, Gary Wilkins.

Editor: William Anderson.

Music: Franz Schubert, Sigismund Thalberg, Arthur Sullivan.

Cast: Susannah Fowle (Laura), Hilary Ryan (Evelyn), Terence Donovan (Tom Macnamara), Patricia Kennedy (Miss Chapman), Sheila Helpmann (Mrs Gurley), Candy Raymond (Miss Zielinski), Barry Humphries (Reverend Strachey), John Waters (Reverend Shepherd), Julia Blake (Isabella Shepherd), Dorothy Bradley (Miss Hicks).

The Getting of Wisdom is set in Victoria in the 1890s and concerns Laura's school days at Melbourne's exclusive Presbyterian Ladies College. It is based on Henry Handel Richardson's second novel and recounts her own adolescent experiences. A drama of human relationships charged with emotion and sexuality, it is the only one of Richardson's works to reveal a strong comic streak. A story of obsession and rebellion, *The Getting of Wisdom* is a closely observed study of the absurdly pompous social values of the time.

Ghosts ... of the Civil Dead

John Hillcoat

Colour, 35mm, 93 mins, 1989

Correctional Services Inc. & Outlaw Values.

Producer: Evan English.

Scriptwriters: Gene Conkie, John Hillcoat, Evan English, Nick Cave, Hugo Race.

Directors of photography: Paul Goldman, Graham Wood.

Production designer: Chris Kennedy.

Sound recordist: Bronwyn Murphy.

Editor: Stewart Young.

Music: Nick Cave, Mick Harvey, Blixa Bargeld.

Cast: Dave Field (Wenzil), Mike Bishop (David Yale), Chris De Rose (Grezner), Nick Cave (Maynard), Freddo Dierck (Robbins), Vincent Gil (Ruben), Bogdan Koca (Waychek), Kevin Mackey (Glover), Dave Mason (Lilly), M. E. Duncan (Junkie 1).

The horrors of the prison system in the not-too-distant (American?) future? Blood and violence colour the non-relationship between prisoner and warder, between the repressed and the oppressor, in a world where the rule of order is perhaps crueller than the punished crime.

A Girl's Own Story

Jane Campion

Black and white, 16mm, 27 mins, 1983

Australian Film and Television School.

Producer: Jane Campion.

Scriptwriter: Jane Campion.

Director of photography: Sally Bongers.

Production designers: Susie Pullen, Maria Ferro.

Sound recordist: Noel Cunnington.

Editor: Chris Lancaster.

Composers: Alexander Proyas; Jane Campion (words).

Cast: Gabrielle Shornegg (Pam), Geraldine Haywood (Stella), Marina Knight (Gloria), John Godden (Graeme), Colleen Fitzpatrick (Mother), Paul Chubb (Father), Joanne Gabbe (Sister), Jane Edwards (Deidre), Cynthia Turner (Nun 1), Valda Diamond (Nun 2), Katherine Cullen (Little Pam).

Girls without boys; the nightmare of parents; incest; and the battle to keep emotionally warm in a cold, uncaring world: these are images from a stark short film by Jane Campion.

Goodbye Paradise

Carl Schultz

Colour, 35mm, 119 mins, 1983 (shot 1981)

Petersham Pictures in association with the NSW Film Corporation.

Producer: Jane Scott.

Scriptwriters: Bob Ellis, Denny Lawrence. Original idea by Denny Lawrence.

Director of photography: John Seale.

Production designer: George Liddle.

Sound recordist: Syd Butterworth.

Editor: Richard Francis-Bruce.

Composer: Peter Best.

Evelyn (Hilary Ryan) and schoolgirls. Bruce Beresford's *The Getting of Wisdom* (1977).

Maynard (Nick Cave). John Hillcoat's *Ghosts . . . of the Civil Dead* (1989).

Con (Lex Marinos) and Michael Stacey (Ray Barrett). Carl Schultz's *Goodbye Paradise* (1983).

Cast: Ray Barrett (Michael Stacey), Robyn Nevin (Kate), Carole Skinner (Landlady), Peter Lawless (Soldier), Lex Marinos (Con), Ray Shaw (Entertainer), Don Pascoe (Les McCredie), Holly Brown (Drag Queen), Kris McQuade (Hooker), Frank Gallacher (Keith).

Michael Stacey is an ex-cop who wakes up one morning in Surfers Paradise to find his publisher has lost interest in the exposé he has written on police corruption. Seeking solace in a piano bar where Kate, an old lover, sings, Stacey bumps into Senator Les McCredie. To avoid a scandal that might cost him his number two position on the Senate ticket, McCredie asks Stacey to find his daughter, Cathy. In the process, Stacey discovers and helps foil a planned military coup.

The Good Woman of Bangkok

Dennis O'Rourke

Colour, 35mm (including blow-up from Video 8). 82 mins, 1992

O'Rourke & Associates Filmmakers.

Producer: Dennis O'Rourke.

Scriptwriter: Dennis O'Rourke.

Director of photography: Dennis O'Rourke.

Sound recordist: Dennis O'Rourke.

Editor: Tim Litchfield.

Cast: Yagwalak Chonchanakun (Aoi).

A story about Aoi, a Bangkok prostitute, and the impossibility of being good in a very bad world.

Green Card

Peter Weir

Colour, 35mm, 102 mins, 1991

Greencard Productions.

Producers: Peter Weir, Jean Contier.

Scriptwriter: Peter Weir.

Director of photography: Geoffrey Simpson.

Production designer: Wendy Stites.

Sound recordist: Pierre Gamet.

Editor: William Anderson.

Composer: Hans Zimmer.

Cast: Gérard Depardieu (Georges), Andie MacDowell (Brontë), Bebe Neuwirth (Lauren), Gregg Edelman (Phil), Robert Prosky (Brontë's lawyer), Jessie Keosian (Mrs Bird), Ethan Phillips (Gorsky), Mary Louise Wilson (Mrs Sheehan); Lois Smith, Conrad McLaren (Brontë's Neighbours).

Georges, a Frenchman, wants a green card so that he can stay and work in the US. For that, he needs to marry an American. Brontë, a New Yorker, wants an apartment with a greenhouse. For that, she needs to have a husband. Can their arranged marriage keep romance at bay?

Grievous Bodily Harm

Mark Joffe

Colour, 35mm, 96 mins, 1988

FGH–Smiley Films.

Producer: Richard Brennan.

Scriptwriter: Warwick Hind.

Director of photography: Ellery Ryan.

Production designer: Roger Ford.

Sound recordist: Andrew Ramage.

Editor: Marc Van Buuren.

Composer: Chris Neal.

Cast: Colin Friels (Tom Stewart), John Waters (Morris Martin), Bruno Lawrence (Det. Sgt Ray Birch), Joy Bell (Claudine), Chris Stalker (Allen), Kim Gyngell (Mick), Shane Briant (Stephen Enderby), Caz Lederman (Vivian Enderby), John Flaus (Bradshaw).

When ambitious young crime reporter Tom Stewart stumbles onto a promising lead for a good story, he finds himself investigating the strange world of Morris Martin, a school teacher obsessed with the recent death of his young wife. Morris cannot accept she is dead and believes a conspiracy is involved. Both Morris and Tom soon find themselves caught up in a series of murders, a high-class brothel in the Blue Mountains and police corruption that makes justice seem a long way off.

H

Half Life: A Parable for the Nuclear Age

Dennis O'Rourke
Colour, 16mm, 86 mins, 1985
Dennis O'Rourke & Associates.
Producer: Dennis O'Rourke.
Scriptwriter: Dennis O'Rourke.
Director of photography: Dennis O'Rourke.
Sound recordists: Martin Cohen, Gary Kildea.
Editor: Tim Litchfield.
Composer: Bob Brozman.

Soon after dropping atomic bombs on Hiroshima and Nagasaki, the American military began looking for an 'appropriate' place to test its nuclear weapons. It chose the tiny Marshall Islands in the mid-Pacific. Of all the nuclear tests carried out between 1946 and 1958, one has come to symbolise the dark threat of nuclear weapons: 'Bravo', the code-name for America's first deliverable hydrogen bomb.

Heatwave

Phillip Noyce
Colour, 35mm, 93 mins, 1982
Preston Crothers in association with M & L.
Producer: Hilary Linstead.
Scriptwriters: Marc Rosenberg, Phillip Noyce. Based on an original screenplay by Mark Stiles, Tim Gooding.
Director of photography: Vince Monton.
Production designer: Ross Major.
Sound recordist: Lloyd Carrick.
Editor: John Scott.
Composer: Cameron Allan.

Cast: Judy Davis (Kate Dean), Richard Moir (Stephen West), Chris Haywood (Peter Houseman), Bill Hunter (Robert Duncan), John Gregg (Phillip Lawson), Anna Jemison (Victoria West), John Meillon (Freddy Dwyer), Dennis Miller (Mick Davis), Peter Hehir (Cigar-smoking Bodyguard), Gillian Jones (Barbie Lee Taylor).

As Christmas approaches, a blistering heatwave hits Sydney. Architect Stephen West has just landed his first major brief, but he finds that many others don't want his $100 million residential complex to go ahead. One is Kate, an individualist who sides with the residents who will lose their homes. Attracted to each other, but on opposite sides, Stephen and Kate find themselves relentlessly drawn into an ominous vortex of violence and terror.

The Hero of the Dardanelles

Alfred Rolfe
Black and white, 4000 ft [?], 1915
Australasian Films.
Scriptwriters: Phillip Gell, Loris Brown.

Cast: Guy Hastings (William Brown), Loma Rossmore (Lily Brunton), C. Throoby (Mr Brown), Ruth Wainwright (Mrs Brown), Fred Francis (Gordon Brown).

'The central incident in *The Hero of the Dardanelles* was the landing of the Anzacs at Gaba Tepe, which was restaged at Tamarama Bay near Sydney just weeks after the actual event. The story presents. . .the careers of two brothers, one who has already enlisted, and another, William, who soon follows his example.. . .Made at a time of intense public enthusiasm for the war, the film seemed to express for many people the romantic heroism of Australia's role in the war.'

Pike and Cooper, *Australian Film 1900–1977*, pp. 71, 72.

Hightide

Gillian Armstrong
Colour, 35mm, 104 mins, 1987
Hemdale Film Corporation presents an FGH/SJL Production.
Producer: Sandra Levy.
Executive producers: Antony I. Ginnane, Joseph Skrzynski.
Associate producer: Greg Ricketson.
Scriptwriter: Laura Jones.
Director of photography: Russell Boyd.
Production designer: Sally Campbell.
Editor: Nick Beauman.
Sound recordist: Ben Osmo.
Composer: Peter Best.

Cast: Judy Davis (Lilli), Jan Adele (Bet), Claudia Karvan (Ally), Frankie J. Holden (Lester), John Clayton (Col), Colin Friels (Mick), Toni Scanlon (Mary), Monica Trapaga (Tracey), Barry Rugless (Club Manager), 'Cowboy' Bob Purtell (Joe).

A story of love lost and found in a remote and wintry coastal town in Australia. Lilli, a back-up singer for a touring rock 'n' roll singer, comes across the daughter she has abandoned. Lilli must come to terms with motherhood and a sense of her own personal worth.

Holidays on the River Yarra

Leo Berkeley
Colour, 35mm, 88 mins, 1991
Jungle Pictures.

Lilli (Judy Davis). Gillian Armstrong's *Hightide* (1987).

Producer: Fiona Cochrane.

Scriptwriter: Leo Berkeley.

Director of photography: Brendan Lavelle.

Production designers: Margaret Eastgate, Adele Flere.

Sound recordist: Mark Tarpey.

Editor: Leo Berkeley.

Composer: Sam Mallet.

Cast: Craig Adams (Eddie), Luke Elliot (Mick), Alex Menglet (Big Mac), Tahir Cambis (Stewie), Claudia Karvan (Elsa), Ian Scott (Frank), Sheryl Munks (Valerie), Angela McKenna (Mother); Chris Askey, John Brumpton, Jacek Koman (Mercenaries).

Eddie and Mick are out-of-work teenagers. They become involved with a gang of would-be mercenaries who are heading for Africa. What they hope will be a great adventure soon goes horribly wrong.

Homesdale

Peter Weir

Black and white, 16mm, 52 mins, 1971

Experimental Film Fund.

Producers: Richard Brennan, Grahame Bond.

Scriptwriters: Peter Weir, Piers Davies.

Director of photography: Anthony Wallis.

Sound recordist: Ken Hammond.

Editor: Wayne Le Clos.

Composers: Grahame Bond, Rory O'Donoghue.

Cast: Geoff Malone (Mr Malfry), Grahame Bond (Mr Kevin), Kate Fitzpatrick (Miss Greenoak), Barry Donnelly (Mr Vaughn), Doreen Warburton (Mrs Sharpe), James Lear (Mr Levy), James Dellit (Manager), Kosta Akon (Chief Robert), Richard Brennan (Robert I), Peter Weir (Robert 2).

The short feature *Homesdale* is a black comedy about a guest-house on a remote island where visitors are encouraged to act out private fantasies, under the 'supervision' of some rather strange orderlies. It was one of the earliest successes of the Experimental Film Fund.

The Hungry Miles

Keith Gow

Black and white, 16mm, 1955

Waterside Workers' Federation Film Unit.

'[The Waterside Workers'] Federation's film unit, led by Jock Levy, Keith Gow and Norman Disher, spoke out against the Menzies government and explored social problems that the government would rather have forgotten; but their films, such as *The Hungry Miles* and *Pensions for Veterans*, were not widely shown, for the most effective outlets for 16 mm films were controlled by the government and were cautious of left-wing content.'

Pike and Cooper, *Australian Film 1900–1977*, p. 264.

I

Indonesia Calling

Joris Ivens

Black and white, 16mm, 1946

Waterside Workers' Federation Film Unit.

The Waterside Workers' Federation in Sydney sponsored a series of rough-hewn films by a small group of dedicated people that expressed far more passion than was possible in government productions. An initial impetus was given by Joris Ivens, who made a clandestine documentary, *Indonesia Calling*, for the Federation to express its solidarity with the Indonesian independence movement.

In the Grip of Polar Ice

Frank Hurley

Black and white, 1917

In January 1915, following a British expedition led by Ernest Shackleton, Frank Hurley was again in Antarctica, and it was on this harrowing two-year trip that Hurley took his most famous photographs and film, depicting the destruction of the ship *Endurance* in pack-ice and the crew's long struggle for survival through a polar winter. The footage was released as *In the Grip of Polar Ice* in 1917 and again, in 1933, as *Endurance*.

In the Wake of the Bounty

Charles Chauvel

Black and white, 35mm, 66 mins, 1933

Expeditionary Films.

Producer: Charles Chauvel.

Scriptwriter: Charles Chauvel.

Director of photography: Tasman Higgins.

Sound recordists: Arthur Smith, Clive Cross.

Editor: William Shepherd.

Cast: Mayne Lynton (Lieutenant Bligh), Errol Flynn (Fletcher Christian), Victor Gouriet (Michael Byrne, the Blind Fiddler), John Warwick (Midshipman Young).

Chauvel's first talkie is a boldly devised entertainment merging documentary footage and dramatic historical reconstruction. The film re-enacts the mutiny led by Fletcher Christian in 1789 against the master of the *Bounty*, William Bligh, and depicts the fate of the mutineers on Tahiti and remote Pitcairn Island. At the same time, it provides a unique and spectacular record of life of the isolated community of Pitcairn in 1932, where most of the inhabitants are descendants of the *Bounty* mutineers.

In This Life's Body

Corinne Cantrill, Arthur Cantrill

Colour, 16mm, 147 mins, 1984

Arthur & Corinne Cantrill.

Joris Ivens' *Indonesia Calling* (1946).

Producers: Arthur Cantrill, Corinne Cantrill.

Scriptwriter: Corinne Cantrill.

Directors of photography: Corinne Cantrill, Arthur Cantrill.

Editors: Corinne Cantrill, Arthur Cantrill.

Narrator: Corinne Cantrill.

Photographers: Corinne Cantrill, Ponch Hawkes, Fred Harden, Phillip Noyce, Bernard Poinssot, Arthur Cantrill, Ivor Cantrill.

'The film pursues a formal idea to its wholly uncompromising limit: virtually two-and-a-half hours of still photographs accompanied by one continuous autobiographical voice-over...The film is about "life's body", the body as a vessel of lived experience both cerebral and sensual. But this vessel is not bound to a single identity or destiny; rather, it is discontinuous, relative, forever open to the possibility of transformation from within and without.'

Adrian Martin, 'Nurturing the next Wave', in *Back of Beyond: Discovering Australian Film and Television*, Scott Murray (ed.), Australian Film Commission, Sydney, 1988, p. 95.

J

Jedda

Charles Chauvel

Colour, 35mm, 101 mins, 1955 (shot 1953)

Charles Chauvel Productions.

Producer: Charles Chauvel.

Scriptwriters: Charles Chauvel, Elsa Chauvel.

Director of photography: Carl Kayser.

Production designer: Ronald McDonald.

Sound recordist: Arthur Browne.

Editors: Alex Ezard, Jack Gardiner, Pam Bosworth.

Composer: Isadore Goodman.

Cast: Ngarla Kunoth (Jedda), Robert Tudawali (Marbuck), Betty Suttor (Sarah McMann), Paul Reynall (Joe), George Simpson-Lyttle (Douglas McMann), Tas Fitzer (Peter Wallis), Wason

Jedda (Ngarla Kunoth) and Marbuck (Robert Tudawali). Charles Chauvel's *Jedda* (1955).

Byers (Felix Romeo), Willie Farrar (Little Joe), Margaret Dingle (Little Jedda).

'On a lonely cattle station in the Northern Territory, a newly born Aboriginal baby is adopted by a white woman, Sarah McMann, in place of her own child who had died. Sarah names the baby Jedda, after a wild bird, and raises her as a white child, forbidding contact with the Aborigines of the station. Years pass, and Jedda, a beautiful teenage girl, is drawn by the mysteries of the Aboriginal people but restrained by her upbringing.'

Pike and Cooper, *Australian Film 1900–1977*, p. 288.

K

Kangaroo

Tim Burstall

Colour, 35mm, 110 mins, 1987 (shot 1985)

Ross Dimsey.

Producer: Ross Dimsey.

Scriptwriter: Evan Jones. Based on the novel by D. H. Lawrence.

Director of photography: Dan Burstall.

Production designer: Tracy Watt.

Sound recordist: Paul Clark.

Editor: Edward McQueen-Mason.

Composer: Nathan Waks.

Cast: Colin Friels (Richard Somers), Judy Davis (Harriet Somers), John Walton (Jack Calcott), Julie Nihill (Vicki Calcott), Hugh Keays-Byrne (Kangaroo), Peter Hehir (Jaz), Peter Cummins (Struthers), Tim Robertson (O'Neill), Malcolm Robertson (Publisher), David Hutchins (Cornwall Detective).

Kangaroo is the story of a British couple who travel to Australia with the intention of settling here. They form a close friendship with an Australian couple. Through them, they meet the leader of a clandestine fascist organisation, made up largely of returned servicemen from World War I. This leader, a strange

Harriet Somers (Judy Davis) and Richard Somers (Colin Friels). Tim Burstall's *Kangaroo* (1987).

character called Kangaroo, aims to set up a dictatorship in Australia.

The Kid Stakes

Tal Ordell

Black and white, 5000 ft, 1927

Ordell-Coyle Productions.

Producers: Tal Ordell, Virgil Coyle.

Scriptwriter: Tal Ordell. Based on comic strip characters created by Syd Nicholls.

Director of photography: Arthur Higgins.

Cast: 'Pop' Ordell (Fatty Finn), Charles Roberts (Tiny King), Ray Salmon (Jimmy Kelly), Frank Boyd (Bruiser Murphy), Edward Stevens (Shooey Shugg), Billy Ireland ('Seasy'), Stanley Funnelle (Headlights Hogan), Gwenda Hemus (Betty Briggs), Leonard Durell (Constable Claffey), Joyce Hazeldine (Kitty Kelly).

'Fatty Finn is the leader of a group of scruffy, irrepressible Woolloomooloo children. They enter Fatty's pet goat, Hector, in a derby but a rival gang, led by Bruiser Murphy, sets Hector loose on the morning of the race. After a series of adventures, Fatty finds the runaway goat and persuades a friendly aviator to fly him to the race-track in time for the main event.'

Pike and Cooper, *Australian Film 1900–1977*, p. 178.

The Killing of Angel Street

Don Crombie

Colour, 35mm, 96 mins, 1981

Forest Home Films presents in association with the Australian Film Commission, G.U.O Film Distributors & Endeavour Communications.

Producer: Anthony Buckley.

Scriptwriters: Evan Jones, Michael Craig, Cecil Holmes. Based on an original story by Michael Craig.

Director of photography: Peter James.

Production designer: David Copping.

Sound recordist: John Phillips.

Editor: Tim Wellburn.

Composer: Brian May.

Cast: Elizabeth Alexander (Jessica Simmonds), John Hargreaves (Elliott), Reg Lye (Riley), Alexander Archdale (B. C. Simmonds), David Downer (Alan Simmonds), Gordon McDougall (Sir Arthur Wadham), Ric Herbert (Ben), Brendon Lunney (Scott), Caz Lederman (Nancy), Allan Bickford (Collins).

Jessica Simmonds returns from overseas and discovers that her street, including the family home, is in the process of being destroyed by property developers. When her campaigning father dies under suspicious circumstances, Jessica decides to take on the fight to save the street. She enlists the help of some residents and the local union official, Elliott, but in the end the fight is her own.

Kodakers and Koories

Walter Saunders, Michael Leigh

Colour, 16mm, 100 mins, 1988

Compilation film which includes:

Year	Director	Subject
1898	Alfred Cort Haddon	Torres Strait Islanders
1901	Walter Baldwin Spencer	Arrente Tribe—Charlotte Waters
1912	Walter Baldwin Spencer	Arnhem Land—Camp Life
1913	T. J. West (?)	Lake Tyers Mission—Victoria
1913	Eric Mjoeberg	Cape York, Queensland
1917	W. J. Jackson	Australia's Wild Nor' West

Tal Ordell's *The Kid Stakes* (1927).

1922	E. Brooke Nicholls	Kodak's Native Australia
1922	Francis Birtles	Coorab on the Island of Ghosts
1930s	E. O. Stocker, Board for Anthropological Research, University of South Australia	Pintubi Meeting Ngalia—Kangaroo Hunting—The Board at Work
1936	N. F. Nelson, Presbyterian Church	A Walkabout—Life on a Church Run Aboriginal Mission

Kokoda Front Line

Damien Parer

Black and white, 1942

Cinesound Review.

Producer: Ken G. Hall.

Academy Award-winning documentary about Australian soldiers fighting the Japanese in New Guinea during World War II.

L

The Last Days of Chez Nous

Gillian Armstrong

Colour, 35mm, 93 mins, 1992

Jan Chapman Productions.

Producer: Jan Chapman.

Prostitute (Denise Drysdale) and Horse (Dennis Miller). Tim Burstall's *The Last of the Knucklemen* (1979).

Scriptwriter: Helen Garner.

Director of photography: Geoffrey Simpson.

Production designer: Janet Patterson.

Editor: Nicholas Beauman.

Composer: Paul Grabowsky.

Sound recordist: Ben Osmo.

Cast: Lisa Harrow (Beth), Bruno Ganz (JP), Kerry Fox (Vicki), Miranda Otto (Annie), Kiri Paramore (Tim), Bill Hunter (Beth's Father), Lex Marinos (Angelo), Mickey Camilleri (Sally), Lynne Murphy (Beth's Mother), Claire Haywood (Janet).

A study of the relationships between Beth, a writer, her younger sister, Vicki, and Beth's French lover, JP, who share a house and an unusual lifestyle.

The Last Harvest

Jeff Bruer

Colour, 16mm, 50 mins, 1977

A girl, an old man and a young stranger…A 'lost gem' of Australian cinema, *The Last Harvest* is a visually and aurally austere film set in the wind-swept outback of South Australia.

The Last of the Knucklemen

Tim Burstall

Colour, 35mm, 93 mins, 1979

Hexagon in association with the Victorian Film Corporation & the New South Wales Film Corporation.

Producer: Tim Burstall.

Scriptwriter: Tim Burstall. Based on the play by John Powers.

Director of photography: Dan Burstall.

Production designer: Leslie Binns.

Sound recordist: John Phillips.

Editor: Edward McQueen-Mason.

Composer: Bruce Smeaton.

Cast: Gerard Kennedy (Tarzan), Michael Preston (Pansy), Peter Hehir (Tom), Michael Duffield (Methuselah), Dennis Miller (Horse), Stephen Bisley (Mad Dog), Michael Caton (Monk), Stewart Faichney (Tassie), Steve Rackman (Carl), Gerry Duggan (Old Arthur).

Set in the Australian desert, the film tells the story of a gang of wild-cat miners. The boss of the gang is Tarzan, who controls these violent, undisciplined men by force alone. Their camp is a scorching inferno of heat and dust where tempers fray easily.

David Burton (Richard Chamberlain). Peter Weir's *The Last Wave* (1977).

Boozing, brawling, gambling and the odd passing prostitute are their only relief from monotony. Then one day a new miner arrives and the old order is faced with change.

The Last Wave

Peter Weir

Colour, 35mm, 106 mins, 1977

Ayer Productions.

Producers: Hal McElroy, Jim McElroy.

Scriptwriters: Peter Weir, Tony Morphett, Petru Popescu. Based on a story by Peter Weir.

Director of photography: Russell Boyd.

Production designer: Goran Warff.

Sound recordist: Don Connolly.

Editor: Max Lemon.

Composer: Charles Wain.

Cast: Richard Chamberlain (David Burton), Olivia Hamnett (Annie Burton), David Gulpilil (Chris Lee), Fred Parslow (Reverend Burton), Vivean Gray (Dr Whitburn), Nandjiwarra Amagula (Charlie), Walter Amagula (Gerry Lee), Roy Bara (Larry), Cedric Lalara (Lindsey), Morris Lalara (Jacko).

David Burton is a happily married Sydney lawyer specialising in corporate law. Unexpectedly, he is asked to act as a defence attorney for some Aborigines in what appears to be a straightforward murder trial. David finds himself mysteriously drawn to the case, and soon he becomes convinced that this is not a mere murder, and that something unusual and weird is occurring. Odd things then start happening to the weather...

Lonely Hearts

Paul Cox

Colour, 35mm, 95 mins, 1982

Adams Packer Film Productions.

Producer: John B. Murray.

Scriptwriters: Paul Cox, John Clarke.

Director of photography: Yuri Sokol.

Production designer: Neil Angwin.

Sound recordist: Ken Hammond.

Editor: Tim Lewis.

Music arranged and performed by: Norman Kaye.

Cast: Wendy Hughes (Patricia), Norman Kaye (Peter), Jon Finlayson (George), Julia Blake (Pamela), Jonathan Hardy (Bruce), Irene Inescort and Vic Gordon (Patricia's Parents), Ted Grove-Rogers (Peter's Father), Ronald Falk (Wig Salesman), Chris Haywood (The Detective).

Painfully aware of what he considers to be the futility of his existence, Peter, a middle-aged piano-tuner, decides to embark upon an adventure. He goes to a lonely hearts club and pays $50 for 'an introduction'. He is shown the photograph of Patricia, a comparatively young and attractive woman. On being reassured that Patricia wants an older man, he invests in a new toupee. For Patricia, also a victim of a smothering family, their first meeting requires some courage. Painfully shy and sexually inhibited, she embarks on a tentative relationship with Peter.

Love Letters from Teralba Road

Stephen Wallace

Colour, 16mm, 50 mins, 1977

Producer: Richard Brennan.

Scriptwriter: Stephen Wallace.

Director of photography: Tom Cowan.

Sound recordist: Laurie Fitzgerald.

Editor: Moya Wood.

Composer: Ralph Schneider.

Stella Raff (Shirley Ann Richards). Ken G. Hall's *Lovers and Luggers* (1937).

Cast: Kris McQuade (Barbara), Bryan Brown (Len), Gia Carides (Maureen), Joy Hruby (Len's Mother), Kevin Leslie (Barbara's Father), Ashe Venn (Norma), Don Chapman (Foreman).

Lovers and Luggers (US: Vengeance of the Deep)

Ken G. Hall

Black and white, 35mm, 99 mins, 1937

Cinesound Productions.

Producer: Ken G. Hall.

Scriptwriters: Frank Harvey, Edmund Barclay. Based on the novel by Gurney Slade.

Directors of photography: George Heath, Frank Hurley.

Cast: Lloyd Hughes (Daubenny Carshott), Shirley Ann Richards (Stella Raff); Sidney Wheeler, Elaine Hamill, Frank Harvey, Ronald Whelan.

Daubenny Carshott is a celebrated London pianist infatuated with an ambitious socialite, Stella Raff. She insists that he prove himself a man by bringing her a pearl with his own hands from the waters off Thursday Island. Blinded by passion, Daubenny travels to the island, where he befriends Craig Henderson, who later turns out to be another of Stella's lovers on a similar mission.

M

Mad Dog Morgan

Philippe Mora

Colour, 35mm, 102 mins, 1976

Motion Picture Productions.

Producer: Jeremy Thomas.

Scriptwriter: Philippe Mora. Based on the book Morgan by Margaret Carnegie.

Director of photography: Mike Molloy.

Editor: John Scott.

Production designer: Robert Hilditch.

Sound recordist: Ken Hammond.

Composer: Patrick Flynn.

Aboriginal songs, didgeridoo: David Gulpilil.

Cast: Dennis Hopper (Daniel Morgan), Jack Thompson (Detective Manwaring), David Gulpilil (Billy), Frank Thring (Superintendent Cobham), Michael Pate (Superintendent Winch), Wallas Eaton (Macpherson), Bill Hunter (Sergeant Smith), John Hargeaves (Baylis), Martin Harris (Wendlan), Robin Ramsay (Roget).

In 1853, a 20-year-old youth named Daniel Morgan joins the fevered rush for gold. But disillusioned and penniless, Morgan drifts into petty crime. In 1854, he is caught and sentenced to twelve years' hard labour. On his release, he retreats to the hills with an Aboriginal boy, Billy, who teaches him bushcraft. Then,

for the next two years, they stage daring and successful hold-ups across the countryside. Finally shot by the police, the police superintendent cuts off Morgan's scrotum and makes a tobacco pouch out of it.

Mad Max

George Miller

Colour, 35mm, Todd AO, 89 mins, 1979

Kennedy Miller Productions.

Producer: Byron Kennedy.

Associate producer: Bill Miller.

Scriptwriters: James McCausland, George Miller. Based on a story by George Miller, Byron Kennedy.

Director of photography: David Eggby.

Production designer: Jon Dowding.

Sound recordist: Gary Wilkins.

Editors: Tony Paterson, Cliff Hayes.

Composer: Brian May.

Cast: Mel Gibson (Max Rockatansky), Joanne Samuel (Jessie Rockatansky), Hugh Keays-Byrne (Toecutter), Steve Bisley (Jim Goose), Tim Burns (Johnny), Roger Ward (Fifi Macafee), Vincent Gil (Nightrider), Geoff Parry (Bubba Zawetti), David Bracks (Mudguts), Paul Johnstone (Cundalini).

Australia, a few years from now, and urban society is in a state of terminal decay. The inter-city highways have become white-line nightmares, the arena for a strange, apocalyptic game between nomad bikers and a handful of young cops in souped-up pursuit cars.

Mad Max Beyond Thunderdome

George Miller, George Ogilvie

Colour, 35mm, 106 mins, 1985

Kennedy Miller Productions.

Producer: George Miller.

Scriptwriters: Terry Hayes, George Miller.

Director of photography: Dean Semler.

Production designer: Graham 'Grace' Walker.

Production sound recordist: Lloyd Carrick.

Editor: Richard Francis-Bruce.

Composer: Maurice Jarre.

Cast: Mel Gibson (Mad Max), Tina Turner (Aunty Entity), Helen Buday (Savannah Nix), Frank Thring (The Collector), Bruce Spence (Jedediah the Pilot), Robert Grubb (Pig Killer), Angelo Rossitto (The Master), Angry Anderson (Ironbar), George Spartels (Blackfinger), Edwin Hodgeman (Dr Dealgood).

Civilisation has been destroyed and a new society has risen in the desert. Ancient rituals have been renewed and refined with mechanical ingenuity. In the thriving market city of Bartertown, everything is subject to trade: a glass of water, a human life. Max arrives seeking his stolen camel train and possessions. These

269

Daniel Morgan (Dennis Hopper). Philippe Mora's *Mad Dog Morgan* (1976).

will be returned to him provided that he do one small favour, which will take him to a lost world where a tribe of children is waiting for its saviour.

Mad Max 2 (US: **The Road Warrior**)

George Miller

Colour, 35mm, 94 mins, 1981

Kennedy Miller.

Producer: Byron Kennedy.

Scriptwriters: Terry Hayes, George Miller, Brian Hannant.

Director of photography: Dean Semler.

Production designer: Graham 'Grace' Walker.

Sound recordist: Lloyd Carrick.

Editors: David Stiven, Tim Wellburn, Michael Balson.

Composer: Brian May.

Cast: Mel Gibson (Max), Bruce Spence (The Gyro Captain), Mike Preston (Pappagallo), Max Phipps (Toadie), Vernon Wells (Wez), Emil Minty (The Feral Kid), Kjell Nilsson (The Humungus), Virginia Hey (Warrior Woman), William Zappa (Zetta), Arkie Whiteley (The Captain's Girl).

In the new dark age, amid the decay of modern technological civilisation, the world's known oil reserves have all run dry. The

Malcolm (Colin Friels). Nadia Tass' *Malcolm* (1986).

remaining barrels of fuel are the new currency by which life is measured. And outside one such last reserve, the Humungus and his gang are holding its owners under siege. But Max arrives and, aided by Gyro Pilot and Feral Child, a dash to freedom begins.

Malcolm

Nadia Tass

Colour, 90 mins, 1986

Cascade Films.

Producers: [not listed; atb Nadia Tass, David Parker.]

Scriptwriter: David Parker. The character of Malcolm was inspired by John Tassopoulos.

Director of photography: David Parker.

Sound recordist: Paul Clark.

Editor: Ken Sallows.

Composer: Simon Jeffes.

Cast: Colin Friels (Malcolm), John Hargreaves (Frank), Lindy Davies (Judith), Chris Haywood (Willy), Charles 'Bud' Tingwell (Tramways Supervisor), Beverley Phillips (Mrs T.), Judith Stratford (Jenny), Heather Mitchell (Barmaid), Tony Mahood (Tram Conductor), David Lander (Restaurant Hoon #1).

Malcolm is a man whose mechanical aptitude is highly developed, but, through the efforts of an overbearing mother, his emotional and social development stopped a long time before. He takes in a boarder, Frank, who turns out to be a crim and who inadvertently uses Malcolm's abilities to further his career. The combination of Malcolm's amazing inventions with Frank's criminal mind results in a spate of unique but unsuccessful attempts at robbery.

The Man from Snowy River

George Miller

Colour, 35mm, 106 mins, 1982

Michael Edgley International & Cambridge Films present a Geoff Burrowes–George Miller Production.

271

Psychiatrist (Bob Ellis) and Charles Brenner (Norman Kaye). Paul Cox's *Man of Flowers* (1983).

Producer: Geoff Burrowes.

Scriptwriter: John Dixon. From a script by Fred Cul Cullen. Based on the poem by A. B. 'Banjo' Paterson.

Director of photography: Keith Wagstaff.

Production designer: Leslie Binns.

Sound recordist: Gary Wilkins.

Editor: Adrian Carr.

Composer: Bruce Rowland.

Cast: Kirk Douglas (Spur; Harrison), Jack Thompson (Clancy), Tom Burlinson (Jim Craig), Sigrid Thornton (Jessica), Lorraine Bayly (Rosemary), Terence Donovan (Henry Craig), June Jago (Mrs Bailey), Gus Mercurio (Frew), David Bradshaw (Banjo Paterson), Tony Bonner (Kane).

The event described in Banjo Paterson's ballad—the pursuit and capture of the colt from Old Regret—is the climax of the film. But the core of the film is 'the man'; Paterson's bare description of his hero—'a stripling'—is developed into the story of an 18-year-old lad who becomes a man and then a legend in a furious, never-to-be-forgotten ride.

Man of Flowers

Paul Cox

Colour, 35mm, 91 mins, 1983

Producers: Jane Ballantyne, Paul Cox.

Scriptwriter: Paul Cox.

Dialogue: Bob Ellis.

Director of photography: Yuri Sokol.

Production designer: Asher Bilu.

Sound recordist: Lloyd Carrick.

Editor: Tim Lewis.

Cast: Norman Kaye (Charles Bremer), Alyson Best (Lisa), Chris Haywood (David), Sarah Walker (Jane), Julia Blake (Art Teacher), Bob Ellis (Pyschiatrist), Barry Dickins (Postman), Patrick Cook (Coppershop Man), Victoria Eagger (Angela), Werner Herzog (Father).

Charles Bremer is a recluse, and a collector of rare flowers and objets d'art. Loved and smothered by his mother, the past remains as real to him as his present life. Each Wednesday, Charles takes Lisa, an artist's model, to his sumptuous house and pays her handsomely to do a striptease to the 'Love Duet' from Donizetti's *Lucia Di Lammermoor*. He then leaves quickly and plays the organ alone in the church across the road from his house. Murder soon follows.

The Martyrdom of Nurse Cavell

John Gavin, C. Post Mason

Black and white, 4000 ft, 1916

Australian Famous Feature Company.

Scriptwriter: Agnes Gavin.

Director of photography: Lacey Percival.

Cast: Vera Pearce (Nurse Cavell), Harrington Reynolds (Reverend Thomas Gerard), C. Post Mason (Georges Renard), Percy Walshe (Baron Von Bissell), John Gavin (Captain Von Hoffberg), Charles Villiers (Herr Cries), George Portus (Dr Schultz), Roland Stavely (American Ambassador), James Martin (Monsieur Renard), Robert Floyd (Monsieur Fouchard).

'On 12 October 1915 an English nurse, Edith Cavell, was executed in Brussels by a German firing squad for allegedly assisting the Belgian resistance movement. News of the German action shocked the world and she became an instant legend in the anti-German propaganda of the Allied countries. Australia was the first to tell her story (or a version of it) on film, and it proved as popular overseas as it did at home, with a world market ripe for an expression of anger against the Germans.'

Pike and Cooper, *Australian Film 1900–1977*, p. 78.

Mike and Stefani

Ron Maslyn Williams

Black and white, 64 mins, 1952 (shot 1949)

Commonwealth Film Unit, Department of the Interior–Film Australia.

Producer: Stanley Hawes.

Director of photography: R. G. Pearse.

Editors: Ted Hunter, Brett Porter.

'When war breaks out, a young Ukrainian couple, Mike and Stefani, are taken away to separate German labour camps. With the declaration of peace, Stefani finds herself one of eight million "displaced persons" in Europe. After months of loneliness

Nora (Noni Hazlehurst) and Javo (Colin Friels). Ken Cameron's *Monkey Grip* (1982).

and despair, she is re-united with Mike at a refugee camp. . . In 1959. . .they undertake the long process of seeking resettlement in Australia.'

Pike and Cooper, *Australian Film 1900–1977*, p. 278.

Monkey Grip

Ken Cameron

Colour, 35mm, 99 mins, 1982

Pavilion Films.

Producer: Patricia Lovell.

Scriptwriter: Ken Cameron, in association with Helen Garner. Based on the novel by Helen Garner.

Director of photography: David Gribble.

Production designer: Clark Munro.

Sound recordist: Mark Lewis.

Editor: David Huggett.

Composer: Bruce Smeaton.

Cast: Noni Hazlehurst (Nora), Colin Friels (Javo), Alice Garner (Gracie), Harold Hopkins (Willie), Candy Raymond (Lillian), Michael Caton (Clive), Tim Burns (Martin), Christina Amphlett (Angela), Don Miller-Robinson (Gerald), Lisa Peers (Rita).

Nora is in her early thirties, recently divorced and caring for her 10-year-old daughter, Gracie. She is a woman trying to live free of the compromises of conventional domesticity and dependence on men. In spite of this, she is drawn into a dangerously obsessive relationship with Javo, an actor addicted to heroin. The film takes place from one summer to the next as Nora attempts to gain control over her life.

Mr. Chedworth Steps Out

Ken G. Hall

Black and white, 35mm, 92 mins, 1939

Cinesound Productions.

Producer: Ken G Hall.

Scriptwriter: Frank Harvey. Based on the novel by Francis Morton Howard.

Director of photography: George Heath.

Production designer: Eric Thompson.

Sound recordist: Clive Cross.

Editor: William Shepherd.

Composer: Hamilton Webber.

Cast: Cecil Kellaway (George Chedworth), James Raglan (Brian Carford), Joan Deering (Gwen Chedworth), Rita Pauncefort (Mrs Chedworth), Jean Hatton (Susie Chedworth), Peter Finch (Arthur Chedworth), Rodney Jacobs (Fred Chedworth), Sidney Wheeler (Leon Fencott), Ronald Whelan (Benny), Leslie Victor (Leslie).

'Chedworth, a mild-mannered clerk, is underpaid and abused by everyone. . .When his employers are forced to reduce staff, Chedworth is demoted and becomes caretaker of an old warehouse. He despairs of his financial situation but one day finds a bag of money, which, unknown to him, is counterfeit. He starts to take a new interest in life and soon wins a fortune. . . Chedworth surrenders the counterfeit hoard but retains his legitimate fortune and his new self-confidence.'

Pike and Cooper, *Australian Film 1900–1977*, p. 241

My Brilliant Career

Gill Armstrong

Colour, 35mm, 100 mins, 1979

The New South Wales Film Corporation & GUO Film Distributors present Margaret Fink's Production.

Producer: Margaret Fink.

Scriptwriter: Eleanor Witcombe. Based on the novel by Miles Franklin.

Director of photography: Don McAlpine.

Production designer: Luciana Arrighi.

Sound recordist: Don Connolly.

Editor: Nicholas Beauman.

Composer: Nathan Waks.

Cast: Judy Davis (Sybylla Melvyn), Sam Neill (Harry Beecham), Wendy Hughes (Aunt Helen), Robert Grubb (Frank Hawden), Max Cullen (Mr McSwat), Aileen Britton (Grandma Bossier), Peter Whitford (Uncle Julius), Patricia Kennedy (Aunt Gussie), Alan Hopgood (Father), Julia Blake (Mother).

Market Researcher (Graeme Blundell) and transexual showgirl. John B. Murray's *The Naked Bunyip* (1970).

Sybylla Melvyn, a sensitive and passionate teenager who cannot bear the dull life on her parents' farm, leaves for her grandmother's home, where she begins to yearn for an artistic life. There she meets, and is drawn to, landowner Harry Beecham. The film ends with Sybylla's being faced with a decision between her less-than-perfect love for Harry, and her desire to pursue an independent life.

My First Wife

Paul Cox

Colour, 35mm, 95 mins, 1984

Dofine.

Producers: Jane Ballantyne, Paul Cox.

Scenario: Paul Cox.

Screen adaptation: Paul Cox, Bob Ellis.

Director of photography: Yuri Sokol.

Art director: Asher Bilu.

Sound recordist: Ken Hammond.

Editor: Tim Lewis.

Cast: John Hargreaves (John), Wendy Hughes (Helen), Lucy Charlotte Angwin (Lucy), David Cameron (Tom), Anna Jemison (Hilary), Betty Lucas (Helen's Mother), Lucy Uralov (John's Mother), Robin Lovejoy (John's Father), Charles Tingwell (Helen's Father), Jon Finlayson (Bernard).

My First Wife is the story of the collapse of the marriage between John and Helen. Helen has decided to leave, and it is John who lacks the inner resources to cope with the impending tragedy. Slowly he is sucked into a tunnel of despair, fighting his conservative nature and the romantic memories of his married life. There is, too, the matter of who should have custody of the child.

N

The Naked Bunyip

John B. Murray

Colour, 16mm, 136 mins, 1970

Southern Cross Films.

Producer: John B. Murray.

Scriptwriters: Ray Taylor, John B. Murray, Phillip Adams.

Director of photography: Bruce McNaughton.

Editor: Brian Kavanagh.

Composers: Janet Laurie, Gerald Lester.

Song: 'Let's Make Love', lyrics by John Romeril.

Cast: Graeme Blundell (Market Researcher), Gordon Rumph (Computer Chief), Barry Humphries (Edna Everage).

A shy and introverted young man is chosen by an advertising agency to conduct a survey on sex in Australia. He is soon adrift in a sea of sexual experience as he investigates homosexuality, transvestites, prostitution, strip clubs, pack-rape, permissive morality, pornography—everything, in fact, except 'normal' heterosexuality.

The Navigator: A Medieval Odyssey

Vincent Ward

Colour, 35mm, 91 mins, 1988

Arena Film and the Film Investment Corporation of New Zealand present an Australian–New Zealand Co-Production produced with the assistance of the AFC and the NZ Film Commisssion.

Producer: John Maynard.

Scriptwriters: Vincent Ward, Kely Lyons, Geoff Chapple. Based on an original idea by Vincent Ward.

Director of photography: Geoffrey Simpson.

Production designer: Sally Campbell.

Sound recordist: Dick Reade.

Editor: John Scott.

Composer: Davood A. Tabrizi.

Cast: Bruce Lyons (Connor), Chris Haywood (Arno), Hamish McFarlane (Griffin), Marshall Napier (Searle), Noel Appleby (Ulf), Paul Livingson (Martin), Sarah Pierse (Linnet), Mark Wheatley (Tog 1), Tony Herbert (Tog 2), Jessica Cardiff-Smith (Esme).

It is Cumbria 1348, the year of the Black Death. Griffin's older brother returns from the outside world in a state of despair, until Griffin tells of his dream and reveals their only source of survival: before dawn, make a tribute to God and place a spire on a distant cathedral. Griffin sets out on a bizarre journey with Connor and four mining friends. Together they tunnel through the earth to a new world: New Zealand, 1988. But Griffin has a chilling new premonition: who will fall from the cathedral?

New Guinea Patrol

Peter Diamond

Colour, 43 mins, 1958 (shot 1955)

Commonwealth Film Unit, Department of the Interior–Film Australia.

Producer: Ron Maslyn Williams.

Director of photography: John Leake.

Composer: John Antill.

One of the more notable Department of Information documentaries of the 1950s.

Newsfront

Phillip Noyce

Colour, 35mm, 110 minutes, 1978

Palm Beach Pictures in association with the NSW Film Corporation, Australian Film Commission and Village Roadshow.

Producer: David Elfick.

Scriptwriter[s]: Phillip Noyce [and, uncredited, Bob Ellis]. Based on an original screenplay by Bob Ellis. From a concept by David Elfick [and, uncredited, Philippe Mora].

Director of photography: Vincent Monton.

Connor (Bruce Lyons), Griffin (Hamish McFarlane), Searle (Marshall Napier), Ulf (Noel Appleby) and Arno (Chris Haywood). Vincent Ward's *The Navigator: A Medieval Odyssey* (1988).

Frank Maguire (Gerard Kennedy) and Amy McKenzie (Wendy Hughes). Phillip Noyce's *Newsfront* (1978).

Production designer: Lissa Coote.

Sound recordist: Tim Lloyd.

Editor: John Scott.

Composer: William Motzing.

Cast: Bill Hunter (Len Maguire), Wendy Hughes (Amy McKenzie), Gerard Kennedy (Frank Maguire), Chris Haywood (Chris Hewitt), John Ewart (Charlie Henderson), Angela Punch (Fay Maguire), Don Crosby (A. G. Marwood), Bryan Brown (Geoff the Editor), John Clayton (Cliff the Production Manager), Lorna Lesley (Ellie).

Newsfront is the dramatic story of the newsreel cameramen who lived and worked in Australia during the golden era of the newsreel from 1948 to 1956. Len Maguire is a top cameraman whose devotion to his work and loyalty to his company bring him into conflict. Len's brother, Frank, heads the Australian branch of an American newsreel company in competition with Len's company. The lives of these people are played out against a backdrop of reality, the film capturing the historic moments of two turbulent decades.

Nirvana Street Murder

Aleksi Vellis

Colour, 35mm, 75 mins, 1991

Aleksi Vellis.

Producer: Fiona Cochrane.

Scriptwriter: Aleksi Vellis.

Director of photography: Mark Lane.

Production designer: Lisa Thompson.

Sound recordist: Mark Atkin.

Editor: Aleksi Vellis.

Cast: Mark Little (Boady), Ben Mendelsohn (Luke), Mary Coustas (Helen), Sheila Florance (Molly), Tamara Saulwick (Penny), Yiorgo (Smeg), Roberto Micale (Hector), Russell Gilbert (Boss), Tibor Gyapjas (Vas), George Zogopoulas (Jim).

A black comedy about two brothers who work at the local abattoirs. Boady is childish, violent and mentally unstable; Luke is normal.

"Norman Loves Rose"

Henri Safran

Colour, 35mm, 98 mins, 1982

Norman Films.

Producers: Henri Safran, Basil Appleby.

Scriptwriter: Henri Safran.

Director of photography: Vince Monton.

Production designer: Darrell Lass.

Sound recordist: Ross Linton.

Editor: Dan Saunders.

Composer: Mike Perjanik.

Cast: Carol Kane (Rose), Tony Owen (Norman), Myra De Groot (Mother), David Downer (Michael), Barry Otto (Charles), Sandy Gore (Maureen), Warren Mitchell (Morris), Virginia Hey (The Girlfriend), Louise Pajo (Shirley), Valerie Newstead (1st Lady).

"Norman Loves Rose" is not a typical love story. Norman is a sensitive, precocious thirteen year old preparing for the formal entry into Jewish manhood, the Bar Mitzvah. Rose is his sister-in-law and the object of his passion. When the story begins, Rose is pregnant. Could Norman be responsible?

O

The Odd Angry Shot

Tom Jeffrey

Colour, 35mm, 92 mins, 1979

A Samson Film.

Producers: Sue Milliken, Tom Jeffrey.

Scriptwriter: Tom Jeffrey. Based on the novel by William Nagle.

Director of photography: Don McAlpine.

Production designer: Bernard Hides.

Sound recordist: Don Connolly.

Editor: Brian Kavanagh.

Composer: Michael Carlos.

Cast: Graham Kennedy (Harry), Bryan Brown (Rogers), John Hargreaves (Bung), John Jarratt (Bill), Graeme Blundell (Dawson), Ian Gilmour (Scott), Richard Moir (Medic), Graham Rouse (The Cook), John Allen (Lieut Golonka), Tony Barry (Black Ronnie).

A comedy which follows a group of Australian regular army soldiers—members of the élite Special Air Service—through a year's tour of duty in Vietnam in the late 1960s. It shows how they cope with the closeness and frustration of camp life, punctuated by patrols into the jungle to fire 'the odd angry shot'.

Boady (Mark Little) and Luke (Ben Mendelsohn). Aleksi Vellis' *Nirvana Street Murder* (1991).

Rogers (Bryan Brown). Tom Jeffrey's *The Odd Angry Shot* (1979).

One Hundred a Day

Gill Armstrong

Black and white, 16mm, 8 mins, 1973

Australian Film and Television School.

Scriptwriter: Gillian Armstrong. Based on 'How Beautiful are Thy Feet' by Alan Marshall.

Directors of photography: Ross King, Bill Constable.

Production designer: Chris French.

Sound recordists: Tim Lloyd, Barry Brown.

Editor: David Stiven.

Cast: Rosalie Fletcher (Main Character); Jenee Welsh, Virginia Portingale, Even Wynne, Beth Child, Sue Piggott.

Based on Alan Marshall's 'How Beautiful are Thy Feet', *One Hundred a Day* is set during the 1930s and concerns a girl struggling to survive the working day at a shoe factory after she has had a backyard abortion.

On Our Selection

Raymond Longford

Black and white, 6890 ft, 1920

Producer: E. J. Carroll.

Scriptwriter: Raymond Longford. Based on the stories by Steele Rudd.

Director of photography: Arthur Higgins.

Cast: Percy Walshe (Dad Rudd), Beatrice Esmond (Mrs Rudd), Tal Ordell (Dave), Arthur Greenaway (Sandy Taylor), Evelyn Johnson (Kate), Fred Coleman (Dan), Charlotte Beaumont (Sarah), Arthur Wilson (Joe), Olga Willard (Nellie), Bisell (Mrs Anderson).

'Mrs Rudd and the younger of her six children go to join Dad and their eldest son, Dave, on the family's selection, where Dad and Dave have made a clearing and built a slab and bark hut. The family gradually adjusts to bush life and everyone helps to till the field. . .Later, romance develops between the Rudds' eldest daughter, Kate, and a neighbour, Sandy Taylor, and the film ends with the celebration of Kate's wedding, and the handing over to the Rudds of the deeds to the selection.'

Pike and Cooper, *Australian Film 1900–1977*, p. 132.

On Our Selection

Ken G. Hall

Black and white, 35mm, 99 mins, 1932

Cinesound Productions.

Producer: Bert Bailey.

Scriptwriters: Bert Bailey, Ken G. Hall. Based on the works of Steele Rudd.

Director of photography: Walter Sully.

Sound recordists: Arthur Smith, Clive Cross.

Editor: George Malcolm.

Cast: Bert Bailey (Dad Rudd), Fred MacDonald (Dave), Alfreda Bevan (Mum), John McGowan (Maloney), Molly Raynor (Kate), Dick Fair (Sandy), John Warwick (Jim Carey), Billy Driscoll (Uncle), Lilias Adeson (Lil), Len Budrick (Old Carey).

An affectionate and personal portrait of life in the Australian bush—not the life on the big stations or of the powerful squatters, but the daily toil of the small selector who struggles to make a living from his few acres, reliant not on capital but on his own wit and physical labour. The Rudds became the archetypal bush family for most Australians after the publication in 1895 of the first story of 'Steele Rudd' (pseud. of Arthur Hoey Davis) in *The Bulletin*.

Moira Davidson (Ava Gardner) in Stanley Kramer's *On the Beach* (1959).

Girl (Rosalie Fletcher). Gill Armstrong's *One Hundred a Day* (1973).

On the Beach

Stanley Kramer	
Black and white, 35mm, 134 mins, 1959	
Lomitas Productions.	

Producer: Stanley Kramer.

Scriptwriters: John Paxton, James Lee Barrett. Based on the novel by Nevil Shute.

Director of photography: Giuseppe Rotunno.

Production designer: Fernando Carrere.

Sound recordist: Hans Wetzel.

Editor: Frederic Knudston.

Composer: Ernest Gold.

Cast: Gregory Peck (Dwight Towers), Ava Gardner (Moira Davidson), Fred Astaire (Julian Osborn), Anthony Perkins (Peter Holmes), Donna Anderson (Mary Holmes), John Tate (Admiral Birdie), Lola Brooks (Lieutenant Hosgood), Guy Doleman (Farrel), John Meillon (Swain), Harp McGuire (Sundstrom).

'The time is five years in the future (1964) and Melbourne has not yet succumbed to the drifting radioactive fall-out caused by atomic war in the northern hemisphere. The story follows five people in their preparation for death.'

Pike and Cooper, *Australian Film 1900–1977*, p. 298.

Or Forever Hold Your Peace

Kit Guyatt and others	
Black and white, 16mm, 1970	
AFC Experimental Film and Television Fund.	

Producer: Richard Brennan.

A Sydney documentary about the growing anti-Vietnam and anti-war protests in the last 1960s and early 1970s. For a Melbourne perspective, see *Beginnings* (Rod Bishop, Gordon Glenn, Scott Murray, Andrew Pecze, 1971).

Our Friends, the Hayseeds (aka: The Hayseeds)

Beaumont Smith	
Black and white, 5000 ft, 1917	
Beaumont Smith's Productions.	

Producer: Beaumont Smith.

Scriptwriter: Beaumont Smith.

Director of photography: Harry Krischock.

Cast: Roy Redgrave (Dad Hayseed), Walter Cornock (Joe Hayseed), Pearl Hellmrich (Pansy Duggan), Margaret Gordon (Mrs Hayseed), J. Plumpton Wilson (Parson), H. H. Wallace (Dan Hayseed), Vera Spaull (Poppy Hayseed), Cecil Haines (Lizzie Hayseed), Jack Radford (Tommie Hayseed), Peter Ward (Peter Hayseed).

This, the first of seven Hayseeds adventures, deals primarily with the rivalry between the Hayseeds and the Duggans, neighbours on adjoining selections in the bush. Joe Hayseed and Pansy Duggan are keen to be married but a quarrel between the two fathers arises when the Hayseeds' cow gets into the Duggans' corn. The young lovers are forbidden to see each other.

The Overlanders

Harry Watts	
Black and white, 35mm, 91 mins, 1946	
Ealing Studios.	

Producer: Michael Balcon.

Scriptwriter: Harry Watts.

Director of photography: Osmond Borradaile.

Sound recordist: Beresford Hallett.

Editor: Inman Hunter.

Composer: John Ireland.

Cast: Chips Rafferty (Dan McAlpine) John Nugent Hayward (Bill Parsons), Daphne Campbell (Mary Parsons), Jean Blue (Mrs Parsons), Helen Grieve (Helen Parsons), John Fernside (Corky), Peter Pagan (Sinbad), Frank Ransome (Charlie), Stan Tolhurst (Bert), Marshall Crosby (Minister).

The story of the gigantic cattle drive that took place in 1942 as part of a 'scorched earth' policy in northern Australia to remove food supplies from the reach of the Japanese. Altogether,

85 000 cattle were driven from the north of Western Australia to the Queensland coast, a 2000-mile trek taking nearly two years to complete. Elements of romance and comedy are woven lightly into Watt's screenplay to provide commercial ballast, but the film is primarily documentary in spirit.

P

Palm Beach

Albie Thoms

Colour, 16mm, 88 mins, 1980 (shot 1978)

Albie Thoms Productions.

Producer: Albie Thoms.

Scriptwriter: Albie Thoms.

Director of photography: Oscar Scherl.

Editor: Albie Thoms.

Sound recordists: Michael Moore, Rick Creaser.

Composer: Terry Hannigan.

Cast: Nat Young (Nick Taylor), Ken Brown (Joe Ryan), Amanda Berry (Leilani Adams), Bryan Brown (Paul Kite), Julie Mc-Gregor (Kate O'Brien), John Flaus (Larry Kent), Bronwyn Stevens-Jones (Wendy Naylor), David Lourie (Zane Green), Peter Wright (Rupert Roberts).

A tale of surf, drugs and rock 'n' roll in Sydney's northern beaches. Three stories intertwine: a surfer, from Maroubra, heads north to Palm Beach to see his old friend, Ned, and get hold of some acid; Leilani from Dee Why has run away from home; while Paul from Mona Vale is unemployed and angry. Their lives are observed over a 48-hour period.

The Passionate Industry

Joan Long

Black and white, 16mm, 59 mins, 1973

Film Australia.

Producer: Frank Bagnal.

Scriptwriter: Joan Long.

Directors of photography: Mick Von Bornemann, Michael Edols.

Editor: Ian Walker.

Sound recordists: Julian Ellingworth, Howard Spry.

Composer: Al Franks.

Documentary record of Australia's early cinema.

Passionless Moments: Recorded in Sydney Australia Sunday October 2nd

Jane Campion, Gerard Lee

Black and white, 16mm, 12.5 mins, 1984

Australian Film and Television School.

Producers: Jane Campion, Gerard Lee.

Scriptwriter: Gerard Lee, assisted by Jane Campion.

Directors of photography: Jane Campion, Alexander Proyas.

Editor: Veronika Haussler.

Production designer: Keith Holmes.

Sound recordists: Moppo, Ged Boy Lee [Gerard Lee].

Cast: David Benton (Ed Turnbury), Ann Berriman (Gwen Gilbert), Alan Brown (Neighbour), Sean Callinan (Jim Newbury), Paul Chubb (Jim Simpson), Sue Collie (Angela Elliott), Haedyn Cunningham (Board Member), Ron Gobert (Board Member), Elias Ibrahim (Ibrahim Ibrahim), Paul Melchert (Arnold).

Dark and funny vignettes of a life perceived to be happening somewhere in Sydney in 1984. Directed by Jane Campion and Gerard Lee, who also co-wrote *Sweetie*. The Campion–Lee collaborations make an interesting comparison to Campion's work without Lee, such as *2 Friends* (tele-feature, 1986) and *An Angel at My Table* (mini-series, 1990).

Patrick

Richard Franklin

Colour, 35mm, 115 mins, 1978

AIFC and Antony I. Ginnane in association with Filmways Australia present for Australian International Film Corporation.

Producers: Antony I. Ginnane, Richard Franklin.

Scriptwriter: Everett de Roche.

Director of photography: Don McAlpine.

Production designer: Leslie Binns.

Sound recordist: Paul Clark.

Editor: Edward McQueen-Mason.

Composer: Brian May.

Cast: Susan Penhaligon (Kathy Jacquard), Robert Helpmann (Dr Roget), Rod Mullinar (Ed Jacquard), Julia Blake (Matron Cassidy), Helen Hemingway (Sister Williams), Bruce Barry (Brian Wright), Robert Thompson (Patrick), Maria Mercedes (Nurse Panicale), Walter Pym (Captain Fraser), Frank Wilson (Detective Sgt Grant).

'Patrick has been in a coma in a Melbourne hospital for three years after killing his mother and her lover. Kathy Jacquard, separated from her husband Ed, is a nurse at the hospital which is run by Dr Roget. Kathy begins to feel that Patrick is trying to communicate with her...Inexplicable events [start] to happen and Patrick is able to talk to Kathy via an electric typewriter...'

David Stratton, *The Last New Wave: The Australian Film Revival*, Angus & Robertson, Sydney, 1980, p. 251.

Patrick White's The Night the Prowler

Jim Sharman

Colour, 35mm, 90 mins, 1979

Paul Kite (Bryan Brown). Albie Thoms` *Palm Beach* (1980).

Chariot Films.

Producer: Anthony Buckley.

Scriptwriter: Patrick White. Based on White's play.

Director of photography: David Sanderson.

Production designer: Luciana Arrighi.

Sound recordist: Don Connolly.

Editor: Sara Bennett.

Composer: Cameron Allan.

Cast: Ruth Cracknell (Doris Bannister), John Frawley (Humphrey Bannister), Kerry Walker (Felicity Bannister), John Derum (John Galbraith), Maggie Kirkpatrick (Madge Hopkirk), Terry Camilleri (Prowler), Alexander Archdale (Sir Roland).

Exploiting the furore surrounding her attempted rape, a young woman emerges from the claustrophobia of a wealthy conservative family and turns from victim to criminal, stalking the streets of Sydney by night in relentless pursuit of her own liberation. Based on a play by Patrick White.

Pearls and Savages

Frank Hurley

Black and white, 1921

Stoll Hurley Productions.

'In December 1920 [Hurley] left Australia to record the work of Anglican missions in Papua and to make a "travelogue entertainment". The result was *Pearls and Savages*, a documentary released in Sydney in December 1921, with Hurley lecturing from the stage as the film was screened. ... [Hurley made] another major trip to Papua to secure additional footage. The expanded film, *With the Headhunters in Papua*, was released in Sydney in October 1923.'

Pike and Cooper, *Australian Film 1900–1977*, p. 171.

Peel

Jane Campion

Colour, 16mm, 9 mins, 1982

Australian Film and Television School.

Executive producer: Ulle Ryghe.

Scriptwriter: Jane Campion.

Director of photography: Sally Bongers.

Sound recordists: Sue Kerr, Kay Dineen, Ian Yates.

Editor: Jane Campion.

Composer: Ralph Tyrrell.

Cast: Tim Pye (Father), Katie Pye (Sister), Ben Pye (Martin).

A family takes a tense car trip, during which the peel of an orange takes on ominous significance. Winner of the Palme d'Or for Best Short Film at the Cannes Film Festival in 1986.

A Personal History of the Australian Surf: Being the Confessions of a Straight Poofter

Michael Blakemore

Colour, 16mm, 52 mins, 1981

Adams-Packer Film Productions.

Producer: Jeremy Cornford.

Scriptwriter: Michael Blakemore.

Director of photography: Tony Wilson.

Production designer: Roger Wood.

Sound recordist: Ian Wilson.

Editor: David Pulbrook.

Composer: Peter Best.

Cast: Michael Blakemore (Himself and His Father), Leaf Nowland (Michael Blakemore aged Seven), Mathew Watkin (Michael aged Ten), Daniel Matz (Michael aged Thirteen), Michael Shearman (Michael aged Eighteen); Colin Angus, Angela Anton, Helen Anton, Spiro Anton, Dennis Ashdown, Cynthia Cooper.

'Michael Blakemore's irresistibly attractive *A Personal History of the Australian Surf* [: *Being the Confessions of a Straight Poofter*] is a dramatised documentary of his own childhood and adolescence. It draws on most of the aspects of growing up...father-son conflict, European influences...school and university which offered little stimulus to an imagination saturated with the movies, and sexual frustrations—and does so with grace and wit.'

Brian McFarlane, *Australian Cinema 1970–1985*, William Heinemann Australia, Melbourne, pp. 154, 155.

Petersen

Tim Burstall

Colour, 35mm, 107 mins, 1974

Hexagon Productions.

Producer: Tim Burstall.

Scriptwriter: David Williamson.

Director of photography: Robin Copping.

Production designer: Bill Hutchinson.

Sound recordist: Ken Hammond.

Editor: David Bilcock.

Composer: Peter Best.

Cast: Jack Thompson (Tony Petersen), Jacki Weaver (Susie Petersen), Wendy Hughes (Trish Kent), Belinda Giblin (Moira), Arthur Dignam (Charles Kent), Charles Tingwell (Reverend Petersen), Helen Morse (Jane), John Ewart (Pete), David Phillips (Heinz), Christine Amor (Annie).

Tony Petersen, an electrical tradesman and former football star, reacts against the values of suburbia and enrols at university in the arts faculty. In this new milieu, he is quickly involved in a public demonstration of lovemaking as a protest against sexual

Harry Telford (Martin Vaughan), holding hat, at Melbourne Cup. Simon Wincer's *Phar Lap* (1983).

conventions, a fight with bikies at a party and an affair with his tutor, Trish Kent. In all of these activities, Petersen is welcomed for his ingenuous, extroverted manner and his physical aggression, but ultimately he finds himself betrayed. He rapes Trish then returns to his life as a tradesman.

Phar Lap (US: **A Horse Called Phar Lap**)

Simon Wincer

Colour, 35mm, 118 mins, 1983

John Sexton Productions, in association with Michael Edgley International.

Producer: John Sexton.

Scriptwriter: David Williamson.

Director of photography: Russell Boyd.

Production designer: Laurence Eastwood.

Sound recordist: Gary Wilkins.

Editor: Tony Paterson.

Composer: Bruce Rowland.

Cast: Tom Burlinson (Tommy Woodcock), Martin Vaughan (Harry Telford), Judy Morris (Bea Davis), Celia de Burgh (Vi Telford), Ron Liebman (Dave Davis), Vincent Ball (Lachlan McKinnon), John Stanton (Eric Connolly), Peter Whitford (Bert Wolfe), Robert Grubb (William Nielson), Richard Morgan ('Cashy' Martin).

The next great Australian legend after 'The Man from Snowy River' is the saga of Phar Lap, the legendary New Zealand racehorse which won the Melbourne Cup in 1932. Phar Lap started 51 times for 37 wins and five placings between 1929 and 1932, before dying mysteriously in California in 1932. Newspaper placards of 6 April 1932 said simply: 'HE'S DEAD'! Flags flew at half-mast, while pavement artists drew portraits of their champ. Wincer's film is a loving tribute to the legend.

The Piano

Jane Campion

Colour, 35mm, 120 mins, 1993

Jan Chapman Productions. French-financed Australia-New Zealand co-production.

Producer: Jan Chapman.

Scriptwriter: Jane Campion.

Director of photography: Stuart Dryburgh.

Production designer: Andrew McAlpine.

Sound recordist: Lee Smith.

Editor: Veronika Jenet.

Composer: Michael Nyman.

Cast: Holly Hunter (Ada), Harvey Keitel (George Baines), Sam Neill (Stewart), Anna Paquin (Flora), Kerry Walker (Aunt Morag), Genevieve Lemon (Nessie), Tungia Baker (Hira), Te Whatanui Skipwith (Chief Nihe), Ian Mune (Reverend).

Ada arrives, with her nine-year-old daughter and her piano, to an arranged marriage in the remote bush of nineteenth-century New Zealand. Of all her belongings, her husband refuses to transport the piano and it is left behind on the beach. Unable to bear its certain destruction, Ada strikes a bargain with an illiterate neighbour. She may have her piano back if she allows him to do certain things while she plays. The arrangement draws all three deeper into an emotional and sexual bond remarkable for its naive passion and frightening disregard for limits.

Picnic at Hanging Rock

Peter Weir

Colour, 35mm, 115 mins, 1975

Picnic Productions.

Alan Anderson's *The Pictures That Moved* (1968).

Producers: Hal McElroy, Jim McElroy, in association with Pat Lovell.

Scriptwriter: Cliff Green. Based on the novel by Joan Lindsay.

Director of photography: Russell Boyd.

Production designer: David Copping.

Sound recordist: Don Connolly.

Editor: Max Lemon.

Composer: Bruce Smeaton.

Cast: Rachel Roberts (Mrs Appleyard), Dominic Guard (Michael Fitzhubert), Helen Morse (Diane de Poitiers), Jacki Weaver (Minnie), Vivean Gray (Miss McCraw), Kirsty Child (Dora Lumley), Anne Lambert (Miranda), Karen Robson (Irma), Jane Vallis (Marion), Christine Schuler (Edith).

A tale of mystery and menace in a sunny Australian landscape. The story of a group of late-Victorian era schoolgirls and one of their teachers who vanish while exploring Hanging Rock. Based on the best-selling novel by Joan Lindsay, the film has spawned many explanations for its mystery, including a witty book by Yvonne Rousseau.

The Pictures That Moved

Alan Anderson

Black and white, 16mm, 46 mins, 1968 (shot 1964)

Film Australia.

Producer: Frank Bagnall.

Scriptwriter: Joan Long.

Director of photography: George Alexander.

Sound recordist: Gordon Wraxall.

Composer: Al Franks.

A documentary record of Australia's silent cinema.

The Plains of Heaven

Ian Pringle

Colour, 16mm, 80 mins, 1982

286

Max (Ivar Kants) and Jill Cowper (Judy Morris). Peter Weir's *The Plumber* (1979).

Producer: John Cruthers.

Scriptwriters: Ian Pringle, Doug Ling, Elizabeth Parsons.

Director of photography: Ray Argall.

Production designer: Elizabeth Stirling.

Sound recordist: Bruce Emery.

Editor: Ray Argall.

Composer: Andrew Duffield.

Cast: Richard Moir (Barker), Reg Evans (Cunningham), Gerard Kennedy (Lenko), John Flaus (Landrover Owner), Jenny Cartwright (Nurse), Brian McKenzie (Lewis), Adam Biscombe (Soldier on Train), Joe Ford (Video producer), Bryce Menzies (ISC Man), Bid Nosal (Secretary).

Two men work on a satellite relay station on the Bogong High Plains, each obsessed in his own way. The film follows the working out of these obsessions in the men's response to the vast and elemental landscape of the plains of heaven.

The Plumber

Peter Weir

Colour, 16mm, 76 mins, 1979

Producer: Matt Carroll.

Scriptwriter: Peter Weir.

Director of photography: David Sanderson.

Production designer: Wendy Weir.

Sound recordist: Ken Hammond.

Editor: G. Turney-Smith.

Composer: Gerry Tolland.

Cast: Judy Morris (Jill Cowper), Ivar Kants (Max), Robert Coleby (Brian Cowper), Candy Raymond (Meg), Henri Szeps (Dept Head).

An insolent plumber arrives at the door of two thin-skinned academic types who haven't called him. He persuades the young wife that her bathroom needs fixing. Soon, strange noises are coming from the bathroom. . .

Proof

Jocelyn Moorhouse

Colour, 35mm, 86 mins, 1991

House & Moorhouse Films.

Producer: Lynda House.

Scriptwriter: Jocelyn Moorhouse.

Director of photography: Martin McGrath.

Production designer: Patrick Reardon.

Sound recordist: Lloyd Carrick.

Editor: Ken Sallows.

Music: Not Drowning, Waving.

Cast: Hugo Weaving (Martin), Genevieve Picot (Celia), Russell Crowe (Andy), Heather Mitchell (Mother), Jeffrey Walker (Young Martin), Daniel Pollock (Punk), Frankie J. Holden (Brian), Frank Gallacher (Vet), Saskia Post (Waitress), Belinda Davey (Doctor).

Martin, a blind photographer, uses his photographs to prove that people are not lying to him. It is the story of a man obsessed with honesty but who hides from the truth.

Puberty Blues

Bruce Beresford

Colour, 35mm, 83 mins, 1981

Limelight Productions.

Producers: Joan Long, Margaret Kelly.

Scriptwriter: Margaret Kelly. Based on the novel by Kathy Lette and Gabrielle Carey.

Director of photography: Don McAlpine.

Production designer: David Copping.

Sound recordist: Gary Wilkins.

Editors: William Anderson, Jeanine Chialvo.

Composers: Les Gock; Tim Finn (theme song).

Cast: Nell Schofield (Debbie), Jad Capelja (Sue), Geoff Rhoe (Garry), Tony Hughes (Danny), Sandy Paul (Tracey), Leander Brett (Cheryl), Jay Hackett (Bruce), Ned Lander (Strach), Joanne Olsen (Vicki), Julie Medana (Kim).

Debbie (Nell Schofield) and Sue (Jad Capelja) watch a surfing ritual. Bruce Beresford's *Puberty Blues* (1981).

The story of Debbie and Sue's growing up in a Sydney beach-side suburb and their revolt against their parents, their school and adult society. The girls fling themselves into new experiences by joining a surfie gang. Evading parental disapproval by subterfuge, they manage to carve a secret life of their own, coping with inept sex, teacher misunderstanding, alcohol, drugs, first love and the threat of pregnancy.

Pure S. . .

Bert Deling

Colour, 16mm, 83 mins, 1975

Apogee Films.

Producer: Bob Weis.

Scriptwriter: Bert Deling and cast.

Director of photography: Tom Cowan.

Sound recordist: Lloyd Carrick.

Editor: John Scott.

Cast: Gary Waddell (Lou), Ann Heatherington (Sandy), Carol Porter (Gerry), John Laurie (John), Max Gillies (Dr Wolf), Tim Robertson (Television Interviewer), Helen Garner (Jo); Phil Motherwell.

One night in the life of four junkies in search of a hit and some excitement to their lives in staid Melbourne. A low-budget,

'underground' classic, it caused considerable controversy for supposedly advocating drug use. The Commonwealth Censor stepped in by replacing three letters of the title with an ellipsis.

R

The Rats of Tobruk

Charles Chauvel

Black and white, 35mm, 95 mins, 1944

Chamun Productions.

Producer: Charles Chauvel.

Scriptwriters: Charles and Elsa Chauvel.

Director of photography: George Heath.

Editor: Gus Lowry.

Production designers: Edmund Barrie, Eric Thompson.

Sound recordists: Jack Bruce, L. J. Stuart.

Composer: Lindley Evans.

Cast: Grant Taylor (Bluey Donkin), Peter Finch (Peter Linton), Chips Rafferty (Milo Trent), Pauline Garrick (Kate Carmody), Mary Gay (Sister Mary Ellis), George Wallace (Barber of Tobruk), Joe Valli (Northumberland Fusilier), Toni Villa (Japanese Soldier); John Sherwood, Walter Pym.

John (John Laurie) and Lou (Gary Waddell). Bert Deling's *Pure S...* (1975).

'Three men—Bluey, a tough, "two-fisted" drover; Milo, a laconic dingo-trapper; and Peter, an intellectual English "new chum"—join the A.I.F. at the outbreak of war. Together they serve in North Africa against Rommel and take part in the defence of Tobruk during the long months of the siege. Peter is killed in action shortly before the end of the siege. Bluey and Milo later serve in New Guinea where Milo too is killed. Bluey returns home alone to the girl who has been waiting for him.'

Pike and Cooper, *Australian Film 1900–1977*, p. 257.

Reckless Kelly

Yahoo Serious

Colour, 35mm, 90 mins, 1993

Producers: Warwick Ross, Yahoo Serious.

Scriptwriter: Yahoo Serious.

Director of photography: Kevin Hayward.

Production designer: Graham 'Grace' Walker.

Sound recordist: Tim Lloyd.

Editor: Robert Gibson.

Cast: Yahoo Serious (Ned Kelly), Melora Hardin (Robin Banks); Alexei Sayle, Hugo Weaving, Bob Maza, Anthony Ackroyd, Adam Bowen, Russell Cheek, Steve Cox.

Ned Kelly, a modern-day bank-robber who rides a powerful, home-made motorbike, has to save his paradise island from a greedy developer.

Return Home

Ray Argall

Colour, 16mm, 87 mins, 1990

289

Composeral Films.

Producer: Cristina Pozzan.

Scriptwriter: Ray Argall.

Director of photography: Mandy Walker.

Production designer: Kerith Holmes.

Sound recordist: Bronwyn Murphy.

Editor: Ken Sallows.

Music: Joe Camilleri, Celibate Rifles, Young Moderns, Bored, This Is Serious Mum.

Cast: Dennis Coard (Noel McKenzie), Frankie J. Holden (Steve McKenzie), Ben Mendelsohn (Gary Wilson), Micki Camilleri (Judy McKenzie), Rachel Rains (Wendy), Alan Fletcher (Barry Marshall), Paul Nestor (Brian), Michelle Stanley (Gail).

Return Home is the story of one man's coming to terms with his past, and the responsibility and rewards of family love. Noel, in his late thirties, is a successful insurance broker in Melbourne who returns home one summer to the Adelaide suburb of his childhood. There, he stays with his elder brother, Steve, wife Judy and their two children. Steve runs a garage in a shopping centre that is going backward financially in the age of American franchise and a dearth of customer service. Both he and the ideals he stands for are on borrowed time.

290

Roadgames

Richard Franklin

Colour, 35mm, 101 mins, 1981

An Essaness Pictures Presentation.

Producer: Richard Franklin.

Scriptwriter: Everett de Roche.

Director of photography: Vincent Monton.

Production designer: Jon Dowding.

Sound recordists: Paul Clark, Raymond Phillips.

Editor: Edward McQueen-Mason.

Composer: Brian May.

Cast: Stacy Keach (Pat Quid), Jamie Lee Curtis (Hitch), Marion Edward (Frita), Grant Page (Smith or Jones), Thaddeus Smith (Police [sic]), Stephen Millichamp (Police [sic]), Alan Hopgood (Lester), John Murphy (Benny Balls), Bill Stacey (Captain Careful), Robert Thompson (Sleezy Rider).

Pat Quid is an eccentric truck driver on the tough Nullarbor route. One day, he realises there is a psychopathic killer sharing his territory, raping and murdering young 'ladies of the road'. Suspected by the police, and aided only by Hitch, a runaway

Hitch (Jamie Lee Curtis). Richard Franklin's *Roadgames* (1981).

heiress, Quid is caught in a race against time to catch the murderer before being arrested himself.

The Rocky Horror Picture Show

Jim Sharman

Colour, 35mm, 100 mins, 1975

Twentieth Century Fox (UK).

Producer: Michael White.

Scriptwriters: Jim Sharman, Richard O'Brien.

Director of photography: Peter Suschitzky.

Production designer: Brian Thomson.

Editor: Graeme Clifford.

Composer: Richard Hartley. Original musical play, music and lyrics by Richard O'Brien.

Cast: Tim Curry, Susan Sarandon, Barry Bostwick, Meatloaf, Richard O'Brien, Patricia Quinn, Little Nell, Jonathan Adams, Peter Hinwood, Charles Gray.

Filmed version of the hit stage musical, shot in London. 'Both show and play revel in the thoroughly bizarre mixture of gay lib, trans-sexuality, Frankenstein, Flash Gordon and B-movies. . .'

David Stratton, *The Last New Wave*, p. 163.

The Romantic Story of Margaret Catchpole

Raymond Longford

Black and white, 3000 (?) ft, 1911

Bill (Arthur Tauchert) and Doreen (Lottie Lyell). Raymond Longford's *The Sentimental Bloke* (1919).

Spencer's Pictures.

Director of photography: Ernest Higgins.

Cast: Lottie Lyell (Margaret Catchpole), Raymond Longford (Will Laud), Augustus Neville (Lieutenant Barry), Sybil Wilde (Little Kitty), William Coulter (Lord Chief Justice), E. Melville (Justice Heath), Fred Hardy (Chaloner Archdeckne).

'Margaret is arrested for horse-stealing and transported to Botany Bay. During her seven years as a convict she begins working in a children's hospital. Meanwhile, Barry [a former suitor] comes to settle in Sydney. Eventually he finds Margaret, woos and weds her, and they live happily at Windsor, where Margaret is well-loved and respected for her hospital work.'

Pike and Cooper, *Australian Film 1900–1977*, p. 30.

Romper Stomper

Geoffrey Wright

Colour, 35mm, 94 mins, 1992

Seon Films.

Producers: Daniel Scharf, Ian Pringle.

Scriptwriter: Geoffrey Wright.

Director of photography: Ron Hagen.

Production designer: Steven Jones-Evans.

Sound recordist: David Lee.

Editor: Bill Murphy.

Composer: John Clifford White.

Cast: Russell Crowe (Hando), Daniel Pollock (Davey), Jacqueline McKenzie (Gabe), Alex Scott (Martin), Leigh Russell (Sonny Jim), Daniel Wylie (Cockles), James McKenna (Bubs), Samantha Bladon (Tracy), Josephine Keen (Megan), John Brumpton (Magoo).

The story of the disintegration of an urban street gang that professes the tenets of racial cleansing.

S

The Sentimental Bloke

Raymond Longford

Black and white, 6700 ft, 1919

Southern Cross Feature Film Company.

Producer: Raymond Longford.

Scriptwriter: Raymond Longford. Based on the verse narrative, *The Song of a Sentimental Bloke*, by C. J. Dennis.

Director of photography: Arthur Higgins.

Cast: Arthur Tauchert (Bill, The Bloke), Lottie Lyell (Doreen), Gilbert Emery (Ginger Mick), Stanley Robinson (The Bloke's Friend), Harry Young (The Stror 'at Coot), Margaret Reid (Doreen's Mother), Charles Keegan (Parson), William Coulter (Uncle Jim), Helen Fergus (Nurse), C. J. Dennis (Himself).

The Bloke, a larrikin from Woolloomooloo in Sydney, 'decides to reform after a spell in jail for "stoushing Johns" during a police raid on an illegal two-up game. He sees his "ideal tart" in the market and learns that her name is Doreen. A friend arranges an introduction and the romance begins. . .Doreen and Bloke are married. With reluctance, the Bloke forsakes his drinking mate, Ginger Mick, and becomes a faithful husband.'

Pike and Cooper, *Australian Film 1900–1977*, p. 119.

Shame

Steve Jodrell

Colour, Super 16, 94 mins, 1988 (shot 1986)

Barron Films and UAA Films.

Producers: Damien Parer, Paul D. Barron.

Scriptwriters: Beverly Blankenship, Michael Brindley.

Director of photography: Joseph Pickering.

Production designer: Phil Peters.

Sound recordist: David Glasser.

Editor: Kerry Regan.

Composer: Mario Millo.

Cast: Deborra-Lee Furness (Asta Cadell), Tony Barry (Tim Curtis), Simone Buchanan (Lizzie Curtis), Gillian Jones (Tina Farrel), Peter Aanensen (Sergeant Wal Cuddy), Margaret Ford (Norma Curtis), David Franklin (Danny Fiske), Bill McClusky (Ross), Allison Taylor (Penny), Phil Dean (Gary).

When her motorcycle is damaged in a road accident, Asta Cadell, a disillusioned barrister, finds herself stuck in the small isolated country town of Ginborak. She gradually becomes aware of a conspiracy of silence: everyone knows what the boys do at night but no one dares to speak out or resist. Those who do are beaten or ostracised. But Asta is a fighter with a real sense of justice, and has no intention of being part of that silence.

Silver City

Sophia Turkiewicz

Colour, 35mm, 101 mins, 1984

Limelight Productions.

Producer: Joan Long.

Scriptwriters: Sophia Turkiewicz, Thomas Keneally.

Director of photography: John Seale.

Art director: Igor Nay.

Sound recordist: Mark Lewis.

Editor: Don Saunders.

Composer: William Motzing.

Cast: Gosia Dobrowolska (Nina), Ivar Kants (Julian), Anna Jemison (Anna), Steve Bisley (Viktor), Debra Lawrance (Helena), Ewa Brok (Mrs Bronowska), Joel Cohen (Young Daniel), Tim McKenzie (Mr Roy), Halina Abramowicz (Ella), Dennis Miller (Max).

A love story set against the epic background of postwar migration to Australia. It is 1949. Nina, 21 years old and alone in the world, arrives in Australia from Europe with a shipload of displaced

Julian (Ivar Kants), Nina (Gosia Dobrowolska) and Customs Official 1 (Robert Newman). Sophia Turkiewicz's *Silver City* (1984).

persons. She finds herself in a camp, ironically dubbed by the migrants as 'Silver City', which is row upon row of corrugated iron huts housing human hopes, despairs and dreams.

Soldiers of the Cross

Joseph Perry, Herbert Booth

Black and white, multimedia, 135 mins (approx.), 1900

The Salvation Army.

Scriptwriters: Joseph Perry, Herbert Booth.

This two-and-a-quarter-hour religious epic is a complex display interrelating thirteen short films, 200 slides and an elaborate music score using themes from hymns and the popular classics. The intention was to convey the suffering and the sorrow, the gladness and the triumph, of the early Christian martyrs, and through this emotional presentation not only to win souls but to raise funds and attract new recruits for the Salvation Army.

Sons of Matthew

Charles Chauvel

Black and white, 35mm, 107 mins, 1949 (shot 1947)

Greater Union Theatres–Universal Pictures.

Producer: Charles Chauvel.

Scriptwriters: Charles and Elsa Chauvel, Maxwell Dunn.

Directors of photography: Bert Nicholas, Carl Kayser.

Production designer: George Hurst.

Sound recordists: Allyn Barnes, Clive Cross.

Editor: Terry Banks.

Composer: Henry Krips.

Cast: Michael Pate (Shane), Ken Wayne (Barney), Tommy Burns (Luke), John Unicomb (Terry), John Ewart (Mickey). Wendy Gibb (Cathy McAllister), John O'Malley (Matthew O'Riordan), Thelma Scott (Jane O'Riordan), Dorothy Alison (Rose O'Riordan), Diane Proctor (Mary O'Riordan).

The 'epic story of Australian pioneer life, tracing the story of three generations of settlers in rugged frontier land. . . Queensland was Chauvel's home state and he had long been inspired by the life story of the pioneering O'Reilly family, who had settled in the mountains in the south-east of the state.'

Pike and Cooper, *Australian Film 1900–1977*, p. 273.

Spotswood

Mark Joffe

Colour, 35mm, 90 mins, 1992

Meridian Films in association with Smiley Films.

Producers: Richard Brennan, Timothy White.

Scriptwriters: Max Dann, Andrew Knight.

Director of photography: Ellery Ryan.

Production designer: Chris Kennedy.

Sound recordists: Lloyd Carrick (location); Angus Robertson (post-sync dia.).

Editor: Nicholas Beauman.

Composer: Ricky Fataar.

Cast: Anthony Hopkins (Wallace), Ben Mendelsohn (Carey), Alwyn Kurts (Mr Ball), Bruno Lawrence (Robert), John Walton (Finn), Rebecca Rigg (Cheryl), Toni Collette (Wendy), Russell Crowe (Kim), Angela Punch McGregor (Caroline), Daniel Wylie (Fletcher).

In the late 1960s, a time-and-motion expert is called in to modernise Ball's moccasin factory. Amid the upheaval, an 18-year-old youth attempts a major romantic take-over.

Stork

Tim Burstall

Colour, 16mm, 90 mins, 1971

Tim Burstall and Associates–Bilcock and Copping Film Productions.

Producer: Tim Burstall.

Scriptwriter: David Williamson. Based on Williamson's play, *The Coming of Stork*.

Director of photography: Robin Copping.

Production designer: Leslie Binns.

Sound recordist: Ron Green.

Editor: Edward McQueen-Mason.

Composer: Hans Poulsen.

Cast: Bruce Spence (Graham 'Stork' Wallace), Graeme Blundell (Westy), Sean McEuan (Tony), Helmut Bakaitis (Clyde), Jacki Weaver (Anna), Peter Green (Clergyman), Madeleine Orr (Stork's Mother), Peter Cummins (Sculptor), Michael Duffield (Judge), Alan Finney (Tailor).

Filmed version of David Williamson's La Mama play, *The Coming of Stork*, about a group of people sharing a house in Carlton during the late 1960s. A comedy, rejoicing in its own ockerism, it sends up many of the prevailing values of its time.

Storm Boy

Henri Safran

Colour, 35mm, 87 mins, 1976

South Australian Film Corporation.

Producer: Matt Carroll.

Scriptwriter: Sonia Borg. Based on the novel by Colin Thiele.

Director of photography: Geoff Burton.

Production designer: David Copping.

Sound recordist: Ken Hammond.

Editor: G. Turney-Smith.

Composer: Michael Carlos.

Cast: Greg Rowe (Storm Boy), Peter Cummins (Hideaway Tom), David Gulpilil (Fingerbone Bill), Judy Dick (Miss Walker), Tony Allison (Ranger), Michael Moody (Boat Master).

Storm Boy (Greg Rowe). Henri Safran's *Storm Boy* (1976).

Storm Boy lives in isolation with his fisherman father in a storm-swept wilderness area of surf and sand dunes on the south coast of South Australia. He knows no other world. One day he discovers another human being living in a wildlife sanctuary among the giant dunes: Fingerbone Bill, an Aborigine. Fingerbone teaches the boy many things about the land, the sea and his people.

The Story of the Kelly Gang

Charles Tait
Black and white, 4000 (?) ft, 1906
J & N Tait–Johnson & Gibson.

Producers: John Tait, Nevin Tait, Millard Johnson, W. A. Gibson.

Scriptwriter: Charles Tait.

Directors of photography: Millard Johnson, Orrie Perry, Reg Perry.

Cast: Elizabeth Tait (Kate Kelly), John Tait (School Master).

'In the hour or more that it lasted on the screen, [the film] presented the highlights from the bushranging career of the Kelly brothers. Using no intertitles, it was entirely dependent on an on-stage lecturer, or often a group of actors, to provide continuity and to identify the characters...the 1906 film openly presented the Kellys as gallant heroes, with the police as the enemy, and no attempt was made to apologise for the cheerful celebration of the outlawry...By September 1907 it was screening in New Zealand, and had reached England, where it toured as "the longest film ever made".'

Pike and Cooper, *Australia Film 1900–1977*, pp. 8, 9.

A Street to Die

Bill Bennett
Colour, 16mm, 91 mins, 1985
Mermaid Beach Productions.

Producer: Bill Bennett.

Scriptwriter: Bill Bennett.

Director of photography: Geoff Burton.

Production designer: Igor Nay.

Sound recordist: Leo Sullivan.

Editor: Denise Hunter.

Composers: Michael Atkinson, Michael Spicer.

Cast: Chris Haywood (Colin Turner), Jennifer Cluff (Lorraine Turner), Peter Hehir (Peter Townley), Andrew Chirgwin (Paul Turner), Peter Chirgwin (Jason Turner), Malcolm Keith (Real Estate Boss), Robin Ramsay (Tom), Steven Shaw (Factory Worker), Susannah Fowle (Julie), Peter Kowitz (Craig).

Colin Turner, a returned Vietnam veteran, and his wife, Lorraine, buy a war-service home in one of Sydney's western suburbs. After moving in, they discover their neighbours are affected by psychological and physiological disorders. When Colin is diagnosed as having incurable cancer, he suspects that there is an underlying cause which links him and his neighbours, all Vietnam veterans.

Strictly Ballroom

Baz Luhrmann
Colour, 35mm, 94 mins, 1992
M & A Film Corporation.

Producer: Tristram Miall.

Scriptwriters: Baz Luhrmann, Craig Pearce.

Director of photography: Steve Mason.

Production designer: Catherin Martin.

Sound recordist: Ben Osmo.

Editor: Jill Bilcock.

Composer: David Hirshfelder.

Cast: Paul Mercurio (Scott Hastings), Tara Morice (Fran), Bill Hunter (Barry Fife), Barry Otto (Doug Hastings), Pat Thomson (Shirley Hastings), Peter Whitford (Les Kendall), Gia Carides (Liz Holt), John Hannan (Ken Railings), Sonia Kruger-Taylor (Tina Sparkle), Pip Mushin (Wayne Burns).

When 21-year-old ballroom dancing champion Scott Hastings commits the cardinal sin of dancing his own steps, and not those laid down by the all-powerful Federation, retribution is swift. But help comes from an unexpected quarter.

Strikebound

Richard Lowenstein
Colour, 16mm, 101 mins, 1984
TRM Productions.

Producers: Miranda Bain, Timothy White.

Scriptwriter: Richard Lowenstein. Based on the book *Dead Men Don't Dig Coal* by Wendy Lowenstein.

Director of photography: Andrew de Groot.

Production designer: Tracy Watt.

Sound recordist: Dean Gawen.

Editor: Jill Bilcock.

Composer: Declan Affley.

Cast: Chris Haywood (Wattie Doig), Carol Burns (Agnes Doig), Hugh Keays-Byrne (Idris Williams), Rob Steele (Charlie Nelson), Nik Foster (Harry Bell), David Kendall (Birch), Anthony Hawkins (Police Sergeant), Marion Edward (Meg), Jo Camilleri (Italian Miner), John Flaus (Militant Miner).

Set in the Depression, in the small mining town of Wonthaggi, *Strikebound* is the dramatised story of two Scottish immigrants, Agnes and Wattie Doig, who organised the first 'stay-in' strike in Australian history. It is a dramatic story, seen through their eyes, of the build-up to the strike and the tensions that surface in the small town.

Struck by Lightning

Jerzy Domaradzki
Colour, 35mm, 105 mins, 1990
Dark Horse Pictures.

Ken Railings (John Hannan) and Tina Sparkle (Sonia Kruger-Taylor) in Baz Luhrmann's *Strictly Ballroom* (1992).

A funeral procession in Richard Lowenstein's *Strikebound* (1984).

Pat Cannizzaro (Brian Vriends), Jody (Jocelyn Betheras) and Ollie Rennie (Garry McDonald). Jerzy Domaradzki's *Struck by Lightning* (1990).

Co-producers: Terry J. Charatsis, Trevor Farrant.

Scriptwriter: Trevor Farrant.

Director of photography: Yuri Sokol.

Production designer: Peta Lawson.

Sound recordist: Toivo Lember.

Editor: Simon James.

Composer: Paul Smyth.

Cast: Garry McDonald (Ollie Rennie), Brian Vriends (Pat Cannizzaro), Catherine McClements (Jill McHugh), Henry Salter (Noel), Denis Moore (Foster), Briony Williams (Gail), Syd Williams (Spencer), Brian M. Logan (Kevin), Peter Douglas (Colin), Jocelyn Betheras (Jody).

A comedy about independence and dignity set in a workshop for the mentally handicapped. Rennie and Cannizzaro, the new physical education teacher, may battle over the same woman, but they also find new and better ways for every one to live.

Summer of the Seventeenth Doll

Leslie Norman

Black and white, 35mm, 94 mins, 1959

Hecht–Hill–Lancaster (Australia).

Producer: Leslie Norman.

Scriptwriter: John Dighton. Based on the play by Ray Lawler.

Director of photography: Paul Beeson.

Production designer: Jim Morahan.

Sound recordists: Alan Allen, Red Law.

Editor: Gordon Hales.

Composer: Benjamin Frankel.

Cast: Ernest Borgnine (Roo), Anne Baxter (Olive), John Mills (Barney), Angela Lansbury (Pearl), Ethel Gabriel (Emma), Vincent Ball (Dowd) Janette Craig (Bubba), Deryck Barnes (Bluey), Frank Wilson (Vince), Al Garcia (Dino), Jessica Noad (Nancy), Al Thomas (Spruiker), Tom Lurich (Atom Bomber), Dana Wilson (Little Girl).

'Roo and Barney are Queensland canecutters who spend the off-season each year in Sydney. For sixteen years Roo has spent the summer with Olive, a barmaid, each year bringing her a kewpie doll as a symbol of their union. In the seventeenth summer, however, things fail to run as smoothly as in the past.'

Pike and Cooper, *Australian Film 19–1977*, p. 297.

Sumner Locke Elliott's Careful He Might Hear You

Carl Schultz

Colour, 35mm, 110 mins, 1983

Syme International Productions in association with the NSW Film Corporation.

Producer: Jill Robb.

Scriptwriter: Michael Jenkins.

Director of photography: John Seale.

Production designers: John Carroll, John Wingrove.

Sound recordist: Syd Butterworth.

Editor: Richard Francis-Bruce.

Composer: Ray Cook.

Cast: Wendy Hughes (Vanessa), Robyn Nevin (Lila), Nicholas Gledhill (PS), John Hargreaves (Logan), Geraldine Turner (Vere), Isabelle Anderson (Agnes), Peter Whitford (George), Colleen Clifford (Ettie), Edward Howell (Judge), Jacqueline Kott (Miss Pile).

The story of the bitter struggle between two sisters to gain possession of PS, a 6-year-old boy, in the 1930s. PS's small world crashes around him when Aunt Vanessa sweeps in from England, rips him out of his comfortable home with Aunt Lila and cloisters him away in an exotic but cold Sydney mansion. The web of deceit between the sisters grows more elaborate and PS is forced to act as the go-between.

Sunday Too Far Away

Ken Hannam

Colour, 35mm, 94 mins, 1975

South Australian Film Corporation.

Producers: Gil Brealey, Matt Carroll.

Scriptwriter: John Dingwall.

Director of photography: Geoff Burton.

Production designer: David Copping.

Sound recordist: Barry Brown.

Editor: Rod Adamson.

Composer: Patrick Flynn.

Cast: Jack Thompson (Foley), Max Cullen (Tim King), Robert Bruning (Tom West), Jerry Thomas (Basher), Peter Cummins (Arthur Black), John Ewart (Ugly), Sean Scully (Beresford), Reg Lye (Old Garth), Graham Smith (Jim the Learner), Laurie Rankin (Old Station Hand), Lisa Peers (Sheila).

Set on one of the vast sheep stations of inland Australia in 1956, the action centres on one of the many groups of shearers which travel the country to find work. The rivalry between the men borders on madness, accentuated by the heat, the repetitious work, alcohol and isolation. The film reaches its climax with a confrontation between the shearers, who go on strike, and the non-union labour, which is brought in by the station owners to handle shearing.

The Sundowners

Fred Zinnemann

Colour, 35mm, 133 mins, 1960

Warner Bros. Productions.

Producer: Gerry Blattner.

Scriptwriter: Isobel Lennart. Based on the novel by Jon Cleary.

Director of photography: Jack Hildyard.

Production designer: Michael Stringer.

Olive (Anne Baxter), Roo (Ernest Borgnine), Pearl (Angela Lansbury) and Barney (John Mills) in Leslie Norman's *Summer of the Seventeenth Doll* (1959).

PS (Nicholas Gledhill), Lila (Robyn Nevin) and George (Peter Whitford). Carl Schultz's *Sumner Locke Elliott's Careful He Might Hear You* (1983).

Sound recordist: David Hildyard.

Editor: Jack Harris.

Composer: Dimitri Tiomkin.

Cast: Deborah Kerr (Ida Carmody), Robert Mitchum (Paddy Carmody), Peter Ustinov (Venneker), Glynis Johns (Mrs Firth), Dina Merrill (Jean Halstead), Chips Rafferty (Quinlan), Michael Anderson Jr (Sean Carmody), Lola Brooks (Liz), Wylie Watson (Herb Johnson), John Meillon (Bluey), Ronald Fraser (Ocker).

'Paddy Carmody is an itinerant farm labourer in the Australian outback. His wife, Ida, and their teenage son, Sean, want him to save money and settle down, but he always manages to elude their pressures. . .In the end Ida realizes that she cannot change Paddy's love for the free, nomadic life, and the family sets off once again in their wagon.'

Pike and Cooper, *Australian Film 1900–1977*, p. 300.

Sweetie

Jane Campion

Colour, 35mm, 97 mins, 1989

Arenafilm.

Producer: John Maynard.

Scriptwriters: Jane Campion, Gerard Lee.

Director of photography: Sally Bongers.

Production designer: Peter Harris.

Sound recordist: Leo Sullivan.

Editor: Veronika Haussler.

Composer: Martin Armiger.

Cast: Genevieve Lemon (Dawn (Sweetie)), Karen Colston (Kay), Tom Lycos (Louis), Jon Darling (Gordon), Dorothy Barry (Flo), Michael Lake (Bob), Andre Pataczek (Clayton).

Kay and Louis are at a relationship dead end, their future as bleak as that of the infant tree hidden under the bed. Then there are the nightmares of family life, and a dominating sister who has an appetite for life but runs round naked. *Sweetie* is a film filled with disturbing images and themes, and Kay is liberated only by the death of Sweetie, who is a bizarre manifestation of social/family control.

T

The Tale of Ruby Rose

Roger Scholes

Colour, 16mm, 101 mins, 1988 (shot 1986)

Hemdale Film Corporation in association with Antony I. Ginnane and FGH, a Seon Film production.

Producers: Bryce Menzies, Andrew Wiseman.

Scriptwriter: Roger Scholes.

Director of photography: Steve Mason.

Production designer: Bryce Perrin.

Sound recordist: Bob Cutcher.

Editor: Roger Scholes.

Composer: Paul Schutze.

Cast: Melita Jurisic (Ruby Rose), Chris Haywood (Henry Rose), Rod Zuanic (Gem), Martyn Sanderson (Bennett), Sheila Florance (Grandma), Sheila Kennelly (Cook), John McKelvey (Tasker), Wilkie Collins (Father), Nell Dobson (Mrs Bennett), Terry Garcia (Vassi).

Located among the haunting peaks and brooding mists of Tasmania's central highlands, *The Tale of Ruby Rose* is the story of a woman overcoming an intense fear of the dark. Ruby lives with her husband and their adopted son in primitive conditions, earning a living from fur trapping. In search of her past, she surmounts her phobia, and leaves the mountain to go down into the valley.

They're a Weird Mob

Michael Powell

Colour, 35mm, 112 mins, 1966

Williamson-Powell International Films.

Producer: Michael Powell.

Scriptwriter: Richard Imrie (pseud. of Emeric Pressburger). Based on the novel by Nino Culotta.

Director of photography: Arthur Grant.

Production designer: Dennis Gentle.

Sound recordist: Alan Allen.

Editor: G. Turney-Smith.

Composers: Lawrence Leonard, Alan Boustead.

Songs: 'Big Country' and 'In this Man's Country' by Reen Devereaux; 'I Kiss You, You Kiss Me' by Walter Chiari; 'Cretan Dance' by Mikis Theodorakis, from *III Met by Moonlight*.

Cast: Walter Chiari (Nino Culotta), Clare Dunne (Kay Kelly), Chips Rafferty (Harry Kelly), Alida Chelli (Giuliana), Ed Devereaux (Joe), Slim de Grey (Pat), John Meillon (Dennis), Charles Little (Jimmy), Anne Haddy (Barmaid), Jack Allen (Fat Man in Bar).

A comedy about an Italian's coming to Australia and coping with all manner of cultural differences. Nino, a journalist at home, becomes a labourer and falls in love with an Australian woman, Kay. After overcoming racial opposition from her father, the film ends with a marriage celebration.

Three in One

Cecil Holmes

Black and white, 35mm, 89 mins, 1957 (shot 1955)

Australian Tradition Films.

Producer: Cecil Holmes.

Director of photography: Ross Wood.

Sound recordist: Hans Wetzel.

Editor: A William Copeland.

Composer: Raymond Hanson.

The film consists of three stories:

'Joe Wilson's Mates'

Scriptwriter: Rex Rienits. Based on the short story, 'The Union Buries Its Dead', by Henry Lawson.

Cast: Edmund Wilson (Tom Stevens), Reg Lye (Swaggie), Alexander Archdale (Firbank), Charles Tasman (Undertaker), Don McNiven (Patrick Rooney), Jerold Wells (Wally), Chris Kempster (Longun), Brian Anderson (Joe), Kenneth Warren (Andy), Evelyn Docker (Maggie).

In the 1890s, Joe is a stranger in town who dies alone without friends or family. Because he carries a union card, however, the local union members give him the honour of a decent burial.

'The Load of Wood'

Scriptwriter: Rex Rienits. Based on a story by Frank Hardy.

Cast: Jock Levy (Darkie), Leonard Thiele (Ernie), Ossie Wenban (Sniffy), John Armstrong (Chilla), Jim Doone (Joe), Ted Smith (Coulson), Edward Lovell (Tye), Keith Howard (Shea), Eileen Ryan (Mrs Johnson).

During the Depression of the 1930s, a group of unemployed men in a small country town are given relief work on the roads, but they still cannot afford to buy enough fuel to keep their families warm. Two of the men steal a truck-load of wood from a rich man's estate, and deliver it to the needy around town.

'The City'

Scriptwriter: Ralph Peterson.

Cast: Joan Landor (Kathie), Brian Vicary (Ted), Betty Lucas (Freda), Gordon Glenwright (Alex), Ken Wayne (First Cab Driver), Stewart Ginn (Second Cab Driver), Alan Trevor (Preacher); Pat Martin and Margaret Christensen (Customers); John Fernside (Vagrant), Alastair Roberts (Bodgie).

A young factory worker and a shop assistant plan to marry but are frustrated by the high costs of housing. After quarrelling and spending the night separately in the city streets, they realise that their love is more important than money.

Three to Go

Peter Weir, Brian Hannant, Oliver Howes

Black and white, 89 mins, 1970

Commonwealth Film Unit.

Producer: Gil Brealey.

Director of photography: Kerry Brown.

Sound recordists: Gordon Wraxall, Julian Ellingworth.

Editor: Wayne Le Clos.

The film consists of three stories:

'Michael'

Scriptwriter: Peter Weir.

Composer: The Cleves.

Cast: Matthew Burton (Michael). Grahame Bond (Grahame), Peter Colville (Neville Trantor), Georgina West (Georgina), Berry Lucas (Mother), Judy McBurney (Judy).

'A young man faces a choice between the life represented by his wealthy middle-class parents and the alternative of a permissive pot-smoking group of radicals.'

'Judy'

Scriptwriter: Brian Hannant.

Composers: Grahame Bond, Rory O'Donoghue.

Cast: Judy Morris (Judy), Serge Lazareff (Mike), Mary Ann Severne (Margaret), Gary Day (David), Penny Ramsey (Heather), Wendy Playfair (Mother), Brian Anderson (Father), Cliff Neate (Mr Vickery).

A 'teenage country girl persists, against the wishes of her parents and boyfriend, with her decision to go to the city in search of a more exciting life'.

'Toula'

Scriptwriter: Oliver Howes.

Music: Mozart, edited by James McCarthy.

Cast: Rina Ioannou (Toula), Erica Crowne (Assimina), Andrew Pappas (Stavros), Joe Hasham (John), Gabriel Battikha (Nick), Theo Coulouris (Father), Ketty Coulouris (Mother), Yaya Laudeas (Grandmother).

Toula 'explores the culture clash between Australian and traditional Greek communities in Sydney, with a young girl from a Greek family trying to reconcile her affection for an Australian boy with the social restraint expected by her parents'.

Pike and Cooper, *Australian Film 1900–1977*, p. 327.

Thunderbolt

John Gavin

Black and white, 3000 (?) ft, 1910

Southern Cross Motion Pictures.

Producer: H. A. Forsyth. Based on the novel *Three Years with Thunderbolt* by Ambrose Pratt.

Director of photography: A. J. Moulton.

Cast: John Gavin (Thunderbolt); Ruby Butler, H. A. Forsyth.

'Frederick Ward is a young citizen of Windsor, N.S.W., who goes droving to earn money for his wedding. He is suspected of cattle duffing, is arrested and sentenced to seven years' imprisonment. He escapes from prison. . .and vows to wreak vengeance on the law. . .The film continues with the story of his life as the notorious bushranger, Captain Thunderbolt. . .'

Pike and Cooper, *Australian Film 1900–1977*, p. 14.

Travelling North

Carl Schultz

Colour, 35mm, 95 mins, 1987

Ben Gannon.

Producer: Ben Gannon.

Scriptwriter: David Williamson. Based on Williamson's play.

Director of photography: Julian Penney.

Production designer: Owen Patterson.

Sound recordist: Syd Butterworth.

Editor: Henry Dangar.

Music co-ordinator: Alan John.

Frank (Leo McKern). Carl Schultz's *Travelling North* (1987).

Bill (Robert McDarra). Esben Storm's *27A* (1974).

Cast: Leo McKern (Frank), Julia Blake (Frances), Henri Szeps (Saul), Michele Fawdon (Helen), Diane Craig (Sophie), Andrea Moor (Joan), Drew Forsythe (Martin), John Gregg (Jim), Graham Kennedy (Freddy), Rob Steele (Syd).

Fed up with bickering adult children, the aged Frank and Frances decide to move north from Melbourne to Queensland. In yet another story about people leaving a bleak Melbourne, play-wright–scriptwriter David Williamson paints an affectionate picture of the emotional tensions of new beginnings and the characters one meets along life's way.

27A

Esben Storm

Colour, 16mm, 86 mins, 1974

Smart Street Films.

Producer: Haydn Keenan.

Scriptwriter: Esben Storm.

Director of photography: Michael Edols.

Production designer: Peter Minnett.

Sound recordists: Laurie Fitzgerald, Peter Cherny.

Editor: Richard Moir.

Music: Winsome Evans (recorder); Michael Norton (guitar).

Cast: Robert McDarra (Bill), Bill Hunter (Cornish), Graham Corry (Peter Newman), T. Richard Moir (Richard), James Kemp (Slats), Kris Olsen (Gloria), Brian Doyle (Lynch), Richard Creaser (Jeremy), Michael Norton (Mark), Haydn Keenan (Jeffrey).

Bill is a middle-aged metho-drinker sentenced to six weeks in prison for a minor offence. There, he volunteers for psychiatric treatment for his alcoholism and is committed to a hospital for the criminally insane, supposedly only for the duration of his prison sentence. He finds, however, that under section 27A of Queensland's Mental Health Act he can be held there until the hospital authorities declare him eligible for release.

2 Friends

Jane Campion

Colour, 35mm, 80 mins, 1986

ABC TV.

Producer: Jan Chapman.

Scriptwriter: Helen Garner.

Director of photography: Julian Penney.

Production designer: Janet Patterson.

Sound recordist: Chris Alderton.

Editor: Bill Russo.

Composer: Martin Armiger.

Cast: Emma Coles (Louise), Kris Bidenko (Kelly), Kris McQuade (Janet), Stephen Leeder (Jim), Peter Hehir (Malcolm), Tony Barry (Charlie), Steve Bisley (Kevin), John Sheerin (Dead Girl's Father), Sean Travers (Matthew), Kerry Dywer (Alison).

In a tele-feature that moves progressively backwards in time, two friends move from separation to becoming friends. Louise and Kelly are schoolgirls who believe that their friendship will endure for ever but, in a modern world, emotions fall prey to disruption.

Two Thousand Weeks

Tim Burstall

Black and white, 35mm, 89 mins, 1969

Eltham Film Productions–Senior Film Productions.

Producers: Patrick Ryan, David Bilcock Snr.

Scriptwriters: Tim Burstall, Patrick Ryan.

Director of photography: Robin Copping.

Production designer: Rosemary Ryan.

Sound recordist: Russell Hurley.

Editor: David Bilcock Jnr.

Composer: Don Burrowes.

Cast: Mark McManus (Will Gardiner), Jeanie Drynan (Jacky Lewis), Eileen Chapman (Sarah Gardiner), David Turnbull (Noel Oakshot), Michael Duffield (Will's Father), Stephen Dattner (Sir George Turnbull), Bruce Anderson (Rex Stapleton), Dominic Ryan (Young Will), Nicholas McCallum (Young Noel), Anne Charleston (Will's Mother), Graeme Blundell (Journalist).

The film presents a subjective view of a crisis in the life of a writer in his early thirties, who calculates that he has two thousand weeks left in his life to fulfil himself. The crisis is both personal and professional: he is faced with a choice between his wife and his mistress, and a deepening despair about the creative emptiness of his work as a journalist accentuated by a re-union with a boyhood friend who left Australia and became a successful television producer in England.

U

Unfinished Business

Bob Ellis

Colour, 16mm, 78 mins, 1986

A film by Bob Ellis, Andrew Lesnie, Michele Fawdon, John Clayton, Norman Kaye, Rebel Penfold-Russell, Andrena Finlay, Patric Juillet, Jake Atkinson, June Henman, (et al.)

Producer: Rebel Penfold-Russell.

Scriptwriter: Bob Ellis.

Director of photography: Andrew Lesnie.

Production designer: Jane Johnston.

Sound recordist: Gerry Nucifora.

Editor: Amanda Robson.

Musical arranger: Norman Kaye.

Cast: Michele Fawdon (Maureen), John Clayton (Geoff), Norman Kaye (George), Call Ricketson (Alice Benson); Jack and Jennie Ellis and Katie Hughes (Her Children); Tom Ellis (Baby), Andrew Lesnie (Telegram Boy).

Former lovers Maureen and Geoff reunite after fifteen years. When Maureen confesses that her husband is sterile and that she wants a baby, Geoff offers his help, believing this is the way to win her back. But on an idyll at Palm Beach irreconcilable tensions emerge and they part. A year later, Geoff visits Maureen and meets her husband and new child.

V

Violence in the Cinema ... Part 1

George Miller

Colour, 16mm, 14 mins, 1972

Producer: George Miller.

Scriptwriters: George Miller, Byron Kennedy.

Director of photography: Byron Kennedy.

Sound recordist: Mike Maxwell.

Editors: Byron Kennedy, George Miller.

Cast: Arthur Dignam (Dr Fyne), Victoria Annoux (Woman), Mallory Pettit (Kid), George Miller (Hanged Man); Karl Avis, Stuart McQueen.

A short film send-up of the way academics analyse violence in the cinema. Here, Dr Fyne calmly delivers his lecture on the subject while violence erupts all around and even when things turn decidely nasty for him.

W

Waiting

Jackie McKimmie

Colour, 35mm, 95 mins, 1991

A Filmside Production.

Producer: Ross Matthews.

Scriptwriter: Jackie McKimmie.

Director of photography: Steve Mason.

Production designer: Murray Picknett.

Sound recordist: Nick Wood.

Editor: Michael Honey.

Composer: Martin Armiger.

Cast: Noni Hazlehurst (Clare), Deborra-Lee Furness (Diane), Frank Whitten (Michael), Helen Jones (Sandy), Denis Moore (Bill), Fiona Press (Therese), Ray Barrett (Frank), Noga Bernstein (Rosie), Peter Tu Tran (Tan), Brian Simpson (Booroomil), Matthew Fargher (Steve), Alan Glover (Policeman), Kaye Stevenson (Midwife), Mariette Rups-Donnelly (Gym Instructor), Justin King (Muscle Man), Jeanette Cronin (Social Worker), Connie Spinks (Woman Driver), Himself (Bazza), Chloe (Scarlet).

An assortment of old friends converges at an isolated farm house to await the birth of a baby.

"Wake in Fright"

Ted Kotcheff

Colour, 35mm, 109 mins, 1971

NLT Productions–Group W Films.

Producer: George Willoughby.

Scriptwriter: Evan Jones. Based on the novel by Kenneth Cook.

Director of photography: Brian West.

Production designer: Dennis Gentle.

Sound recordist: John Appleton.

Editor: Anthony Buckley.

Composer: John Scott.

Cast: Gary Bond (John Grant), Donald Pleasence (Doc Tydon), Chips Rafferty (Jock Crawford), Sylvia Kay (Janette Hynes), Jack Thompson (Dick), Peter Whittle (Joe), Al Thomas (Tim Hynes), John Meillon (Charlie), John Armstrong (Atkins), Slim de Grey (Jarvis).

John Grant is an English teacher in an outback school. On his way to Sydney for a holiday, he stops at a pub in the rough mining town of Bundanyabba, loses his money in a two-up game and finds himself stranded. Gradually, he is overwhelmed by the nightmare of life in the 'Yabba', especially the perpetual beery stupor of the locals and their insistent and claustrophobic 'mateship'. In despair, after participating in a violent kangaroo hunt and being homosexually assaulted by an alcoholic doctor, Grant is driven to attempt suicide.

Walkabout

Nicolas Roeg

Colour, 35mm, 100 mins, 1971 (shot 1969)

Max L. Raab–Si Litvinoff Films.

Producer: Si Litvinoff.

Scriptwriter: Edward Bond. Based on the novel by James Vance Marshall.

Director of photography: Nicolas Roeg.

Production designer: Brian Eatwell.

Sound recordist: Barry Brown.

Editors: Anthony Gibbs, Alan Patillo.

Composer: John Barry.

Cast: Jenny Agutter (Girl), Lucien John (Brother), David Gulpilil (Aboriginal), John Meillon (Father), Peter Carver (No-hoper), John Illingsworth (Husband), Barry Donnelly (Australian Scientist), Noelene Brown (German Scientist), Carlo Manchini (Italian Scientist).

Overwhelmed by pressures in the city, a father drives his children into the desert and tries to kill them before shooting himself. The 14-year-old girl and the 6-year-old boy wander aimlessly until they meet an Aboriginal boy who is on a solitary walkabout as part of his tribal initiation into manhood. The three become travelling companions and gradually sexual tension grows between the girl and the Aborigine.

Dr Fyne (Arthur Dignam). George Miller's *Violence in the Cinema . . . Part 1* (1972).

Clare (Noni Hazlehurst), Diane (Deborra-Lee Furness), Sandy (Helen Jones) and Therese (Fiona Press). Jacki McKimmie's *Waiting* (1991).

Warm Nights on a Slow Moving Train

Bob Ellis

Colour, 35mm, 91 mins, 1988 (shot 1986)

Western Pacific Films presents a Ross Dimsey Production.

Producers: Ross Dimsey, Patric Juillet.

Scriptwriters: Bob Ellis, Denny Lawrence.

Director of photography: Yuri Sokol.

Production designer: Tracy Watt.

Sound recordist: Gary Wilkins.

Editor: Tim Lewis.

Composer: Peter Sullivan.

Cast: Wendy Hughes (Girl), Colin Friels (Man), Norman Kaye (Salesman), John Clayton (Football Coach), Lewis Fitz-Gerald (Brian), Rod Zuanic (Young Soldier), Steve J. Spears (Singer), Grant Tilly (Politician), Peter Whitford (Steward), Peter Sullivan (Piano-playing Steward).

She is an art teacher at a quiet suburban Catholic girl school: attractive, well mannered and worldly. Yet, during the weekend, she rides the overnight express, transforming from teacher to predator. Each week she changes her appearance, mannerisms, personality and target. Her one rule is not to get involved with her clients. But one client is different and becomes her lover, drawing her into the twilight world of intelligence, into a web of seduction, intrigue and murder.

Whatever Happened to Green Valley?

Peter Weir

Colour, 16mm, 57 mins, 1973

Film Australia.

Producer: Tony Buckley.

Scriptwriter: Peter Weir.

Director of photography: Nick Ardizzone.

Editor: Barry Williams.

Sound recordists: Tony Patterson, Julian Ellingworth.

A documentary record.

Winter of Our Dreams

John Duigan

Colour, 35mm, 89 mins, 1981

Vega Film Productions.

Producer: Richard Mason.

Scriptwriter: John Duigan.

Director of photography: Tom Cowan.

Production designer: Lee Whitmore.

Sound recordist: Lloyd Carrick.

Editor: Henry Dangar.

Composer: Sharon Calcraft.

Cast: Judy Davis (Lou), Bryan Brown (Rob), Cathy Downes (Gretel McGregor), Baz Luhrmann (Pete), Peter Mochrie (Tim), Mervyn Drake (Mick), Margie McCrae (Lisa Blaine), Mercia Deane-Johns (Angela), Kim Deacon (Michelle), Virginia Duigan (Sylvia).

Rob, the owner of an inner-city bookshop, hears of the suicide of Lisa Blaine, an old girlfriend. While tracing the events surrounding her death, he meets a prostitute, Lou, a close friend of Lisa's and, like her, a junkie. Initially, Rob is interested in what Lou can tell him about Lisa, but she also arouses his curiosity. What to Rob is casual interest, however, becomes something much more significant for Lou.

A Woman's Tale

Paul Cox

Colour, 35mm, 93 mins, 1991

Illumination Films.

Producers: Paul Cox, Santhana Naidu.

Scriptwriters: Paul Cox, Barry Dickins. Based on a concept by Paul Cox.

Director of photography: Nino Martinetti.

Production designer: Neil Angwin.

Sound recordist: Russell Hurley.

Editor: Russell Hurley.

Composer: Paul Grabowsky.

Cast: Sheila Florance (Martha), Gosia Dobrowolska (Anna), Norman Kaye (Billy), Chris Haywood (Jonathan), Ernest Gray (Peter), Myrtle Woods (Miss Inchley), Bruce Myles (Con 1), Alex Menglet (Con 2); François Bernard, Manuel Bachet (Neighbours).

An 80-year-old woman, still full of imagination and spirit, faces a crisis when the authorities want to commit her to a home for the aged.

The Woman Suffers

Raymond Longford

Black and white, 8000 ft, 1918

Southern Cross Feature Film Company.

Scriptwriter: Raymond Longford.

Director of photography: Arthur Higgins.

Cast: Lottie Lyell (Marjory Manton), Boyd Irwin (Phillip Masters), Roland Conway (Ralph Manton), Connie Martyn (Marion Masters), Paul Baxter (Little Phillip), C. R. Stanford (John Stockdale), Ida Gresham (Mrs Stockdale), Evelyn Black (Joan Stockdale), Charles H. Francis (Stephen Manton).

'"The woman suffers...while the man goes free". To illustrate this tragic irony, the story takes the concept of primitive justice—an eye for an eye and a tooth for a tooth—and extends it to a sister for a sister.'

Pike and Cooper, *Australian Film 1900–1977*, p. 102.

Lou (Judy Davis). John Duigan's *Winter of Our Dreams* (1981).

Anna (Gosia Dobrowolska) and Martha (Sheila Florance). Paul Cox's *A Woman's Tale* (1991).

Wrong Side of the Road

Ned Lander

Colour, 16mm, 80 mins, 1981

Inma Productions.

Producer: Ned Lander.

Scriptwriters: Graeme Issac, Ned Lander.

Director of photography: Louis Irving.

Production designer: Jan Mackay.

Sound recordist: Lloyd Carrick.

Editor: John Scott.

Music: No Fixed Address, Us Mob.

Cast: Bart Willoughby, Chris Jones, John Miller, Veronica Rankine (No Fixed Address); Ronnie Ansell, Peter Butler, Wally McArthur, Carol Karpanny (Us Mob); Leila Rankine, Gayle Rankine, Veronica Brodie, Donna Drover.

What is it like to be young and black in Australia? *Wrong Side of the Road* introduces two black rock reggae bands—No Fixed Address and Us Mob—and follows them through two days on the road. The bands' members play themselves, acting out inci-dents from their lives and those of their friends. The film does not dwell on injustices; it shows a gutsy people's standing up to a racist society, and explores the unique qualities of the Aboriginal community.

Wrong World

Ian Pringle

Colour, 16mm, 97 mins, 1986 (shot 1984)

Producer: Bryce Menzies.

Scriptwriters: Doug Ling, Ian Pringle.

Director of photography: Ray Argall.

Production designer: Christine Johnson.

Sound recordist: Bruce Emery.

Editor: Ray Argall.

Composer: Eric Gradman, with Dave Cahill, Nick Rischbieth.

Cast: Richard Moir (David Trueman), Jo Kennedy (Mary), Nicolas Lathouris (Rangott), Robbie McGregor (Robert), Esben Storm (Lawrence), Tim Robinson (Psychiatrist), Cliff Ellen (Old Man), Elise McCleod (Girl at Service Station).

David Trueman (Richard Moir). Ian Pringle's *Wrong World* (1986).

Eight years of fighting poverty and disease in South America have taken their toll on Dr David Trueman. His spirits drained, his ideals in shreds, he returns home to Melbourne in the hope of piecing his life together. But home, too, seems to have disintegrated during his years away. Then, he meets Mary, like him gripped by drug addiction, but rough and impulsive and hell-bent on escape. Together, doctor and street kid scrounge some money and hit the road. . .

Y

Yackity Yack

Dave Jones	
Black and white, 16mm, 86 mins, 1974 (shot 1972)	
Acme Films.	
Producer: Dave Jones.	
Scriptwriter: Dave Jones.	
Director of photography: Gordon Glenn.	

Sound recordists: Peter Beilby, Lloyd Carrick.

Editor: Dave Jones.

Cast: Dave Jones (Maurice), John Flaus (Steve; Himself), Peter Carmody (Zig), Peggy Cole (Caroline), John Cleary (Building Manager), Jerzy Toeplitz (Man in the Street), Doug White (Socrates), Rod Nicholls (Kirilov), Andy Miller (Mishima).

A low-budget black comedy about entropy by Canadian film lecturer Dave Jones, who was working at the Media Centre of LaTrobe University. The less-than-linear plot concerns chickens, nudity and political revolution, to name only a few of its many idiosyncratic elements.

The Year My Voice Broke

John Duigan	
Colour, 35mm, 105 mins, 1987	
A Kennedy Miller production.	
Producers: Terry Hayes, Doug Mitchell, George Miller.	
Scriptwriter: John Duigan.	
Director of photography: Geoff Burton.	
Production designer: Roger Ford.	
Sound recordist: Ross Linton.	
Editor: Neil Thumpston.	
Music: Vaughan Williams.	

Cast: Noah Taylor (Danny), Loene Carmen (Freya), Ben Mendelsohn (Trevor), Graeme Blundell (Nils Olson), Lynette Curran (Anne Olson), Malcolm Robertson (Bruce Embling), Judi Farr (Sheila Embling), Tim Robertson (Bob Leishman), Bruce Spence (Jonah), Harold Hopkins (Tom Alcock).

Fifteen-year-old Danny, the son of a publican in a small country town, is in love from a distance with 16-year-old Freya. Freya, the adopted daughter of the Olsons, was once Danny's playmate, but the one year difference in age became an unbridgeable gap. Danny can only watch helplessly as Freya's relationship with the school fullback, Trevor, gradually blooms. When Trevor is killed in a police car chase, Freya learns from Danny that, for her own survival, she must leave the town for good.

The Year of Living Dangerously

Peter Weir	
Colour, 35mm, 113 mins, 1982	
Metro-Goldwyn-Mayer presents a Freddie Fields presentation of a McElroy & McElroy production.	
Producer: Jim McElroy.	
Scriptwriters: David Williamson, Peter Weir, C. J. Koch. Based on the novel by C. J. Koch.	
Director of photography: Russell Boyd.	
Design co-ordinator: Wendy Weir.	
Production designer: Herbert Pinter.	
Sound recordist: Gary Wilkins.	
Editor: William Anderson.	
Composer: Maurice Jarre.	

Tom Alcock (Harold Hopkins), Danny (Noah Taylor) and Jonah (Bruce Spence). John Duigan's *The Year My Voice Broke* (1987).

Cast: Mel Gibson (Guy Hamilton), Sigourney Weaver (Jill Bryant), Linda Hunt (Billy Kwan), Bill Kerr (Colonel Henderson), Noel Ferrier (Wally O'Sullivan), Paul Sonkkila (Kevin Condon), Bembol Roco (Kumar), Kuh Ledesma (Tiger Lily), Domingo Landicho (Hortono), Cecily Polson (Moira).

In the year 1965 Indonesia ran wild, on a collision course with the whole Western world. Against a backdrop of violence, international intrigue and terror, a small group of newsmen report from the centre of the political stage. This is the setting for a story of love and anguish, of the strange three-way relationship between successful correspondent Guy Hamilton, his extraordinary Chinese-Australian cameraman, Billy Kwan, and the woman they both love, Jill Bryant.

Young Einstein

Yahoo Serious

Colour, 35mm, 91 mins (reduced version), 1988 (mostly shot 1985)

A Serious Film.

Producers: Yahoo Serious, Warwick Ross, David Roach.

Scriptwriters: Yahoo Serious, David Roach.

Director of photography: Jeff 'Ace' Darling.

Production designers: Steve Marr, Laurie Faen, Colin Gibson, Ron Highfield.

Sound recordists: Geoff Grist, Max Hensser, Paul Brincat.

Editors: Yahoo Serious, David Roach, Neil Thumpston, Peter Whitmore, Amanda Robson.

Composers: William Motzing, Martin Armiger, Tommy Tycho.

Cast: Yahoo Serious (Albert Einstein), Odile Le Clezio (Marie Curie) John Howard (Preston Preston), Peewee Wilson (Mr Einstein), Su Cruickshank (Mrs Einstein), Lulu Pinkus (Blonde), Kaarin Fairfax (Brunette), Michael Lake (Manager), Jonathan Coleman (Wolfgang Bavarian).

The incredible untold story of Australia's most unsung hero: the Tasmanian genius, Albert Einstein. This comedy reveals his birth to a Tasmanian apple farmer, the premature discovery of rock 'n' roll and the joys of the birth of relativity. It is also the saga of his love affair with a beautiful and highly intelligent Marie Curie.

Albert Einstein (Yahoo Serious) and Marie Curie (Odile Le Clezio). Yahoo Serious' *Young Einstein* (1988).

10
Dictionary of directors

Scott Murray and Raffaele Caputo

All films are features unless otherwise noted. Datings on Australian features are for the year of Australian theatrical release, tele-features for the year of Australian television premiere. If there has been a long delay between completion of production and first release, this is usually noted.

Gillian Armstrong

Born 1950, Melbourne. Among the first intake of students at the Swinburne Film and Television School in 1971. Won scholarship to the Australian Film and Television School (now Australian Film Television & Radio School, or AFTRS) in 1973. First woman since the 1930s to direct a 35mm Australian feature.

As director (features):
1979 *My Brilliant Career* (as Gill Armstrong)
1982 *Star Struck*
1984 *Mrs Soffel* (US)
1987 *Hightide*
1991 *Fires Within* (US)
1992 *The Last Days of Chez Nous*

Gillian Armstrong

318

As director (other):
1968 *Storytime* (short)
1969 *Four Walls* (short)
1969 Several films of one to five minutes, completed only to double head, including an animation. Made at Swinburne Film School
1969 *Old Man and Dog* (short)
1970 *The Roof Needs Mowing* (short)
1971 *Shit Commercial* (short)
1972 *Decision* (short)
1973 *One Hundred a Day* (short)—also writer
1973 *Satdee Night* (short)—also writer
1973 *Gretel* (short)—also writer
1976 *The Singer and the Dancer* (short)—also co-writer, producer
1976 *Smokes and Lollies* (documentary)
1978 *A Busy Kind of Bloke* (documentary)
1980 *Touch Wood* (documentary)
1981 *14's Good, 18's Better* (documentary)—also a producer. A shorter version of this film is called *More Smokes, More Lollies*
1983 *Bop Girl* (short)
1983 *Not Just a Pretty Face* (documentary)
1986 *Hard to Handle* (documentary)
1988 *Bingo Bridesmaids & Braces* (documentary)

Also,
1972 *New Life New South Wales* (documentary)—editor
1972 *Ballina Country Town* (documentary)—editor
1972 Promotional film for Levi's—editor
1975 *Promised Woman* (feature)—art director
1975 *The Removalists* (feature)—assistant designer
1976 *The Trespassers* (feature)—art director
1977 *A Time and a Place* (documentary)—editor

Bill Bennett

Born 1953, Sydney. Began career as a cadet journalist at the ABC in 1972. From 1981–85 directed and wrote documentaries for television.

As director (features):
1985 *A Street to Die*—also writer, producer
1986 *Backlash*—also writer (with dialogue improvised by the actors)
Unrel. *Dear Cardholder*—also writer. Made in 1986; released to video in 1989
Unrel. *Jilted*—also writer, co-producer. Made in 1987; released to video in 1990

As director (other):
1981 *The Australians* (documentary series)
1982 *A Big Country* (documentary series)
1983 *Cattle King* (documentary)
1984 *Shipwrecked* (documentary)—also producer
1987 *Bango and the Bard* (docu-drama)—also co-producer, writer
1989 *Malpractice* (tele-feature)
1989 *Mortgage* (tele-feature)—also writer
1992 *You Have No Secrets* (docudrama)—also writer
Also,
1992 *The Last Man Hanged* (docu-drama)—producer

Bruce Beresford

Born 1940, Sydney. Spent two years with a film unit in Nigeria then became head of film production at the British Film Institute, 1966–72.

Bruce Beresford

As director (features):
1972   *The Adventures of Barry McKenzie*—also co-writer, producer
1974   *Barry McKenzie Holds His Own*—also co-writer, producer
1975   *Side by Side* (UK)—also co-writer
1976   *Don's Party*
1977   *The Getting of Wisdom*
1979   *Money Movers*—also writer
1980   *'Breaker' Morant*—also co-writer
1980   *David Williamson's The Club*
1981   *Puberty Blues*
1983   *Tender Mercies* (US)
1985   *King David* (US)
1986   *Crimes of the Heart* (US)
1986   *The Fringe Dwellers*
1987   *Aria* (UK)—a director
1988   *Her Alibi* (US)
1989   *Driving Miss Daisy* (US)
1990   *Mister Johnston* (Kenya)
1991   *Black Robe* (Canada)
1992   *Rich in Love*

Tim Burstall

As director (other):
1958   *Revenge of the Earwig* (short)—also producer
1960   *The Hunters* (short)—also co-writer, co-director of photography, co-producer
1962   *The Devil to Pay* (short)
1963   *Clement Meadmore* (documentary)—also writer, editor, producer
1963   *It Droppeth as the Gentle Rain* (short)—co-director (with Albie Thoms)
1965   *Film for Guitar* (short)—also editor, producer
1965   *Traditional Dance* (short)
1965   *Eastern Nigerian Newsreel No. 30* (documentary)
1966   *King Size Woman* (short)
1968   *Extravaganza* (short)—also director of photography, editor
1968   *Lichtenstein in London* (short)—also director of photography, editor
1968   *Barbara Hepworth at the Tate* (short)—also director of photography
1968   *Martin Agrippa* (short)
1968   *Rene Magritte* (short)
1970   *Cinema of Raymond Fark* (short)—also co-writer, director of photography, editor
1970   *Arts of Village India* (short)—also director of photography
1971   *View from the Satellite* (documentary)—also writer, editor, producer
1973   *Poor Fella Me* (television)—also writer
1974   *Wreck of the Batavia* (television)—also co-editor
1974   *Million Dollar Baby* (television)
1974   *Barry McKenzie Holds His Own Promotional Film* (short)
1975   *Barry McKenzie Stage Show Film* (documentary)

Also,
1953   *Time of Crisis* (short)—director of photography
1978   *Blue Fin*—uncredited standby director

Tim Burstall

Born 1927, England. Came to Australia in 1937. Worked as journalist and editor before forming Eltham Films in 1959. Most of his films throughout the 1970s made through Hexagon Productions, formed in 1972.

As director (features):
1969   *Two Thousand Weeks*—also co-writer
1971   *Stork*—also producer
1973   *Libido*—'The Child' episode
1973   *Alvin Purple*—also producer
1974   *Petersen*—also producer
1975   *End Play*—also producer
1976   *A Faithful Narrative of the Capture, Sufferings and Mira-
        culous Escape of Eliza Fraser*—also producer
1979   *The Last of the Knucklemen*—also writer, producer
1982   *Attack Force Z*
1982   *Duet for Four*—also co-producer
1985   *Morris West's The Naked Country*—also writer, pro-
        ducer
1987   *Kangaroo*

As director (other):
1959   *The Prize* (short)—also writer, producer
1959   *The Gold Digger's Ballad* (short)—also writer
1960   *The Black Man and His Bride* (short)—also writer
1960   *Ned Kelly* (short)
1962   *Dance of the Angels* (short)—also writer
1963   *Australia Felix* (short)—also writer
1963   *The Crucifixion* (short)—also writer
1963   *The Explorer* (short)—also writer
1963   *The Legend of Byamee* (short)—also writer
1963   *Melbourne Timetable* (short)—also writer
1963   *On Three Moon Creek* (short)—also writer
1963   *The Pioneers* (short)—also lyrics
1963   *Adventures of Sebastian Fox* (tele-series)
1964   *Nullabor Hideout* (short)
1965   *Painting People* (documentary)—also writer
1965   *The Making of a Gallery* (documentary)—also writer
1966   *Blues from the Jungle* (documentary)—also producer
1969   *Sculpture Australia 69* (documentary)—also writer,
        narrator
1970   *The Hot Centre of the World* (short)—also co-writer
1970   *Getting Back to Nothing* (documentary)
1973   *Mouse* (short)
1974   *Three Old Friends* (short)—also producer
1983   *Descant for Gossips* (tele-series)
1984   *Special Squad* (tele-series)—a director
1987   *Great Expectations—The Untold Story* (mini-series)—
        also writer. Shortened into a feature released only on
        video
1987   *Nightmare at Bitter Creek* (television special)

Also,
1970   *Nothing Like Experience* (short)—actor
1974   *Alvin Rides Again*—producer
1975   *The Love Epidemic*—co-executive producer
1977   *High Rolling*—producer

Ken Cameron

Born 1946, Sydney. Graduated from Sydney University with
Bachelor of Arts in 1968. Taught at AFTRS, 1974–75.

As director (features):
1982   *Monkey Grip*—also co-writer
1984   *Fast Talking*—also writer
1987   *Peter Kenna's The Umbrella Woman* [aka: *Peter Kenna's
        The Good Wife*]

As director (other):
1974   *Sailing to Brooklyn* (short)—also writer
1977   *Out of It* (short)—also writer, producer
1978   *Temperament Unsuited* (short)—also writer
1979   *Fernando Armendariz* (documentary)—also writer

Jane Campion

1980   *Chase that Dream* (short)—also writer
1984   *Crime of the Decade* (tele-feature)
1985   *On the Loose*—also co-writer
1985   *Special Squad* (tele-series)—a director
1987   *The Clean Machine* (tele-feature)—also co-writer
1987   *Stringer* (mini-series)—co-director (with Kathy Mueller,
        Chris Thomson)
1989   *Bangkok Hilton* (mini-series)
1991   *Brides of Christ* (mini-series)

Jane Campion

Born 1955, New Zealand. Gained Bachelor of Arts Anthropology in Wellington and Diploma of Fine Arts at Chelsea School
of Arts, London. Graduate of AFTRS in 1984.

As director (feature):
1989   *Sweetie*—also co-writer
1993   *The Piano*—also writer

As director (other):
198[?] *Tissues* (Super 8 short)
198[?] *Mishaps: Seduction and Conquest* (video)
1982   *Peel* (short)—also writer
1983   *A Girl's Own Story* (short)—also writer, producer
1984   *Passionless Moments: Recorded in Sydney Australia
        Sunday October 2nd* (short)—co-director(with Gerard
        Lee), also co-writer, co-producer
1984   *After Hours* (short)—also writer
1985   *Dancing Daze* (mini-series)
1986   *2 Friends* (tele-feature)
1990   *An Angel at My Table* (mini-series)—also released
        theatrically

Charles Chauvel

Born 1897, died 1959. Legendary Queensland director who
started as production assistant and actor, went to Hollywood,
then returned to make epic films until he died.

As director (features):
1926   *The Moth of Moonbi*—also actor, writer
1926   *Greenhide*—also writer

Paul Cox

1933   *In the Wake of the Bounty*—also writer
1935   *Heritage*—also writer
1936   *Uncivilised*—also co-writer
1940   *Forty Thousand Horsemen*—also co-writer, producer
1944   *Rats of Tobruk*—also co-writer, producer
1949   *Sons of Matthew*—also co-writer, producer
1955   *Jedda*—also co-writer, producer

As director (other):
1942   *Soldiers Without Uniforms* (documentary)—also producer
1942   *The Power to Win* (documentary)—also producer
1943   *While There Is Still Time* (documentary)—also producer
1943   *A Mountain Goes to Sea* (documentary)—also producer
1943   *Russia Aflame* (documentary)—also producer
1958   *Australian Walkabout* (tele-series)—also director of photography. Thirteen documentaries in all

Also,
1920   *Robbery Under Arms*—actor
1920   *Shadow of Lightning Ridge*—actor
1920   *Jackeroo of Coolabong*—actor
1921   *Fly by Night*—actor
1922   *The Man from the Desert*—actor
1922   *Strangers of the Night*—assistant director
1922   *A Rough Passage*—assistant director
1936   *Rangle River*—co-writer

Paul Cox

Born 1940, The Netherlands. Arrived in Australia 1963. Stills photographer before commencing career in film-making.

As director (features):
1976   *Illuminations*—also co-director of photography, co-editor, writer
1977   *Inside Looking Out*—also editor, co-writer, co-producer
1979   *Kostas*—also wrote original idea
1982   *Lonely Hearts*—also co-writer
1983   *Man of Flowers*—also wrote original scenario
1984   *My First Wife*—also writer, co-producer
1986   *Cactus*—writer, co-producer
1989   *Island*—also writer, co-producer

1991   *Golden Braid*—also co-writer
1991   *A Woman's Tale*—also co-writer
1993   *The Nun and the Bandit*—also writer
Prod. *Exile*—also writer

As director (other):
1965   *Matuta* (short)
1966   *Time Past* (short)
1968   *Skin Deep* (short)
1969   *Marcel* (short)
1969   *Symphony* (short)
1970   *Mirka* (short)
1970   *Phyllis* (short)
1972   *The Journey* (short)
1975   *Island* (short)
1975   *All Set Backstage* (short)
1977   *Ritual* (short)
1977   *Ways of Seeing* (short)
1979   *For a Child Called Michael* (documentary)
1981   *The Kingdom of Nek* (documentary)
1982   *Underdog* (documentary)
1985   *Death and Destiny—A Journey into Ancient Egypt* (documentary)
1985   *Winners* (tele-series)—'The Paper Boy' episode
1986   *Kaboodle* (tele-series)—'The Secret Life of Trees' episode
1987   *Touch the Sun* (tele-series)—'The Gift' episode
1987   *Vincent: The Life and Death of Vincent Van Gogh* (documentary)—also director of photography

Donald Crombie

Born 1942, Queensland. Entered first production course at National Institute of Dramatic Art (NIDA) in 1961 and commenced work at the Commonwealth Film Unit (now Film Australia) in 1963.

As director (features):
1976   *Caddie*
1978   *The Irishman*—also writer
1979   *Cathy's Child*
1981   *The Killing of Angel Street*
1983   *Kitty and the Bagman*
1986   *Playing Beatie Bow*

As director (other):
1966   *Aircraft at Work* (documentary)—also writer
1966   *It's So Easy* (documentary)—also writer, editor
1967   *Is Anybody Doing Anything About It?* (short)—also writer
1968   *Canberra* (documentary)—co-director
1968   *Sailor* (documentary)
1969   *Plane Mates* (short)
1970   *Personnel or People* (short)
1970   *Turnover* (short)
1970   *Top End* (documentary)
1971   *The Choice* (short)
1972   *Our Land Australia* (documentary)—also producer, co-writer
1972   *The Three-Metre Lifeline* (documentary)
1973   *The Fifth Facade* (short)
1973   *I Need More Staff* (short)
1973   *Kilkenny Primary School* (short)
1973   *One Good Reason* (short)
1973   *Stradbroke Infants School South Australia* (documentary)
1974   *Three Workshop Films* (short)—co-director
1974   *Who Killed Jenny Langby?* (documentary)—also co-writer

321

1976   *Do I Have to Kill My Child?* (tele-feature)—also
       co-writer
1980   *Slippery Slide* (tele-feature)—a director, also writer
1985   *Robbery Under Arms* (mini-series)—co-director (with
       Ken Hannam). Also released as a shortened feature
1986   *Tracy* (mini-series)
1987   *The Alien Years* (mini-series)
198[?] *The Secret* (documentary)
198[?] *Parents and Teachers* (documentary)—also writer
1988   *The Heroes* (mini-series)
1989   *The Saint in Australia* (tele-feature)
1991   *The River Kings* (mini-series)
1991   *Heroes II* (mini-series)

Also,
1972   *Australia's North West* (documentary)—producer
1972   *A City Family* (documentary)—producer

Rolf de Heer

Born 1951, the Netherlands. Graduate of AFTRS.

As director (features):
1984   *Tail of a Tiger*—also writer
1989   *Incident at Raven's Gate* (aka: *Encounter at Raven's
       Gate*)—also co-writer, co-producer
1991   *Dingo*—also a producer
1993   *Bad Boy Bubby*

As director (other):
1987   *Thank You Jack* (tele-feature)

John Dingwall

Born 1940, Queensland. Recipient of eleven Australian writing
awards.

As director (features):
1990   *Phobia*—also writer
1993   *The Custodian*—also writer

Also,
1970s *Homicide* (tele-series)—a writer
1970s *Division 4* (tele-series)—a writer
1970s *Matlock Police* (tele-series)—a writer
1970s *Pike in a Poke* (series)—co-writer
1975   *Sunday Too Far Away*—writer
1984   *Buddies*—writer, producer

Roger Donaldson

Born in Ballarat. Went to New Zealand when twenty. Apart
from making features there, had a successful career in advertising, before leaving for the US.

1977   *Sleeping Dogs* (New Zealand)
1981   *Smash Palace* (New Zealand)
1984   *The Bounty* (US)
1985   *Marie* (US)
1987   *No Way Out* (US)
1988   *Cocktail* (US)
1990   *Cadillac Man* (US)
1992   *White Sands* (US)

John Duigan

Born 1949, UK. Arrived in Australia 1961. Graduated from
Melbourne University with Masters in Philosophy. A published
novelist, he now lives in England.

John Duigan

As director (features):
1975   *The Firm Man*—also writer, composer, producer
1976   *The Trespassers*—also writer, producer
1978   *Mouth to Mouth*—also writer, co-producer
1979   *Dimboola*
1981   *Winter of Our Dreams*—also writer
1982   *Far East*—also writer
1984   *One Night Stand*—also writer
1987   *The Year My Voice Broke*—also writer
1989   *Romero* (Mexico)
1991   *Flirting*—also writer
1992   *Wide Sargasso Sea* (US)
1993   *Sirens*—also writer

As director (other):
1985   *Winners* (tele-series)—'Room to Move' episode
1987   *Vietnam* (mini-series)—a director, also co-writer
1988   *Fragments of War: The Story of Damien Parer* (tele-
       feature)—also writer
1989   *Bitter Rice* (documentary)

Also,
1970   *Brake Fluid* (short)—actor
1971   *Bonjour Balwyn*—actor
1973   *Dalmas*—actor
1974   *Children of the Moon*—actor

John Farrow

Born 10 February 1904, Sydney. Educated in Australia by private tutors, as well as at Newington College. Later, he went to England and Winchester College, before entering the Royal Naval Academy. Took part in several scientific expeditions. Made almost all his features in the US.

1937 *Men in Exile*
1937 *West of Shanghai*
1938 *She Loved a Fireman*
1938 *The Invisible Menace*
1938 *Little Miss Thoroughbred*
1938 *My Bill*
1938 *Broadway Musketeers*
1939 *The Saint Strikes Back*
1939 *Women in the Wind*
1939 *Sorority House* (UK: *That Girl from College*)
1939 *Five Came Back*
1939 *Full Confession*
1939 *Reno*
1940 *Married and in Love*
1940 *A Bill of Divorcement* (aka: *Never to Love*)
1942 *Wake Island*
1942 *Commandos Strike at Dawn*
1943 *China*
1944 *The Hitler Gang*
1945 *You Came Along*
1946 *Two Years Before the Mast*
1946 *California*
1947 *Easy Come, Easy Go*
1947 *Blaze of Noon*
1947 *Calcutta*
1948 *The Big Clock*
1948 *Beyond Glory*
1948 *Night Has a Thousand Eyes*
1949 *Alias Nick Beal* (UK: *The Contact Man*)
1949 *Red, Hot and Blue*—also co-writer
1950 *Copper Canyon*
1950 *Where Danger Lives*—also producer
1951 *His Kind of Woman*
1951 *Submarine Command*
1953 *Ride, Vaquero!*
1953 *Botany Bay*
1953 *Plunder in the Sun*
1953 *Hondo*
1954 *A Bullet is Waiting*
1955 *The Sea Chase*—also producer
1956 *Back from Eternity*—also producer
1957 *The Unholy Wife*—also producer
1959 *John Paul Jones*

As director (other):
1934 *The Spectacle Maker* (short)—based on a Farrow short story
1934 *War Lord*
1951 *Red Mountain*—uncredited direction when director was ill
1962 *Empire* (television)—directed several episodes

As other:
1927 *White Gold*—co-titles
1927 *The Wreck of the Hesperus*—story
1928 *The Showdown*—titles
1928 *The Blue Danube*—story
1928 *Ladies of the Mob*—writer
1928 *The First Kiss*—adaptation
1928 *Three Weekends*—adaptation
1928 *The Woman from Moscow*—writer, titles

1929 *Wolf Song*—writer
1929 *A Dangerous Woman*—adaptation
1929 *The Four Feathers*—co-titles
1929 *The Wheel of Life*—adaptation
1930 *Seven Days Leave* (UK: *Medals*)—co-writer
1930 *The Shadow of the Law*—writer
1930 *Inside the Lines*—dialogue
1931 *The Common Law*—story
1931 *A Woman of Experience*—co-writer, author original play
1932 *Woman in Chains* (aka: *Woman in Bondage*; UK: *The Impassive Footman*)—co-writer
1933 *Adventures of Don Quixote*—collaborator on English version
1936 *Last of the Pagans*—writer, author original short story
1936 *Tarzan Escapes*—writer, author original short story
1949 *Red, Hot and Blue*—co-writer
1956 *Around the World in 80 Days*—co-writer
1961 *King of Kings*—uncredited writer of original screenplay, some of which may have been used in film

Ross Gibson

Born 1956, Brisbane. Academic whose main area of research and writing has been the depiction of Australian landscape in the arts.

As director (features):
Unrel. *Dead to the World*—also writer; finished 1991

As director (other):
1986 *Camera Natura* (short)—also writer
Prod: *Wild Acres* (documentary)

Ken G. Hall

Born 1901. Started as reporter, publicist and cinema manager. Head of Cinesound, 1932–56. Television executive, 1956–68. Published reminiscences in later life.

1932 *On Our Selection*—co-writer
1933 *The Squatter's Daughter*—also producer
1934 *The Silence of Dean Maitland*—also producer
1934 *Strike Me Lucky*
1935 *Grandad Rudd* (UK: *Ruling the Roost*)—also a producer
1936 *Thoroughbred*—also producer
1936 *Orphan of the Wilderness* (aka: *Chut*; UK: *Orphan of the Wilderness*; US *Wild Innocence*)—also producer
1937 *It Isn't Done*—also producer
1937 *Tall Timbers*—also producer
1937 *Lovers and Luggers* (US: *Vengeance of the Deep*)—also producer
1938 *The Broken Melody* (UK: *The Vagabond Violinist*)—also producer
1938 *Let George Do It* (UK: *In the Nick of Time*)—also producer
1938 *Dad and Dave Come to Town* (UK: *The Rudd Family Goes to Town*)—also producer, original story
1939 *Mr. Chedworth Steps Out*—also producer
1939 *Gone to the Dogs*—also producer
1939 *Come Up Smiling* (aka: *Ants in His Pants*)—also writer (under pseudonym of John Addison Chandler), producer
1940 *Dad Rudd, MP*—also producer
1946 *Smithy* (UK: *Southern Cross*; US: *Pacific Adventure*)—also co-writer (under pseudonym of John Chandler)

As director (other):
1929 *Exploits of the Emden* (documentary)—co-director, also writer, editor, producer
1934 *Cinesound Varieties* (short)—also producer

323

1942 *100 000 Cobbers* (documentary)—also producer
1942 *Anzacs in Overalls* (documentary)—also producer
1943 *South West Pacific* (documentary)
1952 *Bushland Symphony* (documentary)
1953 *South Pacific Playground* (documentary—also producer
1957 *The Kurnell Story*—also producer

Also,
1946 *Australia's Bushland Symphony* (documentary)—producer
1954 *Tough Assignment* (documentary)—co-producer
1954 *Overland Adventure* (documentary)—producer
1954 *Haven on the Hill*—producer

NB: Hall directed hundreds of short films, the titles mostly unknown.

Ken Hannam

Born 1929, Melbourne. Worked extensively in radio, theatre and television as announcer, actor, writer and director before moving to London in 1968. Since then, has returned to Australia several times to direct features.

As director (features):
1975 *Sunday Too Far Away*
1976 *Break of Day*
1977 *Summerfield*
1979 *Dawn!*

As director (other):
1974 *Luke's Kingdom* (tele-series)—a director
1979 *Mismatch* (tele-feature)
1984 *Lovejoy* (UK tele-series)—a director
1985 *Bergerac* (UK tele-series)—a director
1985 *Call Me Mister* (UK tele-series)—a director
1985 *Robbery Under Arms* (mini-series)—co-director (with Donald Crombie). Also released as a shortened feature
1986 *Boon* (UK tele-series)—a director
1987 *Cross Fire* (UK tele-series)—a director
1987 *Return of Sherlock Homes* (UK tele-series)—a director
1988 *Crimesquad* (UK tele-series)—a director
1988 *Hannay* (UK tele-series)—a director
1989 *Campion* (UK tele-series)—a director
1990 *Lovejoy* (UK tele-series)—a director
1990 *Paradise Club* (UK tele-series)—a director
1992 *House of Elliott* (UK tele-series)—a director
1992 *Strathblair* (UK tele-series)—a director

John Heyer

Born 1916, Tasmania. Documentary film-maker. Was sound engineer with Efftee and Cinesound, producer with ANFB and producer-in-charge of Australian branch of Shell Film Unit. Executive producer for Shell in London, 1956–67. Awarded OBE.

As director:
1939 *2000 Below* (documentary)—also writer
1939 *Silver Soil* (documentary)—also writer
1940 *New Pastures* (documentary)—also writer
1943 *Jungle Conquest* (documentary)—also writer
1945 *Native Earth* (documentary)—also writer
1946 *Turn of the Soil* (documentary)
1946 *Born in the Sun* (documentary)
1947 *The Canecutter* (documentary)
1947 *Men and Mobs* (documentary)
1948 *The Valley is Ours* (documentary)
1951 *The Dealer Plan* (documentary)

1952 *Playing With Water* (documentary)
1954 *The Back of Beyond* (feature documentary)—also co-writer, co-dialogist, co-narrator, editor, producer
1955 *The Forerunner* (documentary)
1958 *Man's Head* (short documentary)
1958 *Dream Sound* (short)
1959 *The Professor* (short)
1959 *The Paying Bay* (documentary)
1960 *Duel* (short)
1960 *Jack* (short)
1960 *Chameleon* (short)
1961 *Hands* (short)
1962 *Tumut Pond* (documentary)
1962 *The Waste Land* (documentary)
1965 *TMO 135* (documentary)
1971 *The South Seas* (documentary)—also producer
1976 *The Reef* (feature documentary)—also producer

Also,
1940 *Forty Thousand Horsemen*—director of photography (exteriors)
1946 *The Overlanders*—second unit director
1950 *Rankin's Spring is West* (documentary)—producer
1957 *The Forming of Metals* (documentary)—executive producer
1958 *Coupe des Alpes* (documentary)—executive producer
1959 *Tough on a Two-Stroke* (documentary)—executive producer
1961 *Kerosene* (documentary)—executive producer
1962 *Shell Spirit* (short)—producer
1962 *Boot* (short)—producer
1963 *Like New* (short)—producer
1963 *How the Motor Car Works* (documentary)
1963 *Quality Control* (documentary)—executive producer
1964 *Servishell* (documentary)—producer
1964 *The Kerosene Flame* (documentary)—producer
1964 *Aviation Research Report* (documentary)—executive producer
1964 *Years of Adventure* (documentary)—executive producer
1965 *A History of Motor Racing* (documentary series)—executive producer
1966 *Kuala Lumpur Airport* (documentary)—producer
1967 *The Sleeper* (short)—producer
1967 *Visible Manifestations* (documentary)—producer
1969 *The Infinite Pacific* (documentary)—producer

John Hillcoat

Born 1961, Queensland. Spent most of his early life in Canada. Returned to Australia in the late 1970s and soon after attended Swinburne Institute of Technology. Director of numerous rock music videos.

As director (feature):
1989 *Ghosts . . . of the Civil Dead*

Frank Hurley

Born 1885, died 1962. Documentary film-maker. Shot footage in the Antarctic, tropical north of Australia and Papua New Guinea. Was official photographer in World War I and leader of Australia's official war correspondents in the Middle East during World War II.

As director (features):
1926 *Jungle Woman*—also writer, director of photography, producer

1926 *Hound of the Deep*—also writer, director of photography, producer

As director and director of photography (documentary):
1913 *Home of the Blizzard*
1913 *Dr Mawson in the Antarctic*
1913 *Life in the Antarctic*
1915 *Into Australia's Unknown*
1917 *In the Grip of Polar Ice*
1919 *Australians in Palestine*
1920 *The Ross Smith Flight*
1921 *Pearls and Savages*
1923 *With the Headhunters in Papua*
1929 *Southward Ho with Mawson*
1931 *Siege of the South*
1931 *With Mawson to the Frozen South*
1932 *Jewel of the Pacific*
1932 *Symphony in Steel*
1933 *Oasis*
1933 *Endurance* (re-release of *In the Grip of Polar Ice*)
1934 *Here Is Paradise*
1934 *Treasures of Katoomba*
1937 *A Nation Is Built*
1944 *Isle of Many Waters*
1945 *Mid East*

Also,
1933 *Squatter's Daughter*—director of photography
1934 *The Silence of Dean Maitland*—director of photography
1934 *Strike Me Lucky*—director of photography
1935 *Grandad Rudd*—director of photography
1937 *Lovers and Luggers*—director of photography
1937 *Tall Timbers*—writer (original story)
1940 *Forty Thousand Horsemen*—co-director of photography
1944 *Isle of Many Waters* (documentary)—producer
1944 *Scenes That Are Brightest* (documentary)—producer
1949 *Brown Coal to Briquettes* (documentary)—producer
1949 *Brown Coal to Kilowatts* (documentary)—producer
1949 *Magic of Electricity* (documentary)—producer
1949 *Pageant of Power* (documentary)—producer
1949 *Power from Kiewa Waters* (documentary)—producer
1949 *Romance of Brown Coal* (documentary)—producer
1952 *Eternal Forest* (documentary)—producer
1961 *Mawson Expedition to the Antarctic* (documentary)—narrator
1962 *Antarctic Pioneers* (documentary)—co-director of photography, narrator

Ray Lawrence

Born 1947, UK. Emigrated to Australia as a young boy. Began career in commercials industry in the UK.

As director (feature):
1985 *Bliss*

Raymond Longford

Born 1878, Victoria; died 1959. Spent early life at sea, then was a medical orderly in the Boer War and a stage actor in India, New Zealand and Australia. Formed production team with Lottie Lyell. Last years of his life were as a nightwatchman in Sydney.

As director:
1911 *The Fatal Wedding*—also actor
1911 *The Romantic Story of Margaret Catchpole*—also writer, actor
1911 *Sweet Nell of Old Drury*—possibly also writer

1912 *The Tide of Death*—also writer
1912 *The Midnight Wedding*—also writer
1913 *Australia Calls*—also writer
1913 *Naming the Federal Capital of Australia* (documentary)
1913 *Pommy Arrives in Australia* (aka: *Pommy, the Funny Little New Chum*)—also writer
1913 *'Neath Australian Skies*—also writer
1914 *The Swagman's Story*
1914 *The Silence of Dean Maitland*
1914 *Taking His Chance*—also writer
1914 *Trooper Campbell*—also writer
1915 *We'll Take the Children in Amongst Our Own*
1915 *Ma Hogan's Boarder*—also writer
1916 *A Maori Maid's Love*—also co-writer
1916 *The Mutiny on the Bounty*—also writer
1917 *The Church and the Woman*—also writer
1918 *The Woman Suffers*—also writer
1919 *The Sentimental Bloke*—also writer
1920 *Ginger Mick*—also writer
1920 *On Our Selection*—also writer
1921 *Rudd's New Selection*—also writer
1921 *The Blue Mountains Mystery*—co-director (with Lottie Lyell)
1923 *The Dinkum Bloke*—also co-writer
1923 *Australia Calls* (semi-documentary)
1923 *An Australian by Marriage* (semi-documentary)
1923 *Australia Land of Sunshine*—also writer
1924 *Fisher's Ghost*—also writer
1925 *The Bushwackers*—also co-writer
1925 *On the Trail of the Kangaroo* (documentary)
1926 *Peter Vernon's Silence*—also writer
1926 *The Pioneers*
1926 *Sunrise*—Longford completed this F. Stuart-White film
1926 *Hills of Hate*
1934 *The Man They Could Not Hang*

Also,
1909 *Life and Adventures of John Vane, the (Notorious) Australian Bushranger*—actor
1911 *Captain Midnight—The Bush King*—actor
1911 *Captain Starlight—A Gentleman of the Road*—actor
1911 *Life of Rufus Dawes*—actor
1932 *The Sentimental Bloke*—associate director
1932 *His Royal Highness*—associate director
1933 *Diggers in Blighty*—actor
1933 *Harmony Row*—associate director
1933 *Waltzing Matilda*—associate director
1933 *The Hayseeds*—associate director
1934 *Splendid Fellows*—Longford claimed to be associated
1937 *The Avenger*—actor
1938 *Dad and Dave Come to Town*—actor
1939 *The Pyjama Girl Mystery*—actor
1940 *Dad Rudd, MP*—actor
1940 *Wings of Destiny*—actor
1941 *That Certain Something*—actor
1941 *Racing Luck*—actor
1941 *The Power and the Glory*—actor

Richard Lowenstein

Born 1960, Melbourne. Graduate of Swinburne Film & Television School. Directed many rock music videos.

As director (features):
1984 *Strikebound*—also writer

Richard Lowenstein

Baz Luhrmann

1987　*Dogs in Space*—also writer
1993　*Say a Little Prayer*—also writer

As director (other):
1979　*Evictions* (short)
1986　*White City* (short)
1988　*Australian Made* (feature documentary)

Also,
1978　*Astral Projections* (short)—second assistant camera
1978　*Bingo* (short)—third assistant camera, co-grip, co-lighting, stills photographer
1978　*Welding* (short)—focus puller, camera assistant, second unit photography, stills photographer
1980　*Freya* (short)—assistant director
1981　*His Master's Voice* (short)—sound recordist

Baz Luhrmann

Born 17 September 1962. After working as an actor, Luhrmann went to NIDA, where he workshopped the original stage version of *Strictly Ballroom*. After a successful run at Sydney's Wharf Theatre, the play was taken to Bratislava, Czechoslovakia,

where it won Best Play and Best Direction. Back in Sydney, Luhrmann has continued to work as a director in theatre and at the Australian Opera. Has also directed several video clips.

As director (feature):
1992　*Strictly Ballroom*—also co-writer

As director (other):
1982　*Kids of the Cross* (television)

Also,
1981　*Winter of Our Dreams* (feature)—actor

Paulette McDonaugh

Died 1978. With sisters Phyllis and Isobel ventured into film production in the 1920s with their own company McD Productions, funding the films themselves.

1926　*Those Who Love*—co-director (with P. J. Ramster)
1928　*The Far Paradise*—also writer, producer
1930　*The Cheaters*—also writer
1933　*Two Minutes Silence*

George Miller

George Miller

Born 1945, Brisbane. Graduated in medicine from University of NSW in 1970. Formed Kennedy Miller production company with producer Byron Kennedy in 1979.

As director (features):
1979   *Mad Max*—also co-writer
1981   *Mad Max 2* (aka: *The Road Warrior*)—also co-writer
1983   *Twilight Zone: The Movie* (US)—'Nightmare at 20,000 Feet' episode
1985   *Mad Max Beyond Thunderdome*—co-director (with George Ogilvie), also co-writer, a producer
1987   *The Witches of Eastwick* (US)
1992   *Lorenzo's Oil* (US)—also co-writer

As director (other):
1972   *Violence in the Cinema . . . Part 1* (short)—also writer, actor
1973   *Devil in Evening Dress* (documentary)—also writer
1983   *The Dismissal* (mini-series)—a director, also an executive producer

Also,
1973   *Frieze—An Underground Film* (short)—editor
1980   *The Chain Reaction*—second unit director, an associate producer
1984   *Bodyline* (mini-series)—a producer
1985   *The Cowra Breakout* (mini-series)—a producer
1985   *The Making of Mad Max Beyond Thunderdome* (documentary)—an executive producer

George Miller

1987   *Vietnam* (mini-series)—a producer
1987   *The Year My Voice Broke*—a producer
1988   *The Dirtwater Dynasty* (mini-series)—a producer
1988   *Sportz Crazy* (documentary series)—a producer
1988   *The Clean Machine* (tele-feature)—a producer
1988   *The Riddle of the Stinson* (tele-feature)—a producer
1988   *Fragments of War: The Story of Damien Parer* (tele-feature)—a producer
1989   *Dead Calm*—a producer
1989   *Bangkok Hilton* (mini-series)—a producer
1991   *Flirting*—a producer

George Miller

Born 1943, Scotland. Moved to Melbourne as a child. Commenced work as television director at Crawford Productions in 1972.

As director (features):
1982   *The Man from Snowy River*
1984   *The Aviator* (Yugoslavia)
1986   *Cool Change*
1987   *Les Patterson Saves the World*
1987   *Bushfire Moon*
1990   *The Neverending Story II* (Germany)
1991   *Frozen Assets* (US)
1993   *Gross Misconduct*

As director (other):
1976   *Cash and Company* (tele-series)
1978   *Against the Wind* (tele-series)
1979   *High Country* (documentary)
1980   *The Last Outlaw* (tele-series)
1983   *All the Rivers Run* (mini-series)
1984   *Five Mile Creek* (mini-series)
1985   *Anzacs* (mini-series)
1985   *The Far Country* (mini-series)
1985   *Spooner* (US tele-feature)
1988   *Goodbye Miss Liberty* (US tele-feature)

Jocelyn Moorhouse

Also,
1978   *The Making of Anna* (documentary)—actor
1979   *In Search of Anna*—assistant director

Jocelyn Moorhouse

Jocelyn Moorhouse attended the Australian Film Television & Radio School between 1981 and 1983, where she majored in Direction and Screenwriting. Previous to her award-winning debut feature, *Proof*, Moorhouse worked in television as a writer and director, specialising in serial dramas and children's programmes.

As director (feature):
1991   *Proof*

As director (other):
1987   *The Bartons* (mini-series)—a director
1988   *Secrets* (television)—a director
1991   *The Flying Doctors* (television)—a director

Also,
1988   *House Rules* (television)—a writer
1989   *Inside Running* (television)—a writer
1989   *Roundabout* (television)—a writer

Philippe Mora

Born 1949, Paris. Moved to Melbourne with his family at the age of two. Had a career as an artist and painter in the early 1970s, and held a number of exhibitions in Australia and England.

As director (features):
1976   *Mad Dog Morgan*—also writer
1982   *The Return of Captain Invincible*
1982   *The Beast Within* (US)
1984   *A Breed Apart* (US)

Philippe Mora

1984   *The Howling: Part 2: Your Sister Is a Werewolf* (US)
1986   *Death of a Soldier*
1986   *Howling III: The Marsupials*—also co-producer
1988   *Communion* (US)

As director (other):
1969   *Trouble in Molopolis* (UK, short)—also writer
1973   *Swastika* (UK, documentary)—also co-writer
1974   *Brother, Can You Spare a Dime?* (documentary)—also co-writer
1976   *To Shoot a Mad Dog* (documentary)—also co-writer, narration

Also,
1972   *The Double-Headed Eagle* (UK, documentary)—co-writer

Russell Mulcahy

Born 1953, Melbourne. Commenced career at ABC in 1969. Directed many rock music videos.

As director (features):
1984   *Razorback*
1986   *The Highlander* (UK)
1991   *Highlander II: The Quickening* (Argentina)
1991   *Ricochet*

Scott Murray

As director (other):
1976 *Delicious Dreams Despite Depression* (short)
1988 *Cyberforce* (US pilot)

Scott Murray

Born 1951, Melbourne. Graduated from Latrobe University after majoring in formal logic. One of Australia's most prolific writers and publishers on the subject of film. Co-founded *Cinema Papers* in 1973.

As director (features):
1989 *Devil in the Flesh* (aka: *Beyond Innocence*)—also writer. Released overseas in 1986

As director (other):
1971 *Beginnings* (documentary)—co-director (with Rod Bishop, Gordon Glenn, Andrew Pecze), also co-editor
1973 *Paola* (short)—also writer, editor
1975 *Denial* (short)—also writer, editor
1977 *Summer Shadows* (short)—also writer, editor
1983 *Australian Movies to the World* (television documentary)—co-director, also co-writer

Also,
1992 *No. 7* (short)—editor

Phillip Noyce

Born 1950, NSW. Manager of Sydney Filmmakers Co-op in 1970. Among first intake at AFTRS in 1973.

Phillip Noyce

As director (features):
1977 *Backroads*—also co-writer, producer
1978 *Newsfront*—also writer
1982 *Heatwave*—also co-writer
Unrel. *Echoes of Paradise*—made in 1987; released to video in 1989
1989 *Dead Calm*—co-writer, director
1989 *Blind Fury* (US)
1992 *Patriot Games* (US)
1993 *Sliver* (US)

As director (other):
1969 *Better to Reign in Hell* (short)—also writer, producer
1970 *Intersechon* (short)
1970 *Just a Little Note* (short)—co-director
1971 *Camera Class* (short)
1971 *Sun* (short)
1971 *Memories* (short)
1972 *Who Are These People and What Are These Films* (documentary)
1973 *Caravan Park* (short)—also writer
1973 *That's Showbiz* (short)—also writer, actor
1973 *Cinemusic* (documentary)—co-director
1974 *Castor and Pollux* (documentary)—also director of photography, co-editor

329

1974 *Renegades* (documentary)—also writer, director of photography, editor, producer
1975 *God Knows Why But It Works* (short)—also co-writer
1975 *Finks Make Movies* (documentary)
1976 Support programmes for *Let the Balloon Go*
1977 *Why Can't They Be Like We Were* (tele-series)—a director
1978 *Tulau Dewata* (documentary)—also writer
1980 *Three Vietnamese Stories* (documentary)
1980 *Fact and Fiction* (documentary)
1981 *Another Saturday Night* (short)
1983 *Survival* (documentary)
1983 *The Dismissal* (mini-series)—co-director, also co-writer
1985 *The Cowra Breakout* (mini-series)—co-director, also co-writer
1987 *The Hitchhiker* (US tele-series)—a director

Also,
1970 *Style of Champions* (documentary)—production assistant
1971 *Homesdale* (short)—actor
1973 *One Hundred a Day* (short)—production assistant
1974 *Matchless* (short)—production assistant
1974 *I Happen to Be a Girl* (documentary)—director of photography, editor
1975 *The Golden Cage*—production manager, assistant director
1976 *Let the Balloon Go*—second assistant director
1976 *A Calendar of Dreamings* (short)—editor
1976 *Zizzem Zam* (short)—production assistant
1980 *Attack Force Z*—replaced as director the day before shooting. Some of his script involvement remains
1981 *The Thirsty Season* (documentary)—co-writer

George Ogilvie

Born 1931. Began career as an actor in the UK. Taught at Central School of Drama. Has worked in all fields of the performing arts as a director.

As director (features):
1985 *Mad Max Beyond Thunderdome*—co-director (with George Miller)
1986 *Short Changed*
1987 *The Place at the Coast*
1990 *The Crossing*

As director (other):
1982 *The Dismissal* (mini-series)—a director
1983 *Bodyline* (mini-series)—a director
1988 *Touch the Sun* (television)—the 'Princess Kate' episode
1988 *Michael Willesee's Australians* (tele-series)—'Soldier Settler' episode
1988 *The Shiralee* (mini-series)
1992 *The Battlers* (tele-series)

Dennis O'Rourke

Born 1945, Brisbane. Has specialised in the ethnographic/essay form of film-making. Recipient of Byron Kennedy Award in 1990.

As director:
1976 *Yumi Yet: Independence for Papua New Guinea* (documentary)
1978 *Iliksen: Politics in Papua New Guinea* (documentary)
1980 *Yap. . .How Did You Know We'd Like TV?* (aka: *South Seas and Soft Soap*) (documentary)

1982 *The Sharkcallers of Kontu* (documentary)
1984 *'. . .Couldn't be Fairer'* (documentary)
1986 *Half Life: A Parable for the Nuclear Age* (documentary)—also writer, director of photography, producer
1988 *"Cannibal Tours"* (documentary)
1992 *The Good Woman of Bangkok*

Ian Pringle

Born 1953, Melbourne. Began career at the ABC. Founded Seon Films. Now partially based in Europe.

As director (features):
1980 *Wronsky*—also co-writer, producer
1982 *The Plains of Heaven*—also writer
1986 *Wrong World*—also writer
1990 *The Prisoner of St Petersburg*—also co-writer. Made in 1988
1992 *Isabelle Eberhardt*

As director (other):
1977 *Flights* (short)—also writer, producer
1979 *The Cartographer and the Waiter* (short)—also writer, producer
1979 *Bare Is His Back Who Has No Brother* (documentary)—also producer
1981 *Desiderius Orban* (documentary)
1986 *Islomania* (documentary)

Also,
1988 *The Tale of Ruby Rose*—associate producer
1989 *Lover Boy* (short)—associate producer
1990 *Celia*—associate producer
1992 *Romper Stomper*—associate producer

John Ruane

Born 1952, Melbourne. Graduated Swinburne Film and Television School in 1975. Directs television commercials.

As director (features):
1991 *Death in Brunswick* (aka: *Nothing to Lose*)
Prod. *That Eye the Sky*—also writer

As director (other):
1976 *Queensland* (short)—also co-writer
1982 *Man into Woman—The Transsexual Experience* (documentary)
1984 *Interpreting for Lawyers* (video)—also writer
Unrel. *Hanging Together* (tele-feature)—made in 1985
1987 *Feathers* (short)—also writer
1989 *Warriors* (documentary series)—'I Hope the War Will Be Over Soon' episode
1989 *Protecting Your Rights* (video short)

Also,
1973 *Where Is This Dream of Your Youth?* (short)—co-producer
1976 *Melanie and Me* (short)—sound recordist
1976 *Last Drive-In Movie* (short)—camera assistant
1976 *Out of the Past* (short)—lighting camera; unfinished
1977 *Rodeo* (short)—writer; unfinished
1979 *Energy and Agriculture* (documentary)—director of photography
1979 *Fight that Fire* (documentary)—director of photography
1980 *Blood Money*—co-writer, stills photographer
1981 *Undermining Australia* (short)—director of photography
1989 *Justice for All* (video short)—writer
1989 *Under the Skin* (tele-series)—writer 'Nino Where You Been?' episode
Unrel. *Cassandra*—co-writer. Made in 1981

Henri Safran

Born 1932, Paris. Educated at Turgot College. Studied acting, singing and ballet up to conscription in the army in 1952. Came to Australia in 1960 and signed a contract with the ABC to produce and direct documentaries.

As director (features):
1975   *Elephant Boy* (UK)
1976   *Storm Boy*
1982   *"Norman Loves Rose"*—also writer, co-producer
1983   *Bush Christmas*
1984   *The Wild Duck*—also co-writer

As director (other):
196[?]   *Traveller without Luggage* (documentary)
196[?]   *A Local Boy* (documentary)
196[?]   *Tartuffe* (documentary)
196[?]   *Rape of the Belt* (documentary)
196[?]   *Point of Departure* (documentary)
196[?]   *A Season in Hell* (documentary)
1966   *Champion House* (UK television)—also producer
1968   *The Trouble Shooters* (UK tele-series)—also producer
1969   *Somerset Maugham* (UK documentary)—also producer
1971   *30-Minute Theatre* (UK television)—also producer
1971   *Castaways* (UK tele-series)
1972   *Tales of Unease* (UK television)—also producer
1972   *The Inheritors* (UK television)—also producer
1972   *The Frighteners* (UK television)—also producer
1974   *Trouble Shooter* (tele-series)
1975   *Softly Softly* (UK tele-series)—also producer
1976   *Love Story* (UK tele-series)—also producer
1976   *Democracy* (short)
1977   *Listen to the Lion* (short)
1979   *Golden Soak* (mini-series)
1984   *A Fortunate Life* (mini-series)
1985   *The Lancaster–Miller Affair* (mini-series)
1987   *Edge of Power* (tele-feature)
1987   *Simpson* (tele-feature)
1987   *Michael Willesee's Australians* (documentary series)
1989   *Wildfire* (tele-feature)
1989   *Flair* (mini-series)
1990   *Bony* (tele-feature)

Also,
1962   *River of Life* (documentary)—producer
19[?]   *Baby Love* (feature)—writer
1985   *Relatives* (feature)—producer

Fred Schepisi

Born 1939, Melbourne. Left school at fifteen to work in an advertising agency. Joined Cinesound (Melbourne) in 1963, buying the company in 1966 and changing its name to The Film House (still operating).

As director (features):
1973   *Libido*—'The Priest' episode
1976   *The Devil's Playground*—also writer, producer
1978   *The Chant of Jimmie Blacksmith*—also writer, producer
1982   *Barbarosa* (US)
1984   *Iceman* (US)
1985   *Plenty* (UK)
1987   *Roxanne* (US)
1988   *Evil Angels* (aka: *A Cry in the Dark*)
1990   *The Russia House* (US)
1992   *Mr Baseball* (Japan)
1993   *Six Degrees of Separation* (US)
Prod.   *I.Q.* (US)

Fred Schepisi

As director (other):
1966   *Camera Corner* (series of shorts)
1965   *Breaking the Language Barrier* (short)
1965   *The Shape of Quality* (documentary)
1965   *People Make Papers* (documentary)—also writer
1966   *And One Was Gold* (documentary)—also writer
1966   *Up and Over Down Under* (documentary)
1967   *Switch On* (documentary)
1970   *The Plus Factor* (documentary)—also producer
1972   *Tomorrow's Canberra* (documentary)—also writer

Carl Schultz

Born 1939, Hungary. Settled in Australia as a teenager. Drama director at the ABC, 1972–78.

As director (features):
1978   *Blue Fin*
1983   *Goodbye Paradise*
1983   *Sumner Locke Elliott's Careful He Might Hear You*
1987   *Travelling North*
1988   *The Seventh Sign* (US)
1989   *Bullseye*—made in 1985

As director (other):
1975   *The Tichborne Affair* (tele-feature)
1976   *The Outsiders* (tele-series)
1978   *Earth Patrol* (short)
1978   *Run from the Morning* (mini-series)
1979   *A Place in the World* (mini-series)
1979   *Ride on Stranger* (mini-series)
1981   *The Levkas Man* (mini-series)
1983   *The Dismissal* (mini-series)—a director
1984   *Bodyline* (mini-series)—a director
1985   *Winners* (tele-series)—'Top Kid' episode

Nadia Tass

Yahoo Serious

Born Greg Pead, 1953, Hunter Valley. Began directing documentaries and experimental comedy films while studying painting at the National Art School.

As director (features):
1988   *Young Einstein*—also co-writer, editor, co-producer
1993   *Reckless Kelly*

As director (other):
1985   *Coaltown* (documentary)—also writer, editor, producer
1977   *Lifestyle* (documentary series)—also editor, producer
1981   *Australia Seriously* (television special)—also writer, editor, actor, producer
1984   *Knightmare* (short)
1989   *The Big Serious Show* (tele-series)—also writer, actor, producer

Nadia Tass

Born Nadia Tassopolous, 1956, Greece. Theatre actor and director.

As director (features):
1986   *Malcolm*—also a producer
1988   *Rikky and Pete*—also a producer
1990   *The Big Steal*—also a producer
1991   *Pure Luck* (US)

As director (other):
1993   *Stark* (mini-series)

Albie Thoms

Born 1941, Sydney. Attended Sydney University in 1959 and studied dramatic theory. Helped in formation of the Ubu group

in Sydney. Subsequently worked as a writer and director on television series and avant-garde films.

As director (features):
1969   *Marinetti*—also writer, producer, editor
1973   *Sunshine City*—also writer, producer, editor, director of photography
1980   *Palm Beach*—also writer, producer, editor

As director (other):
1963   *It Droppeth as the Gentle Rain* (short)—co-director (with Bruce Beresford), producer, co-writer
1965   *Spurt of Blood* (short)—also producer, co-editor
1966   *Man and His World* (short)—also producer
1966   *Blunderball* (short)—also producer
1966   *Rita and Dundi* (short)—also producer
1966   *The Film* (short)
1966   *Nice 'n' Juicy* (television)
1967   *Bluto* (short)—also producer
1967   *Bolero* (short)—also producer
1967   *Moon Virility* (documentary)—also producer
1967   *In Key* (short)—also producer
1967   *Tribute to America* (documentary)—also producer
1967   *Australian Playhouse* (tele-series)
1968   *David Perry* (short)—also producer
1968   *Tripartite Adventure in Redfern* (short)
1968   *Tobias Icarus Age Four* (short)
1968   *Looby* (short)
1968   *Vision for a New World* (short)
1968   *Contrabandits* (tele-series)
1969   *Petfoods is a Serious Business* (documentary)
1969   *Skippy* (tele-series)
1970   *Octopus* (short)
1971   *Yellow TV* (short)
1974   *Hot Rats/Blue Poles* (short)
1974   *Words and Music* (short)
1974   *Journey to the Centre of the Earth* (short)
1975   *GTK* (tele-series)
1975   *Yesterday's Hero* (short)
1975   *The Boy from the Stars* (short)
1975   *Living in the Seventies* (short)
1975   *Lucy in the Sky with Diamonds* (short)
1975   *Aborigine* (short)
1975   *Autobahn* (short)
1975   *Peppermint Twist* (short)
1975   *Target* (television)
1976   *Hollywood Expanded* (short)
1976   *Funky Road* (tele-series)
1977   *Something Old—Something New* (documentary)—also producer
1977   *Neu Australische Film* (documentary)—also producer
1981   *Surf Movie/Australian Surfing Phenomenon* (documentary)—also writer, producer
1982   *Rock Around the World* (documentary)
1983   *Johnny O'Keefe—The Wild One* (documentary)—also producer
1983   *The Bradman Era* (documentary)—also producer
1985   *From Neck-to-Nude* (feature–documentary)
1988   *The Australian Image* (documentary)
1988   *The Red and the Gold* (documentary)
1989   *Getting Straight* (documentary)
1990   *Bradman* (documentary)
1990   *Polygenesis* (short)

Also,
1965   *Poem 25* (documentary)—co-producer
1969   *Hair*—effects
1971   *Alpha and Omega*—camera operator

1972   *The Second Bardo* (documentary)—co-producer
1972   *Morning of the Earth* (documentary)—editor, effects
1975   *Surfabout* (documentary)—producer
1976   *Levi Strauss Story* (documentary)—production manager

Michael Thornhill

Born 1941, Sydney. In 1968 started writing film criticism for the first national newspaper, *The Australian*, a position held for three years. Became one of the first directors of the New South Wales Film Corporation in 1977.

As director (features):
1974   *Between Wars*—also producer
1977   *The FJ Holden*—also co-writer, producer
1979   *The Journalist*—also co-writer
1988   *The Everlasting Secret Family*—also producer

As director (other):
1969   *The Esperance Story* (documentary)
1969   *The American Poet's Visit* (short)—also co-writer, co-producer
1969   *Leonard French's Stained Glass Screens* (documentary)
1970   *The Girl from the Family of Man* (short)—also producer
1971   *The Machine Gun* (short)—also producer
1971   *Mister Fixit My Dad* (documentary)—also co-writer
1972   *Kevin and Cheryl* (documentary)—also co-writer
1978   *Harvest of Hate* (tele-feature)
1985   *Robbery* (tele-feature)—also producer

Also,
1963   *The Explorer* (short)—editor
1976   *Summer of Secrets* (feature)—producer
1982   *Greed* (documentary)—executive producer
1983   *The Secret Discovery of Australia* (documentary)—executive producer
1984   *The Disappearance of Azaria Chamberlain* (tele-feature)—executive producer
1984   *The Great Gold Swindle* (mini-series)—executive producer

Ann Turner

Born 1960, Adelaide. Graduate of Swinburne Film and Television School.

As director (features):
1989   *Celia*—also writer
Unrel. *Hammers over the Anvil*
Prod.   *Dallas Doll*

As director (other):
1979   *Aids* (video)
1979   *Dry Reaching* (video)
1980   *Mama Crow Wears Dresses Now* (short)
1980   *Espoused Carcass/Grey Shores* (short)
1981   *Flesh on Glass* (short)
1990   *Rescue* (tele-series)—'L.P.G.' episode

Also,
1990   *Embassy* (tele-series)—a writer
1990   *Rescue* (tele-series)—a writer
1992   *Turtle Beach*—writer

Stephen Wallace

Born 1943, Sydney. Former production assistant and documentary writer–director at Film Australia.

As director (features):
1980   *Stir*
Unrel. *The Boy Who Had Everything*—also writer. Made in 1984
1986   *For Love Alone*—also writer
1990   *Blood Oath*
1992   *Turtle Beach*—shot in 1990

As director (other):
1968   *Just Below* (documentary)
1969   *Balmain* (documentary)—also co-editor
1970   *The Look* (short)
1972   *Patterns of Time and Distance* (documentary)—also co-writer
1973   *Brittle Weather Journey* (short)—also writer
1975   *Break-Up* (short)—also writer
1976   *Zizzem Zam* (short)—assistant director
1977   *Love Letters from Teralba Road* (short)—also writer
1979   *Conman Harry and the Others* (short)—also writer
1980   *Women of the Sun* (mini-series)—'Nerida Anderson' episode
1981   *Captives of Care* (short)
1981   *So You're Getting a Divorce* (short)
1982   *There's a Little Bit of Cowboy in Everyone* (documentary)
1983   *Women Who Kill* (documentary)
1984   *A Bride for All Reasons*
1984   *Mail Order Bride* (tele-feature)
1985   *Winners* (tele-series)—'Quest Beyond Time' episode
1986   *Hunger* (tele-feature)
1987   *Olive* (tele-feature)
1988   *Michael Willesee's Australians* (tele-series)—'Gordon Bennett' episode
1991   *Flying Doctors* (tele-series)—a director
1992   *Sins* (mini-series)—a director

Vincent Ward

Born 1956, New Zealand. Trained as artist prior to commencing career in film industry.

As director (features):
1984   *Vigil* (New Zealand)
1988   *The Navigator: A Medieval Odyssey* (New Zealand–Australia)
1993   *Map of the Human Heart* (Canada–Australia–New Zealand–France)

As director (other):
1978   *A State of Siege* (short)
1980   *In Spring One Plants Alone* (documentary)

Peter Weir

Born 1944, Sydney. Commenced work at Channel 7 in Sydney, then joined the Commonwealth Film Unit in 1969.

As director (features):
1971   *Three to Go*—the 'Michael' episode; also writer
1974   *The Cars that Ate Paris*—also co-writer
1975   *Picnic at Hanging Rock*
1977   *The Last Wave*—also co-writer. Based on an original idea by Peter Weir
1981   *Gallipoli*—also wrote story
1982   *The Year of Living Dangerously*—also co-writer
1985   *Witness* (US)
1986   *The Mosquito Coast* (US)
1989   *Dead Poets Society* (US)

Peter Weir

Geoffrey Wright

1990   *Green Card* (US, though officially a French–Australia co-production)—also writer
1993   *Fearless* (US)

As director (other):
1967   *Count Vim's Last Exercise* (short)
1968   *The Life and Flight of Reverend Buckshotte* (short)
1969   *Stirring the Pool* (documentary)
1971   *Homesdale* (short)—also actor, co-writer
1971   *Tempo: Australia in the 70s* (documentary)—also co-writer
1972   *Australian Colour Diary No. 43: Two Directions in Australian Pop Music* (documentary)
1972   *Boat Building* (short)
1972   *The Billiard Room* (short)
1972   *The Computer Centre* (short)
1972   *The Field Day* (short)
1972   *Incredible Floridas* (documentary)
1973   *Whatever Happened to Green Valley?* (documentary)—also writer
1979   *The Plumber* (tele-feature)—also writer
1975   *Three Workshop Films* (short)—co-director

Also,
1973   *The Fifth Facade* (documentary)—writer
1974   *Fugue* (short)—writer

Simon Wincer

Born 1943, Sydney. Began career at ABC and spent 1966–69 in UK as television director and stage manager. Joined Crawford Productions in 1970.

1979   *Snapshot*
1980   *Harlequin*
1983   *Phar Lap* (US: *A Horse Called Phar Lap*)
1985   *D.A.R.Y.L.* (US)
1987   *The Lighthorsemen*
1991   *Quigley* (US: *Quigley Down Under*)
1992   *Harley Davidson and the Marlboro Man*
1993   *Free Willy* (US)
Prod. *Lightning Jack*

As director (other):
1970s *Division 4* (tele-series)—a director
1970s *Homicide* (tele-series)—a director
1976   *Cash and Company* (tele-series)—a director
1976   *Tandarra* (tele-series)—a director
1976   *The Sullivans* (tele-series)—a director
1977   *Chopper Squad* (tele-series)—a director
1978   *Against the Wind* (tele-series)—a director
1983   *Phar Lap Trailer* (short)
1986   *The Girl Who Spelled Freedom* (US tele-feature)
1986   *The Last Frontier* (mini-series)
1988   *Blue Grass* (US mini-series)
1989   *Lonesome Dove* (US mini-series)
1992   *Young Indiana Jones* (US tele-series)—a director

Also,
1982 *The Man from Snowy River*—co-executive producer,
      co-second unit director
1984 *One Night Stand*—executive producer

Geoffrey Wright

In 1989, Geoffrey Wright wrote and directed the short film *Lover Boy*. It won the Best Short Fiction awards at the Melbourne International Film Festival and the Sydney Film Festival, and was invited to the festivals of Venice, Milan and Hoff that same year. Previously, Wright worked as a film critic for Radio 3AW, *The Melbourne Times* and *The Age*'s *E.G.*

As director (feature):
1992 *Romper Stomper*—also writer

As director (other):
1979 *Arrivederci Roma* (short)—also writer
1989 *Lover Boy* (short)—also writer

Australian films shown at the Centre Georges Pompidou

The following is a list of those films selected for Le Cinéma Australien at the Centre Georges Pompidou in Paris in 1991. The title of each Australian-based film is followed by the director's name and the year of Australian release. The dates given for films made overseas by Australian film-makers is that of first world release. If the film is not a feature, there is a brief annotation ('documentary', 'short', etc.).

Among the Hardwoods (Lacey Percival, documentary, 1936)
Backlash (Bill Bennett, 1988)
Back of Beyond, The (John Heyer, documentary, 1954)
Bismark Convoy Smashed (Damien Parer, documentary, 1944)
Bitter Springs (Ralph Smart, 1950)
Bliss (Ray Lawrance, 1985)
Blood Oath (Stephen Wallace, 1990)
'Breaker' Morant (Bruce Beresford, 1980)
Camera Natura (Ross Gibson, cinematic essay, 1985)
Cars that Ate Paris, The (Peter Weir, 1974)
Celia (Ann Turner, 1989)
Celso and Cora (Gary Kildea, documentary, 1983)
Chant of Jimmie Blacksmith, The (Fred Schepisi, 1978)
Cheaters, The (Paulette McDonagh, 1930)
Crocodile Dundee (Peter Faiman, 1986)
Dad and Dave Come to Town (Ken G. Hall, 1938)
Dead Calm (Phillip Noyce, 1989)
Dead Poets Society (Peter Weir, 1989)
Dead to the World (Ross Gibson, unreleased, 1991)
Devil in the Flesh (Scott Murray, 1989)
Devil's Playground, The (Fred Schepisi, 1976)
Dingo (Rolf de Heer, 1992)
Dogs in Space (Richard Lowenstein, 1987)
Don's Party (Bruce Beresford, 1976)
Driving Miss Daisy (Bruce Beresford, 1989)
Evil Angels (Fred Schepisi, 1988)
FJ Holden, The (Michael Thornhill, 1977)
For the Term of his Natural Life (Norman Dawn, 1927)
Forty Thousand Horsemen (Charles Chauvel, 1940)
Fran (Glenda Hambly, 1985)
Gallipoli (Peter Weir, 1981)
Getting Wet (Paul J. Hogan, short, 1989)
Ghosts . . . of the Civil Dead (John Hillcoat, 1989)
Girl's Own Story, A (Jane Campion, short, 1983)
Goodbye Paradise (Carl Schultz, 1983)
Green Card (Peter Weir, 1991)
Half Life: A Parable of the Nuclear Age (Dennis O'Rourke, documentary, 1985)
Hightide (Gillian Armstrong, 1987)
His Kind of Woman (John Farrow, 1951)
Holidays on the River Yarra (Leo Berkeley, 1991)
Homesdale (Peter Weir, short, 1971)
Hungry Miles, The (WWF Film Unit, documentary, 1955)
Incredible Floridas (Peter Weir, documentary, 1972)
Indonesia Calling (Joris Ivens, documentary, 1946)
In the Wake of the Bounty (Charles Chauvel, 1933)
Jedda (Charles Chauvel, 1955)
Kid Stakes, The (Tal Ordell, 1927)

Killing of Angel Street, The (Don Crombie, 1981)
Kokoda Front Line (uncredited, newsreel, 1942)
Last Wave, The (Peter Weir, 1977)
Lonely Hearts (Paul Cox, 1982)
Mad Max (George Miller, 1979)
Mad Max 2 (George Miller, 1981)
Malcolm (Nadia Tass, 1986)
Man from Snowy River, The (George Miller, 1982)
Man of Flowers (Paul Cox, 1983)
Melbourne Cup, The (actuality, 1896)
'Michael' (episode of the portmanteau *Three to Go*, Peter Weir, 1969)
Mike and Stefani (R. Maslyn Williams, 1952)
Monkey Grip (Ken Cameron, 1982)
Mosquito Coast, The (Peter Weir, 1986)
Mrs. Soffel (Gillian Armstrong, 1984)
My Brilliant Career (Gill Armstrong, 1979)
Navigator: A Medieval Odyssey, The (Vincent Ward, 1988)
New Guinea Patrol (Ron Maslyn Williams, documentary, 1958)
Newsfront (Phil Noyce, 1978)
Night Cries: A Rural Tragedy (Tracey Moffatt, short, 1990)
On the Beach (Stanley Kramer, 1959)
On the Waves of the Adriatic (Brian McKenzie, documentary, 1991)
Overlanders, The (Harry Watt, 1946)
Passionless Moments: Recorded in Sydney Australia Sunday October 2nd (Jane Campion and Gerard Lee, short, 1984)
Patrick (Richard Franklin, 1978)
Pearls and Savages (Frank Hurley, documentary, 1921)
Peel (Jane Campion, short, 1982)
Personal History of the Australian Surf: Being the Confessions of a Straight Poofter, A (Michael Blakemore, 1981)
Picnic at Hanging Rock (Peter Weir, 1975)
Plumber, The (Peter Weir, 1979)
Proof (Jocelyn Moorhouse, 1991)
Quigley (Simon Wincer, 1991)
Return Home (Ray Argall, 1990)
Rocky Horror Picture Show, The (Jim Sharman, 1975)
Russia House, The (Fred Schepisi, 1991)
Sentimental Bloke, The (Raymond Longford, 1919)
Shame (Steve Jodrell, 1988)
Song of Air, A (Merilee Bennett, short, 1987)
Storm Boy (Henri Safran, 1976)
Story of the Kelly Gang, The (Charles Tait, 1906)
Street to Die, A (Bill Bennett, 1985)
Summer of the Seventeenth Doll (Leslie Norman, 1959)
Sumner Locke Elliott's Careful He Might Hear You (Carl Schultz, 1983)
Sunday Too Far Away (Ken Hannam, 1975)
Sundowners, The (Fred Zinnemann, 1960)
Surfer, The (Frank Shields, 1988)
Sweetie (Jane Campion, 1989)
They're a Weird Mob (Michael Powell, 1966)
Three in One (Cecil Holmes, 1957)
Unfinished Business (Bob Ellis, 1986)
Violence in the Cinema . . . Part One (George Miller, short, 1972)
"Wake in Fright" (Ted Kotcheff, 1971)
Walkabout (Nicolas Roeg, 1971)
Whatever Happened to Green Valley? (Peter Weir, documentary, 1973)
Where Danger Lives (John Farrow, 1950)
Witches of Eastwick, The (George Miller, 1987)
Witness (Peter Weir, 1985)
Wrong World (Ian Pringle, 1986)
Year My Voice Broke, The (John Duigan, 1987)
Year of Living Dangerously, The (Peter Weir, 1982)
Young Einstein (Yahoo Serious, 1988)

Select bibliography

Australian Copyright Council, *Film and Copyright*, Sydney, 1990

Australian Council of Government Film Libraries, *Focus on Reel Australia*, in association with the National Film & Sound Archive, Canberra, 1990

Australian Film Commission. *Australian Film Data: Selected Film, Video and Television Statistics from the Australian Film Database*, Sydney, 1988

Adamson, Judith. *Australian Film Posters 1906–1960*, Currency Press & the Australian Film Institute, Sydney, 1978

Baxter, John. *The Australian Cinema*, Angus & Robertson, Sydney, 1970

Beilby, Peter (ed.). *Australian Motion Picture Year Book 1980*, Cinema Papers in association with the New South Wales Film Corporation, Melbourne, 1980

—— *Australian Motion Picture Year Book 1981/82*, Cinema Papers in association with the New South Wales Film Corporation, Melbourne, 1981

Beilby, Peter & Lansell, Ross (eds). *Australian Motion Picture Year Book 1983*, Four Seasons in association with Cinema Papers, Melbourne, 1982

Bertrand, Ina. *Australian Film Studies: Efftee Productions*, Centre for the Study of Educational Communication and Media, La Trobe University, Melbourne, 1977

—— (ed.). *Cinema in Australia: A Documentary History*, New South Wales University Press, Sydney, 1989

—— *Film Censorship in Australia*, University of Queensland Press, Brisbane, 1978

Bertrand, Ina & Collins, Diane. *Government and Film in Australia*, Currency Press & the Australian Film Institute, Sydney, 1981

Blonski, Annette, Creed, Barbara & Freiberg, Freda (eds). *Don't Shoot Darling!: Women's Independent Filmmaking in Australia*, Greenhouse Publications, Melbourne, 1987

Brand, Simon. *The Australian Film Book: 1930—Today*, Dreamweaver Books, Sydney, 1985

—— *Picture Palaces and Flea-Pits: Eighty Years of Australians at the Pictures*, Dreamweaver Books, Sydney, 1983

Buesst, Nigel. *Melbourne Film Makers Resource Book*, printed with the assistance of Film Victoria, Melbourne, 1991

Carlsson, Susanne Chauvel. *Charles & Elsa Chauvel: Movie Pioneers*, University of Queensland Press, Brisbane, 1989

Chauvel, Charles. *In the Wake of the Bounty*, Endeavour Press, Sydney, 1933

Chauvel, Elsa. *My Life With Charles Chauvel*, Shakespeare Head Press, Sydney, 1973

Clark, Al (ed.). *The Film Yearbook: Volume Two*, Australian section edited by Tom Ryan, Currey O'Neil Ross, Melbourne, 1984

—— *The Film Yearbook 1985*, Australian section edited by Tom Ryan, Currey O'Neil Ross, Melbourne, 1984

Collins, Diane. *Hollywood Down Under: Australians at the Movies: 1896 to the Present Day*, Angus & Robertson Publishers, Sydney, 1987

Cruthers, John (ed.). 'Case Studies in Independent Production' in *Taking Care of Business! A Practical Guide to Independent Film and Video Production: Volume 2*, Australian Film Television & Radio School & the Australian Film Commission, Sydney, 1988–89

Cruthers, John, Scollor, Andrew & Duncan, (Janice) Digby, 'Production Budgeting and Accounting' in, *Taking Care of Business: A Practical Guide to Independent Film and Video Production: Volume 1*, John Cruthers (ed.), Australian Film Television & Radio School & the Australian Film Commission, Sydney, 1988–89

Cunningham, Stuart. *Featuring Australia: The Cinema of Charles Chauvel*, Allen & Unwin, Sydney, 1991

Cunningham, Stuart & Turner, Graeme. *The Media in Australia: Industries, Texts, Audiences*, Allen & Unwin, Sydney, 1993

Dawson, Jonathan & Molloy, Bruce (eds). *Queensland Images in Film and Television*, University of Queensland Press, 1990

Dermody, Susan & Jacka, Elizabeth. *The Imaginary Industry: Australian Film in the Late '80s*, Australian Film Television & Radio School, Sydney, 1988

—— *The Screening of Australia Volume 1: Anatomy of a Film Industry*, Currency Press, Sydney, 1987

—— *The Screening of Australia Volume 2: Anatomy of a National Cinema*, Currency Press, Sydney, 1988

Dunn, Maxwell. *How They Made Sons of Matthew*, Angus & Robertson, Sydney, 1949

Edmondson, Ray & Pike, Andrew. *Australia's Lost Films: The Loss and Rescue of Australia's Silent Cinema*, National Library of Australia, Canberra, 1982

Fraser, Bryce. *The Macquarie Book of Events*, film section written by Graham Shirley, the Macquarie Library, Sydney, 1983

Frow, John & Morris, Meaghan. *Australian Cultural Studies: A Reader*, Allen & Unwin, Sydney, 1993

Hall, Ken G. *Australian Film: The Inside Story*, Summit Books, Sydney, 1980

—— *Directed by Ken G. Hall: Autobiography of an Australian Film Maker*, Lansdowne Press, Melbourne, 1977

Hall, Sandra. *Critical Business: The New Australian Cinema in Review*, Rigby Publishers, Adelaide, 1985

—— *Supertoy*, Sun Books, Melbourne, 1970

Hamilton, Peter & Mathews, Sue. *American Dreams: Australian Movies*, Currency Press, Sydney, 1986

Herd, Nick. *Independent Filmmaking in Australia 1960–1980*, Australian Film Television & Radio School, Sydney, 1983

Hutton, Anne (ed.). *The First Australian History and Film Conference Papers*, the History and Film Conference & the Australian Film and Television School, Sydney, 1982

Jacka, Elizabeth. *The ABC of Drama 1975–1990*, Australian Film Television & Radio School, Sydney, 1991

Jennings, Karen. *Sites of Difference: Cinematic Representation of Aboriginality and Gender*, Australian Film Institute, Melbourne, 1993

Jones, Ross. *Cut! Protection of Australia's Film and Television Industries*, the Centre for Independent Studies, NSW, 1991

Kathner, Rupert. *Let's Make a Movie*, Currawong Publishing, Sydney, 1945

Langton, Marcia. '*Well, I heard it on the radio and I saw it on television . . .*', Australian Film Commission, Sydney, 1993

Lansell, Ross & Beilby, Peter (eds). *The Documentary Film in Australia*, Cinema Papers in association with Film Victoria, Melbourne, 1982

Legg, Frank. *The Eyes of Damien Parer*, Rigby, Adelaide, 1963

Legg, Frank & Hurley, Toni. *Once More On My Adventure*, Ure Smith, Sydney, 1966

Levy, Wayne, Cutts, Graeme & Stockbridge, Sally. *The Second Australian History and Film Conference Papers*, the History and Film Conference & the Australian Film and Television School, Sydney, 1984

Long, Joan & Long, Martin. *The Pictures That Moved: A Picture History of the Australian Cinema 1896–1929*, Hutchinson Group, Melbourne, 1982

Lyle, Valda, Politis, Tom & Stell, Ross. *Stanley Hawes: Documentary Filmmaker*, WEA Film Study Group, Sydney, 1980

McFarlane, Brian. *Australian Cinema 1970–1985*, William Heinemann Australia, Melbourne, 1987

—— *Words and Images: Australian Novels into Film*, Heinemann Publishers in association with Cinema Papers, Melbourne, 1980

McFarlane, Brian & Mayer, Geoff. *New Australian Cinema: Sources and Parallels in American and British Cinema*, Cambridge University Press, Melbourne, 1992

McMurchy, Megan & Stott, Jennifer (eds). *Signs of Independents: Ten Years of the Creative Development Fund*, Australian Film Commission, Sydney, 1988

Marsh, Marion & Pip, Chris (eds). *Women in Australian Film, Video and Television Production*, Australian Film Commission and the Australian Film Television & Radio School, Sydney, 1987

Mathews, Sue. *35 mm Dreams: Conversations with Five Australian Directors*, Penguin Books Australia, Melbourne, 1984

Moran, Albert. *Australian Television Drama Series: 1956–1981*, Australian Film Television & Radio School, Sydney, 1989

—— *Images and Industry: Television Drama Production in Australia*, Currency Press, Sydney, 1985

—— *Making a TV Series: the Bellamy Project*, Currency Press, Sydney, 1983

—— *Projecting Australia: Government Film Since 1945*, Currency Press, Sydney, 1991

Moran, Albert & O'Regan, Tom (eds). *An Australian Film Reader*, Currency Press, Sydney, 1985

—— *The Australian Screen*, Penguin Books Australia, Melbourne, 1989

Moran, Albert & Tulloch, John. *A Country Practice: 'Quality Soap'*, Currency Press, Sydney, 1986

Murray, Scott (ed.). *Australian Film 1978–1992: A Survey of Theatrical Features*, Oxford University Press, in association with the Australian Film Commission and Cinema Papers, Melbourne, 1993

—— *Back of Beyond: Discovering Australian Film and Television*, Australian Film Commission, Sydney, 1988

—— *The New Australian Cinema*, Thomas Nelson Australia in association with Cinema Papers, Melbourne, 1980

Pike, Andrew & Cooper, Ross. *Australian Film 1900–1977: A Guide to Feature Film Production*, Oxford University Press in association with the Australian Film Institute, Melbourne, 1980

Porter, Hal. *Stars of Australian Stage and Screen*, Rigby, Adelaide, 1965

Reade, Eric. *The Australian Screen: A Pictorial History of Australian Film Making*, Lansdowne Press, Melbourne, 1975

—— *Australian Silent Films*, Lansdowne Press, Melbourne, 1970

—— *History and Heartburn: The Saga of Australian Film, 1896–1978*, Harper & Row, Sydney, 1979

—— *The Talkies Era*, Lansdowne Press, Melbourne, 1972

Ryan, Penny, Eliot, Margaret and Appleton, Gil (eds). *Women in Australian Film Production*, Women's Film Fund (Australian Film Commission) & the Australian Film Television & Radio School, Sydney, 1983

Schou, Kirsten. *Policies for the Australian Film Industry: Part A: Rationale for assistance and direct government subsidy*, Australian Film and Television School, Sydney, 1982

—— *The Structure and Operation of the Film Industry in Australia*, Australian Film and Television School, Sydney, 1982

Shand, John & Wellington, Tony. *Don't Shoot the Best Boy!: The Film Crew at Work*, Currency Press, Sydney, 1988

Shaw, Sylvie. *No Koalas Please: Issues for Film-makers in Asia and Australia*, Asialink, Melbourne, 1990

Shirley, Graham & Adams, Brian. *Australian Cinema: The First Eighty Years*, Angus & Robertson in association with Currency Press, Sydney, 1983

Spear, Peta (ed.). *Get the Picture: Essential Data on Australian Film, Television and Video*, Australian Film Commission, Sydney, 1989

Stewart, John. *An Encyclopaedia of Australian Film*, Reed Books, Sydney, 1984

Stott, Jennifer. 'Marketing and Distribution' in *Taking Care of Business: A Practical Guide to Independent Film and Video Production: Volume 3*, Australian Film Television & Radio School & the Australian Film Commission, Sydney, 1988–89

Stratton, David. *The Avocado Plantation: Boom and Bust in the Australian Film Industry*, Pan Macmillan, Sydney, 1990

—— *The Last New Wave: The Australian Film Revival*, Angus & Robertson, Sydney, 1980

Thoms, Albie. *Polemics for a New Cinema*, Wild & Woolley, Sydney, 1978

Thorne, Ross. *Picture Palace Architecture in Australia*, Sun Books, Melbourne, 1976

Treole, Victoria (ed.). *Australian Independent Film*, Australian Film Commission, Sydney, 1982

Tulloch, John. *Australian Cinema: Industry, Narrative and Meaning*, George Allen & Unwin Australia, Sydney, 1982

—— *Conflict and Control in the Cinema: A Reader in Film and Society*, Macmillan, Melbourne, 1977

—— *Legends on the Screen: The Australian Narrative Cinema 1919–1929*, Currency Press and the Australian Film Institute, Sydney, 1981

Turner, Graeme. *National Fictions: Literature Film and the Construction of Australian Narrative*, Allen & Unwin, Sydney, 1993, revised edition

Wasson, Mervyn. *The Beginnings of Australian Cinema*, Australian Film Institute, Melbourne, 1964

White, David. *Australian Movies to the World: The International Success of Australian Films Since 1970*, Fontana Australia, Sydney, & Cinema Papers, Melbourne, 1984

Wright, Andrëe. *Brilliant Careers: Women in Australian Cinema*, Pan Books, Sydney, 1986.

Index

Compiled by Scott Murray

This index covers all names, titles and organisations in the text and notes. When there are variants in a person's name (Gill and Gillian Armstrong), they have been standardised to the most common form (Gillian), except after a film's title where the exact spelling on the film is known (Gill Armstrong on *My Brilliant Career*). All films are features and Australian unless otherwise noted.

Only film titles and directors have been indexed for 'Filmography': one hundred and fifty Australian films' and directors for 'Dictionary of Directors'. Entries for the former have a 'c' after the page number (indicating major credits for the film in question, or for a film made by that director); for the latter, an 'f' (meaning a director's filmography). A 'p' after a page number indicates the film referred to was shown at the Centre Georges Pompidou in Paris. Italicised page numbers refer to a photograph from the film or of the person cited. In-sequence page numbers are only given when a continuous text reference is not broken by full page illustrations.

All entries have been sorted in strict alphabetical order, ignoring word breaks. Thus,

New South Wales Film Corporation (NSWFC) 67
Newton, Thandie 120, *250*
New York (magazine) 132, 146n